WRITE GREAT CODE, Volume 3

Property of the
Boston Public Library

WRITE GREAT CODE

VOLUME 3

Engineering Software

by Randall Hyde

no starch press

San Francisco

WRITE GREAT CODE, Volume 3: Engineering Software
Copyright © 2020 by Randall Hyde.

All rights reserved. No part of this work may be reproduced or transmitted in any form or by any means, electronic or mechanical, including photocopying, recording, or by any information storage or retrieval system, without the prior written permission of the copyright owner and the publisher.

Printed in USA

First printing

24 23 22 21 20   1 2 3 4 5 6 7 8 9

ISBN-10: 1-59327-979-5
ISBN-13: 978-1-59327-979-0

Publisher: William Pollock
Executive Editor: Barbara Yien
Production Editor: Rachel Monaghan
Developmental Editors: Liz Chadwick, Neville Young, and Athabasca Witschi
Project Editor: Dapinder Dosanjh
Cover and Interior Design: Octopod Studios
Technical Reviewer: Anthony Tribelli
Copyeditor: Rachel Monaghan
Compositor: Danielle Foster
Proofreader: James Fraleigh
Illustrator: David Van Ness

For information on distribution, translations, or bulk sales, please contact No Starch Press, Inc. directly:
No Starch Press, Inc.
245 8th Street, San Francisco, CA 94103
phone: 1.415.863.9900; info@nostarch.com
www.nostarch.com

The Library of Congress issued the following Cataloging-in-Publication Data for the first edition of Volume 1:

```
Hyde, Randall.
   Write great code : understanding the machine / Randall Hyde.
       p. cm.
   ISBN 1-59327-003-8
 1. Computer programming.  2. Computer architecture.  I. Title.
    QA76.6.H94 2004
    005.1--dc22
                                       2003017502
```

No Starch Press and the No Starch Press logo are registered trademarks of No Starch Press, Inc. Other product and company names mentioned herein may be the trademarks of their respective owners. Rather than use a trademark symbol with every occurrence of a trademarked name, we are using the names only in an editorial fashion and to the benefit of the trademark owner, with no intention of infringement of the trademark.

The information in this book is distributed on an "As Is" basis, without warranty. While every precaution has been taken in the preparation of this work, neither the author nor No Starch Press, Inc. shall have any liability to any person or entity with respect to any loss or damage caused or alleged to be caused directly or indirectly by the information contained in it.

About the Author

Randall Hyde is the author of *The Art of Assembly Language* and *Write Great Code, Volumes 1, 2,* and *3* (all from No Starch Press), as well as *Using 6502 Assembly Language* and *P-Source* (Datamost). He is also the coauthor of *Microsoft Macro Assembler 6.0 Bible* (The Waite Group). Over the past 40 years, Hyde has worked as an embedded software/hardware engineer developing instrumentation for nuclear reactors, traffic control systems, and other consumer electronics devices. He has also taught computer science at California State Polytechnic University, Pomona, and at the University of California, Riverside. His website is *www.randallhyde.com/*.

About the Technical Reviewer

Tony Tribelli has more than 35 years of experience in software development, including work on embedded device kernels and molecular modeling. He developed video games for 10 years at Blizzard Entertainment. He is currently a software development consultant and privately develops applications utilizing computer vision.

BRIEF CONTENTS

Acknowledgments xvii

Introduction xix

PART I: PERSONAL SOFTWARE ENGINEERING 1

Chapter 1: Software Development Metaphors 3

Chapter 2: Productivity 17

Chapter 3: Software Development Models 39

PART II: UML 71

Chapter 4: An Introduction to UML and Use Cases 73

Chapter 5: UML Activity Diagrams 89

Chapter 6: UML Class Diagrams 103

Chapter 7: UML Interaction Diagrams 127

Chapter 8: Miscellaneous UML Diagrams 155

PART III: DOCUMENTATION 167

Chapter 9: System Documentation 169

Chapter 10: Requirements Documentation 185

Chapter 11: Software Design Description Documentation 227

Chapter 12: Software Test Documentation 261

Afterword: Designing Great Code 317

Glossary 319

Index 327

CONTENTS IN DETAIL

ACKNOWLEDGMENTS xvii

INTRODUCTION xix
Assumptions and Prerequisites xxi
What Is Great Code? xxi
Programmer Classifications xxii
    Amateurs xxii
    Programmers xxii
    Software Engineers xxiv
    Great Programmers xxiv
So You Want to Be a Great Programmer xxv
A Final Note on Ethics and Character xxv
For More Information xxvi

PART I: PERSONAL SOFTWARE ENGINEERING 1

1
SOFTWARE DEVELOPMENT METAPHORS 3
1.1 What Is Software? 3
    1.1.1 Software Is Not Manufactured 4
    1.1.2 Software Doesn't Wear Out 4
    1.1.3 Most Software Is Custom 4
    1.1.4 Software Can Be Easily Upgraded 5
    1.1.5 Software Is Not an Independent Entity 5
1.2 Parallels to Other Fields 5
    1.2.1 Programmer as Artist 5
    1.2.2 Programmer as Architect 6
    1.2.3 Programmer as Engineer 7
    1.2.4 Programmer as Craftsman 7
    1.2.5 Artist, Architect, Engineer, or Craftsman? 8
1.3 Software Engineering 8
    1.3.1 A Formal Definition 9
    1.3.2 Project Size 10
    1.3.3 Where Software Engineering Fails 12
1.4 Software Craftsmanship 13
    1.4.1 Education 13
    1.4.2 Apprenticeship 13
    1.4.3 The Software Journeyman 14
    1.4.4 The Master Craftsman 15
    1.4.5 Where Software Craftsmanship Fails 15

| 1.5 | The Path to Writing Great Code | 15 |
| 1.6 | For More Information | 16 |

2
PRODUCTIVITY   17

2.1	What Is Productivity?	17
2.2	Programmer Productivity vs. Team Productivity	18
2.3	Man-Hours and Real Time	19
2.4	Conceptual and Scope Complexity	20
2.5	Predicting Productivity	21
2.6	Metrics and Why We Need Them	22
	2.6.1 Executable Size Metric	22
	2.6.2 Machine Instructions Metric	23
	2.6.3 Lines of Code Metric	23
	2.6.4 Statement Count Metric	24
	2.6.5 Function Point Analysis	24
	2.6.6 McCabe's Cyclomatic Complexity Metric	24
	2.6.7 Other Metrics	25
	2.6.8 The Problem with Metrics	25
2.7	How Do We Beat 10 Lines per Day?	26
2.8	Estimating Development Time	27
	2.8.1 Estimating Small Project Development Time	27
	2.8.2 Estimating Medium and Large Project Development Time	28
	2.8.3 Problems with Estimating Development Time	29
2.9	Crisis Mode Project Management	30
2.10	How to Be More Productive	31
	2.10.1 Choose Software Development Tools Wisely	31
	2.10.2 Manage Overhead	33
	2.10.3 Set Clear Goals and Milestones	33
	2.10.4 Practice Self-Motivation	34
	2.10.5 Focus and Eliminate Distractions	34
	2.10.6 If You're Bored, Work on Something Else	35
	2.10.7 Be as Self-Sufficient as Possible	35
	2.10.8 Recognize When You Need Help	36
	2.10.9 Overcome Poor Morale	36
2.11	For More Information	37

3
SOFTWARE DEVELOPMENT MODELS   39

3.1	The Software Development Life Cycle	39
3.2	The Software Development Model	42
	3.2.1 The Informal Model	43
	3.2.2 The Waterfall Model	44
	3.2.3 The V Model	45
	3.2.4 The Iterative Model	46
	3.2.5 The Spiral Model	48
	3.2.6 The Rapid Application Development Model	49
	3.2.7 The Incremental Model	51

3.3 Software Development Methodologies 52
        3.3.1   Traditional (Predictive) Methodologies 52
        3.3.2   Adaptive Methodologies. 52
        3.3.3   Agile 52
        3.3.4   Extreme Programming 55
        3.3.5   Scrum 65
        3.3.6   Feature-Driven Development 66
3.4 Models and Methodologies for the Great Programmer 68
3.5 For More Information 69

PART II: UML   71

4
AN INTRODUCTION TO UML AND USE CASES   73

4.1 The UML Standard 73
4.2 The UML Use Case Model 74
        4.2.1   Use Case Diagram Elements 74
        4.2.2   Use Case Packages 76
        4.2.3   Use Case Inclusion 76
        4.2.4   Use Case Generalization 77
        4.2.5   Use Case Extension 79
        4.2.6   Use Case Narratives 80
        4.2.7   Use Case Scenarios 86
4.3 The UML System Boundary Diagrams 87
4.4 Beyond Use Cases 88
4.5 For More Information 88

5
UML ACTIVITY DIAGRAMS   89

5.1 UML Activity State Symbols 89
        5.1.1   Start and Stop States 90
        5.1.2   Activities 90
        5.1.3   States 91
        5.1.4   Transitions 91
        5.1.5   Conditionals 91
        5.1.6   Merge Points 93
        5.1.7   Events and Triggers 94
        5.1.8   Forks and Joins (Synchronization) 96
        5.1.9   Call Symbols 96
        5.1.10 Partitions 97
        5.1.11 Comments and Annotations 98
        5.1.12 Connectors 98
        5.1.13 Additional Activity Diagram Symbols 98
5.2 Extending UML Activity Diagrams 99
5.3 For More Information 100

6
UML CLASS DIAGRAMS — 103

- 6.1 Object-Oriented Analysis and Design in UML 103
- 6.2 Visibility in a Class Diagram 105
    - 6.2.1 Public Class Visibility 105
    - 6.2.2 Private Class Visibility 106
    - 6.2.3 Protected Class Visibility 107
    - 6.2.4 Package Class Visibility 107
    - 6.2.5 Unsupported Visibility Types 108
- 6.3 Class Attributes 108
    - 6.3.1 Attribute Visibility 109
    - 6.3.2 Attribute Derived Values 109
    - 6.3.3 Attribute Names 109
    - 6.3.4 Attribute Data Types 110
    - 6.3.5 Operation Data Types (Return Values) 110
    - 6.3.6 Attribute Multiplicity 111
    - 6.3.7 Default Attribute Values 111
    - 6.3.8 Property Strings 112
    - 6.3.9 Attribute Syntax 112
- 6.4 Class Operations 112
- 6.5 UML Class Relationships 114
    - 6.5.1 Class Dependency Relationships 114
    - 6.5.2 Class Association Relationships 115
    - 6.5.3 Class Aggregation Relationships 116
    - 6.5.4 Class Composition Relationships 117
    - 6.5.5 Relationship Features 117
    - 6.5.6 Class Inheritance Relationships 125
- 6.6 Objects 125
- 6.7 For More Information 126

7
UML INTERACTION DIAGRAMS — 127

- 7.1 Sequence Diagrams 128
    - 7.1.1 Lifelines 128
    - 7.1.2 Message Types 129
    - 7.1.3 Message Labels 130
    - 7.1.4 Message Numbers 130
    - 7.1.5 Guard Conditions 131
    - 7.1.6 Iterations 132
    - 7.1.7 Long Delays and Time Constraints 132
    - 7.1.8 External Objects 133
    - 7.1.9 Activation Bars 133
    - 7.1.10 Branching 134
    - 7.1.11 Alternative Flows 135
    - 7.1.12 Object Creation and Destruction 136
    - 7.1.13 Sequence Fragments 137
- 7.2 Collaboration Diagrams 152
- 7.3 For More Information 153

8
MISCELLANEOUS UML DIAGRAMS   155

8.1   Component Diagrams 155
8.2   Package Diagrams. 158
8.3   Deployment Diagrams 159
8.4   Composite Structure Diagrams. 160
8.5   Statechart Diagrams. 163
8.6   More UML 165
8.7   For More Information 165

PART III: DOCUMENTATION   167

9
SYSTEM DOCUMENTATION   169

9.1   System Documentation Types. 170
9.2   Traceability 171
     9.2.1   Ways to Build Traceability into Your Documentation 172
     9.2.2   Tag Formats 172
     9.2.3   The Requirements/Reverse Traceability Matrix. 178
9.3   Validation, Verification, and Reviews 181
9.4   Reducing Development Costs Using Documentation 182
     9.4.1   Reducing Costs via Validation 182
     9.4.2   Reducing Costs via Verification 183
9.5   For More Information 184

10
REQUIREMENTS DOCUMENTATION   185

10.1   Requirement Origins and Traceability. 185
     10.1.1   A Suggested Requirements Format 186
     10.1.2   Characteristics of Good Requirements 187
10.2   Design Goals 193
10.3   The System Requirements Specification Document 193
10.4   The Software Requirements Specification Document 194
     10.4.1   Introduction. 195
     10.4.2   Overall Description 196
     10.4.3   Specific Requirements. 199
     10.4.4   Supporting Information 203
     10.4.5   A Sample Software Requirements Specification 203
10.5   Creating Requirements 212
10.6   Use Cases. 214
     10.6.1   Enable/Disable Debug Mode 215
     10.6.2   Enable/Disable Ethernet 216
     10.6.3   Enable/Disable RS-232 218
     10.6.4   Enable/Disable Test Mode 218
     10.6.5   Enable/Disable USB 218
     10.6.6   Read DIP Switches 218

10.7 Creating DAQ Software Requirements from the Use Cases 218
10.8 (Selected) DAQ Software Requirements (from SRS). 219
10.9 Updating the Traceability Matrix with Requirement Information 222
        10.9.1 Requirements to Be Verified by Review. 223
        10.9.2 Requirements to Be Verified by Testing 225
10.10 For More Information 225

11
SOFTWARE DESIGN DESCRIPTION DOCUMENTATION   227

11.1 IEEE Std 1016-1998 vs. IEEE Std 1016-2009. 228
11.2 IEEE 1016-2009 Conceptual Model. 228
        11.2.1 Design Concerns and Design Stakeholders 228
        11.2.2 Design Viewpoints and Design Elements 229
        11.2.3 Design Views, Overlays, and Rationales. 239
        11.2.4 The IEEE Std 1016-2009 Conceptual Model. 242
11.3 SDD Required Contents 244
        11.3.1 SDD Identification 244
        11.3.2 Design Stakeholders and Their Design Concerns 244
        11.3.3 Design Views, Viewpoints, Overlays, and Rationales 245
11.4 SDD Traceability and Tags 245
11.5 A Suggested SDD Outline. 245
11.6 A Sample SDD 247
11.7 Updating the Traceability Matrix with Design Information 259
11.8 Creating a Software Design 260
11.9 For More Information 260

12
SOFTWARE TEST DOCUMENTATION   261

12.1 The Software Test Documents in Std 829 262
        12.1.1 Process Support. 262
        12.1.2 Integrity Levels and Risk Assessment 263
        12.1.3 Software Development Testing Levels 265
12.2 Test Plans 266
        12.2.1 Master Test Plan 266
        12.2.2 *Level* Test Plan 267
        12.2.3 *Level* Test Design Documentation 269
12.3 Software Review List Documentation. 270
        12.3.1 Sample SRL Outline 270
        12.3.2 Sample SRL. 271
        12.3.3 Adding SRL Items to the Traceability Matrix. 274
12.4 Software Test Case Documentation 274
        12.4.1 Introduction in the STC Document. 277
        12.4.2 Details 278
        12.4.3 General 280
        12.4.4 A Sample Software Test Case Document. 281
        12.4.5 Updating the RTM with STC Information 288
12.5 Software Test Procedure Documentation 288
        12.5.1 The IEEE Std 829-2009 Software Test Procedure 289
        12.5.2 Extended Outline for Software Test Procedure 290
        12.5.3 Introduction in the STP Document. 292

		12.5.4	Test Procedures	294
		12.5.5	General	296
		12.5.6	Index	297
		12.5.7	A Sample STP	297
		12.5.8	Updating the RTM with STP Information	302
12.6	*Level* Test Logs			303
		12.6.1	Introduction in the *Level* Test Logs Document	304
		12.6.2	Details	305
		12.6.3	Glossary	305
		12.6.4	A Few Comments on Test Logs	305
12.7	Anomaly Reports			308
		12.7.1	Introduction in the Anomaly Reports Document	309
		12.7.2	Details	310
		12.7.3	A Few Comments on Anomaly Reports	311
12.8	Test Reports			312
		12.8.1	Brief Mention of the Master Test Report	313
		12.8.2	*Level* Test Reports	313
12.9	Do You Really Need All of This?			315
12.10	For More Information			315

AFTERWORD: DESIGNING GREAT CODE 317

GLOSSARY 319

INDEX 327

ACKNOWLEDGMENTS

Many people have read and reread every word, symbol, and punctuation mark in this book in order to produce a better result. Kudos to the following people for their careful work on the second edition: development editor Athabasca Witschi, copyeditor/production editor Rachel Monaghan, and proofreader James Fraleigh.

I would like to take the opportunity to graciously thank Anthony Tribelli, a longtime friend, who went well beyond the call of duty when doing a technical review of this book. He pulled every line of code out of this book (including snippets) and compiled and ran it to make sure it worked properly. His suggestions and opinions throughout the technical review process have dramatically improved the quality of this work.

Thanks to all of you,
Randall Hyde

INTRODUCTION

In the late 1960s, the need for computer software was outpacing the capability of technical schools, colleges, and universities to produce trained computer professionals to create that software—a phenomenon that became known as the *software crisis.* Increasing the output of colleges and universities wasn't a practical approach; too few qualified students were enrolling in computer science programs to satisfy the demand. At the time, researchers determined that a better solution was to increase the productivity of existing computer programmers. Noticing similarities between software development and other engineering activities, these researchers concluded that the procedures and policies that worked for other engineering disciplines could solve the software crisis. Thus, *software engineering* was born.

Until the field of software engineering blossomed, software development was a mysterious craft practiced by gurus with varying abilities and accomplishments. Up to that point, a software project's success depended entirely upon the abilities of one or two key programmers rather than those of the entire team. Software engineering sought to balance the skills of software teams to make them more productive and less reliant upon those one or two highly talented individuals.

To a large extent, the practice of software engineering has been successful. Large projects built by teams of programmers could never have been completed with the ad hoc organizational methods of the past. But at the same time, important qualities were lost. Software engineering encourages team productivity at the expense of individual creativity, skill, and growth. Although software engineering techniques have the potential to turn poor programmers into good programmers, they can also restrict great programmers from doing their best work. The world has too few great programmers. The last thing we want to do is to discourage a programmer from reaching their potential; however, this is what the software engineering regimen often does.

The *Write Great Code* series is an effort to restore some of that lost individual creativity, skill, and growth. It covers what I call *personal software engineering*, or how a programmer can improve the quality of their code. Specifically, it describes how you can produce great code—code that's easy to maintain, enhance, test and debug, document, deploy, and even retire—from mediocre code. Great code is devoid of the kludges and hacks that are often the result of unreasonable pressure or ill planning on the engineer's or management's part. Great code is code you can be proud of.

As I completed *Write Great Code, Volume 2: Thinking Low-Level, Writing High-Level (WGC2)*, I had intended to incorporate more information in this book. In the last chapter of *WGC2*, I wrote the following:

> [*Write Great Code, Volume 3: Engineering Software*] begins discussing the *personal software engineering* aspects of programming. The software engineering field focuses primarily on the management of large software systems. Personal software engineering, on the other hand, covers those topics germane to writing great code at a personal level—craftsmanship, art, and pride in workmanship. So, in *Engineering Software*, we'll consider those aspects through discussions on software development metaphors, software developer metaphors, and *system documentation* [emphasis added], among other topics.

System documentation (including requirements, test procedures, design documents, and the like) is a huge part of software engineering. Therefore, a book on the subject must provide, at the very least, an overview of these subjects. Well, about seven chapters into this book I realized there wasn't enough room to cover all this material in a single book. In the end, I wound up splitting this volume, *Engineering Software*, into four volumes. The first of these four volumes is this one, which is the third volume of the *Write Great Code* series. It concentrates on software development models and system documentation. The fourth volume of the series will teach software design; the fifth volume will develop the great-coding theme further; and a sixth volume will deal with testing.

As I write this, it's been 10 years since I completed Volume 2 of the *Write Great Code* series. It was time to complete Volume 3, even if it meant splitting the original information across two or more volumes. If you've read my earlier books, you know I like to cover subjects in depth; I'm not interested in writing books that barely touch on the subject matter. Thus, I was faced with either splitting the work across multiple volumes and getting them out the door or producing a 2,000-page tome that, as history has oft demonstrated, might never be completed. I apologize to those who expected this book to cover additional subjects. Fear not—the information will arrive in future volumes. You're just getting the first part of it sooner in this book.

Assumptions and Prerequisites

In order to concentrate on engineering software, this book has to make certain assumptions. Although I've tried to keep those to a minimum, you'll benefit most from this book if your personal skill set fulfills some prerequisites.

You should be reasonably competent in at least one imperative (procedural) or object-oriented programming language. This includes C and C++, C#, Swift, Pascal, BASIC, Java, and assembly. You should know how to take a small problem description and work through the design and implementation of its software solution. A typical semester or quarter course at a college or university or several months' experience on your own should be sufficient for using this book.

You should also have a basic grasp of machine organization and data representation. For example, you should understand hexadecimal and binary numbering systems, and how computers represent various high-level data types, such as signed integers, characters, and strings in memory. *Write Great Code, Volume 1: Understanding the Machine (WGC1)* fully covers machine organization if you feel your knowledge in this area is weak. Although I might refer to material in *WGC1*, you should have no problem reading this book independently of that one.

What Is Great Code?

Great code is software that follows a set of rules that guide the decisions a programmer makes when implementing an algorithm as source code. Great code is written with other programmers in mind—with documentation that allows others to read, comprehend, and maintain the software. I call this the *Golden Rule of Software Development*, and it holds the key to software engineering.

Taking things down a level, great code:

- Is fast and uses the CPU, system resources, and memory efficiently
- Is well documented and easy to read, maintain, and enhance
- Follows a consistent set of style guidelines
- Uses an explicit design that follows established software engineering conventions
- Is well tested and robust
- Is produced on time and under budget

While Volumes 1 and 2 of the *Write Great Code* series deal with many of the efficiency aspects associated with great code, the remaining books in the series, starting with this one, focus specifically on creating code that meets the preceding criteria.

Programmer Classifications

In order to understand what makes a programmer great, let's first consider the differences between amateurs, programmers at various levels, and software engineers.

Amateurs

The amateur programmer is self-taught, with only a small amount of experience, and as such is the antithesis of the great programmer. In the early days of computers, these programmers were known as *hackers*. That term has morphed into several different meanings today that don't necessarily describe a programmer without sufficient education or experience to do professional-level software engineering.

The problem with code written by amateur programmers is that typically they write it for themselves or for friends; thus, it doesn't usually adhere to contemporary standards for software engineering projects. However, amateur programmers can improve their status with a little education (which the *WGC* series can help provide).

Programmers

Computer programmers have a wide range of experiences and responsibilities, which is often reflected in titles like junior programmer, coder, Programmer I and II, analyst/system analyst, and system architect. Here we explore some of these roles and how they differ.

Interns

Typically, interns are students working part-time who are assigned so-called *grunt work*—tasks such as running a set of canned test procedures on the code or documenting the software.

Junior Programmer

Recent graduates typically fill the junior programmer position. Often, they work on testing or maintenance tasks. Rarely do they get the opportunity to work on new projects; instead, most of their programming time is spent reworking existing statements or dealing with legacy code.

Coder

A programmer advances to the coder level when they gain sufficient experience for management to trust them with developing new code for projects.

A more senior programmer assigns (less complex) subcomponents of a larger project to the coder to help complete the project faster.

Programmer I and II

As a programmer gains more experience and is capable of handling complex implementation tasks on their own, they progress from coder to Programmer I and then Programmer II. A system analyst can often provide a Programmer I or II with a general idea of what they want, and the programmer is able to fill in the missing details and produce an application in line with the system analyst's expectations.

System Analyst

A system analyst studies a problem and determines the best way to implement a solution. Often, the system analyst chooses the major algorithms to use and creates the final application's organization.

System Architect

The system architect chooses how the components designed by a system analyst in a large-scale system will work together. Often, the system architect specifies processes, hardware, and other non-software-related items as part of the total solution.

The Complete Programmer

A *complete programmer* is the amalgamation of all these subdivisions. That is, a complete programmer is capable of studying a problem, designing a solution, implementing that solution in a programming language, and testing the result.

THE PROBLEM WITH PROGRAMMER CLASSIFICATION

In reality, most of these programmer categories are artificial; they exist simply to justify a different pay scale for beginning programmers and experienced programmers. For example, a system analyst designs the algorithms and overall data flow for a particular application, then hands off the design to a coder, who implements that design in a particular programming language. We normally associate both tasks with *programming*, but junior members of the programming staff don't have the proper experience to design large systems from scratch, although they're perfectly capable of taking a design and converting it into an appropriate programming language. The system analysts and architects usually have the experience and ability to handle the entire project. However, management generally finds it more cost-effective to use them on those portions of the project that require their experience rather than having them do the low-level coding that a recent graduate could do (at lower cost).

Software Engineers

In the engineering fields, engineers approach a specified problem by following a prescribed set of rules, building a custom solution from a combination of predetermined solutions. This approach allows even less talented engineers to produce working solutions without having to develop a system from scratch. Software engineering emerged as an effort to maximize the value of the entire programming team by applying traditional engineering concepts to software development. For the most part, the software engineering revolution has been successful. Software engineers with the proper training and leadership can produce high-quality code in less time and for less money than was possible before.

Pure software engineering discourages divergent thinking, because it risks wasting time and leading the engineer down an unsuccessful path (resulting in higher development costs and longer development times). In general, software engineering is more concerned with developing an application *on time and under budget* than with writing code the *best possible way*. But if software engineering practitioners never try anything new, they often miss opportunities to produce a great design, never develop any new practices to incorporate into their rule book, and never become great programmers.

Great Programmers

Great programmers are cognizant of the budgetary issues, but they also realize that exploring new ideas and methodologies is important to advance the field. They know when it's essential to follow the rules but also when it's okay to break (or at least bend) them. But most important of all, great programmers use their skill sets to their fullest, achieving results that wouldn't be possible by simply thinking inside the box. Hackers are born, software engineers are made, and great programmers are a bit of both. They have three main characteristics: a genuine love for the work, ongoing education and training, and the ability to think outside the box when solving problems.

Loving What You Do, Doing What You Love

People tend to excel at tasks they love and do poorly on activities they dislike. The bottom line is that if you hate computer programming, you won't make a very good computer programmer. If you weren't born with the desire to solve problems and overcome challenges, no amount of education and training will change your disposition. Thus, the most important prerequisite to becoming a great programmer is that you really love to write computer programs.

Prioritizing Education and Training

Great programmers enjoy the types of tasks the field demands, but they also need something else—formal education and training. We'll discuss education and training in greater depth in later chapters, but for now it suffices to say that great programmers are well educated (perhaps possessing a postsecondary degree) and continue their education throughout their careers.

Thinking Outside the Box

As mentioned, following a predetermined set of rules to produce code is the typical expectation of a software engineer. However, as you'll see in Chapter 1, to become a great programmer (a "Grand Master Programmer"), you need to be willing and able to devise new programming techniques that come only from divergent thinking rather than blindly following rules. Great programmers have an innate desire to push boundaries and explore new solutions to the problems they face.

So You Want to Be a Great Programmer

To summarize, if you want to be a truly great programmer and inspire awe from your peers, you'll need the following:

- A love of computer programming and problem solving
- A wide range of computer science knowledge based on a college or university degree[1]
- A lifelong commitment to education and training
- The ability and willingness to think outside the box when exploring solutions
- The personal desire and motivation to excel at a task and always produce the best possible work

With these attributes, the only thing keeping you from becoming a great programmer is more knowledge. That's where this book comes in.

A Final Note on Ethics and Character

The software engineer's job is to create the best possible product given conflicting requirements by making appropriate compromises in a system's design. During this process, the engineer must prioritize requirements and choose the best solution to the problem given the project's constraints. Ethics and personal character often impact decisions individuals make while working on complex projects, particularly stressful ones. Being intellectually dishonest (for example, fudging project estimates or claiming a piece of software works without fully testing it), pirating software development tools (or other software), introducing undocumented features in software (such as backdoors) without management approval, or adopting an elitist attitude (thinking you're better than other team members) are all cases of software engineering ethical lapses. Exercising sound moral judgment and practicing good ethics will make you both a better person and a better programmer.

---

1. Or equivalent self-study, which is very rarely accomplished in reality despite honest intentions.

For More Information

Barger, Robert N. *Computer Ethics: A Case-Based Approach.* Cambridge, UK: Cambridge University Press, 2008.

Floridi, Luciano, ed. *The Cambridge Handbook of Information and Computer Ethics.* Cambridge, UK: Cambridge University Press, 2006.

Forester, Tom, and Perry Morrison. *Computer Ethics: Cautionary Tales and Ethical Dilemmas in Computing.* 2nd ed. Cambridge, MA: MIT Press, 1993.

Parker, Donn B. "Rules of Ethics in Information Processing." *Communications of the ACM* 11, no. 3 (1968): 198–201. *https://dl.acm.org/doi/10.1145/362929.362987.*

Wiener, Norbert. *The Human Use of Human Beings: Cybernetics and Society.* Boston: Houghton Mifflin Harcourt, 1950.

WikiWikiWeb. "Grand Master Programmer." Last updated November 23, 2014. *http://c2.com/cgi/wiki?GrandMasterProgrammer/.*

PART I

PERSONAL SOFTWARE ENGINEERING

1

SOFTWARE DEVELOPMENT METAPHORS

How do we define the software development process? This might seem like a silly question. Why not just say "software development is software development" and leave it at that? Well, if we can draw analogies between software development tasks and other professional endeavors, we can gain insight into the software development process. Then we can refine the process by studying process improvements in related fields. To that end, this chapter explores some of the common ways of understanding software development.

1.1 What Is Software?

To better understand how programmers create software, we can compare software to other things people create. Doing so will provide important insight into why certain creative metaphors apply, or don't apply, to software development.

In his book, *Software Engineering: A Beginner's Approach*, Robert Pressman identifies several characteristics of software. This section explores those characteristics to illuminate the nature of software and how it defines a computer programmer's work.

1.1.1 Software Is Not Manufactured

> *Software is developed or engineered; it is not manufactured in the classical sense.*
>
> —Robert Pressman

Compared to hardware products, the manufacturing cost of a software product is very low: stamping out a CD or DVD costs only a few pennies, plus a small amount for shipping and handling (and electronic distribution is even less expensive). Also, the software design has very little impact on the quality or final cost of the manufactured CD/DVD. Assuming reasonable quality controls at the manufacturing plant, a computer programmer rarely has to consider manufacturing issues when designing a software application.[1] Contrast this with other engineering professions where the engineer has to design in *manufacturability* of the product.

1.1.2 Software Doesn't Wear Out

Both software and hardware suffer from failures due to poor design early in the products' lives. However, if we could eliminate design flaws in the products (that is, deliver a defect-free piece of software or hardware), the differences between the two become obvious. Once a piece of software is correct, it doesn't ever fail or "wear out." As long as the underlying computer system is functioning properly, the software will continue to work.[2] The software engineer, unlike the hardware engineer, doesn't have to worry about designing in the ability to easily replace components that fail over time.

1.1.3 Most Software Is Custom

> *Most software is custom built rather than being assembled from existing [standard] components.*
>
> —Robert Pressman

Although many attempts have been made to create similarly standardized software components that software engineers can assemble into large applications, the concept of a *software IC* (that is, the equivalent of an electronic integrated circuit) has never been realized. Software libraries and object-oriented programming techniques encourage reusing prewritten code, but the premise of constructing large software systems from smaller preassembled components has failed to produce anything close to what's possible in hardware design.

---

1. Probably the only time this consideration comes up in software development is when the program becomes so large that it requires multiple CDs, DVDs, or other media for distribution.

2. Arguably, we could say software "wears out" when the hardware it requires becomes obsolete and eventually fails without any way of being replaced.

1.1.4 Software Can Be Easily Upgraded

In many cases, it's possible to completely replace an existing software application in the field with a new version (or even a completely different application) without incurring a huge cost.[3] The application's end user can simply replace the old software with the new and enjoy the benefits of the upgraded version. In fact, most modern software systems and applications auto-update via the internet during normal operation.

1.1.5 Software Is Not an Independent Entity

Software is not a stand-alone product. An electrical engineer can design a hardware device that can operate completely on its own. However, software depends upon something else (typically a computer system) for proper operation. Therefore, a software developer must live with the constraints imposed by external systems (computer systems, operating systems, programming languages, and so on) when designing and implementing a software application.

1.2 Parallels to Other Fields

Computer programmers are often compared to artists, craftsmen, engineers, architects, and technicians. Although computer programming doesn't match any of these professions exactly, we can draw useful parallels to these fields and gain insight from the techniques they employ.

1.2.1 Programmer as Artist

In the early days of computer programming, software development was considered an art. The ability to write software—to make sense of so much nonsense to create a working program—seemed to be a God-given talent exercised by a select few, akin to master painters or musical virtuosos. (In fact, considerable anecdotal evidence suggests that musicians and computer programmers use the same areas of their brains for their creative activities, and a decent percentage of programmers were, or are, musicians.[4])

But is software development an actual art form? An *artist* is typically defined as someone blessed with certain talents and the skill to use them in a creative way. The key word here is *talent*, which is a natural ability. Because not everyone is born with the same talents, not everyone can be an artist. To apply the analogy, it would seem that if you want to be a programmer, you have to be born that way; indeed, some people seem to be born with a natural talent or aptitude for programming.

---

3. We'll ignore the cost of development, marketing, and upgrade fees here, and simply consider the cost of doing a field upgrade of a piece of software.

4. Kathleen Melymuka, "Why Musicians May Make the Best Tech Workers," CNN.com, July 31, 1998.

The "programmer as artist" comparison seems to apply to the very best programmers. Although artists follow their own set of rules to produce quality art, they often produce their most exceptional art when they bend the rules and explore new creative ground. Similarly, the very best programmers are familiar with good software development rules but are also willing to experiment with new techniques to try to improve the development process. Just as true artists are not content with duplicating existing work or styles, the "programmer as artist" is happier creating new applications than grinding out yet another version of an old one.

NOTE *One of the most well-respected textbook series on computer science is Donald Knuth's* The Art of Computer Programming. *Clearly, the notion of programming as an art form is well entrenched in the computer science field.*

1.2.2 Programmer as Architect

The artist metaphor works great for small projects where the artist creates the idea and implements a work of art, much like a programmer designs and implements a small software system. However, for larger software systems, the "programmer as architect" analogy is probably a better fit. An architect designs the structure but leaves the implementation to others (because often it's logistically impossible for one person to build it). In computer science, those who design a system for others to implement are often called *programmer/analysts*.

An architect exercises large-scale creative control over a project. For example, an architect designing a fancy building defines how it will look, what materials to use, and the guidelines for the construction workers to follow, but doesn't handle the construction itself. An architect might supervise the build (much like a programmer/analyst would review modules others add to their software system); however, the architect doesn't wield a hammer or operate a crane.

It might seem that this analogy doesn't apply to small projects, but it can if you allow an individual to "change hats." That is, during the first phase of the project, the programmer puts on their architect/programmer/analyst hat and creates the design for the system. Then the programmer switches hats and puts on their programmer/coder hat to implement the system.

What the "programmer as architect" paradigm adds over and above the "programmer as artist" model is verification and safety measures. When an artist paints an image, composes a piece of music, or sculpts an object, they generally don't worry about whether that work meets any requirements other than their own. Also, they don't have to worry about how that art might physically hurt life or property.[5] An architect, on the other hand, must consider physical realities and the fact that a bad design can lead to injury or harm. The "programmer as architect" paradigm introduces personal responsibility, review (testing), and safety to the programmer's task.

---

5. An exception might be a performance artwork, such as a fireworks display.

1.2.3 Programmer as Engineer

A NATO conference in 1968 challenged the notion that good programmers are born, not made. As mentioned in this book's introduction, the world was facing a software crisis—new software applications were needed faster than programmers could be trained to create them. So NATO sponsored the 1968 conference, coining the term *software engineering* to describe how to tackle the problem by applying engineering principles to the wild world of computer programming.

Engineers are interested in solving practical problems cost-effectively, in terms of both the design effort and the cost of production. For this reason, coupled with the fact that the engineering profession has been around for a very long time (particularly mechanical and chemical engineering), a large number of procedures and policies have been created for engineers over the years to streamline their work.

In many engineering fields today, an engineer's task is to construct a large system from smaller, predesigned building blocks. An electrical engineer who wants to design a computer system doesn't start by designing custom transistors or other small components; instead, they use predesigned CPUs, memory elements, and I/O devices, assembling them into a complete system. Similarly, a mechanical engineer can use predesigned trusses and pedestals to design a new bridge. Design reuse is the hallmark of the engineering profession. It's one of the key elements to producing safe, reliable, functional, and cost-effective designs as rapidly as possible.

Software engineers also follow a set of well-defined procedures and policies to construct large systems from smaller predefined systems. Indeed, the Institute of Electrical and Electronics Engineers (IEEE) defines *software engineering* as follows:

> The application of a systematic, disciplined, quantifiable approach to development, operation, and maintenance of software; that is, the application of engineering to software.

1.2.4 Programmer as Craftsman

The craftsman model lies somewhere between the artist and the engineer. Central to this paradigm is the idea of programmers as individuals; that is, the software craftsman metaphor recognizes that people matter. Throwing more people and restrictive rules at a problem doesn't produce higher-quality software, but training individuals better and allowing them to apply their natural talents and skills does.

There are parallels between the traditional craftsman's development process and that of the software craftsman. Like all craftsmen, a software craftsman starts as an *apprentice* or an *intern*. An apprentice works under the close guidance of another craftsman. After learning the ropes, the apprentice programmer becomes a *journeyman*, usually working with teams of other programmers under the supervision of a software craftsman. Ultimately, the programmer's skills increase to the point that they become a *master craftsman*.

The craftsman model provides the best metaphor for programmers intent upon becoming great programmers. I'll return to the discussion of this metaphor later in this chapter, in the section "Software Craftsmanship" on page 13.

1.2.5 Artist, Architect, Engineer, or Craftsman?

To write great code, you must understand what makes code great. You need to use the best tools, coding techniques, procedures, processes, and policies when writing code. In addition, you must constantly increase your knowledge and improve the development processes you use to enhance the quality of the software you develop. That's why it's important to consider different approaches to software development, understand the software product, and choose the best approach.

You need to work hard to learn how to write great code and then work hard at actually writing it. A great software developer adopts ideas that work from each of the fields just discussed and dispenses with those that don't work. To summarize:

- *Great artists* practice their skills to develop their talents. They engage in divergent thinking to explore new ways of presenting their message.
- *Great architects* know how to build upon existing designs using standard components to create custom objects. They understand cost constraints, safety issues, requirements, and the need for overdesign to ensure reliable operation. Great architects understand the relationship between form and function, as well as the need to fulfill customer requirements.
- *Great engineers* recognize the benefit of consistency. They document and automate development steps to avoid missing steps in the process. Like architects, engineers encourage the reuse of existing designs to deliver more robust and cost-effective solutions. Engineering provides procedures and policies to help overcome personal limitations in a project.
- *Great craftsmen* train and practice skills under the tutelage of a master with the ultimate goal of becoming a master craftsman. This metaphor emphasizes the qualities of the individual such as their problem-solving and organizational abilities.

1.3 Software Engineering

Since its emergence in the late 1960s, software engineering has become an unqualified success. Today, few professional programmers would accept the coding horrors that were "standard procedure" at the dawn of the field. Concepts that modern programmers take for granted—such as structured programming, proper program layout (like indentation), commenting, and good naming policies—are all due to software engineering research. Indeed, decades of such research have greatly influenced modern programming languages and other programming tools.

Software engineering has been around for so long and has had such an impact on all facets of computer programming that many people assume the term *software engineer* is synonymous with *computer programmer*. It's certainly true that any professional software engineer should also be a capable computer programmer, but computer programming constitutes only a small part of software engineering. Software engineering largely involves economics and project management. Interestingly, those responsible for managing the projects, maintaining the schedules, choosing the methodologies to use, and so on are not called software engineers; they're called managers, project leads, and other titles implying a position of authority. Likewise, the people we call software engineers don't actually do the software engineering—they simply write the code specified by the actual software engineers (managers and project leads). This is, perhaps, why there is so much confusion around the term *software engineering*.

1.3.1 A Formal Definition

No single definition of *software engineering* seems to satisfy everyone. Different authors add their own "spin," making their definition slightly (or greatly) different than those found in other texts. The reason this book is titled *Engineering Software* is because I want to avoid adding yet another definition to the mix. As a reminder, the IEEE defines *software engineering* as

> The application of a systematic, disciplined, quantifiable approach to development, operation, and maintenance of software; that is, the application of engineering to software.

The original software engineering definition, and the one I use, is

> Software engineering is the study of the development and management of large software systems.

The operative term here is *large*. Progress in software engineering has mostly been funded by defense contracts and the like, so it's no surprise that software engineering is synonymous with large systems. The IEEE definition could apply to systems of nearly any size, but because most of the research into software engineering deals with very large systems, I prefer the second definition.

NOTE *To avoid confusion with the generic term* software engineering, *I use a more specialized term*, personal software engineering, *to describe those processes and methodologies that apply to a single programmer working on a small project or a small part of a larger project. My intent is to describe what computer programmers believe is the essence of software engineering without all the extraneous detail that has little to do with writing great code.*

When it comes to software development, people have completely different concepts of what "large" means. An undergraduate in a computer science program might think that a program containing a couple thousand lines of source code is a large system. To a project manager at Boeing (or other large firm), a large system contains well over one million lines of code. The last time I counted (which was a long time ago), Microsoft's Windows operating system (OS) exceeded 50 million lines of source code; no one questions that Windows is a large system!

Because traditional software engineering definitions generally apply to large software systems, we need to come up with a reasonable definition of large (and small) software systems. Although *lines of code (LOC)* is the metric software engineers often use to describe the size of a software system, it is a low-quality metric with almost a two-order-of-magnitude variance.[6] This book will often use the LOC or *thousands of lines of code (KLOC)* metric. But it's not a good idea to base a formal definition on such a poor metric. Doing so weakens the definition.

1.3.2 Project Size

A *small project* is one that an average programmer can complete on their own in a reasonable amount of time (less than two years). A *medium-sized project* is too large for an individual to complete in a reasonable time frame, but a small team of two to five programmers can accomplish it. A *large project* requires a large team of programmers (more than five members). In terms of LOC, a small project contains about 50 to 100 KLOC; medium-sized projects fall into the 50 to 1,000 KLOC (one million lines of source code) range; and large projects start at around 500 to 1,000 KLOC.

Small projects are trivial to manage. Because small projects require no interaction between programmers and very little interaction between the programmer and the outside world, productivity depends almost solely upon the programmer's abilities.

Medium-sized projects introduce new challenges. Because multiple programmers are working on the project, communication can become a problem, but the team is small enough that this overhead is manageable. Nevertheless, the group dynamics require extra support, which increases the cost of each line of code written.

Large projects require a large team of programmers. Communication and other overhead often consume 50 percent of each engineer's productivity. Effective project management is crucial.

Software engineering deals with the methodologies, practices, and policies needed to successfully manage projects requiring large teams of programmers. Unfortunately, practices that work well for individuals, or even small teams, don't scale up to large teams, and large-project methodologies, practices, and policies don't scale down to small and medium-sized projects. Practices that work well for large projects typically inject unreasonable overhead into small and medium-sized projects, reducing the productivity of those small teams.

Let's take a closer look at some benefits and drawbacks of projects of different sizes.

---

6. That is, two software systems with the same approximate complexity could vary by a factor of almost 100 in terms of the number of lines of code.

1.3.2.1 Small Projects

On small projects, a single software engineer is completely responsible for system design, implementation, testing, debugging, deployment, and documentation. On such a project, the lone engineer is accountable for far more tasks than a single engineer would be on a medium-sized or large project. But the tasks are small and therefore manageable. Because a small project requires an individual to perform a wide range of tasks, the programmer must possess a varied skill set. Personal software engineering covers all the activities a developer would do on a small project.

Small projects make the most efficient use of engineering resources. The engineer can employ the most productive approach to solving problems because they don't have to reach a consensus with other engineers on the project. The engineer can also optimize the time they spend on each development phase. In a structured software design regimen, considerable time is spent documenting operations, which doesn't make sense when there's only a single programmer on a project (though a different programmer might need to work with the code later in the product's lifetime).

The drawback, and the trap, of a small project is that an engineer must be capable of handling all the different tasks required. Many small projects fail (or their development cost is too high) because the engineer doesn't have the proper training to handle an entire project. More than any other goal, the purpose of the *Write Great Code* series is to teach programmers how to do small projects properly.

1.3.2.2 Medium-Sized Projects

On a medium-sized project, personal software engineering encompasses those aspects of the project for which a single engineer is responsible. This typically includes the design of their system component, its implementation (coding), and the documentation for that module. Generally, they are also responsible for testing their component (*unit testing*), and then the team as a whole tests the entire system (*integration testing*). Usually, there's one engineer in charge of the complete system design (the *project head* or *lead programmer*) who also handles deployment. Depending on the project, a technical writer might handle system documentation. Because engineers share tasks in a medium-sized project, specialization is possible, and the project doesn't require each engineer to be capable of performing all the individual tasks. The lead programmer can direct the activities of those less experienced to maintain quality throughout the project.

A single engineer on a small project sees the total picture and can optimize certain activities based on their understanding of the entire project. On a large project, a single engineer is unaware of much of the project beyond their small piece of it. Medium-sized projects provide a hybrid of these two extremes: individuals can see much of the entire project and adjust their approach to system implementation. They can also specialize on certain aspects of the system without becoming overwhelmed by the details of the rest of the system.

1.3.2.3 Large Projects

On a large project, various team members have specialized roles, from system design to implementation, testing, documentation, deployment, and system enhancement and maintenance. As with medium-sized projects, in large projects personal software engineering encompasses only those activities for which an individual programmer is responsible. Software engineers on a large project generally do only a few tasks (such as coding and unit testing); therefore, they don't require the wide-ranging skill set of a lone programmer on a small project.

Beyond the scope of activity, the size of a project affects the productivity of its engineers. On a large project, engineers can become very specialized and concentrate on their one area of expertise. This allows them to do their job more efficiently than if they had to use a more generalized skill set. However, large projects must use a common software development approach to be effective, and some engineers may not be as productive if they don't like the approach.

1.3.3 Where Software Engineering Fails

It's possible to apply engineering techniques to software development to produce applications in a more cost-effective manner. However, as Pete McBreen states in *Software Craftsmanship: The New Imperative*, the biggest problem with software engineering is the assumption that a "systematic, disciplined, quantifiable approach" is the only reasonable approach. In fact, he raises a very good question: is it even possible to make software development systematic and quantified? Quoting *http://www.controlchaos.com/*, McBreen says:

> If a process can be fully defined, with all things known about it so that it can be designed and run repeatedly with predictable results, it is known as a defined process, and it can be subjected to automation. If all things about a process aren't fully known—only what generally happens when you mix these inputs and what to measure and control to get the desired output—these are called empirical processes.

Software development is not a defined process; it's an empirical process. As such, software development cannot be fully automated, and it's often difficult to apply engineering principles to software development. Part of the problem is that practical engineering relies so much on the reuse of existing designs. Although a considerable amount of reuse is possible in computer programming, too, it requires much more customization than you find in other engineering professions.

Another significant problem with software engineering, as briefly discussed in the book's introduction, is that software engineering treats software engineers as commodity resources that a manager can swap arbitrarily into and out of a project, which disregards the importance of an individual's talents. The issue isn't that engineering techniques aren't ever valuable, but that management attempts to apply them uniformly to everyone and encourages the use of some current set of "best practices" in software development. This approach can produce quality software, but it doesn't allow for thinking outside the box and creating new practices that might be better.

1.4 Software Craftsmanship

Software craftmanship, where a programmer trains and practices skills under the tutelage of a master, is about lifelong learning to be the best software developer you can be. Following the craftmanship model, a programmer gets an education, completes an apprenticeship, becomes a journeyman programmer, and strives to develop a masterpiece.

1.4.1 Education

Colleges and universities provide the prerequisites that interns need to be software craftsmen. If an internship exposed a beginning programmer (intern/apprentice) to the same information and challenges that a formal education does, the internship might be equivalent to a formal education. Unfortunately, few software craftsmen have the time or ability to train an apprentice from scratch. They're far too busy working on real-world projects to devote the time needed to teach an intern everything they need to know. Therefore, education is the first step on the road to software craftsmanship.

Additionally, a formal education at a college or university accomplishes two main objectives: first, you're forced to study those computer science topics that you'd probably just skip over if you were studying the material on your own; and second, you prove to the world that you're capable of finishing a major commitment that you've started. In particular, after you've completed a formal computer science program, you're ready to *really* start learning about software development.

However, a college degree, no matter how advanced, doesn't automatically qualify you as a software craftsman. A person with a graduate degree, which requires a deeper and more specialized study of computer science, starts out as an intern, just as someone with an undergraduate degree does. The intern with the graduate degree might spend fewer years as an apprentice but still needs considerable training.

1.4.2 Apprenticeship

Completing a formal computer science program prepares you to start learning, at an apprentice level, how to become a craftsman. A typical computer science program teaches you about programming languages (their syntax and semantics), data structures, and the theory of compilers, operating systems, and the like, but doesn't teach you *how to program* beyond the first- or second-semester Introduction to Programming courses. An apprenticeship shows you what programming is about when you enter the real world. The purpose of an apprenticeship is to get the experience necessary to use what you've learned to approach problems in many different ways, and to gain as many different experiences as possible.

An apprentice studies under someone who has mastered advanced programming techniques. This person can be either a *software journeyman* (see the next section) or a *software craftsman*. The "master" assigns tasks to the apprentice, demonstrates how to accomplish the task, and reviews the apprentice's work, making appropriate mid-course corrections to obtain high-quality work. Most important, the apprentice also reviews their master's work. This can take various forms, including testing, structured walk-throughs, and debugging. The important factor is that the apprentice learns how the master's code operates.[7] In doing so, the apprentice picks up programming techniques they would never master on their own.

If an apprentice is lucky, they'll have the opportunity to study under several masters and learn solid techniques from all of them. With each project completed under the tutelage of an advanced programmer, the apprentice nears the end of their apprenticeship and moves on to the next stage in the software craftsman's route: the software journeyman.

In one sense, an apprenticeship never ends. You should always be on the lookout for new techniques and new skills. For example, consider all the software engineers who grew up on structured programming and had to learn object-oriented programming. However, at some point, you reach the stage where you're using your existing skills more often than developing new ones. At that point, you start imparting your wisdom to others rather than learning from others. It's then that the "masters" you're working with feel you're ready to tackle projects on your own without assistance or supervision. That's when you become a software journeyman.

1.4.3 The Software Journeyman

Software journeymen handle the bulk of software development. As the name suggests, they typically move from project to project, applying their skills to solve application problems. Even though a software developer's education never ends, a software journeyman is more focused on application development than on learning how to develop applications.

Another important task that software journeymen take on is training new software apprentices. They review the work of apprentices on their project and share programming techniques and knowledge with them.

A software journeyman constantly looks for new tools and techniques that can improve the software development process. By adopting new (but proven) techniques early on, they stay ahead of the learning curve and keep up with current trends to avoid falling behind. Utilizing industry best practices to create efficient and cost-effective solutions for customers is the hallmark of this stage of craftsmanship. Software journeymen are productive, knowledgeable, and exactly the type of software developer most project managers hope to find when assembling a software team.

---

7. Another advantage to the apprenticeship process is that multiple individuals now understand how the code operates, so if one leaves, another can pick up the project in their place.

1.4.4 The Master Craftsman

The traditional way to become a master craftsman is to create a *masterpiece*, a work that sets you apart from your peers. Some (high-end) examples of software masterpieces include VisiCalc,[8] the Linux operating system, and the vi and emacs text editors. These products were initially the brainchild and creation of a single person, even though they went on to involve dozens or hundreds of different programmers. A masterpiece doesn't have to become famous, like Linux or some GNU tool. However, your immediate peers must recognize your masterpiece as a useful and creative solution to a problem. A masterpiece doesn't have to be a stand-alone original piece of code, either. Writing a complex device driver for an operating system, or extending some other program in several useful ways, could very well qualify as a masterpiece. The purpose of the masterpiece is to create an item in your portfolio that tells the world: "I'm capable of producing serious software—take me seriously!" A masterpiece work lets others know that they should seriously consider your opinions and trust what you have to say.

Generally, the domain of the master craftsman is to determine what current best practices are and invent new ones. Best practices describe the best *known* way, not necessarily the absolute best way, to accomplish a task. The master craftsman investigates whether there's a better approach for designing applications, recognizes the utility of a new technique or methodology as it applies to a wide spectrum of applications, and verifies that a practice is best and communicates that information to others.

1.4.5 Where Software Craftsmanship Fails

Steve McConnell, in his classic software engineering book *Code Complete*, claims that experience is one of those characteristics that doesn't matter as much as people think: "If a programmer hasn't learned C after a year or two, the next three years won't make much difference." He then asks, "If you work for 10 years, do you get 10 years of experience or do you get 1 year of experience 10 times?" McConnell even suggests that book learning might be more important than programming experience. He claims that the computer science field changes so fast that someone with 10 years of programming experience has missed out on all the great research to which new programmers have been exposed during that decade.

1.5 The Path to Writing Great Code

Writing great code doesn't happen because you follow a list of rules. You must make a personal decision to put in the effort to ensure the code you're writing is truly great. Violating well-understood software engineering principles is a good way to ensure that your code is not great, but rigidly following such rules doesn't guarantee greatness, either. A well-experienced and meticulous developer, or software craftsman, can navigate both

---

8. For those too young to remember VisiCalc, it was the precursor to Microsoft Excel.

approaches: following established practices when it's required, but being unafraid to try a different technique or strategy when the need arises.

Unfortunately, a book can only teach you the rules and methodologies. Creativity and wisdom are qualities you need to develop on your own. This book teaches you the rules and suggests when you might consider breaking them. However, it's still up to you to decide whether to do so.

1.6 For More Information

Hunt, Andrew, and David Thomas. *The Pragmatic Programmer*. Upper Saddle River, NJ: Addison-Wesley Professional, 1999.

Kernighan, Brian, and Rob Pike. *The Practice of Programming*. Upper Saddle River, NJ: Addison-Wesley Professional, 1999.

McBreen, Pete. *Software Craftsmanship: The New Imperative*. Upper Saddle River, NJ: Addison-Wesley Professional, 2001.

McConnell, Steve. *Code Complete*. 2nd ed. Redmond, WA: Microsoft Press, 2004.

———. *Rapid Development: Taming Wild Software Schedules*. Redmond, WA: Microsoft Press, 1996.

Pressman, Robert S. *Software Engineering, A Practitioner's Approach*. New York: McGraw-Hill, 2010.

2

PRODUCTIVITY

In the late 1960s, it was clear that training more programmers would not alleviate the software crisis. The only solution was to increase programmer productivity—that is, enable existing programmers to write more code—which is how the software engineering field originated. Therefore, a good place to start studying software engineering is with an understanding of productivity.

2.1 What Is Productivity?

Although the term *productivity* is commonly described as the basis for software engineering, it's amazing how many people have a distorted view of it. Ask any programmer about productivity, and you're bound to hear "lines of code," "function points," "complexity metrics," and so on. The truth is, there is nothing magical or mysterious about the concept of productivity on a software project. We can define productivity as:

> The number of unit tasks completed in a unit amount of time or completed for a given cost.

The challenge with this definition is specifying a *unit task*. One convenient unit task might be a project; however, projects vary wildly in terms of size and complexity. The fact that programmer A has completed three projects in a given amount of time, whereas programmer B has worked only on a small portion of a large project, tells us nothing about the relative productivity of these two programmers. For this reason, the unit task is usually much smaller than an entire project. Typically, it's something like a function, a single line of code, or an even smaller component of the project. The exact metric is irrelevant as long as the unit task is consistent between various projects and a single programmer would be expected to take the same amount of time to complete a unit task on any project. In general, if we say that programmer A is n times more productive than programmer B, programmer A can complete n times as many (equivalent) projects in the same amount of time as it would take programmer B to complete one of those projects.

2.2 Programmer Productivity vs. Team Productivity

In 1968, Sackman, Erikson, and Grant published an eye-opening article claiming that there was a 10 to 20 times difference in productivity among programmers.[1] Later studies and articles have pushed this difference even higher. This means that certain programmers produce as much as 20 (or more) times as much code as some less capable programmers. Some companies even claim a two-order-of-magnitude difference in productivity between various software teams in their organizations. This is an astounding difference! If it's possible for some programmers to be 20 times more productive than others (so-called Grand Master Programmers [GMPs]), is there some technique or methodology we can use to improve the productivity of a typical (or low-productivity) programmer?

Because it's not possible to train every programmer to raise them to the GMP level, most software engineering methodologies use other techniques, such as better management processes, to improve the productivity of a large team. This book series takes the other approach: rather than attempting to increase the productivity of a team, it teaches individual programmers how to increase their own productivity and work toward becoming a GMP.

Although the productivity of individual programmers has the largest impact on a project's delivery schedule, the real world is more concerned with project cost—how long it takes and how much it costs to complete the

---

1. Harold Sackman, W. J. Erikson, and E. E. Grant, "Exploratory Experimental Studies Comparing Online and Offline Programming Performance," *Communications of the ACM* 11, no. 1 (1968): 3–11.

project—than with programmer productivity. Except for small projects, the productivity of the *team* takes priority over the productivity of a *team member*.

Team productivity isn't simply the average of the productivities of each member; it's based on complex interactions between team members. Meetings, communications, personal interactions, and other activities can all have a negative impact on team members' productivity, as can bringing new or less knowledgeable team members up to speed and reworking existing code. (The lack of overhead from these activities is the main reason a programmer is far more productive when working on a small project than when working on a medium- or large-sized project.) Teams can improve their productivity by managing overhead for communication and training, resisting the urge to rework existing code unless it's really necessary, and managing the project so code is written correctly the first time (reducing the need to rework it).

2.3 Man-Hours and Real Time

The definition given earlier provides two measures for productivity: one based on time (productivity is the number of unit tasks completed in a unit amount of time) and one based on cost (productivity is the number of unit tasks completed for a given cost). Sometimes cost is more important than time, and vice versa. To measure cost and time, we can use man-hours and real time, respectively.

From a corporation's view, the portion of a project's cost related to programmer productivity is directly proportional to its *man-hours*, or the number of hours each team member spends working on the project. A *man-day* is approximately 8 man-hours, a *man-month* is approximately 176 man-hours, and a *man-year* is approximately 2,000 man-hours. The total cost of a project is the total number of man-hours spent on that project multiplied by the average hourly wage of each team member.

Real time (also known as *calendar time* or *wall clock time*) is just the progression of time during a project. Project schedules and delivery of the final product are usually based on real time.

Man-hours are the product of real time multiplied by the number of team members concurrently working on the project, but optimizing for one of these quantities doesn't always optimize for the other. For example, suppose you're working on an application needed in a municipal election. The most critical quantity in this case is real time; the software must be completely functional and deployed by the election date regardless of the cost. In contrast, a "basement programmer" working on the world's next killer app can spend more time on the project, thus extending the delivery date in real time, but can't afford to hire additional personnel to complete the app sooner.

One of the biggest mistakes project managers make on large projects is to confuse man-hours with real time. If two programmers can complete a project in 2,000 man-hours (and 1,000 real hours), you might conclude that four programmers can complete the project in 500 real hours. In other words, by doubling the staff on the project, you can get it done in half the time and complete the project on schedule. In reality, this doesn't always work (just like adding a second oven won't bake a cake any faster).

Increasing staff to increase the number of man-hours per calendar hour is generally more successful on large projects than on small and medium-sized projects. Small projects are sufficiently limited in scope that a single programmer can track all the details associated with the project; there's no need for the programmer to consult, coordinate with, or train anyone else to work on the project. Generally speaking, adding programmers to a small project eliminates these advantages and increases the costs dramatically without significantly affecting the delivery schedule. On medium-sized projects, the balance is delicate: two programmers may be more productive than three,[2] but adding more programming resources can help get an understaffed project finished sooner (though, perhaps, at a greater cost). On large software projects, increasing the team size reduces the project's schedule accordingly, but once the team grows beyond a certain point, you might have to add two or three people to do the amount of work usually done by one person.

2.4 Conceptual and Scope Complexity

As projects become more complex,[3] programmer productivity decreases, because a more complex project requires deeper (and longer) thought to understand what is going on. In addition, as project complexity increases, there's a greater likelihood that a software engineer will introduce errors into the system, and that defects introduced early in the system will not be caught until later, when the cost of correcting them is much higher.

Complexity comes in a couple of forms. Consider the following two definitions of *complex*:

1. Having a complicated, involved, or intricate arrangement of parts so as to be hard to understand
2. Composed of many interconnected parts

We can call the first definition *conceptual complexity*. For example, consider a single arithmetic expression in a high-level language (HLL), such as C/C++, which can contain intricate function calls, several weird arithmetic/logical operators with varying levels of precedence, and lots of parentheses that make the expression difficult to comprehend. Conceptual complexity can occur in any software project.

We can call the second definition *scope complexity*, which occurs when there is too much information for a human mind to easily digest. Even if the individual components of the project are simple, the sheer size of the

---

2. Barry W. Boehm, Terence E. Gray, and Thomas Seewaldt, "Prototyping Versus Specifying: A Multiproject Experience," *IEEE Transactions on Software Engineering* 10, no. 3 (1984): 290–303.

3. Generally, this means larger, although conceptual complexity applies as well.

project makes it impossible for one person to understand the whole thing. Scope complexity occurs in medium- and large-scale projects (indeed, it's this form of complexity that differentiates small projects from the others).

Conceptual complexity affects programmer productivity in two ways. First, complex constructs require more thought (and therefore more time) to produce than simple constructs. Second, complex constructs are more likely to contain defects that must be corrected later, producing a corresponding loss in productivity.

Scope complexity introduces different problems. When the project reaches a certain size, a programmer on the project might be completely unaware of what is going on in other parts of the project, and might duplicate code already in the system. Clearly, this reduces programmer productivity, because the programmer wasted time writing that code.[4] Inefficient use of system resources can also occur as a result of scope complexity. When working on a part of the system, a small team of engineers might be testing their piece by itself, but they don't see its interaction with the rest of the system (which might not even be ready yet). As a result, problems with system resource usages (such as CPU cycles or memory) might not be uncovered until later.

With good software engineering practices, it's possible to mitigate some of this complexity. But the general result is the same: as systems become more complex, people must spend more time thinking about them and the opportunity for defects increases dramatically. The end result is reduced productivity.

2.5 Predicting Productivity

Productivity is a project attribute that you can measure and attempt to predict. When a project is complete, it's fairly easy to determine the team's (and its members') productivity, assuming the team kept accurate records of the tasks accomplished during project development. Though success or failure on past projects doesn't guarantee success or failure on future projects, past performance is the best indicator available to predict a software team's future performance. If you want to improve the software development process, you need to track the techniques that work well and those that don't, so you'll know what to do (or *not* to do) on future projects. To track this information, programmers and their support personnel must document all software development activities. This is a good example of *pure overhead* introduced by software engineering: the documentation does almost nothing to help get the current project out the door or improve its quality, but it's an investment in future projects to help predict (and improve) productivity.

---

4. Some large projects appoint a "librarian" whose job is to keep track of reusable code components. Programmers looking for a particular routine can ask the librarian about its availability and spare themselves from having to write that code. The productivity loss is limited to the time the librarian spends to maintain the library and the time the programmer and the librarian spend communicating.

Watts S. Humphrey's *A Discipline for Software Engineering* (Addison-Wesley Professional, 1994) is a great read for those interested in learning about tracking programmer productivity. Humphrey teaches a system of forms, guidelines, and procedures for developing software that he calls the *Personal Software Process (PSP)*. Although the PSP is targeted at individuals, it offers valuable insight into where a programmer's problems lie in the software development process. In turn, this can greatly help them to determine how to attack their next major project.

2.6 Metrics and Why We Need Them

The problem with predicting a team's or an individual's productivity by looking at their past performance on similar projects is that it applies *only to similar projects*. If a new project is significantly different than a team's past projects, past performance might not be a good indicator. Because projects vary greatly in size, measuring productivity across whole projects might not provide sufficient information to predict future performance. Therefore, some system of measurement (a *metric*) at a granularity level below a whole project is needed to better evaluate teams and team members. An ideal metric is independent of the project (team members, programming language chosen, tools used, and other related activities and components); it must be usable across multiple projects to allow for comparison between them. Several metrics do exist, but none is perfect—or even very good. Still, a poor metric is better than no metric, so software engineers will continue to use them until a better measurement comes along. In this section, I'll discuss several of the more common metrics and the problems and benefits of each.

2.6.1 Executable Size Metric

One simple metric that programmers use to specify a software system's complexity is the size of the executables in the final system.[5] The assumption is that complex projects produce large executable files.

The advantages of this metric are:

- It is trivial to compute (typically, you need only look at a directory listing and compute the sum of one or more executable files).
- It doesn't require access to the original source code.

Unfortunately, the executable size metric also has deficiencies that disqualify it for most projects:

- Executable files often contain uninitialized data whose contribution to the file size have little or nothing to do with the complexity of the system.

---

5. Note that a project might contain multiple executable files. In such a case, the "executable file size" is the sum of all the executable components in the system.

- Library functions add to the executable's size, yet they actually reduce the complexity of the project.[6]
- The executable file size metric is not language-independent. For example, assembly language programs tend to be much more compact than HLL executables, yet most people consider assembly programs much more complex than equivalent HLL programs.
- The executable file size metric is not CPU-independent. For example, an executable for an 80x86 CPU is usually smaller than the same program compiled for an ARM (or other RISC) CPU.

2.6.2 Machine Instructions Metric

A major failing of the executable file size metric is that certain executable file formats include space for uninitialized static variables, which means trivial changes to the input source file can dramatically alter the executable file size. One way to solve this problem is to count only the machine instructions in a source file (either the size, in bytes, of the machine instructions or the total number of machine instructions). While this metric solves the problem of uninitialized static arrays, it still exhibits all the other problems of the executable file size metric: it's CPU-dependent, it counts code (such as library code) that wasn't written by the programmer, and it's language-dependent.

2.6.3 Lines of Code Metric

The lines of code (LOC, or KLOC for thousands of lines of code) metric is the most common software metric in use today. As its name suggests, it's a count of the number of lines of source code in a project. The metric has several good qualities, as well as some bad ones.

Simply counting the number of source lines appears to be the most popular form of using the LOC metric. Writing a line count program is fairly trivial, and most word count programs available for operating systems like Linux will compute the line count for you.

Here are some common claims about the LOC metric:

- It takes about the same amount of time to write a single line of source code regardless of the programming language in use.
- The LOC metric is not affected by the use of library routines (or other code reuse) in a project (assuming, of course, you don't count the number of lines in the prewritten library source code).
- The LOC metric is independent of the CPU.

The LOC metric does have some drawbacks:

- It doesn't provide a good indication of how much work the programmer has accomplished. One hundred lines of code in a VHLL accomplishes more than 100 lines of assembly code.

---

6. Assuming, of course, that the library routines existed prior to the project and were not part of the project's development.

- It assumes that the cost of each line of source code is the same. However, this isn't the case. Blank lines have a trivial cost, simple data declarations have a low conceptual complexity, and statements with complex Boolean expressions have a very high conceptual complexity.

2.6.4 Statement Count Metric

The statement count metric counts the number of language statements in a source file. It does not count blank lines or comments, nor does it count a single statement spread across multiple lines as separate entities. As a result, it does a better job than LOC of calculating the amount of programmer effort.

Although the statement count metric provides a better view of program complexity than lines of code, it suffers from many of the same problems. It measures effort rather than work accomplished, it isn't as language-independent as we'd like, and it assumes that each statement in the program requires the same amount of effort to produce.

2.6.5 Function Point Analysis

Function point analysis (FPA) was originally devised as a mechanism for predicting the amount of work a project would require before any source code was written. The basic idea was to consider the number of inputs a program requires, the number of outputs it produces, and the basic computations it must perform, and use this information to determine a project schedule.[7]

FPA offers several advantages over simplistic metrics like line or statement count. It is truly language- and system-independent. It depends upon the functionality of the software rather than its implementation.

FPA does have a few serious drawbacks, though. First, unlike line count or even statement count, it's not straightforward to compute the number of "function points" in a program. The analysis is subjective: the person analyzing the program must decide on the relative complexity of each function. Additionally, FPA has never been successfully automated. How would such a program decide where one calculation ends and another begins? How would it apply different complexity values (again, a subjective assignment) to each function point? Because this manual analysis is rather time-consuming and expensive, FPA is not as popular as other metrics. Largely, FPA is a *postmortem* (end-of-project) tool applied at the completion of a project rather than during development.

2.6.6 McCabe's Cyclomatic Complexity Metric

As mentioned earlier, a fundamental failure of the LOC and statement count metrics is that they assume each statement has equivalent complexity. FPA fares a little better but requires an analyst to assign a complexity rating to each statement. Unfortunately, these metrics don't accurately reflect the

---

7. True function point analysis is based on five components: external inputs, external outputs, external inquiries, internal logical file operations, and external file interfaces. But this basically boils down to tracking the inputs, outputs, and computations.

effort that went into the work being measured, and, therefore fail to document programmer productivity.

Thomas McCabe developed a software metric known as *cyclomatic complexity* to measure the complexity of source code by counting the number of paths through it. It begins with a flowchart of the program. The nodes in the flowchart correspond to statements in the program, and the edges between the nodes correspond to nonsequential control flow in the program. A simple calculation involving the number of nodes, the number of edges, and the number of connected components in the flowchart provides a single cyclomatic complexity rating for the code. Consider a 1,000-line `printf` program (with nothing else); the cyclomatic complexity would be 1, because there is a single path through the program. Now consider a second example, with a large mixture of control structures and other statements; it would have a much higher cyclomatic complexity rating.

The cyclomatic complexity metric is useful because it's an objective measure, and it's possible to write a program to compute this value. Its drawback is that the bulk size of a program is irrelevant; that is, it treats a single `printf` statement the same as 1,000 `printf` statements in a row, even though the second version clearly requires more work (even if that extra work is just a bunch of cut-and-paste operations).

2.6.7 Other Metrics

There's no shortage of metrics we could devise to measure some facet of programmer productivity. One common metric is to count the number of operators in a program. This metric recognizes and adjusts for the fact that some statements (including those that don't involve control paths) are more complex than others, taking more time to write, test, and debug. Another metric is to count the number of tokens (such as identifiers, reserved words, operators, constants, and punctuation) in a program. No matter the metric, though, it will have shortcomings.

Many people attempt to use a combination of metrics (such as line count multiplied by cyclomatic complexity and operator count) to create a more "multidimensional" metric that better measures the amount of work involved in producing a bit of code. Unfortunately, as the complexity of the metric increases, it becomes more difficult to use on a given project. LOC has been successful because you can use the Unix `wc` (word count) utility, which also counts lines, to get a quick idea of program size. Computing a value for one of these other metrics usually requires a specialized, language-dependent application (assuming the metric is automatable). For this reason, although people have proposed a large number of metrics, few have become as universally popular as LOC.

2.6.8 The Problem with Metrics

Metrics that roughly measure the amount of source code for a project provide a good indication of the time spent on a project if we assume that each line or statement in the program takes some average amount of time to write, but only a tenuous relationship exists between lines of code (or statements) and the work accomplished. Unfortunately, metrics measure some physical attributes of the program but rarely measure what we're really interested in knowing: the intellectual effort needed to write the code in the first place.

Another failure of almost every metric is that they all assume that more work produces more (or more complex) code. This is not always true. For example, a great programmer will often expend effort to refactor their code, making it smaller and less complex. In this case, more work produces less code (and less complex code).

Metrics also fail to consider environmental issues concerning the code. For example, are 10 lines of code written for a bare-metal embedded device equivalent to 10 lines of code written for a SQL database application?

All these metrics fail to consider the learning curve for certain projects. Are 10 lines of Windows device driver code equivalent to 10 lines of Java code in a web applet? The LOC values for these two projects are incomparable.

Ultimately, most metrics fail because they measure the *wrong thing*. They measure the *amount of code* a programmer produces rather than the programmer's overall *contribution to the complete project* (productivity). For example, one programmer could use a single statement to accomplish a task (such as a standard library call), whereas a second programmer could write several hundred lines of code to accomplish the same task. Most metrics would suggest the second programmer is the more productive of the two.

For these very reasons, even the most complex software metrics currently in use have fundamental flaws that prevent them from being completely effective. Therefore, choosing a "better" metric often produces results that are no better than using a "flawed" metric. This is yet another reason the LOC metric continues to be so popular (and why this book uses it). It's an amazingly bad metric, but it's not a whole lot worse than many of the other existing metrics, and it's very easy to compute without writing special software.

2.7   How Do We Beat 10 Lines per Day?

Early texts on software engineering claim that a programmer on a major product produces an average of ten lines of code per day. In a 1977 article, Walston and Felix report about 274 LOC per month per developer.[8] Both numbers describe the production of debugged and documented code *over the lifetime* of that product (that is, LOC divided by the amount of time all the programmers spent on the product from first release to retirement), rather than simply time spent writing code from day to day. Even so, the numbers seem low. Why?

At the start of a project, programmers might quickly crank out 1,000 lines of code per day, then slow down to research a solution to a particular

---

8. Claude E. Walston and Charles P. Felix, "A Method of Programming Measurement and Estimation," *IBM Systems Journal* 16, no. 1 (1977): 54–73.

portion of the project, test the code, fix bugs, rewrite half their code, and then document their work. By the product's first release, productivity has dropped tenfold since that first day or two: from 1,000 LOC per day to fewer than 100. Once the first release is out the door, work generally begins on the second release, then the third, and so on. Over the product's lifetime, several different developers will probably work on the code. By the time the project is retired, it has been rewritten several times (a tremendous loss in productivity), and several programmers have spent valuable time learning how the code operates (also sapping their productivity). Therefore, over the lifetime of the product, programmer productivity is down to 10 LOC per day.

One of the most important results from software engineering productivity studies is that the best way to improve productivity is not by inventing some scheme that allows programmers to write twice as many lines of code per unit time, but to *reduce the time wasted on debugging, testing, documenting, and rewriting the code, and on educating new programmers about the code once the first version exists*. To reduce that loss, it's much easier to improve the processes that programmers use on the project than it is to train them to write twice as much code per unit time. Software engineering has always recognized this problem and has attempted to solve it by reducing the time spent by all programmers. Personal software engineering's goal is to reduce the time spent by individual programmers on their portion of the project.

2.8 Estimating Development Time

As noted earlier, while productivity is of interest to management for awarding bonuses, pay raises, or verbal praise, the real purpose for tracking it is to predict development times on future projects. Past results don't guarantee future performance, so you also need to know how to estimate a project schedule (or at least the schedule for your portion of a project). As an individual software engineer, you typically don't have the background, education, and experience to determine what goes into a schedule, so you should meet with your project manager, have them explain what needs to be considered in the schedule (which is more than just the time required to write code), and then build the estimate that way. Though all the details needed to properly estimate a project are beyond the scope of this book (see "For More Information" on page 37 for suggested resources), it's worthwhile to briefly describe how development time estimates differ depending on whether you're working on a small, medium, or large project, or just a portion of a project.

2.8.1 *Estimating Small Project Development Time*

By definition, a small project is one that a single engineer works on. The major influence on the project schedule will be the ability and productivity of that software engineer.

Estimating development time for small projects is much easier and more accurate than for larger projects. Small projects won't involve parallel development, and the schedule only has to consider a single developer's productivity.

Without question, the first step in estimating the development time for a small project is to identify and understand all the work that needs to be done. If some parts of the project are undefined at that point, you introduce considerable error in the schedule when the undefined components inevitably take far more time than you imagined.

For estimating a project's completion time, the design documentation is the most important part of the project. Without a detailed design, it's impossible to know what subtasks make up the project and how much time each will take to accomplish. Once you've broken down the project into suitably sized subtasks (a suitable size is where it's clear how long it will take to complete), all you need to do is add the times for all the subtasks to produce a decent first estimate.

One of the biggest mistakes people make when estimating small projects, however, is that they add the times for the subtasks and call that their schedule, forgetting to include time for meetings, phone calls, emails, and other administrative tasks. They also forget to add in testing time, plus time to correct (and retest) the software when defects are found. Because it's difficult to estimate how many defects will be in the software, and thus how much time it will take to resolve them, most managers scale a schedule's first approximation by a factor of 2 to 4. Assuming the programmer (team) maintains reasonable productivity on the project, this formula produces a good estimate for a small project.

2.8.2   *Estimating Medium and Large Project Development Time*

Conceptually, medium and large projects consist of many small projects (assigned to individual team members) that combine to form the final result. So a first approximation on a large project schedule is to break it down into a bunch of smaller projects, develop estimates for each of those subprojects, and then combine (add) the estimates. It's sort of a bigger version of the small project estimate. Unfortunately, in real life, this form of estimate is fraught with error.

The first problem is that medium and large projects introduce problems that don't exist in small projects. A small project typically has one engineer, and, as noted previously, the schedule completely depends upon that person's productivity and availability. In a larger project, multiple people (including many nonengineers) affect the estimated schedule. One software engineer who has a key piece of knowledge might be on vacation or sick for several days, holding up a second engineer who needs that information to make progress. Engineers on larger projects usually have several meetings a week (unaccounted for in most schedules) that take them offline—that is, they're not programming—for several hours. The team composition can change on large projects; some experienced programmers leave and someone else has to pick up and learn the subtasks, and new programmers join the project and need time to get up to speed. Sometimes even getting a computer workstation for a new hire can take weeks (for example, in a large company with a bureaucratic IT department). Waiting for software tools to be purchased, hardware to be developed, and support from other parts of the organization also creates scheduling problems. The list goes on and on. Few schedule estimates can accurately predict how the time will be consumed in these myriad ways.

Ultimately, creating medium and large project schedule estimates involves four tasks: breaking down the project into smaller projects, running the small project estimations on those, adding in time for integration testing and debugging (that is, combining the small tasks and getting them to work properly together), and then applying a multiplicative factor to that sum. They're not precise, but they're about as good as it gets today.

2.8.3 Problems with Estimating Development Time

Because project schedule estimates involve predicting a development team's future performance, few people believe that a projected schedule will be totally accurate. However, typical software development schedule projections are especially bad. Here are some of the reasons why:

They're research and development projects. R&D projects involve doing something you've never done before. They require a research phase during which the development team analyzes the problem and tries to determine solutions. Usually, there's no way to predict how long the research phase will take.

Management has preconceived schedules. Typically, the marketing department decides that it wants to have a product to sell by a certain date, and management creates project schedules by working backward from that date. Before asking the programming team for their time estimates of the subtasks, management already has some preconceived notions about how long each task should take.

The team's done this before. It's common for management to assume that if you've done something before, it will be easier the second time around (and therefore will take less time). In certain cases, there's an element of truth to this: if a team works on an R&D project, it will be easier to do a second time because they only have to do the development and can skip (at least most of) the research. However, the assumption that a project is always easier the second time is rarely correct.

There isn't enough time or money. In many cases, management sets some sort of monetary or time limit within with a project must be completed or else it will be canceled. That's the *wrong* thing to say to someone whose paycheck depends on the project moving forward. If given a choice between saying, "Yes, we can meet that schedule," or looking for a new job, most people—even knowing the odds are against them—will opt for the first.

Programmers overstate their efficiency. Sometimes when a software engineer is asked if they can complete a project within a certain timeframe, they don't lie about how long it will take, but instead make optimistic estimates of their performance—which rarely hold up during the actual work. When asked how much they can produce when *really pushed*, most software engineers give a figure that represents their maximum output ever achieved over a short period of time (for example, while working in "crisis mode" and putting in 60–70 hours per week) and don't consider unexpected hindrances (such as a really nasty bug that comes along).

Schedules rely on extra hours. Management (and engineers) often assume that programmers can always put in "a few extra hours" when the schedule starts to slip. As a result, schedules tend to be more aggressive than they should be (ignoring the negative repercussions of having engineers put in massive overtime).

Engineers are like building blocks. A common problem with project schedules is that management assumes it can add programmers to a project to achieve an earlier release date. However, as mentioned earlier, this isn't necessarily true. You can't add or remove engineers from a project and expect a proportional change in the project schedule.

Subproject estimates are inaccurate. Realistic project schedules are developed in a top-down fashion. The whole project is divided into smaller subprojects. Then those subprojects are divided into sets of sub-subprojects, and so on until the subproject size is so small that someone can accurately predict the time needed for each tiny part. However, there are three challenges with this approach:

- Being willing to put in the effort to create a schedule this way (that is, to provide a correct and accurate top-down analysis of the project)
- Obtaining accurate estimates for the tiny subprojects (particularly from software engineers who may not have the appropriate management training to understand what must go into their schedule estimates)
- Accepting the results the schedule predicts

2.9 Crisis Mode Project Management

Despite the best intentions of everyone involved, many projects fall significantly behind schedule and management must accelerate development to meet some important milestone. To achieve the deadline, engineers often are expected to put in more time each week to reduce the (real time) delivery date. When this occurs, the project is said to be in "crisis mode."

Crisis mode engineering can be effective for short bursts to handle (rapidly) approaching deadlines, but in general, crisis mode is never that effective, and results in lower productivity, because most people have things to take care of outside of work, and need time off to rest, decompress, and allow their brains to sort out all the problems they've been collecting while putting in long hours. Working while you're tired leads to mistakes that often take far more time to correct later on. It's more efficient in the long run to forgo the crisis mode and stick to 40-hour weeks.

The best way to handle crisis mode schedules is to add milestones throughout the project to generate a series of "small crises" rather than one big crisis at the end. Putting in an extra day or a couple of long days once a month is infinitely better than having to put in several seven-day weeks at the end of the project. Working one or two 16-hour days to meet a deadline won't adversely affect the quality of your life or lead you to the point of exhaustion.

Beyond the health and productivity issues, operating in crisis mode can cause scheduling, ethical, and legal problems:

- A poor schedule can affect future projects as well. If you work 60-hour weeks, management will assume that future projects can also be done in the same amount of (real) time, expecting this pace from you in the future without any additional compensation.
- Technical staff turnover is high on projects that operate for lengthy periods of time in crisis mode, further reducing team productivity.
- There is also the legal issue of putting in lots of extra hours without being paid overtime. Several high-profile lawsuits in the video game industry have shown that engineers are entitled to overtime pay (they are not *salary exempt* employees). Even if your company can survive such lawsuits, the rules for time reporting, administrative overhead, and work schedules will become much more restrictive, leading to productivity drops.

Again, operating in crisis mode can help you meet certain deadlines if managed properly. But the best solution is to work out better schedules to avoid crisis mode altogether.

2.10 How to Be More Productive

This chapter has spent considerable time defining productivity and metrics for measuring it. But it hasn't devoted much time to describing how a programmer can increase their productivity to become a great programmer. Whole books can be (and have been) written on this subject. This section provides an overview of techniques you can use to improve your productivity on individual and team projects.

2.10.1 Choose Software Development Tools Wisely

As a software developer, you'll spend most of your time working with software development tools, and the quality of your tools can have a huge impact on your productivity. Sadly, the main criterion for selecting development tools seems to be familiarity with a tool rather than the applicability of the tool to the current project.

Keep in mind when choosing your tools at the start of the project that you'll probably have to live with them for the life of the project (and maybe beyond that). For example, once you start using a defect tracking system, it might be very difficult to switch to a different one because of incompatible database file formats; the same goes for source code control systems. Fortunately, software development tools (especially IDEs) are relatively mature these days, and a large number of them are interoperable, so it's hard to make a bad choice. Still, careful thought at the beginning of a project can spare you a lot of problems down the road.

The most significant tool choice for a software development project is which programming language and which compilers/interpreters/translators to use. Optimal language choice is a difficult problem to solve. It's easy to justify some programming language because you're familiar with it and you won't lose productivity learning it; however, future engineers new to the product might be far less productive because they're learning the programming language while trying to maintain the code. Furthermore, some language choices could streamline the development process, sufficiently improving productivity to make up for lost time learning the language. As noted earlier, a poor language choice could result in wasted development time using that language until it becomes clear that it is unsuitable for the project and you have to start over.

Compiler performance (how many lines per second it takes to process a common source file) can have a huge impact on your productivity. If your compiler takes two seconds to compile an average source file rather than two minutes, you'll probably be far more productive using the faster compiler (though the faster compiler might be missing some features that completely kill your productivity in other ways). The less time your tools take to process your code, the more time you'll have for designing, testing, debugging, and polishing your code.

It's also important to use a set of tools that work well together. Today, we take for granted *integrated development environments (IDEs)*, which combine an editor, compiler, debugger, source code browser, and other tools into a single program. Being able to quickly make small changes in an editor, recompile a source code module, and run the result in a debugger all within the same window onscreen provides a phenomenal boost in productivity.

However, you'll often have to work on parts of your project outside the IDE. For example, some IDEs don't support source code control facilities or defect tracking directly in the IDE (though many do). Most IDEs don't provide a word processor for writing documentation, nor do they provide simple database or spreadsheet capabilities to maintain requirements lists, design documentation, or user documentation. Most likely, you'll have to use a few programs outside your IDE—word processing, spreadsheet, drawing/graphics, web design, and database programs, to name a few—to do all the work needed on your project.

Running programs outside an IDE isn't a problem. Just make sure the applications you choose are compatible with your development process and the files your IDE produces (and vice versa). Your productivity will decrease if you must constantly run a translator program when moving files between your IDE and an external application.

Can I recommend tools for you to use? No way. There are too many projects with different needs to even consider such suggestions here. My recommendation is to simply be aware of the issues at the start of the project.

But one recommendation I *can* make is to avoid the "Gee whiz, why don't we try this new technology" approach when choosing a development tool. Discovering that a development tool can't do the job after spending six months working with it (and basing your source code on it) can be disastrous. Evaluate your tools apart from your product development, and work in new tools only after you're confident that they'll work for you. A classic example of this is Apple's Swift programming language. Until Swift v5.0 was released (about four years after Swift was first introduced), using Swift was an exercise in frustration. Every year Apple would release a new version that was source code–incompatible with earlier releases, forcing you to go back and change old programs. In addition, many features were missing in early versions of the language, and several features weren't quite ready for "prime time." By version 5.0 (released as this book was being written), the language seems relatively stable. However, the poor souls who jumped on the Swift bandwagon early on paid the price for the immature development of the language.[9]

Sadly, you don't get to choose the development tools on many projects. That decision is an edict from on high, or you inherit tools from earlier products. Complaining about it wastes time and energy, and reduces your productivity. Instead, make the best of the tool set you have, and become an expert at using it.

2.10.2 Manage Overhead

On any project, we can divide the work into two categories: work that is directly associated with the project (such as writing lines of code or documentation for the project) and work that is indirectly related to the project. Indirect activities include meetings, reading and replying to emails, filling out time cards, and updating schedules. These are *overhead* activities: they add time and money to a project's cost but don't directly contribute to getting the work done.

By following Watts S. Humphrey's *Personal Software Engineering* guidelines, you can track where you spend your time during a project and easily see how much is spent directly on the project versus on overhead activities. If your overhead climbs above 10 percent of your total time, reconsider your daily activities. Try to decrease or combine those activities to reduce their impact on your productivity. If you don't track your time outside the project, you'll miss the opportunity to improve your productivity by managing overhead.

2.10.3 Set Clear Goals and Milestones

It's a natural human tendency to relax when no deadlines are looming, and then go into "hypermode" as one approaches. Without goals to achieve, very little productive work ever gets done. Without deadlines to meet, rarely is there any motivation to achieve those goals in a timely manner.

---

9. Today, I don't have a problem recommending Swift. It's a great language, and version 5.0 and later seem relatively stable and reliable. It's moved beyond the "Gee whiz, ain't this a great new language" stage and is now a valid software development tool for real projects.

Therefore, to improve your productivity, be sure to have clear goals and subgoals, and attach hard *milestones* to them.

From a project management viewpoint, a milestone is a marker in a project that determines how far work has progressed. A good manager always sets goals and milestones in the project schedule. However, few schedules provide useful goals for individual programmers. This is where personal software engineering comes into play. To become a superproductive programmer, micromanage your own goals and milestones on your (portion of the) project. Simple goals, such as "I'll finish this function before I take lunch" or "I'll find the source of this error before going home today" can keep you focused. Larger goals, such as "I'll finish testing this module by next Tuesday" or "I'll run at least 20 test procedures today" help you gauge your productivity and determine if you're achieving what you want.

2.10.4 Practice Self-Motivation

Improving your productivity is all about attitude. Although others can help you manage your time better and aid you when you're stuck, the bottom line is that you must have the initiative to better yourself. Always be conscious of your pace and constantly strive to improve your performance. By keeping track of your goals, efforts, and progress, you'll know when you need to "psych yourself up" and work harder to improve your productivity.

A lack of motivation can be one of the greatest impediments to your productivity. If your attitude is "Ugh, I have to work on *that* today," it will probably take you longer to complete the task than if your attitude is "Oh! This is the best part! This will be fun!"

Of course, not every task you work on will be interesting and fun. This is one area where *personal* software engineering kicks in. If you want to maintain higher-than-average productivity, you need to have considerable self-motivation when a project makes you feel "less than motivated." Try to create reasons to make the work appealing. For example, create mini-challenges for yourself and reward yourself for achieving them. A productive software engineer constantly practices self-motivation: the longer you remain motivated to do a project, the more productive you'll be.

2.10.5 Focus and Eliminate Distractions

Staying focused on a task and eliminating distractions is another way to dramatically improve your productivity. Be "in the zone." Software engineers operating this way are more productive than those who are mentally multitasking. To increase your productivity, concentrate on a single task for as long as possible.

Focusing on a task is easiest in a quiet environment without any visual stimulation (other than your display screen). Sometimes, work environments aren't conducive to an extreme focus. In such cases, putting on headphones and playing background music might help remove the distractions. If music is too distracting, try listening to white noise; there are several white noise apps available online.

Whenever you're interrupted in the middle of a task, it will take time to get back in the zone. In fact, it could take as long as half an hour to become fully refocused on your work. When you need to focus and complete a task, put up a sign saying that you should only be interrupted for urgent business, or post "office hours"—times when you can be interrupted—near your workstation; for example, you could allow interruptions at the top of the hour for five minutes. Saving your coworkers 10 minutes by answering a question they could figure out themselves could cost you half an hour of productivity. You do have to work as part of the team and be a good teammate; however, it's just as important to ensure that excessive team interactions don't impair your (and others') productivity.

During a typical workday, there will be many scheduled interruptions: meal breaks, rest breaks, meetings, administrative sessions (for example, handling emails and time accounting), and more. If possible, try to schedule other interruptions around these events. For example, turn off any email alerts; answering emails within a few seconds is *rarely* imperative, and someone can find you in person or call you if it's an emergency. Set an alarm to remind you to check email at fixed times if people do expect quick responses from you (ditto with text messages and other interruptions). If you can get away with it, consider silencing your phone if you get a lot of nonurgent phone calls, checking your messages every hour or so during your breaks. What works for you depends on your personal and professional life. But the fewer interruptions you have, the more productive you'll become.

2.10.6 If You're Bored, Work on Something Else

Sometimes, no matter how self-motivated you are, you'll be bored with what you're working on and have trouble focusing; your productivity will plummet. If you can't get into the zone and focus on the task, take a break from it and work on something else. Don't use boredom as an excuse to flitter from task to task without accomplishing much. But when you're really stuck and can't move forward, switch to something you can be productive doing.

2.10.7 Be as Self-Sufficient as Possible

As much as possible, you should try to handle all tasks assigned to you. This won't improve your productivity; however, if you're constantly seeking help from other engineers, you might be damaging their productivity (remember, they need to stay focused and avoid interruptions, too).

If you're working on a task that requires more knowledge than you currently possess, and you don't want to constantly interrupt other engineers, you have a few options:

- Spend time educating yourself so you can do the task. Although you might hurt your short-term productivity, the knowledge you gain will help you with similar future tasks.
- Meet with your manager and explain the problems you're having. Discuss the possibility of their reassigning the task to someone more experienced and assigning you a task you're better able to handle.

- Arrange with your manager to schedule a meeting to get help from other engineers at a time that won't impact their productivity as much (for example, at the beginning of the workday).

2.10.8 Recognize When You Need Help

You can take the self-supporting attitude a little too far. You can spend an inordinate amount of time working on a problem that a teammate could solve in just a few minutes. One aspect of being a great programmer is recognizing when you're stuck and need help to move forward. When you're stuck, the best approach is to set a timer alarm. After some number of minutes, hours, or even days being stuck on the problem, seek help. If you know who to ask for help, seek that help directly. If you're not sure, talk to your manager. Most likely, your manager can direct you to the right person so you don't interrupt others who wouldn't be able to help you anyway.

Team meetings (daily or weekly) are a good place to seek help from team members. If you have several tasks on your plate and you're stuck on one particular task, set it aside, work on other tasks (if possible), and save your questions for a team meeting. If you run out of work before a meeting, ask your manager to keep you busy so you don't have to interrupt anyone. Further, while working on other tasks, the solution just might come to you.

2.10.9 Overcome Poor Morale

Nothing can kill a project faster than an infestation of bad morale among team members. Here are some suggestions to help you overcome poor morale:

- Understand the business value of your project. By learning about, or reminding yourself of, the real-world practical applications of your project, you'll become more invested and interested in the project.
- Take ownership and responsibility for (your portion of) a project. When you own the project, your pride and reputation are on the line. Regardless of what else might happen, ensure that you can always talk about the contributions you made to the project.
- Avoid becoming emotionally invested in those project components over which you have no control. For example, if management has made some poor decisions that affect the project's schedule or design, work as best as you can within those confines. Don't just sit around thinking bad thoughts about management when you could be putting that effort into solving problems.
- If you're faced with personality differences that are creating morale problems, discuss those issues with your manager and other affected personnel. Communication is key. Allowing problems to continue will only lead to larger morale problems down the road.
- Always be on the lookout for situations and attitudes that could damage morale. Once morale on a project begins to decline, it's often very difficult to restore what was lost. The sooner you deal with morale issues, the easier it will be to resolve them.

Sometimes, financial, resource, or personnel issues decrease morale among the project's participants. Your job as a great programmer is to step in, rise above the issues, and continue writing great code—and encourage those on the project to do the same. This isn't always easy, but no one ever said that becoming a great programmer was easy.

2.11 For More Information

Bellinger, Gene. "Project Systems." Systems Thinking, 2004. *http://systems-thinking.org/prjsys/prjsys.htm.*

Heller, Robert, and Tim Hindle. *Essential Managers: Managing Meetings.* New York: DK Publishing, 1998.

Humphrey, Watts S. *A Discipline for Software Engineering.* Upper Saddle River, NJ: Addison-Wesley Professional, 1994.

Kerzner, Harold. *Project Management: A Systems Approach to Planning, Scheduling, and Controlling.* Hoboken, NJ: Wiley, 2003.

Lencioni, Patrick. *Death by Meeting: A Leadership Fable . . . About Solving the Most Painful Problem in Business.* San Francisco: Jossey-Bass, 2004.

Levasseur, Robert E. *Breakthrough Business Meetings: Shared Leadership in Action.* Lincoln, NE: iUniverse.com, Inc., 2000.

Lewis, James P. *Project Planning, Scheduling, and Control.* New York: McGraw-Hill, 2000.

McConnell, Steve. *Software Project Survival Guide.* Redmond, WA: Microsoft Press, 1997.

Mochal, Tom. "Get Creative to Motivate Project Teams When Morale Is Low." TechRepublic, September, 21, 2001. *http://www.techrepublic.com/article/get-creative-to-motivate-project-teams-when-morale-is-low/.*

Wysocki, Robert K., and Rudd McGary. *Effective Project Management.* Indianapolis: Wiley, 2003.

3

SOFTWARE DEVELOPMENT MODELS

You don't write great code by following a fixed set of rules for every project. For some projects, hacking out a few hundred lines of code might be all you need to produce a great program. Other projects, however, could involve millions of code lines, hundreds of project engineers, and several layers of management or other support personnel; in these cases, the software development process you use will greatly affect the project's success.

In this chapter, we'll look at various development models and when to use them.

3.1 The Software Development Life Cycle

During its life, a piece of software generally goes through eight phases, collectively known as the *Software Development Life Cycle (SDLC)*:

1. Product conceptualization
2. Requirement development and analysis

3. Design
4. Coding (implementation)
5. Testing
6. Deployment
7. Maintenance
8. Retirement

Let's look at each phase in turn.

Product conceptualization

A customer or manager develops an idea for some software and creates a business case justifying its development.

Often, a nonengineer envisions a need for the software and approaches a company or individual who can implement it.

Requirement development and analysis

Once you have a product concept, the product requirements must be outlined. Project managers, stakeholders, and clients (users) meet to discuss and formalize what the software system must do to satisfy everyone. Of course, users will want the software to do everything under the sun. Project managers will temper this expectation based on the available resources (for example, programmers), estimated development times, and costs. Other stakeholders might include venture capitalists (others financing the project), regulatory agencies (for example, the Nuclear Regulatory Commission if you're developing software for a nuclear reactor), and marketing personnel who might provide input on the design to make it saleable.

By meeting, discussing, negotiating, and so on, the interested parties develop requirements based on questions like the following:

- For whom is the system intended?
- What inputs should be provided to the system?
- What output should the system produce (and in what format)?
- What types of calculations will be involved?
- If there is a video display, what screen layouts should the system use?
- What are the *expected* response times between input and output?

From this discussion, the developers will put together the *System Requirements Specification (SyRS)* document, which specifies all the major requirements for hardware, software, and so on. Then the program management and system analysts use the SyRS to produce a *Software Requirements Specification (SRS)* document,[1] which is the

---

1. Depending on the system, they might also produce a *Hardware Requirements Specification (HRS)* document, and other documents as well, all of which are outside the scope of this book.

end result of this phase. As a rule, the SRS is for internal consumption only, used by the software development team, whereas the SyRS is an external document for customer reference. The SRS extracts all the software requirements from the SyRS and expands on them. Chapter 10 discusses these two documents in detail (see "The System Requirements Specification Document" on page 193 and "The Software Requirements Specification Document" on page 194).

Design

The software design architect (software engineer) uses the software requirements from the SRS to prepare the *Software Design Description (SDD)*. The SDD provides some combination, but not necessarily all, of the following items:

- A system overview
- Design goals
- The data (via a *data dictionary*) and databases used
- A data flow (perhaps using data flow diagrams)
- An interface design (how the software interacts with other software and the software's users)
- Any standards that must be followed
- Resource requirements (for example, memory, CPU cycles, and disk capacity)
- Performance requirements
- Security requirements

See Chapter 11 for further details on the contents of the SDD. The design documentation becomes the input for the next phase, coding.

Coding

Coding—writing the actual software—is the step most familiar and fun to software engineers. A software engineer uses the SDD to write the software. *WGC5: Great Coding* will be dedicated to this phase.

Testing

In this phase, the code is tested against the SRS to ensure the product solves the problems listed in the requirements. There are several components in this phase, including:

Unit testing   Checks the individual statements and modules in the program to verify that they behave as expected. This actually occurs during coding but logically belongs in the testing phase.

Integration testing   Verifies that the individual subsystems in the software work well together. This also occurs during the coding phase, usually toward the end.

System testing   Validates the implementation; that is, it shows that the software correctly implements the SRS.

Acceptance testing   Demonstrates to the customer that the software is suitable for its intended purpose.

WGC6: Testing, Debugging, and Quality Assurance will cover the testing phase in detail. Chapter 12 describes the software test case and software test procedure documents you'll create to guide testing.

Deployment

The software product is delivered to the customer(s) for their use.

Maintenance

Once customers begin using the software, chances are fairly high that they'll discover defects and request new functionality. During this time, the software engineers might fix the defects or add the new enhancements, and then deploy new versions of the software to the customer(s).

Retirement

Eventually in some software's life, development will cease, perhaps because the development organization decides to no longer support or work on it, it is replaced by a different version, the company making it goes out of business, or the hardware on which it runs becomes obsolete.

3.2   The Software Development Model

A *software development model* describes how all the phases of the SDLC combine in a software project. Different models are suitable for different circumstances: some emphasize certain phases and deemphasize others, some repeat various phases throughout the development process, and others skip some phases entirely.

There are eight well-respected software development models and dozens, if not hundreds, of variations of these eight models in use today. Why don't developers just pick one popular model and use it for everything? The reason, as noted in Chapter 1, is that practices that work well for individuals or small teams don't *scale up* well to large teams. Likewise, techniques that work well for large projects rarely *scale down* well for small projects. This book will focus on techniques that work well for individuals, but great programmers must be able to work within all design processes if they want to be great programmers on projects of all sizes.

In this chapter I'll describe the eight major software models—their advantages, disadvantages, and how to apply them appropriately. However, in practice, none of these models can be followed blindly or expected to guarantee a successful project. This chapter also discusses what great programmers can do to work around the limitations of a model forced on them and still produce great code.

3.2.1 The Informal Model

The Informal model describes software development with minimal process or discipline: no formal design, no formal testing, and a lack of project management. This model was originally known as *hacking*[2] and those who engaged in it were known as *hackers*. However, as those original hackers grew up and gained experience, education, and skills, they proudly retained the name "hacker," so the term no longer refers to an inexperienced or unskilled programmer.[3] I'll still use the term *hacking* to mean an informal coding process, but I'll use *informal coder* to describe a person who engages in hacking. This will avoid confusion with differing definitions of *hacker*.

In the Informal model, the programmer moves directly from product conceptualization to coding, "hacking away" at the program until something is working (often not well), rather than designing a robust, flexible, readable program.

Hacking has a few advantages: it's fun, done independently (though certainly many people participate in group events like hackathons), and the programmer is responsible for most design decisions and for moving the project along, so they can often get something working faster than could a software engineer following a formal development process.

The problem with the Informal model is that its conscious lack of design may lead to an invalid system that doesn't do what end users want, because their requests weren't considered in the requirements and software specifications—if those even exist—and often the software isn't tested or documented, which makes it difficult for anyone other than the original programmer to use it.

Thus, the Informal model works for small, throwaway programs intended for use only by the programmer who coded them. For such projects, it's far cheaper and more efficient to bang out a couple hundred lines of code for limited and careful use than to go through the full software development process. (Unfortunately, some "throwaway" programs can take on a life of their own and become popular once users discover them. Should this happen, the program should be redesigned and reimplemented so it can be maintained properly.)

Hacking is also useful for developing small prototypes, especially screen displays intended to demonstrate a program in development to a prospective customer. One sticky problem here, though, is that clients and managers may look at the prototype and assume that a large amount of code is already in place, meaning they may push to further develop the hacked code rather than start the development process from the beginning, which will lead to problems down the road.

---

2. The original definition of *hacking*, from *https://www.merriam-webster.com*, is "a person who is inexperienced or unskilled at a particular activity; e.g., a tennis hacker."

3. Of course, along the way the term *hacker* was also redefined to describe someone engaged in criminal activities on computers. We'll ignore that definition here.

3.2.2 The Waterfall Model

The Waterfall model is the granddaddy of software development models, and most models are a variation of it. In the Waterfall model, each step of the SDLC is executed sequentially from beginning to end (see Figure 3-1), with the output from each step forming the input for the next step.

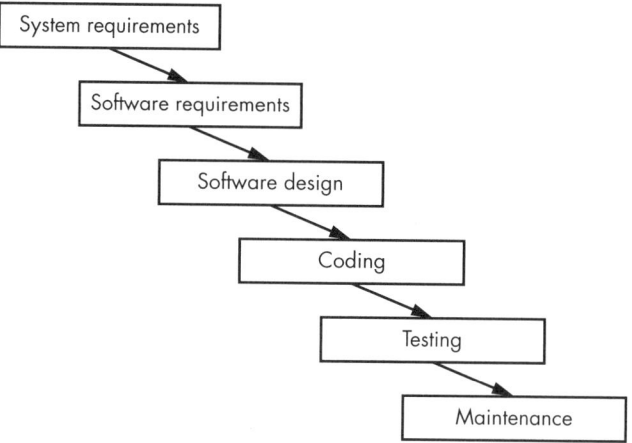

Figure 3-1: The Waterfall model

You begin the Waterfall model by producing the SyRS. Once the system requirements are specified, you produce the SRS from the SyRS. When the software requirements are specified, you produce the SDD from the SRS. You then produce source code from the SDD and test the software. Then you deploy and maintain the software. Everything in the SLDC happens in that order, without deviation.

As the original SDLC model, the Waterfall model is usually very simple to understand and apply to a software development project because each step is distinct, with well-understood inputs and deliverables. It's also relatively easy to review work performed using this model and verify that the project is on track.

However, the Waterfall model suffers from some huge problems. The most important is that it assumes that you perform each step perfectly before progressing to the next step, and that you'll find errors early in one step and make repairs before proceeding. In reality, this is rarely the case: defects in the requirements or design phases are typically not caught until testing or deployment. At that point, it can be very expensive to back up through the system and correct everything.

Another disadvantage is that the Waterfall model doesn't allow you to produce a working system for customers to review until very late in the development process. I can't count the number of times I've shown a client static screenshots or diagrams of how code would work, received their buy-in, and then had them reject the running result. That major disconnect in expectations could have been avoided had I produced a working prototype of the code that would have allowed customers to experiment with certain aspects of the system during the requirements phase.

Ultimately, this model is very risky. Unless you can *exactly* specify what the system will do before you start the process, the Waterfall model is likely inappropriate for your project.

The Waterfall model is appropriate for small projects of, say, less than a few tens of thousands of code lines involving only a couple of programmers; for very large projects (because nothing else works at that level); or when the current project is similar to a previous product that employed the Waterfall model during development (so you can use the existing documentation as a template).

3.2.3 The V Model

The V model, shown in Figure 3-2, follows the same basic steps as the Waterfall model but emphasizes the development of testing criteria early in the development life cycle. The V model is organized so the earlier steps, requirements and design, produce two sets of outputs: one for the step that follows and one for a parallel step during the testing phase.

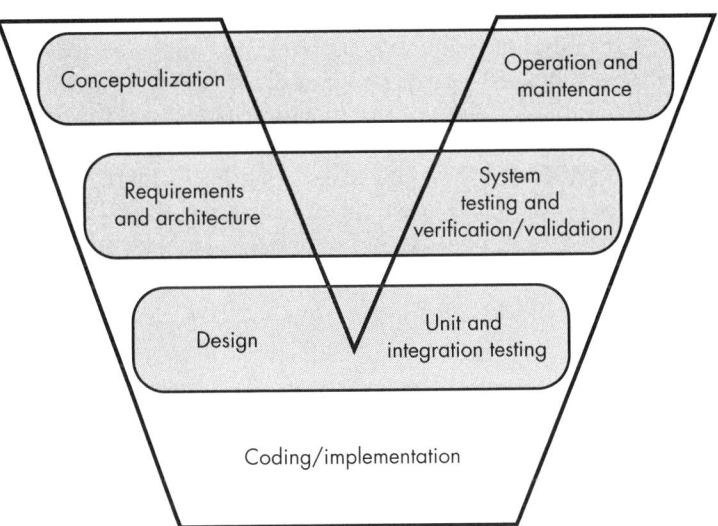

Figure 3-2: The V model

In Figure 3-2, the items on the left side of the V link straight across to the items on the right side: at each design stage, the programmer is thinking about how to test and use the concepts being modeled. For example, during the *requirements and architecture* phase, the system architect designs the system acceptance tests that will verify that the software correctly implements all the requirements. During the *design* phase, the system designer implements the software's unit and integration tests.

The big difference here from the Waterfall model is that the engineer implements test cases and procedures early on, so by the time coding begins, the software engineer can use existing test procedures to verify the code's behavior during development. Known as *test-driven development (TDD)*, in this approach the programmer constantly runs tests throughout the development process. Continuous testing allows you to find bugs much sooner and makes it cheaper and faster to correct them.

That said, the V model is far from perfect. Like its parent, the Waterfall model, the V model is too simple, and requires too much perfection in the early stages in order to prevent disasters in the later stages. For example, a defect in the requirements and architecture phase might not surface until system testing and validation, resulting in expensive backtracking through the development. For this reason, the V model doesn't work well for projects whose requirements are subject to change throughout a product's lifetime.

The model often encourages verification at the expense of validation. *Verification* ensures that a product meets certain requirements (such as its software requirements). It's easy to develop tests that show the software is fulfilling requirements laid out in the SRS and SyRS. In contrast, *validation* shows that the product meets the needs of its end users. Being more open-ended, validation is more difficult to achieve.

It's difficult, for example, to test that the software doesn't crash because it tries to process a NULL pointer. For this reason, validation tests are often entirely missing in the test procedures. Most test cases are requirements-driven, and rarely are there requirements like "no divisions by zero in this section of code" or "no memory leaks in this module" (these are known as *requirement gaps*; coming up with test cases without any requirements to base them on can be challenging, especially for novices).

3.2.4 The Iterative Model

Sequential models like Waterfall and V rely on the assumption that specification, requirements, and design are all perfect before coding occurs, meaning users won't discover design problems until the software is first deployed. By then it's often too costly (or too late) to repair the design, correct the software, and test it. The Iterative model overcomes this problem by taking multiple passes over the development model.

The hallmark of the Iterative model is user feedback. The system designers start with a general idea of the product from the users and stakeholders and create a minimal set of requirements and design documentation. The coders implement and test this minimal implementation. The users then play with this implementation and provide feedback. The system designers produce a new set of requirements and designs based on the user feedback, and the programmers implement and test the changes. Finally, users are given a second version for their evaluation. This process repeats until the users are satisfied or the software meets the original goals.

One big advantage of the Iterative model is that it works reasonably well when it's difficult to completely specify the software's behavior at the beginning of the development cycle. System architects can work from a general road map to design enough of the system for end users to play with and determine which new features are necessary. This avoids spending considerable effort producing features end users want implemented differently or don't want at all.

Another advantage is that the Iterative model reduces *time to market* risk. To get the product to market quickly, you decide on a subset of features the final product will have and develop those first, get the product working (in a minimalist fashion), and ship this *minimum viable product (MVP)*. Then, you add functionality to each new iteration to produce a new enhanced version of the product.

Advantages of the Iterative model include:

- You can achieve minimal functionality very rapidly.
- Managing risk is easier than in sequential models because you don't have to complete the entire program to determine that it won't do the job properly.
- Managing the project as it progresses (toward completion) is easier and more obvious than with sequential models.
- Changing requirements is supported.
- Changing requirements costs less.
- Parallel development is possible with two (or more) sets of teams working on alternate versions.

Here are some disadvantages of the Iterative model:

- Managing the project is more work.
- It doesn't scale down to smaller projects very well.
- It might take more resources (especially if parallel development takes place).
- Defining the iterations might require a "grander" road map of the system (that is, going back to specifying all the requirements before development starts).
- There might be no limit on the number of iterations; hence, it could be impossible to predict when the project will be complete.

3.2.5 The Spiral Model

The Spiral model is also an iterative model that repeats four phases: planning, design, evaluation/risk analysis, and construction (see Figure 3-3).

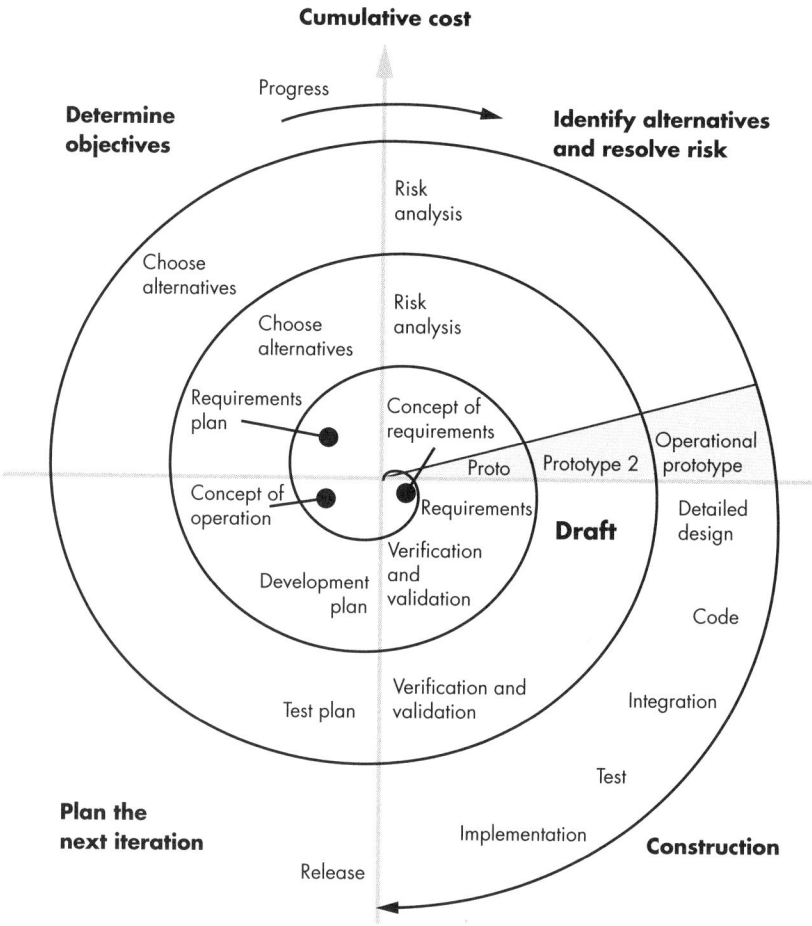

Figure 3-3: The Spiral model

The Spiral model is heavily risk-based: each iteration assesses the risks of going forward with the project. Management chooses which features to add and omit and which approaches to take by analyzing the risk (that is, the likelihood of failure).

The Spiral is often called a *model generator* or *meta model* because you can use further development models—the same type or a different one—on each spiral. The drawback is that the resulting model becomes specific to that project, making it difficult to apply to others.

One key advantage of the Spiral model is that it involves end users with the software early and continuously during development by producing working prototypes on a regular basis. The end user can play with these prototypes, determine if development is on the right track, and redirect the development process if needed. This addresses one of the great shortcomings of the Waterfall and V models.

A drawback of this approach is that it rewards "just good enough" design. If the code can be written "just fast enough" or "just small enough," further optimization is delayed until a later phase when it's necessary. Similarly, testing is done only to a level sufficient to achieve a minimal amount of confidence in the code. Additional testing is considered a waste of time, money, and resources. The Spiral model often leads to compromises in the early work, particularly when it's managed poorly, which leads to problems later in development.

Another downside is that the Spiral model increases management complexity. This model is complex, so project management requires risk analysis experts. Finding managers and engineers with this expertise is difficult, and substituting someone without appropriate experience is usually a disaster.

The Spiral model is suitable only for large, risky projects. The effort (especially with respect to documentation) expended is hard to justify for low-risk projects. Even on larger projects, the Spiral model might cycle indefinitely, never producing the final product, or the budget might be completely consumed while development is still on an intermediate spiral.

Another concern is that engineers spend considerable time developing prototypes and other code needed for intermediate versions that don't appear in the final software release, meaning the Spiral model often costs more than developing software with other methodologies.

Nevertheless, the Spiral model offers some big advantages:

- The requirements don't need to be fully specified before the project starts; the model is ideal for projects with changing requirements.
- It produces working code early in the development cycle.
- It works extremely well with *rapid prototyping* (see the next section, "The Rapid Application Development Model"), affording customers and other stakeholders a good level of comfort with the application early in its development.
- Development can be divided up and the riskier portions can be created early, reducing the overall development risk.
- Because requirements can be created as they're discovered, they are more accurate.
- As in the Iterative model, functionality can be spread out over time, enabling the addition of new features as time/budget allows without impacting the initial release.

3.2.6 The Rapid Application Development Model

Like the Spiral model, the Rapid Application Development (RAD) model emphasizes continuous interaction with users during development. Devised by James Martin, a researcher at IBM in the 1990s, the original RAD model divides software development into four phases (see Figure 3-4).

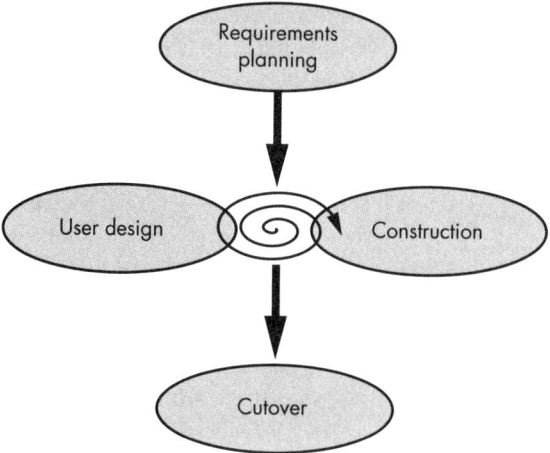

Figure 3-4: The RAD model

Requirements planning   A project's stakeholders come together to discuss business needs, scope, constraints, and system requirements.

User design   End users interact with the development team to produce models and prototypes for the system (detailing inputs, outputs, and computations), typically using *computer-aided software engineering (CASE)* tools.

Construction   The development team builds the software using tools to automatically generate code from the requirements and user design. Users remain involved during this phase, suggesting changes as the UI comes to life.

Cutover   The software is deployed.

RAD is more lightweight than Spiral, with fewer risk mitigation techniques and fairly light documentation needs, meaning it works well for small to medium-sized projects. Unlike other models, traditional RAD heavily depends on very-high-level languages (VHLLs), user interface modeling tools, complex libraries and frameworks of existing code, and CASE tools to automatically generate code from requirements and user interface models. In general, RAD is practical only when there are CASE tools available for the specific project problems. Today, many generic language systems support a high degree of automatic code generation, including Microsoft's Visual Basic and Visual Studio packages, Apple's Xcode/Interface Builder package, Free Pascal/Lazarus, and Embarcadero's Delphi (Object Pascal) package.

The advantages of the RAD model are similar to those of the Spiral model:

- The customer is involved with the product throughout development, resulting in less risk.
- RAD reduces development time because less time is spent writing documentation that must be rewritten later when the specifications inevitably change.

- The RAD model encourages the fast delivery of working code, and testing (and defect mitigation) is more efficient. Developers spend more time running the code, testing for problems.

Like any development model, RAD has some disadvantages as well:

- RAD requires Grand Master–level software engineers who have the experience to short-circuit much of the heavyweight development process found in other models. Such resources are scarce in many organizations.
- RAD requires continuous interaction with end users, which may be limited on many projects.
- RAD may be difficult to schedule and control. Managers who live and die by Microsoft Project will find it difficult to deal with the uncertainties in the RAD model.
- Unless carefully managed, RAD can rapidly devolve into hacking. Software engineers might forgo formal design methodologies and just hack away at the code to make changes. This can be especially troublesome when end users start making suggestions "just to see what the result will look like."[4]
- RAD doesn't work well for large system development.

3.2.7 The Incremental Model

The Incremental model is very similar to the Iterative model, with the main difference being in planning and design. In the Iterative model, the system design is created first and software engineers implement various pieces at each iteration; the initial design defines only the first piece of working code. Once the program is running, new features are designed and added incrementally.

The Incremental model emphasizes the "keep the code working" concept. When a base product is operational, the development team adds a minimal amount of new functionality at each iteration, and the software is tested and kept functional. By limiting new features, the team can more easily locate and solve development problems.

The advantage of the Incremental model is that you always maintain a working product. The model also comes naturally to programmers, especially on small projects. The disadvantage is that it doesn't consider the product's full design in the beginning. Often, new features are simply hacked on to the existing design. This could result in problems down the road when end users request features that were never considered in the original design. The Incremental model is sufficient for small projects but

---

4. I was once tasked with setting up user interface colors on an embedded application. The client requested one set of colors. A week later I showed up with their desired changes, and they didn't like them. So, we tried a second set. They didn't like those. Then a third set, then a fourth set. A month later they decided the initial color set was the best. In the meantime, the project had lost a month.

doesn't scale well to large projects, where the Iterative model might be a better choice.

3.3 Software Development Methodologies

A software development model describes *what* work is done but leaves considerable leeway as to *how* it is done. This section looks at some development methodologies and processes you can apply to many of the models just discussed.

The Belitsoft company blog[5] describes software methodology as follows:

> A system of principles, as well as a set of ideas, concepts, methods, techniques, and tools that define the style of software development.

Thus, we can reduce the concept of software methodology to one word: *style*. There are various styles you can use when developing software.

3.3.1 Traditional (Predictive) Methodologies

The traditional methodology is *predictive*, meaning that management predicts which activities will take place, when they will take place, and who will do them. These methodologies work hand in hand with linear/sequential development models, like the Waterfall or V model. You could use prediction with other models, but those are designed to purposely avoid the problems that predictive methodologies are prone to.

Predictive methodologies fail when it's impossible to predict changes in future requirements, key personnel, or economic conditions (for example, did the company receive the expected additional financing at some milestone in the project?).

3.3.2 Adaptive Methodologies

The Spiral, RAD, Incremental, and Iterative models came about specifically because it's usually difficult to correctly predict requirements for a large software system. Adaptive methodologies handle these unpredictable changes in the workflow and emphasize short-term planning. After all, if you're planning only 30 days in advance on a large project, the worst that can happen is you have to replan for the next 30 days; this is nowhere near the disaster you'd face in the middle of a large Waterfall/Predictive-based project, when a change would force you to resync the entire project.

3.3.3 Agile

Agile is an incremental methodology that focuses on customer collaboration, short development iterations that respond to changes quickly, working software, and support for individuals' contributions and interactions. The Agile methodology was created as an umbrella to cover several

---

5. Sadly, the link to this quote is no longer active. Ah, the joys of the internet. Nevertheless, this is one of the best, most concise definitions I've found that doesn't try to promote a particular methodology.

different "lightweight" (that is, nonpredictive) methodologies, including Extreme Programming, Scrum, Dynamic System Development Model (DSDM), Adaptive Software Development (ASD), Crystal, Feature-Driven Development (FDD), Pragmatic Programming, and others. Most of these methodologies are considered "Agile," although they often cover different aspects of the software development process. Agile has largely proven itself on real-world projects, making it one of the currently most popular methodologies, so we'll dedicate a fair amount of space to it here.

NOTE *For a detailed list of the principles behind Agile, see the Agile Manifesto at* http://agilemanifesto.org/.

3.3.3.1 Agile Is Incremental in Nature

Agile development is incremental, iterative, and evolutionary in nature, and so works best with Incremental or Iterative models (using Spiral or RAD is also possible). A project is broken down into tasks that a team can complete in one to four weeks, which is often called a *sprint*. During each sprint, the development team plans, creates requirements, designs, codes, unit-tests, and acceptance-tests the software with the new features.

At the end of the sprint, the deliverable is a working piece of software that demonstrates the new functionality with as few defects as possible.

3.3.3.2 Agile Requires Face-to-Face Communication

Throughout the sprint, a customer representative must be available to answer questions that arise. Without this, the development process can easily veer off in the wrong direction or get bogged down while the team waits for responses.

Efficient communication in Agile requires a face-to-face conversation.[6] When a developer demonstrates a product directly to the customer, that customer often raises questions that would never come up in an email or if they'd just tried the feature on their own. Sometimes, offhand remarks in a demo can result in a burst of divergent thinking that would never happen if the conversation weren't in person.

3.3.3.3 Agile Is Focused on Quality

Agile emphasizes various quality-enhancing techniques, such as automated unit testing, TDD, design patterns, pair programming, code refactoring, and other well-known best software practices. The idea is to produce code with as few defects as possible (during initial design and coding).

Automated unit testing creates a test framework that a developer can automatically run to verify that the software runs correctly. It's also important for *regression testing*, which tests to ensure the code still works properly after

---

6. Note that although face-to-face communication is more efficient, these meetings can also have a negative impact on engineers' productivity. See "Focus and Eliminate Distractions" on page 34 for more details.

new features have been added. Manually running regression tests is too labor-intensive, so it generally won't happen.

In TDD, developers write automated tests prior to writing the code, which means that the test will initially fail. The developer runs the tests, picks a test that fails, writes the software to fix that failure, and then reruns the tests. As soon as a test succeeds, the developer moves on to the next failing test. Successfully eliminating all the failed tests verifies that the software meets the requirements.

Pair programming, one of Agile's more controversial practices, involves two programmers working on each section of code together. One programmer enters the code while the other watches, catching mistakes onscreen, offering design tips, providing quality control, and keeping the first programmer focused on the project.

3.3.3.4 Agile Sprints (Iterations) Are Short

Agile methodologies work best when the iterations are short—from one week to (at most) a couple of months. This is a nod to the old adage "If it weren't for the last minute, nothing would ever get done." By keeping iterations short, software engineers are always working during the last minute, reducing fatigue and procrastination and increasing project focus.

Hand in hand with short sprints are short feedback cycles. A common Agile feature is a brief daily stand-up meeting, typically no more than 15 minutes,[7] where programmers concisely describe what they're working on, what they're stuck on, and what they've finished. This allows project management to rearrange resources and provide help if the schedule is slipping. The meetings catch any problems early rather than wasting several weeks before the issue comes to project management's attention.

3.3.3.5 Agile Deemphasizes Heavyweight Documentation

One of the Waterfall model's biggest problems is that it produces reams of documentation that is never again read. Overly comprehensive, *heavyweight* documentation has a few problems:

- Documentation must be maintained. Whenever a change is made in the software, the documentation must be updated. Changes in one document have to be reflected in many other documents, increasing workload.
- Many documents are difficult to write prior to the code. More often than not, such documents are updated after the code is written and then never read again (a waste of time and money).
- An iterative development process quickly destroys coherence between code and documentation. Therefore, properly maintaining the documentation at each iteration doesn't fit well with the Agile methodology.

---

7. They're called "stand-up" meetings because everyone who can is required to stand up. This makes everyone physically uncomfortable, which results in shorter meetings.

Agile emphasizes *just barely good enough (JBGE)* documentation—that is, enough documentation so the next programmer can pick up where you left off, but no more (in fact, Agile emphasizes JBGE for most concepts, including design/modeling).

Many books have been written on Agile development (see "For More Information" on page 69). This is not one of them, but we'll look at a couple of the different methodologies under the Agile umbrella. These methodologies are not mutually exclusive; two or more can be combined and used on the same project.

3.3.4 Extreme Programming

Extreme Programming (XP) is perhaps the most widely used Agile methodology. It aims to streamline development practices and processes to deliver working software that provides the desired feature set without unnecessary extras.

XP is guided by five values:

Communication Good communication between the customer and the team, among team members, and between the team and management is essential for success.

Simplicity XP strives to produce the simplest system today, even if it costs more to extend it tomorrow, rather than producing a complicated product that implements features that might never be used.

Feedback XP depends upon continuous feedback: unit and functional tests provide programmers with feedback when they make changes to their code; the customer provides immediate feedback when a new feature is added; and project management tracks the development schedule, providing feedback about estimates.

Respect XP requires that team members respect one another. A programmer will never commit a change to the code base that breaks the compilation or existing unit tests (or do anything else that will delay the work of other team members).

Courage XP's rules and practices don't line up with traditional software development practices. XP requires the commitment of resources (such as an "always available" customer representative or pair programmers) that can be expensive or difficult to justify in older methodologies. Some XP policies like "refactor early, refactor often" run counter to common practice such as "if it ain't broke, don't fix it." Without the courage to fully implement its extreme policies, XP becomes less disciplined and can devolve into hacking.

3.3.4.1 The XP Team

Paramount to the XP process is the XP *whole team* concept: all members of the team work together to produce the final product. Team members are not specialists in one field, but often take on different responsibilities or roles, and different team members might perform the same role at different times. An XP team fills the following roles with various team members.

A customer representative

The customer representative is responsible for keeping the project on the right track, providing validation, writing *user stories* (requirements, features, and use cases) and *functional tests*, and deciding the *priorities* (release planning) for new functionality. The customer representative must be available whenever the team needs them.

Not having an available customer representative is one of the largest impediments to successful XP projects. Without continuous feedback and direction from the customer, XP degenerates into hacking. XP doesn't rely on requirements documentation; instead, the representative is a "living version" of that documentation.

Programmers

Programmers have several responsibilities on an XP team: working with the customer representative to produce user stories, estimating how resources should be allocated for those stories, estimating timelines and costs to implement stories, writing unit tests, and writing the code to implement the stories.

Testers

Testers (programmers who implement or modify a given unit run unit tests) run the functional tests. Often, at least one of the testers is the customer representative.

Coach

The coach is the team leader, typically the lead programmer, whose job is to make sure the project succeeds. The coach ensures the team has the appropriate work environment; fosters good communication; shields the team from the rest of the organization by, for example, acting as a liaison to upper management; helps team members maintain self-discipline; and ensures the team maintains the XP process. When a programmer is having difficulty, coaches provide resources to help them overcome the problem.

Manager/tracker

The XP project manager is responsible for scheduling meetings and recording their results. The tracker is often, but not always, the same as the manager, and is responsible for tracking the project's progress and determining whether the current iteration's schedule can be met. To do so, the tracker checks with each programmer a couple of times a week.

Different XP configurations often include additional team roles, such as analysts, designers, doomsayers, and so on. Because of the small size of XP teams (typically around 15 members) and the fact that (paired) programmers constitute the majority of the team, most roles are shared. See "For More Information" on page 69 for additional references.

3.3.4.2 XP Software Development Activities

XP uses four basic software development activities: coding, testing, listening, and designing.

Coding

XP considers code to be the *only* important output of the development process. Contrary to the "think first, code later" philosophy of serial models like Waterfall, XP programmers start writing code at the beginning of the software development cycle. After all, "at the end of the day, there has to be a working program."[8]

XP programmers don't immediately start coding, but are given a list of small and simple features to implement. They work on a basic design for a particular feature and then code that feature and make sure it's working before expanding in increments, with each increment working correctly to ensure that the main body of code is always running. Programmers make only small changes to the project before integrating those changes into the larger system. XP minimizes all noncode output, such as documentation, because there is very little benefit to it.

Testing

XP emphasizes TDD using automated unit and functional tests. This allows XP engineers to develop the *product right* (verification via automated unit tests) and develop the *right product* (validation via functional tests). *WGC6: Testing, Debugging, and Quality Assurance* will deal more exclusively with testing, so we won't go too far into it here; just know that TDD is very important to the XP process because it ensures that the system is always working.

Testing in XP is always automated. If adding one feature breaks an unrelated feature for some reason, it's critical to immediately catch that. By running a full set of unit (and functional) tests when adding a new feature, you can ensure that your new code doesn't cause a regression.

Listening

XP developers communicate almost constantly with their customers to ensure they're developing the right product (validation).

XP is a *change-driven process*, meaning it expects changes in requirements, resources, technology, and performance, based on feedback from customers as they test the product throughout the process.

Designing

Design occurs constantly throughout the XP process—during release planning, iteration planning, refactoring, and so on. This focus prevents XP from devolving into hacking.

---

8. Wilfrid Hutagalung, "Extreme Programming," *http://www.umsl.edu/~sauterv/analysis/f06Papers/Hutagalung/*.

3.3.4.3 The XP Process

Each cycle of XP produces a software *release*. Frequent releases ensure constant feedback from the customer. Each cycle consists of a couple of fixed-period blocks of time known as iterations (with no more than a couple of weeks for each iteration). Cycles, as shown in Figure 3-5, are necessary for planning; the middle box in this figure represents one or more iterations.

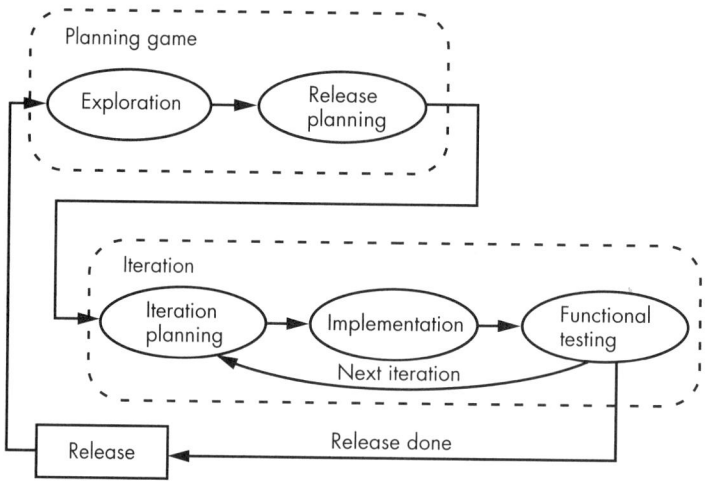

Figure 3-5: An XP cycle

In the planning game, the XP team decides which features to implement, estimates their costs, and plans the release. During the exploration step, the customer defines the feature set and developers estimate costs and time requirements for those features. The next section (under "User stories") describes the mechanism customers use to specify features.

During release planning, the customer negotiates with the developers on the features to implement in the given iteration. The developers commit to the release plan, and engineers are assigned various tasks. At the end of release planning, the process enters the *steering* phase, during which the customer ensures that the project remains on track.

After the overall plan is determined, the process for the current release enters an inner loop consisting of three steps: iteration planning, implementation, and functional testing. Iteration planning is the planning game scaled down for a single feature.

The implementation step is the coding and unit testing of the feature. The developer writes a set of unit tests, implements just enough code to make the unit tests succeed, refactors the code as necessary, and integrates the changes into the common code base.

During the last step of the iteration, customers perform functional testing. Then the process repeats for the next iteration, or a release is produced if all iterations are completed for the current release.

3.3.4.4 XP Software Development Rules

XP implements the four software development activities—coding, testing, listening, and designing—using 12 simple rules:[9]

- User stories (planning game)
- Small releases (building blocks)
- Metaphors (standardized naming schemes)
- Collective ownership
- Coding standard
- Simple design
- Refactoring
- Testing
- Pair programming
- Onsite customer
- Continuous integration
- Sustainable pace

Each rule is described next, along with its advantages and disadvantages.

User stories

User stories describe a simplified set of use cases, written by the customer, that define the system's requirements. The project team uses this set, which should provide only enough detail to estimate how long it will take to implement the feature, to estimate the cost and plan the system's development.

At the beginning of a project, the customer generates 50 to 100 user stories to use during a release planning session. Then the customer and the team negotiate which features the team will implement in the next release. The customer, possibly with help from a developer, also creates functional tests from the user stories.

Small releases

Once a piece of software is functional, the team adds one feature at a time. Other features are not added until that new feature is written, tested, debugged, and incorporated into the main build. The team creates a new build of the system for each feature it adds.

Metaphors

XP projects revolve around a story about the system's operation that all stakeholders can understand. Metaphors are naming conventions used within the software to ensure that operations are obvious to everyone;

---

9. Actually, there are 28 different XP rules, but they can be simplified to these 12.

they replace a complex business process name with a simple name. For example, "train conductor" might describe how a data acquisition system operates.

Collective ownership

In XP, the entire team owns and maintains all source code. At any time, any team member can check out code and modify it. During reviews, no one is singled out for coding mistakes. Collective code ownership prevents delays and means one person's absence doesn't hinder progress.

Coding standard

All XP members must adhere to common coding standards concerning styles and formats. The team can develop the standards or they can come from an outside source, but everyone must follow them. Coding standards make the system easier to read and understand, especially for newcomers getting up to speed with the project, and help the team avoid having to waste time later refactoring the code to bring it into compliance.

Simple design

The simplest design that meets all the requirements is always chosen. At no time does the design anticipate features that have yet to be added—for example, adding "hooks" or application programming interfaces (APIs) that allow future code to interface with the current code. Simple design means *just enough to get the current job done*. The simplest code will pass all the tests for the current iteration. This runs counter to traditional software engineering, where software is designed as generically as possible to handle any future enhancements.

Refactoring

Refactoring code is the process of restructuring or rewriting the code without changing its external behavior, to make the code simpler, more readable, or better by some other improvement metric.

WGC5: Great Coding will go into refactoring in much greater detail. See "For More Information" on page 69 for additional references on refactoring.

Testing

XP uses a TDD methodology, as discussed in "XP Software Development Activities" on page 57.

Pair programming

In pair programming, one programmer (the *driver*) enters code, and the second programmer (the *navigator*) reviews each line of code as it's written. The two engineers change roles throughout and pairs are often created and broken apart.

It's often difficult to convince management that two programmers working together on the same code are more productive than they are working separately on different pieces of code. XP evangelists argue that because the navigator is constantly reviewing the driver's code, a separate review session isn't needed, among other benefits:[10]

Economic benefits   Pairs spend about 15 percent more time on programs than individuals, but the code has 15 percent fewer defects.[11]

Design quality   Two programmers produce a better design because they bring more experiences to the project. They think about the problem in different ways, and they devise the solution differently based on their driver/navigator roles. A better design means the project requires less backtracking and redesign throughout its life cycle.

Satisfaction   A majority of programmers enjoy working in pairs rather than alone. They feel more confident in their work and, as a result, produce better code.

Learning   Pair programming allows pair members to learn from each other, increasing their respective skills. This cannot happen in solo programming.

Team building and communication   Team members share problems and solutions, which helps spread the intellectual property (IP) around and makes it easier for others to work on a given code section.

Overall, the research on the effectiveness of pair programming is a mixed bag. Most published papers from industry sources talk about how well pair programming has worked, but papers describing its failure in industry (versus academic) settings generally don't get published. Research by Kim Man Lui and Andreas Hofer considers three types of pairings in pair programming: expert–expert, novice–novice, and expert–novice.

Expert–expert pairing can produce effective results, but two expert programmers are likely to use "tried and true" methods without introducing any new insight, meaning the effectiveness of this pairing versus two solo expert programmers is questionable.

Novice–novice pairing is often more effective than having the partners work on solo projects. Novices will have greatly varying backgrounds and experiences, and their knowledge is more likely to be complementary than overlapping (as is the case for expert pairs). Two novices working together are likely to work faster on two projects serially rather than they would working independently on their own project in parallel.

Expert–novice pairing is commonly called *mentoring*. Many XP adherents don't consider this to be pair programming, but mentoring is an efficient way to get a junior programmer up to speed with the code base. In mentoring, it's best to have the novice act as the driver so they can interact with and learn from the code.

---

10. *http://en.wikipedia.org/wiki/Pair_programming*

11. *http://collaboration.csc.ncsu.edu/laurie/Papers/dissertation.pdf* and *https://collaboration.csc.ncsu.edu/laurie/Papers/ieeeSoftware.PDF*

GUIDELINES FOR SIMPLE DESIGN

Common phrases associated with simple design include:

Don't repeat yourself (DRY)   Duplicate code is complex code.
Once and only once (OAOO)   All unique functionality should exist as some method/procedure in the code and appear only once in the code (this last point is DRY).
You aren't gonna need it (YAGNI)   Avoid speculative coding. When adding a feature to your code base, make sure it's specified by a user story (requirement). Don't add code in anticipation of future requirements.
Limit APIs and (published) interfaces   If your code interfaces with other systems by publishing an API, limiting the number of interfaces to the bare minimum will make it easier to modify your code in the future (without breaking external code).

Simple design is amazingly difficult to achieve. More often than not, you accomplish it only by writing complex code and then refactoring it repeatedly until you're happy with the result. A few quotes from some famous computer scientists will help drive this point home:

> There are two ways of constructing a software design: one way is to make it so simple that there are obviously no deficiencies, and the other way is to make it so complicated that there are no obvious deficiencies.
> —C. A. R. Hoare

> The cheapest, fastest, and most reliable components are those that aren't there.
> —Gordon Bell

> Deleted code is debugged code.
> —Jeff Sickle

> Debugging is twice as hard as writing the code in the first place. Therefore, if you write the code as cleverly as possible, you are, by definition, not smart enough to debug it.
> —Brian Kernighan and P. J. Plauger

> Any program that tries to be so generalized and configurable that it could handle any kind of task will either fall short of this goal or will be horribly broken.
> —Chris Wenham

> The cost of adding a feature isn't just the time it takes to code it. The cost also includes the addition of an obstacle to future expansion. The trick is to pick the features that don't fight each other.
> —John Carmack

> Simplicity is hard to build, easy to use, and hard to charge for. Complexity is easy to build, hard to use, and easy to charge for.
> —Chris Sacca

Though supporting evidence for pair programming is anecdotal and essentially unproven, XP depends on pair programming to replace formal code reviews, structured walk-throughs, and—to a limited extent—design documentation, so it can't be forgone. As is common in the XP methodology, certain heavyweight processes like code reviews are often folded into other activities like pair programming. Trying to eliminate one rule or subprocess will likely open a gap in the overall methodology.

Not all XP activities are done in pairs. Many nonprogramming activities are done solo—for example, reading (and writing) documentation, dealing with emails, and doing research on the web—and some are always done solo, like writing *code spikes* (throwaway code needed to test a theory or idea). Ultimately, *pair programming is essential for successful XP ventures*. If a team cannot handle pair programming well, it should use a different development methodology.

Onsite customer

As noted many times previously, in XP the customer is part of the development team and must be available at all times.

The onsite customer rule is probably the most difficult to follow. Most customers aren't willing or able to provide this resource. However, without the continuous availability of a customer representative, the software could go off track, encounter delays, or regress from previous working versions. These problems are all solvable, but their solution destroys the benefits of using XP.

Continuous integration

In a traditional software development system like Waterfall, individual components of the system, written by different developers, are not tested together until some big milestone in the project, and the integrated software may fail spectacularly. The problem is that the unit tests don't behave the same as the code that must be integrated with the units, typically due to communication problems or misunderstood requirements.

There will always be miscommunication and misunderstandings, but XP makes integration problems easier to solve via *continuous integration*. As soon as a new feature is implemented, it's merged with the main build and tested. Some tests might fail because a feature has not yet been implemented, but the entire program is run, testing linkages with other units in the application. Software builds are created frequently (several times per day). As a result, you'll discover integration problems early when they're less costly to correct.

Sustainable pace

Numerous studies show that creative people produce their best results when they're not overworked. XP dictates a 40-hour workweek for software engineers. Sometimes a crisis might arise that requires a small amount of overtime. But if management keeps its programming team in constant crisis mode, the quality of the work suffers and the overtime becomes counterproductive.

3.3.4.5 Other Common Practices

In addition to the previous 12 rules, XP promotes several other common practices:

Open workspace and collocation

The XP methodology suggests open work areas for the entire team, who work in pairs at adjacent workstations. Having everyone together promotes constant communication and keeps the team focused.[12] Questions can be quickly asked and answered, and other programmers can inject comments into a discussion as appropriate.

But open workspaces have their challenges. Some people are more easily distracted than others. Loud noise and conversations can be very annoying and break concentration.

Open workspaces are a "best practice" in XP, not an absolute rule. If this setup doesn't work for a particular pair, they can use an office or cubicle and work without distractions.

Retrospectives/debriefings

When a project is complete, the team meets to discuss the successes and failures, disseminating the information to help improve the next project.

Self-directed teams

A self-directed team works on a project without the usual managerial levels (project leads, senior and junior level engineers, and so forth). The team makes decisions on priorities by consensus. XP teams aren't completely unmanaged, but the idea here is that given a set of tasks and appropriate deadlines, the team can manage the task assignments and project progress on its own.

3.3.4.6 Problems with XP

XP is not a panacea. There are several problems with it, including:

- Detailed specifications aren't created or preserved. This makes it difficult to add new programmers later in the project or for a separate programming team to maintain the project.
- Pair programming is required, even if it doesn't work. In some cases, it can be overkill. Having two programmers work on a relatively simple piece of code can double your development costs.
- To be practical, XP typically requires that all team members be GMPs in order to handle the wide range of roles each member must support. This is rarely achievable in real life, except on the smallest of projects.

---

12. This isn't quite the same as having a manager constantly looking over your shoulder because your team isn't explicitly watching what you're doing. Hence, the stress level is quite a bit lower.

- Constant refactoring can introduce as many problems (new bugs) as it solves. It can also waste time when programmers refactor code that doesn't need it.
- No Big Design Up Front (that is, non-Waterfall-like development) often leads to excessive redesign.
- A customer representative is necessary. Often, the customer will assign a junior-level person to this position because of the perceived costs, resulting in a failure point. If the customer representative leaves before the project is complete, all the requirements that aren't written down are lost.
- XP is not scalable to large teams. The limit for a productive XP team is approximately a dozen engineers.
- XP is especially susceptible to "feature creep." The customer can inject new features into the system due to a lack of documented requirements/features.
- Unit tests, even those created by XP programmers, often fail to point out missing features. Unit tests test "the code that is present," not "the code that *should* be present."
- XP is generally considered an "all or nothing" methodology: if you don't follow every tenet of the "XP religion," the process fails. Most XP rules have weaknesses that are covered by the strengths of other rules. If you fail to apply one rule, another rule will likely break (because its weaknesses are no longer covered, and that broken rule will break another, ad nauseam).

This small introduction to XP cannot do the topic justice. For more information on XP, see "For More Information" on page 69.

3.3.5 Scrum

The Scrum methodology is not a software development methodology per se, but an Agile mechanism for *managing* the software development process. More often than not, Scrum is used to manage some other model such as XP.

Beyond engineers, a Scrum team has two special members: the product owner and the scrum master. The *product owner* is responsible for guiding the team toward building the right product by, for example, maintaining requirements and features. The *scrum master* is a coach who guides the team members through the Scrum-based development process, managing team progress, maintaining lists of projects, and ensuring team members aren't held up.

Scrum is an iterative development process like all other Agile methodologies, and each iteration is a one- to four-week sprint. A sprint begins with a planning meeting where the team determines the work to be done. A list of items known as a *backlog* is assembled, and the team estimates how much time is required for each item on the backlog. Once the backlog is created, the sprint can begin.

Each day the team has a short stand-up meeting during which the members briefly mention yesterday's progress and their plans for today. The scrum master notes any progress problems and deals with them after the meeting. No detailed discussions about the project take place during the stand-up meeting.

Team members pick items from the backlog and work on those items. As items are removed from the backlog, the scrum master maintains a Scrum *burn-down chart* that shows the current sprint's progress. When all the items have been implemented to the product owner's satisfaction, or the team determines that some items cannot be finished on time or at all, the team holds an *end meeting*.

At the end meeting, the team demonstrates the features that were implemented and explains the failures of the items not completed. If possible, the scrum master collects unfinished items for the next sprint.

Also part of the end meeting is the sprint *retrospective*, where team members discuss their progress, suggest process improvements, and determine what went well and what went wrong.

Note that Scrum doesn't dictate how the engineers perform their jobs or how the tasks are documented, and doesn't provide a set of rules or best practices to follow during development. Scrum leaves these decisions to the development team. Many teams, for example, employ the XP methodology under Scrum. Any methodology compatible with iterative development will work fine.

Like XP, Scrum works well with small teams fewer than a dozen members and fails to scale to larger teams. Some extensions to Scrum have been made to support larger teams. Specifically, a "scrum-of-scrums" process allows multiple teams to apply a Scrum methodology to a large project. The large project is broken down into multiple teams, and then an ambassador from each team is sent to the daily scrum-of-scrums meeting to discuss their progress. This doesn't solve all the communication problems of a large team, but it does extend the methodology to work for slightly larger projects.

3.3.6 *Feature-Driven Development*

Feature-driven development, one of the more interesting methodologies under the Agile umbrella, is specifically designed to scale up to large projects.

One common thread among most Agile methodologies is that they require expert programmers in order to succeed. FDD, on the other hand, allows for large teams where it is logistically impossible to ensure you have the best person working on every activity of the project, and is worth serious consideration on projects involving more than a dozen software engineers.

FDD uses an iterative model. Three processes take place at the beginning of the project (often called *iteration zero*), and then the remaining two processes are iteratively carried out for the duration of the project. These processes are as follows:

1. Develop an overall model.
2. Build a features list.

3. Plan by feature.
4. Design by feature.
5. Build by feature.

3.3.6.1 Develop an Overall Model

Developing an overall model is a collaborative effort between all the stakeholders—clients, architects, and developers—where all team members work together to understand the system. Unlike the specifications and design documents in the serial methods, the overall model concentrates on breadth rather than depth to fill in as many generalized features as possible to define the entire project, and then fill in the depth of the model design's future iterations, with the purpose of guiding the current project, not documenting it for the future.

The advantage of this approach versus other Agile approaches is that most features are planned from the beginning of the project. Therefore, the design can't take off in a direction that makes certain features difficult or impossible to add at a later date, and new features cannot be added in an ad hoc fashion.

3.3.6.2 Build a Features List

During the second step of FDD, the team documents the feature list devised in the model development step, which is then formalized by the chief programmer for use during design and development. The output of this process is a formal features document. Although not as heavyweight as the SRS document found in other models, the feature descriptions are formal and unambiguous.

3.3.6.3 Plan by Feature

The plan-by-feature process involves creating an initial schedule for the software development that dictates which features will be implemented initially and which features will be implemented on successive iterations.

Plan by feature also assigns sets of features to various chief programmers who, along with their teams, are responsible for implementing them. The chief programmer and associated team members take ownership of these features and the associated code. This deviates somewhat from standard Agile practice, where the entire team owns the code. This is one of the reasons FDD works better for large projects than standard Agile processes: collective code ownership doesn't scale well to large projects.

As a rule, each feature is a small task that a three- to five-person team can develop in two or three weeks (and, more often, just days). Each feature class is independent of the others, so no feature depends on the development of features in classes owned by other teams.

3.3.6.4 Design by Feature

Once the features for a given iteration are selected, the chief programmer who owns each feature set forms a team to design the feature. Feature teams are not static; they're formed and disbanded for each iteration of the design-by-feature and build-by-feature processes.

The feature team analyzes the requirements and designs the feature(s) for the current iteration. The teams decide on that feature's implementation and its interaction with the rest of the system. If the feature is far-reaching, the chief programmer might involve other feature class owners to avoid conflicts with other feature sets.

During the design phase, the feature teams decide on the algorithms and processes to use, and develop and document tests for the features. If necessary, the chief programmer (along with the original set of stakeholders) updates the overall model to reflect the design.

3.3.6.5 Build by Feature

The build-by-feature step involves coding and testing the feature. The developers unit-test their code and feature teams provide formal system testing of the features. FDD doesn't mandate TDD, but it does insist that all features added to the system be tested and reviewed.

FDD requires code reviews (a best practice, but not required by most Agile processes). As Steve McConnell points out in *Code Complete* (Microsoft Press, 2004), well-executed code inspections uncover many defects that testing alone will never find.

3.4 Models and Methodologies for the Great Programmer

A great programmer should be capable of adapting to any software development model or methodology in use by their team. That said, some models are more appropriate than others. If you're given the choice of model, this chapter should guide you in choosing an appropriate one.

No methodology is scalable up *or down*, so you'll need to choose a suitable model and methodology based on the project size. For tiny projects, hacking or a documentation-less version of the Waterfall model is probably a good choice. For medium-sized projects, one of the iterative (Agile) models and methodologies is best. For large projects, the sequential models or FDD are the most successful (although often quite expensive).

More often than not, you won't get to choose the developmental models for projects you work on unless they're your personal projects. The key is to become familiar with the various models so you're comfortable with any model you're asked to use. The following section provides some resources for learning more about the different software development models and methodologies this chapter describes. As always, an internet search will provide considerable information on software development models and methodologies.

3.5 For More Information

Astels, David R. *Test-Driven Development: A Practical Guide.* Upper Saddle River, NJ: Pearson Education, 2003.

Beck, Kent. *Test-Driven Development by Example.* Boston: Addison-Wesley Professional, 2002.

Beck, Kent, with Cynthia Andres. *Extreme Programming Explained: Embrace Change.* 2nd ed. Boston: Addison-Wesley, 2004.

Boehm, Barry. *Spiral Development: Experience, Principles, and Refinements.* (Special Report CMU/SEI-2000-SR-008.) Edited by Wilfred J. Hansen. Pittsburgh: Carnegie Mellon Software Engineering Institute, 2000.

Fowler, Martin. *Refactoring: Improving the Design of Existing Code.* Reading, MA: Addison-Wesley, 1999.

Kerievsky, Joshua. *Refactoring to Patterns.* Boston: Addison-Wesley, 2004.

Martin, James. *Rapid Application Development.* Indianapolis: Macmillan, 1991.

Martin, Robert C. *Agile Software Development, Principles, Patterns, and Practices.* Upper Saddle River, NJ: Pearson Education, 2003.

McConnell, Steve. *Code Complete.* 2nd ed. Redmond, WA: Microsoft Press, 2004.

———. *Rapid Development: Taming Wild Software Schedules.* Redmond, WA: Microsoft Press, 1996.

Mohammed, Nabil, Ali Munassar, and A. Govardhan. "A Comparison Between Five Models of Software Engineering." *IJCSI International Journal of Computer Science Issues* 7, no. 5 (2010).

Pressman, Robert S. *Software Engineering, A Practitioner's Approach.* New York: McGraw-Hill, 2010.

Schwaber, Ken. *Agile Project Management with Scrum (Developer Best Practices).* Redmond, WA: Microsoft Press, 2004.

Shore, James, and Shane Warden. *The Art of Agile Development.* Sebastopol, CA: O'Reilly, 2007.

Stephens, Matt, and Doug Rosenberg. *Extreme Programming Refactored: The Case Against XP.* New York: Apress, 2003.

Wake, William C. *Refactoring Workbook.* Boston: Addison-Wesley Professional, 2004.

Williams, Laurie, and Robert Kessler. *Pair Programming Illuminated.* Reading, MA: Addison-Wesley, 2003.

PART II

UML

4

AN INTRODUCTION TO UML AND USE CASES

The *Unified Modeling Language (UML)* is a graphic-based developmental language used to describe requirements and standards for software design. The latest versions of the Institute of Electrical and Electronics Engineers (IEEE) SDD standard are built around UML concepts, so we'll start by covering the background and features of UML before moving on to how the language implements use cases to help us represent software system designs clearly and consistently.

4.1 The UML Standard

UML started out in the mid-1990s as a collection of three independent modeling languages: the Booch method (Grady Booch), the object modeling technique (Jim Rumbaugh), and the object-oriented software engineering system (Ivar Jacobson). After this initial amalgamation, the Object Management Group (OMG) developed the first UML standard, with input from a multitude of researchers, in 1997. UML remains under OMG's management today. Because UML was essentially designed by unification, it contains many different ways to specify the same thing, resulting in a lot of systemwide redundancy and inconsistency.

So why use UML? Well, despite its shortcomings, it's a rather complete modeling language for object-oriented design. It's also become the de facto IEEE documentation standard to use. So even if you don't intend to use UML for your own projects, you'll need to be able to read it when dealing with documentation from other projects. Because UML has become popular, there's a good chance your project's stakeholders are already familiar with it. It's sort of like the C programming language (or BASIC, if you don't know C): it's ugly as far as language design goes, but everybody knows it.

UML is a very complex language that requires considerable study to master, an educational process that is beyond the scope of this book. Fortunately, dozens of good books are available on the subject, some almost 1,000 pages long (for example, *The UML Bible* by Tom Pender; see "For More Information" on page 88). This chapter and those that follow are not intended to make you an expert on UML, but rather to quickly cover the UML features and concepts that the rest of the book uses. That way, you can refer back to these chapters when you're trying to make sense of UML diagrams later in the book.

With that brief introduction behind us, next we'll discuss how UML enables us to visualize a system's design in a standardized way.

4.2   The UML Use Case Model

UML specifies use cases to describe a system's functionality. A *use case* roughly corresponds to a requirement. Designers create a *use case diagram* to specify what a system does from an external observer's point of view, meaning they specify only *what* a system does, not *how* it does it. They'll then create a use case narrative to fill in the details of the diagram.

4.2.1   Use Case Diagram Elements

Use case diagrams typically contain three elements: an actor, a communication link (or association), and the actual use case:

- *Actors*, typically drawn as stick figures, represent users or external devices and systems that use the system under design.
- *Communication links* are drawn as a line between an actor and a use case, and indicate some form of communication between the two.
- *Use cases* are drawn as ovals with an appropriate description and represent the activities the actors perform on the system.

Figure 4-1 shows an example of a use case diagram.

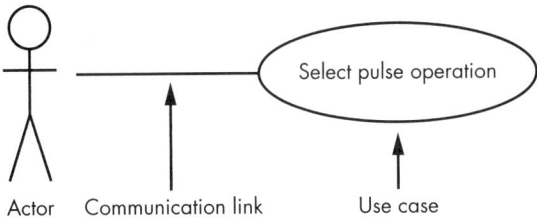

Figure 4-1: A sample use case diagram

Every use case should have a high-level name that concisely and uniquely describes the operation. For example, a nuclear reactor operator might want to select a power input from a nuclear power (NP) channel: "select %Pwr" is a general description, whereas "press the percent power button on the NP device" is probably too specific. How the user selects percent power is more of a design issue, not a system analysis issue (analysis is what we're doing at this stage).

The use case name should be unique, because you'll likely use it to associate the diagram with a use case narrative elsewhere in your UML documentation. One way to achieve uniqueness is by attaching a *tag* (see "Tag Formats" on page 172). However, the whole point of a use case diagram is to make the action obvious to the readers and stakeholders (that is, the external observers), and tags can obfuscate the meaning. One possible solution is to include a descriptive name (or phrase) *and* a tag inside the use case oval, as shown in Figure 4-2.

Figure 4-2: A use case tag combined with a user-friendly name

The tag uniquely identifies the use case narrative, and the user-friendly name makes the diagram easy to read and understand.

A use case diagram can contain multiple actors as well as multiple use cases, as shown in Figure 4-3, which provides use cases for generating Individual Megawatt Hour (MWH) and other reports.

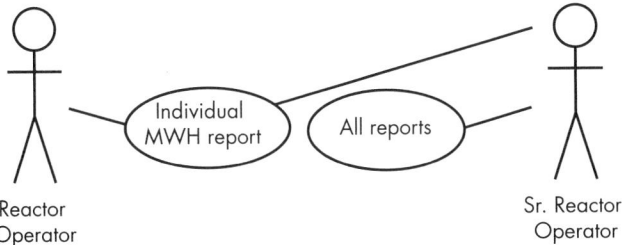

Figure 4-3: Multiple actors and use cases in a use case diagram

Stick figures are useful for making it instantly obvious that you're specifying an actor, but they have some drawbacks. First, a stick figure is rather large and can consume considerable screen (or page) space. Also, in a large and cluttered UML diagram, it can become difficult to associate names and other information with a stick figure actor. For this reason, UML designers often use a stereotype to represent an actor. A *stereotype* is a special UML name (such as "actor") surrounded by guillemets (« and ») and enclosed along with the element's name inside a rectangle, as shown in Figure 4-4. (You can use a pair of angle brackets—less-than and greater-than symbols—if you don't have access to guillemets in your editing system.)

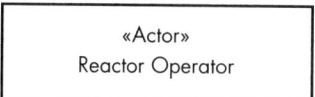

Figure 4-4: An actor stereotype

Stereotypes can apply to any UML element, not just an actor. The stereotype consumes less space and creates less clutter, though its disadvantage is that the type of element isn't as instantly clear as it would be using the actual icon.[1]

4.2.2 Use Case Packages

You can assign use case names to different *packages* by separating the package name from the use case name using a pair of colons. For example, if the aforementioned reactor operator needs to select percent power from two different nuclear power systems (NP and NPP), we could use NP and NPP packages to separate these operations (see Figure 4-5).

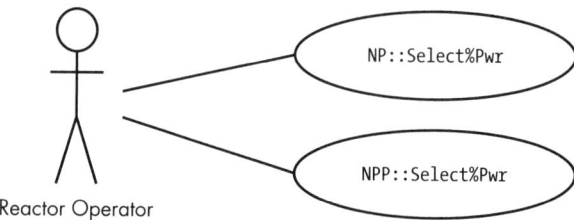

Reactor Operator

Figure 4-5: Package names in a use case

4.2.3 Use Case Inclusion

Sometimes, use cases will replicate information. For example, the use case in Figure 4-5 might correspond to a reactor operator selecting which nuclear power channel to use (the NP or NPP instrument) for a given operation. If the operator must verify that the channel is online before making the selection, presumably either of the use cases for NP::Select%Pwr

---

1. This is a good example of *redundancy* in UML—that is, using two different notations for the same thing.

and `NPP::Select%Pwr` would contain the steps needed to confirm this. When writing the narrative for these two use cases, you'll probably discover that you're duplicating considerable information.

To avoid this replication, UML defines *use case inclusion*, which allows one use case to completely include the functionality of another.

You specify use case inclusion by drawing two use cases with oval icons, and placing a dashed open arrow from the including use case to the included use case. Also attach the label «include» to the dashed arrow, as shown in Figure 4-6.

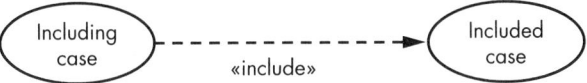

Figure 4-6: Use case inclusion

We could redraw Figure 4-5 using inclusion as shown in Figure 4-7.

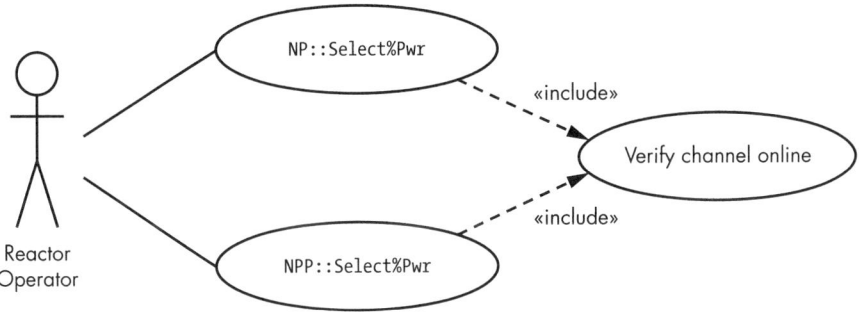

Figure 4-7: Use case inclusion example

An inclusion is the use case diagram equivalent of a function call. Inclusion allows you to reuse a use case from other use cases, thereby reducing redundancy.

4.2.4 Use Case Generalization

Sometimes, two or more use cases share an underlying base design and build upon it to produce different use cases. Revisiting the example from Figure 4-3, the Sr. Reactor Operator actor might produce additional reactor reports (that is, "All reports") beyond those that the Reactor Operator actor produces ("Individual MWH report"). However, both use cases are still an example of the more general "Generate reports" use case and, therefore, they share some common (*inherited*) operations. This relationship is known as *use case generalization*.

We can illustrate use case generalization in a use case diagram by drawing a hollow arrow from a specific use case to the more general use case, as shown in Figure 4-8.

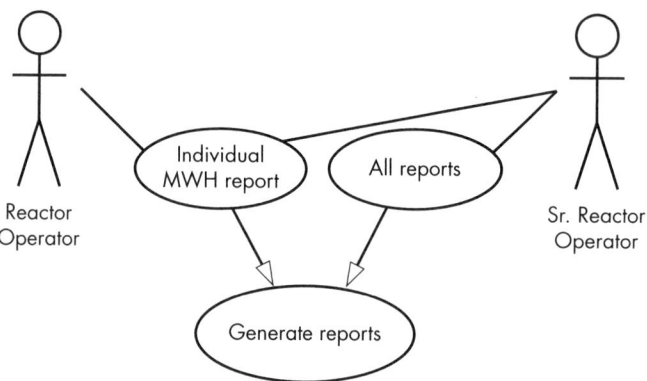

Figure 4-8: Generalization of use cases

This figure tells us that the "Individual MWH report" and "All reports" use cases share some common activities inherited from the "Generate reports" use case.

We can generalize actors in the same fashion by drawing an open arrow from multiple (specific) actors to a generalized actor, as shown in Figure 4-9.

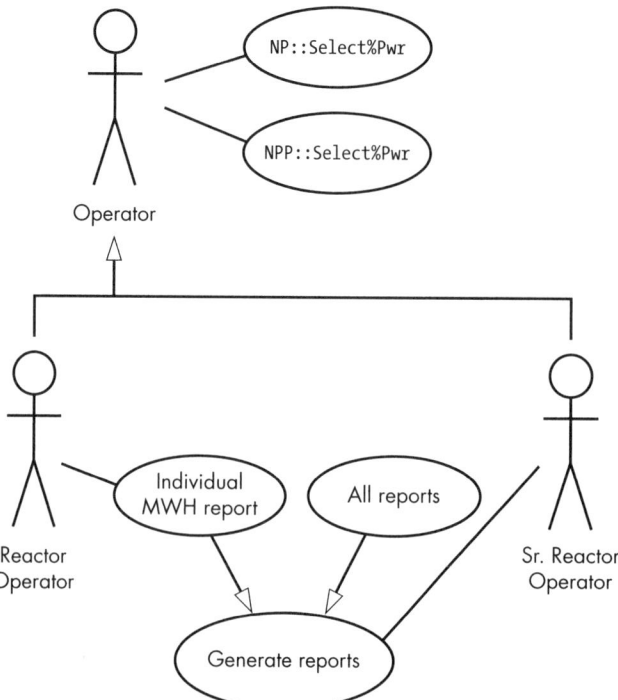

Figure 4-9: Generalization of actors

Generalization (particularly, use case generalization) is equivalent to inheritance in object-oriented systems. The hollow arrow points at the base use case, and the tail of the arrow (that is, the end without the arrowhead) connects to the inheriting, or derived, use case. In Figure 4-9, "Generate reports" is the base use case, and "Individual MWH report" and "All reports" are the derived use cases.

A derived use case inherits all the features and activities of the base use case. That is, all the items and functionality in the base use case are present in the derived use case, along with certain items unique to the derived use case.

In Figure 4-9, the Reactor Operator actor can select only an "Individual MWH report." Therefore, any report generated by the Reactor Operator actor always follows the steps associated with that individual report. The Sr. Reactor Operator actor, on the other hand, can generate any report derived from the "All reports" or "Individual MWH report" use case.

Although generalization might seem very similar to inclusion, there are subtle differences. With inclusion a use case is completely included, but with inheritance the base use case is augmented by the features in the derived use case.

4.2.5 Use Case Extension

The UML *use case extension* allows you to specify the optional (*conditional*) inclusion of some use case. You draw an extension similar to an inclusion except you use the word «extend» rather than «include» and the arrow is a dashed line with a solid arrowhead. Another difference is that the arrowhead points at the extended use case, and the tail points at the extending use case, as shown in Figure 4-10.

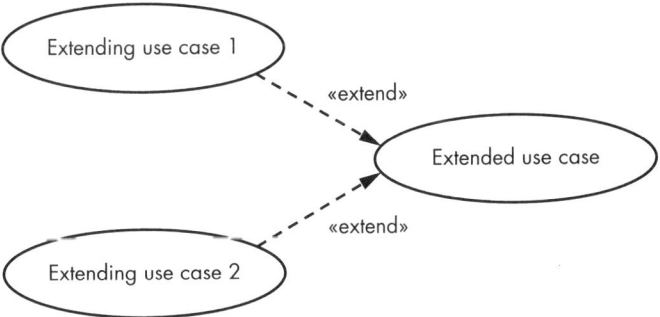

Figure 4-10: Use case extension

Use case extensions are useful when you want to select one of several different use cases based on some internal system/software state. A classic example would be error or exception handling conditions. Suppose you have a small command line processor that recognizes certain commands beginning with a verb (such as `read_digital`). The command syntax might take the form:

```
read_digital port#
```

where *port#* is a numeric string indicating the port to read from. Two things could go wrong when the software processes this command: *port#* could have a syntax error (that is, it doesn't represent a valid numeric value) or the *port#* value could be out of range. Thus, there are three possible outcomes from processing this command: the command is correct and reads the specified port; a syntax error occurs and the system presents an appropriate message to the user; or a range error occurs and the system displays an appropriate error message. Use case extensions easily handle these situations, as shown in Figure 4-11.

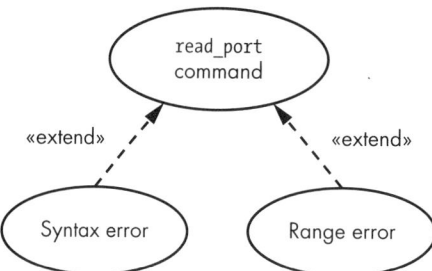

Figure 4-11: Use case extension example

Note that the normal case (no error) is not an extension use case. The read_port command use case handles the nonerror case directly.

4.2.6 Use Case Narratives

By themselves, the use case diagrams you've seen thus far don't explain any details. An actual use case (as opposed to a use case *diagram*) is text, not graphics. The diagrams provide an "executive overview" of the use case and make it easy for external observers to differentiate activities, but the *use case narrative* is where you truly describe a use case. Although there is no defined set of items that appear in a use case narrative, it typically contains the information listed in Table 4-1.

Table 4-1: Use Case Narrative Items

Use case narrative item	Description
Associated requirements	A requirements tag or other indication of the requirement(s) associated with the use case. This provides traceability to the SyRS and SRS documentation.
Actors	A list of the actors that interact with the use case.
Goal/purpose/brief description	A description of the goal (and its context within the system) to clarify the purpose of the use case.
Assumptions and preconditions	A description of what must be true prior to the execution of the use case.
Triggers	External events that start the execution of the use case.

Use case narrative item	Description
Interaction/Flow of Events	The step-by-step description of how an external actor interacts with the system during the execution of the use case.
Optional interactions/Alternative Flow of Events	Alternative interactions from those the interaction steps describe.
Termination	Conditions that result in the termination of a use case.
End conditions	Conditions describing what happens when the use case successfully terminates or when it fails.
Post conditions	Conditions that apply upon completion of the execution of a use case (success or failure).

Additional items (search online for descriptions) might include:[2]

- Minimal guarantees
- Successful guarantees
- Dialog (effectively another name for interactions)
- Secondary actors
- Extensions (another name for optional/conditional interactions)
- Exceptions (that is, error-handling conditions)
- Related use cases (that is, other relevant use cases)
- Stakeholders (people with an interest in the use case)
- Priority (among use cases for implementation)

4.2.6.1 Use Case Narrative Formality

Use case narratives can range in formality from casual to fully dressed.

A casual use case narrative is a natural language (for example, English) description of the use case without much structure. Casual narratives are ideal for small projects, and often vary from use case to use case.

A fully dressed use case narrative is a formal description of the use case, typically created via a form with all the narrative items defined for your project. A fully dressed use case narrative will likely consist of three forms:

- A list of the use case items, exclusive of the Dialog/Flow of Events/Interaction and Alternative Flow of Events/Optional Interactions items
- The main Flow of Events
- The Alternative Flow of Events (extensions)

---

[2]. This is a nonexhaustive list. You may freely add any items specific to your project.

Tables 4-2, 4-3, and 4-4 show an example of a fully dressed use case narrative.

Table 4-2: Select Nuclear Power Source, RCTR_USE_022

Requirement(s)	RCTR_SyRS_022, RCTR_SRS_022_000
Actors	Reactor Operator, Sr. Reactor Operator
Goal	To select the power measurement channel used during automatic operation
Assumptions and preconditions	Operator has logged in to the reactor console
Trigger	Operator presses appropriate button, selecting automatic mode power source
Termination	Operator-specified power source is selected
End conditions	System uses the selected power source for current actual power during automatic operation, if successful; system reverts to original auto-mode power source if unsuccessful
Post condition	System has an operational automatic-mode power source available

Table 4-3: Flow of Events, RCTR_USE_022

Step	Action
1	Operator presses NP selection button
2	System verifies that the NP is online
3	System switches auto-mode power selection to the NP channel

Table 4-4: Alternative Flow of Events (Extensions), RCTR_USE_022

Step	Action
2.1	The NP channel is not online
2.2	The system doesn't switch to using the NP power channel and continues to use the previously selected power channel for automatic mode

4.2.6.2 Alternative Flow of Events

Whenever a step in the Flow of Events table contains a conditional or optional item (an *extension* in UML terminology), you'll have some corresponding entries in the Alternative Flow of Events table that describe the behavior when the conditional item is false. Note that you don't use a separate Alternative Flow of Events table for each condition; you simply use substeps (in this example, 2.1 and 2.2 in Table 4-4) associated with the step number(s) from the Flow of Events table (step 2 in Table 4-3).

This is just one possible example of a fully dressed use case narrative. Many other forms are possible. For example, you could create a fourth table to list all the possible end conditions, as shown in Table 4-5.

Table 4-5: End Conditions, RCTR_USE_022

Condition	Result
Success	The NP channel is selected as the automatic-mode power channel
Failure	The previously selected channel continues to control automatic mode

Adding an end conditions table is especially compelling if there are more than two end conditions.

As another example, consider the read_port use case in Figure 4-11. The narrative for it could be similar to Tables 4-6, 4-7, and 4-8.

Table 4-6: read_port Command

Requirement(s)	DAQ_SyRS_102, DAQ_SRS_102_000
Actors	PC host computer system
Goal	To read a digital data port on the data acquisition system
Assumptions and preconditions	Digital data acquisition ports have been initialized as input ports
Trigger	Receipt of the read_port command
Termination	Data port is read and the value returned to requesting system
End conditions	System returns port value or appropriate error message if the command was malformed
Post condition	The system is ready to accept another command

Table 4-7: Flow of Events, read_port Command

Step	Action
1	The host PC sends a command line beginning with read_port
2	System verifies that there is a second parameter
3	System verifies that the second parameter is a valid numeric string
4	System verifies that the second parameter is a numeric value in the range 0–15
5	System reads the digital data from the specified port
6	System returns the port value to the host PC

Table 4-8: Alternative Flow of Events (Extensions), read_port Command

Step	Action
2.1	Second parameter doesn't exist
2.2	System returns a "syntax error" message to the host PC
3.1	Second parameter isn't a valid numeric string
3.2	System returns a "syntax error" message to the host PC
4.1	Second parameter is outside the range 0–15
4.2	The system returns a "range error" message to the host PC

Table 4-8 actually contains several independent flows of events. The major number to the left of the decimal point specifies the associated step in the Flow of Events table; the minor number to the right of the decimal point is the particular step within the Alternative Flow of Events. The flow occurs only within the steps associated with a single Flow of Events number. That is, the flow from 2.1 to 2.2 ends with 2.2; it doesn't continue into 3.1 (in this example).

Generally, once a system selects an alternative flow (such as the "range error" flow, steps 4.1 and 4.2 in this example), the use case ends with the completion of that alternative flow (that is, at step 4.2). Control doesn't return to the main Flow of Events. Execution to the end of the main Flow of Events list happens only if no alternative flows occur.

The "correct" way to use the Flow of Events and Alternative Flow of Events is to write a straight-line sequence representing the path through the use case that produces the intended result. If multiple viable paths exist, you would typically create multiple use cases, one for each correct path. The alternative flows handle any deviations (usually error paths) from the correct path. Of course, one risk of this approach is that you might wind up with an excessive number of use case diagrams.

For a Flow of Events, diagrams are more expensive to create and maintain than a textual description; even with the proper UML diagramming tools, creating figures generally takes more time and effort than just writing textual descriptions.

4.2.6.3 Conditional Flow of Events

For use cases that have multiple correct paths, you could encode those paths in the main Flow of Events using branches and conditionals, and leave the alternative paths for exceptional conditions. Consider a command for a data acquisition system that supports two different syntaxes:[3]

```
ppdio boards
ppdio boards boardCount
```

The first variant returns the number of PPDIO boards in the system, and the second variant sets the number of PPDIO boards. The technically correct solution to document these two commands is to create two separate use cases, each with its own Flow of Events. However, if the data acquisition system has dozens of different commands, creating individual use cases could clutter your documentation. One solution is to combine these use cases into a single use case by incorporating conditional operations (that is, if..else..endif) into a single Flow of Events, as in the following example.

---

3. This example is from a real-world project: Plantation Productions' "Open Source/Open Hardware Digital Data Acquisition & Control System" (*http://www.plantation-productions.com/Electronics/DAQ/DAQ.html*).

Flow of Events

1. Verify command begins with `ppdio`.
2. Verify second word on command line is `boards`.
3. If no additional parameters appear on command line:
   a. Return number of PPDIO boards in system as response.
4. Verify there is a single numeric parameter on the line.
5. Verify that the numeric parameter is in the range `0..6`.
6. Set the number of PPDIO boards to the value specified by the numeric parameter.

Alternative Flows

1.1 If command doesn't begin with `ppdio`, return `not PPDIO` response.
2.1 If command doesn't begin with `ppdio boards`, return `not PPDIO BOARDS` response.
5.1 Return `syntax error` as the response.
6.1 Return `range error` as the response.

Having conditionals and multiple exit points from a Flow of Events isn't "clean" UML; however, it can reduce the overall size of the documentation (saving time and expenses), so this is a common kludge in use cases.

You could even add `while`, `for`, `switch`, and other high-level-language–style operations to your Flow of Events. But keep in mind that use cases (and their descriptions) should be very general. Once you start embedding programming language concepts into your use cases, you invariably start introducing implementation details, which don't belong in use cases; save those for later UML diagram types (such as activity diagrams).

These examples might seem to suggest that alternative flows are solely for error handling, but you can use them for other purposes as well; any time a conditional branch is out of a main flow, you can use extensions to handle that. However, one problem with using alternative flows for generic conditionals is that concepts that are inherently related wind up separated from one another in your use case descriptions, which can make following the logic in those descriptions more difficult.

4.2.6.4 Generalization vs. Extension

Generalization is often a better tool than extension. For example, suppose you have a generic `port_command` use case and you want to attach `read_port` and `write_port` to it. In theory, you could create an extension to handle this, as shown in Figure 4-12.

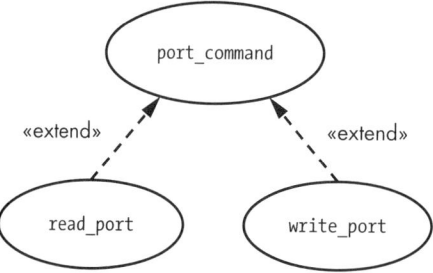

Figure 4-12: Poor example of use case extension

In practice, this particular situation is probably better handled with generalization, because read_port and write_port are special cases of a port_command (rather than being alternative branches from port_command). Figure 4-13 shows the generalization approach.

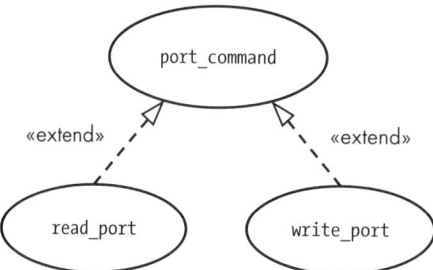

Figure 4-13: Using generalization rather than extension

With generalization, the derived use case follows all the steps in the base use case. When you use extensions, control transfers from the main Flow of Events to the Alternative Flow of Events, and any remaining steps in the main flow don't happen.

4.2.7 Use Case Scenarios

A *scenario* is a single path through a use case. For example, the read_port use case has four scenarios: the success scenario when the command reads a port and returns the port data; two syntax error scenarios (2.1/2.2 and 3.1/3.2 in the Alternative Flow of Events); and one range error scenario (4.1/4.2 in the Alternative Flow of Events). You generate a full scenario by choosing the steps from the Flow of Events and Alternative Flow of Events that complete a specific path. The read_port command has the following scenarios:

Success scenario

1. The host sends a command beginning with read_port.
2. The system verifies that there is a second parameter.

3. The system verifies that the second parameter is a numeric string.
4. The system verifies that the second parameter is a value in the range 0..15.
5. The system reads the data from the specified port.
6. The system returns the port value to the host PC.

Syntax error #1 scenario

1. The host sends a command beginning with `read_port`.
2. The system determines there is no second parameter.
3. The system sends a syntax error to the host PC.

Syntax error #2 scenario

1. The host sends a command beginning with `read_port`.
2. The system verifies that there is a second parameter.
3. The system determines that the second parameter is not a legal numeric string.
4. The system sends a syntax error to the host PC.

Range error scenario

1. The host sends a command beginning with `read_port`.
2. The system verifies that there is a second parameter.
3. The system verifies that the second parameter is a numeric string.
4. The system determines that the numeric string is a value outside the range 0..15.
5. The system sends a range error to the host PC.

You can use scenarios to create test cases and test procedures for your system. You'll have one or more test cases for each scenario.

You can combine use case scenarios by incorporating `if` statements in your Flow of Events. However, because this introduces low-level details into your use case narratives, you should avoid combining scenarios unless the number of use case narratives grows out of control.

4.3 The UML System Boundary Diagrams

When you're drawing a simple use case diagram, it should be obvious which components are internal to the system and which are external. Specifically, actors are external entities, and the use cases are internal. If you're using stereotyped rectangles instead of stick figures for the actors, though, it might not be immediately clear which components are external to the system. Also, if you reference multiple systems in a use case diagram, determining which use cases are part of which system can be challenging. UML system boundary diagrams solve these problems.

A *UML system boundary diagram* is simply a shaded rectangle surrounding the use cases that are internal to a particular system, as shown in Figure 4-14. The system title generally appears near the top of the rectangle.

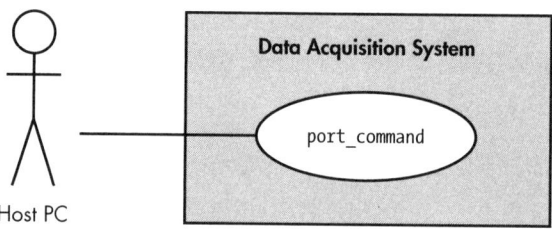

Figure 4-14: A system boundary diagram

4.4 Beyond Use Cases

This chapter introduced UML uses cases, a very important feature of the Unified Modeling Language. However, there are many other components of UML beyond use cases. The next chapter presents UML activity diagrams, which provide a way to model actions within a software design.

4.5 For More Information

Bremer, Michael. *The User Manual Manual: How to Research, Write, Test, Edit, and Produce a Software Manual*. Grass Valley, CA: UnTechnical Press, 1999. A sample chapter is available at *http://www.untechnicalpress.com/Downloads/UMM%20sample%20doc.pdf*.

Larman, Craig. *Applying UML and Patterns: An Introduction to Object-Oriented Analysis and Design and Iterative Development*. 3rd ed. Upper Saddle River, NJ: Prentice Hall, 2004.

Miles, Russ, and Kim Hamilton. *Learning UML 2.0: A Pragmatic Introduction to UML*. Sebastopol, CA: O'Reilly Media, 2003.

Pender, Tom. *UML Bible*. Indianapolis: Wiley, 2003.

Pilone, Dan, and Neil Pitman. *UML 2.0 in a Nutshell: A Desktop Quick Reference*. 2nd ed. Sebastopol, CA: O'Reilly Media, 2005.

Roff, Jason T. *UML: A Beginner's Guide*. Berkeley, CA: McGraw-Hill Education, 2003.

Tutorials Point. "UML Tutorial." *https://www.tutorialspoint.com/uml/*.

5

UML ACTIVITY DIAGRAMS

UML *activity diagrams*, traditionally known as *flowcharts*, illustrate the workflow between different components of a system. Flowcharts were prevalent in the early days of software development and were still used in software design just before the rise of object-oriented programming (OOP). Although the UML object-oriented notation supersedes old-fashioned flowcharting to a large extent, OOP still relies on small methods, functions, and procedures to implement the low-level, nitty-gritty details, and flowcharting is useful for describing control flow in those cases. Hence, UML's designers created activity diagrams as an updated version of flowcharting.

5.1 UML Activity State Symbols

UML activity diagrams use state symbols based on traditional flowchart symbols. This section describes some of the ones you'll commonly use.

> **NOTE** *If you want information on general flowcharting, any web search should yield decent results.*

5.1.1 Start and Stop States

UML diagrams always contain a single *start state*, which represents the start terminal object. This consists of a solid circle with a single arrow (*transition* in UML parlance) coming from it. You might associate the start state with a label, which would be the name of the whole activity diagram.

UML also usually contains *end state* and *end flow* symbols. An end state symbol terminates an entire process, while an end flow symbol terminates a single thread, useful for processes that involve multiple threads of execution. You might associate the end state symbol with a label that indicates the system's state at the end of the process.

Figure 5-1 shows the start state, end state, and end flow symbols.

Figure 5-1: UML starting and ending states

While an activity diagram has only one starting state symbol, it might have multiple ending state symbols (think of a method returning from several points in the code). The labels attached to the various ending states will likely be different, such as "exception exit" and "normal exit."

5.1.2 Activities

Activity symbols in UML are rectangles with semicircular ends (like the terminal symbol in a flowchart) that represent some action, as shown in Figure 5-2.[1]

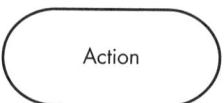

Figure 5-2: UML activities

Activities, as a general rule, correspond to one or more statements (actions) in a programming language that execute sequentially. The text inside the symbol describes the action to perform, such as "read data" or "compute CRC." Generally, a UML activity doesn't include much low-level detail; it's the programmer's job to provide that.

---

1. Some authors use *roundangles*, rectangles with rounded corners, to show activities. However, the UML standard uses roundangles for states.

5.1.3 States

UML activity diagrams also provide intermediate states, in addition to start and end states, which effectively act as milestones indicating some existing condition(s) at the point of the state symbol. State symbols are rounded rectangles (*roundangles*), as shown in Figure 5-3, although the rounded corners are much smaller than those of activity symbols.

Figure 5-3: UML states

The text in the state symbol should describe the state of the system at that given point. For example, if the activity is "compute CRC," you might label the state immediately following it as "CRC computed" or "CRC available." States don't incorporate any action, only the current condition of the system at a given point.

5.1.4 Transitions

Transitions indicate a flow of control from one point in an activity diagram (for example, a state or activity) to another. If a transition flows out of some activity, it means the system makes that transition upon completing most of the actions associated with that activity. If a pair of transitions flows into and out of a state, control flow transfers immediately to wherever the outgoing arrow points. A UML state is effectively a marker in the middle of a transition, and so no action takes place in a UML state, as shown in Figure 5-4.

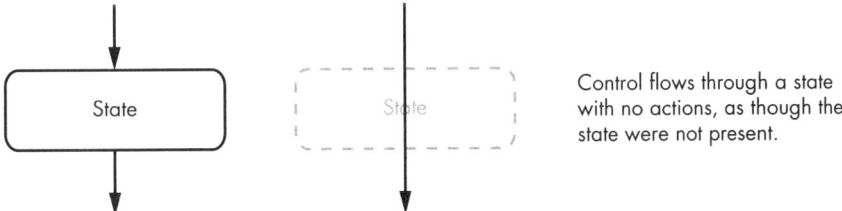

Figure 5-4: Control flow through a state

5.1.5 Conditionals

You can handle conditionals in a couple of different ways in a UML activity diagram: transition guards and decision points.

5.1.5.1 Transition Guards

In conditionals, a Boolean expression is attached to a transition symbol. UML calls these Boolean expressions *guards*. A conditional UML symbol must have at least two guarded transitions, which are labeled with expressions surrounded by square brackets, but might have more than two, as in Figure 5-5 (where the hexagon shape represents an arbitrary UML symbol).

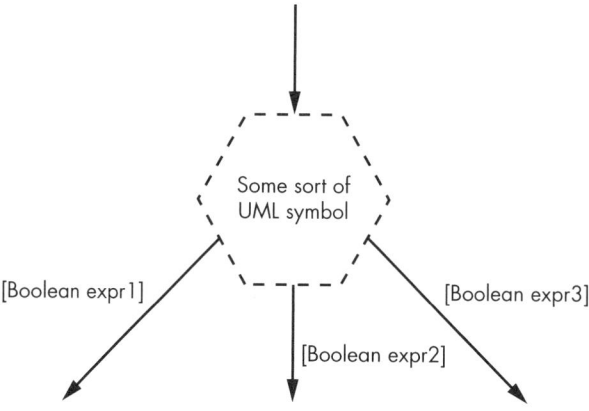

Figure 5-5: Transition guards

The set of Boolean expressions must be mutually exclusive; that is, only one expression can be true at all times. Furthermore, the expression coverage must be *complete*, which in this context means that for all possible combinations of input values, at least one Boolean expression in a set of guarded transitions must evaluate to true (which, combined with the first condition, means *exactly one* Boolean condition must evaluate to true).

If you want a "catch-all" transition to handle any input values that the existing guards don't handle, just attach a word like *else, otherwise,* or *default* to a transition (see Figure 5-6).

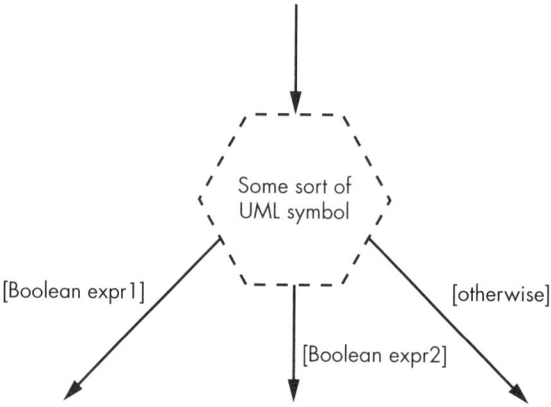

Figure 5-6: Catch-all transition guard

5.1.5.2 Decision Points

Transitions with guards can exit just about any UML symbol; state and action symbols often contain them. Problems can occur, however, if you have several actions or states merging into a single point at which a decision can create divergent paths. For this, UML provides a special symbol, the *decision point*, to cleanly collect and join paths where a decision branch occurs. Decision points use a diamond-shaped symbol, as shown in Figure 5-7.

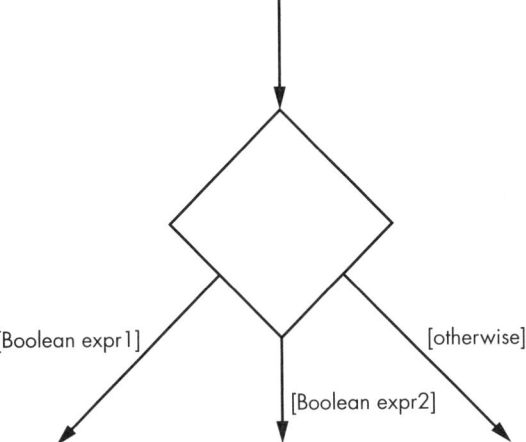

Figure 5-7: A UML decision point

Although UML allows guarded transitions to emanate from any UML symbol, it's good practice to always use a decision point to begin a set of related guarded transitions.

5.1.6 Merge Points

In UML we can also use the diamond shape to collect several incoming transitions into a single outgoing transition, as shown in Figure 5-8; we call this a *merge point*.

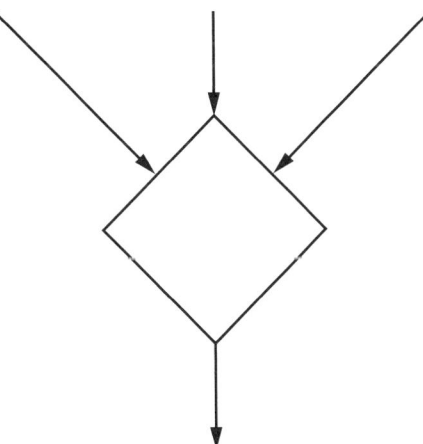

Figure 5-8: A UML merge point

Technically, a merge point and a decision point are the same object type. Essentially, a merge point is an unnamed state object; it takes no action other than passing control from all the incoming transitions to the outgoing transition. A decision point is just a special case of a merge point that has multiple outgoing guarded transitions.

In theory, a merge point could have both multiple incoming and outgoing guarded transitions. However, the result would be so ugly that the common convention is instead to divide the single point into separate merge and decision points, as shown in Figure 5-9. Most of the time, this separation is clearer and easier to read than the alternative.

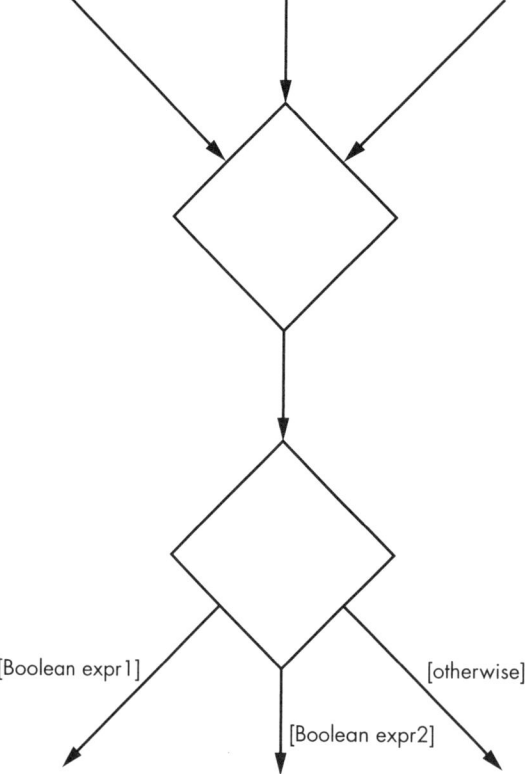

Figure 5-9: UML merge and decision points

5.1.7 Events and Triggers

Events and triggers are actions outside the current flow of control, typically from some other thread of execution or hardware input, that cause some change in it.[2] In UML, event and trigger transitions are syntactically similar to guarded transitions in that they consist of a labeled transition. The difference is that a guarded transition immediately evaluates some Boolean expression and transfers control to the UML symbol at the other end of the transition, whereas an event or trigger transition waits for the event or trigger to occur before transferring control.

---

2. For the most part, an event and a trigger in UML are the same thing—a signal from a source outside the current flow of control that causes a change in it. This book uses the terms *trigger* and *event* interchangeably.

Event and trigger transitions are labeled with the name of the event or trigger along with any necessary parameters provided to the control flow when it occurs (see Figure 5-10).

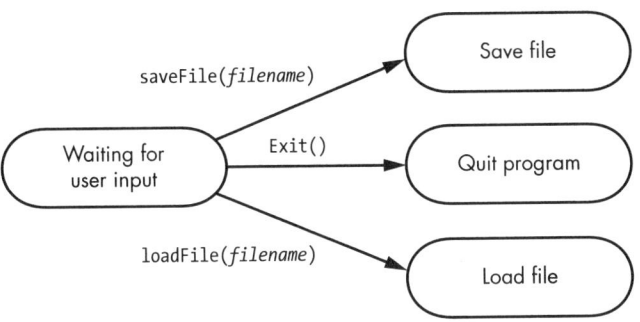

Figure 5-10: UML events or triggers

In this example, the system is waiting for input from the user (perhaps clicking a UI button on the display). When the user activates the save, exit, or load operation, control transfers to the specified action at the end of the event or trigger transition (Save file, Quit program, or Load file, respectively).

You can also attach guard conditions to an event or trigger transition, consisting of a Boolean expression inside square brackets immediately following the trigger or event, as shown in Figure 5-11. When you do so, the transition occurs only when the event or trigger occurs and the guard expression evaluates to true.

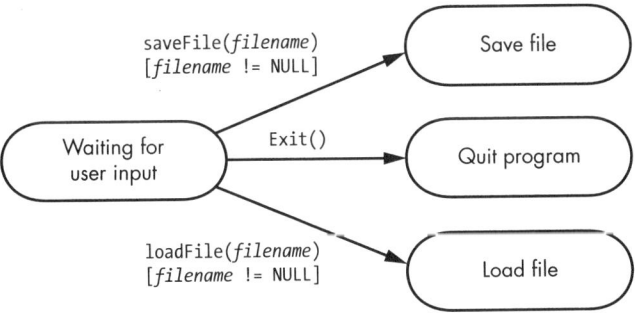

Figure 5-11: Guard conditions on events or triggers

UML events and triggers also support action expressions and multiple actions, which are beyond the scope of this chapter. To find out more, check out examples in Tom Pender's *UML Bible* (see "For More Information" on page 100).

5.1.8 Forks and Joins (Synchronization)

UML offers support for concurrent processing by providing symbols to split a single thread of execution into multiple threads as well as to join multiple threads of execution into a single thread (see Figure 5-12).[3]

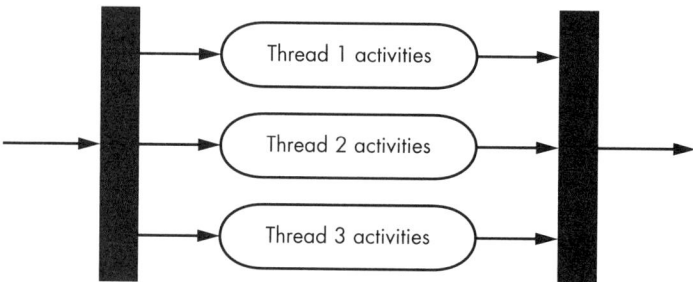

Figure 5-12: Forks and joins

The UML *fork* operation (a thin, solid rectangle) splits a single thread of execution into two or more concurrent operations. The *join* operation (also represented by a thin, solid rectangle) merges multiple sets of threads into a single thread of execution. The join operation also synchronizes the threads: the diagram assumes that all but the last thread entering the join operation will halt until the final thread arrives, at which point a single thread of execution continues on output.

5.1.9 Call Symbols

A call symbol in UML, which looks like a small rake, attaches to an activity to explicitly declare it as an invocation of another UML sequence. You include the call symbol inside the UML activity along with the name of the sequence to invoke, as shown in Figure 5-13.

Elsewhere in your UML document, you'll define that sequence (or *subroutine*) using the invocation name as the activity diagram name, as shown in Figure 5-14.

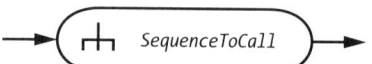

Figure 5-13: A UML sequence invocation

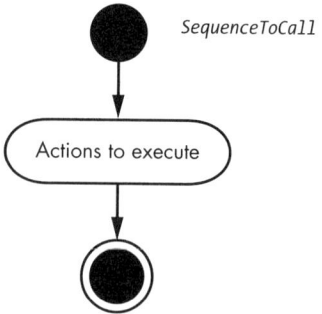

Figure 5-14: A UML subroutine

---

3. Note that UML's thread operations are only a suggestion. When a UML diagram shows multiple threads executing concurrently, it's simply an indication that the separate paths are independent and *could be* executed concurrently. In actual execution, the system could execute the paths serially in any order.

5.1.10 Partitions

Partitions, which organize the steps of a process, consist of several side-by-side rectangular boxes, each labeled at the top with an actor, object, or domain name.[4] The activity diagram transitions between the boxes as each part of the process comes under the control of the owner of a given box, as shown in Figure 5-15.

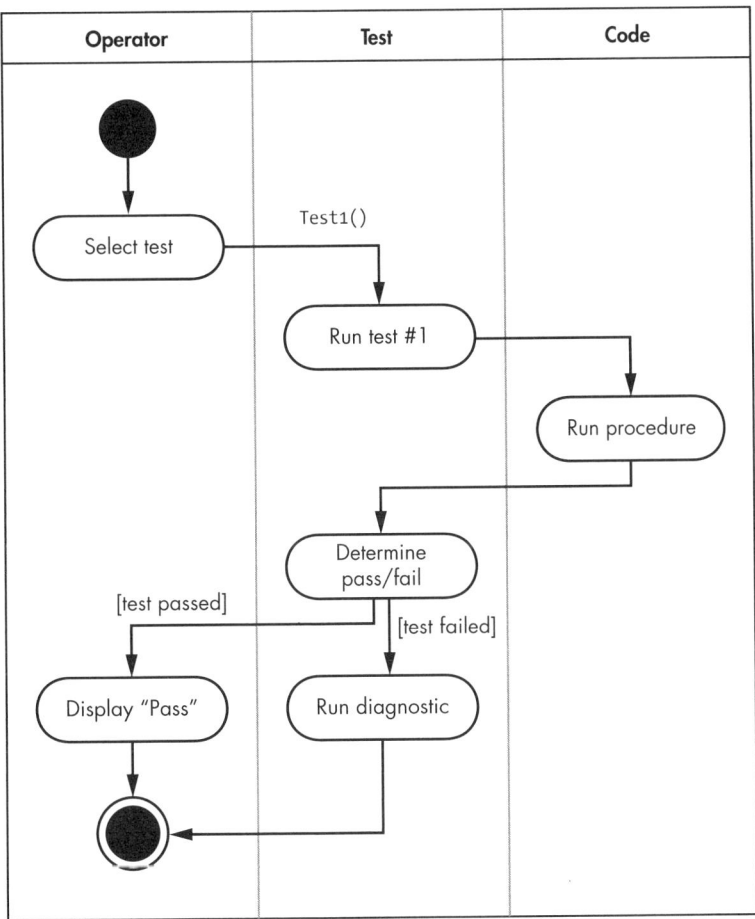

Figure 5-15: A UML partition

The process in Figure 5-15 shows some code under test. An operator selects a test to run, passing control to the test software. An event or trigger then transfers control to the "Run test #1" action. The test software calls the code under test (in the third partition). After the code under test executes, control returns to the test software, which determines whether the test passed or failed. If the test passes, the test code displays "Pass" to the operator; otherwise, the test code runs a diagnostic routine.

---

4. Older versions of UML call partitions *swim lanes*, so you'll see that term used in many books and papers referring to this construct.

5.1.11 Comments and Annotations

Comments and annotations in UML use an icon that looks like a small page with a folded corner, as shown in Figure 5-16. You draw a dashed line from one side of the box to the UML item you want to annotate.

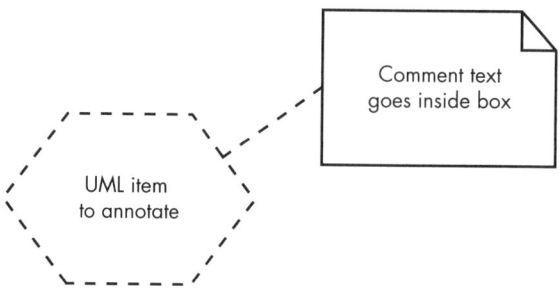

Figure 5-16: A UML comment or annotation

5.1.12 Connectors

Connectors are circles with an internal label, typically a number, that indicate that control transfers to some other point in the diagram with the same label (see Figure 5-17). You'd use the same symbol for on-page and off-page connectors.

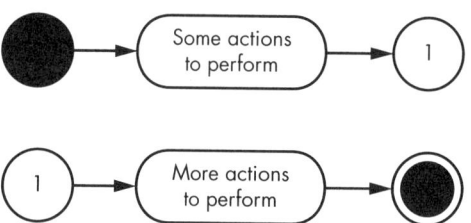

Figure 5-17: UML connectors

When used properly, UML connectors can make an activity diagram easier to read by reducing long or overlapping transition lines. However, keep in mind that connectors are the UML equivalent of a goto statement in a programming language, and overuse can make diagrams more difficult to read.

5.1.13 Additional Activity Diagram Symbols

The full UML 2.0 specification provides many additional symbols you can use in activity diagrams, such as structured activities, expansion regions/nodes, conditional nodes, loop nodes, and more. We don't have space to discuss them all in this book's basic introduction to UML, but if you're interested in more details, see the sources listed in "For More Information" on page 100 or search online for "UML."

5.2 Extending UML Activity Diagrams

Sometimes the UML activity diagram notation just doesn't cut it. In such cases, you might be tempted to come up with your own custom symbols. This is almost always a bad idea, for the following reasons:

- UML is a *standard*. If you extend UML, you're no longer using a well-defined standard. That means all the people who've learned UML won't be able to read your activity diagrams unless they first read your documentation (and will that documentation be available to them in your nonstandard activity diagrams?).
- There are many UML diagramming tools available for creating and editing UML activity diagrams, and most of them can't handle nonstandard symbols and objects.
- Many computer-aided software engineering (CASE) tools can generate code directly from a UML diagram. Again, these CASE tools work only with standard UML and probably won't be able to handle your nonstandard extensions.
- If you can't figure out how to do something in a UML activity diagram, you may be able to use some other scheme. Using a nonstandard way to do a task that you can easily do with standard tools may come across to other UML users as an amateur approach.

All that being said, UML is far from perfect. In rare cases, developing some nonstandard activity diagram objects can vastly simplify your activity diagrams.

As an example, consider a concurrent programming *critical section*, a region of code in which only one thread of execution can take place at a time. UML sequence diagrams (the subject of Chapter 7) use *sequence fragment* notation to describe concurrency with critical regions. Although you could adapt sequence fragment notation to activity diagrams, the result is messy and hard to read and understand. In some activity diagrams I've created for personal projects, I used the custom notation in Figure 5-18 to indicate critical regions.

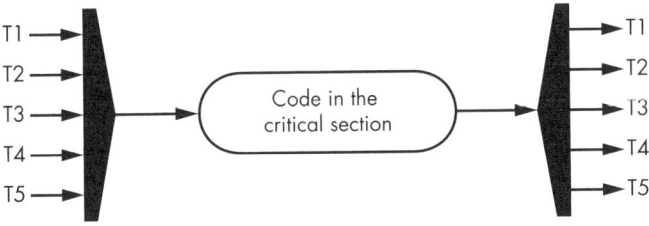

Figure 5-18: A nonstandard critical region diagram

Arrows coming in to the pentagon on the left indicate transitions (generally from different threads) competing for a critical section. The single line out of the pentagon represents the single thread of execution that takes place in the critical section. The pentagon on the right accepts that single thread of execution and routes it back to the original thread (for example, if T1 was the thread that entered the critical section, the close of the critical section routes control back to the T1 transition/flow).

This diagram doesn't imply that there are only five threads that can use this critical section. Instead, it conveys that there are five activity diagram flows (T1–T5) that could compete for the critical resource. In fact, there could be multiple threads executing any one of these flows that are also competing for the critical region. For example, there could be three threads all executing the T1 flow and waiting for the critical region to be available.

Because multiple threads could be executing on the same flow in the critical section diagram, it's quite possible to have only a single flow entering the critical region (see Figure 5-19).

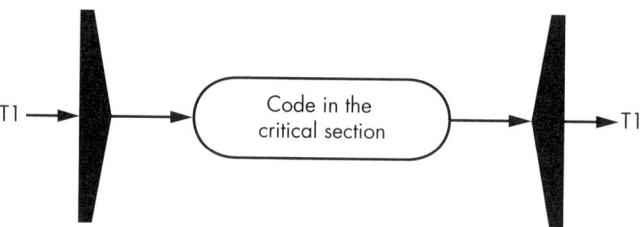

Figure 5-19: A single-flow critical region diagram

This example requires that multiple threads execute the same flow (T1) for this diagram to make any sense.

As you can see, even a simple diagram like this requires a fair amount of documentation to describe and validate it. If that documentation isn't readily available (that is, if it's not embedded directly in your UML activity diagrams), readers probably won't find it when they're trying to understand your diagram. Annotating a nonstandard object directly within the diagram is the only reasonable approach. Placing meaningful documentation in a separate section of the document containing the activity diagrams (such as the SDD document), or in a separate document altogether, makes this information unavailable when someone cuts and pastes your diagram into a different document.

NOTE *The critical region diagram in Figure 5-19 is simply an example of how you might extend UML activity diagrams. In general, I don't recommend adopting it in your own diagrams, nor do I recommend extending UML notation. However, you should know that the option is available if you really need it.*

5.3 For More Information

Bremer, Michael. *The User Manual Manual: How to Research, Write, Test, Edit, and Produce a Software Manual.* Grass Valley, CA: UnTechnical Press, 1999. A sample chapter is available at *http://www.untechnicalpress.com/Downloads/UMM%20sample%20doc.pdf.*

Larman, Craig. *Applying UML and Patterns: An Introduction to Object-Oriented Analysis and Design and Iterative Development.* 3rd ed. Upper Saddle River, NJ: Prentice Hall, 2004.

Miles, Russ, and Kim Hamilton. *Learning UML 2.0: A Pragmatic Introduction to UML.* Sebastopol, CA: O'Reilly Media, 2003.

Pender, Tom. *UML Bible.* Indianapolis: Wiley, 2003.

Pilone, Dan, and Neil Pitman. *UML 2.0 in a Nutshell: A Desktop Quick Reference.* 2nd ed. Sebastopol, CA: O'Reilly Media, 2005.

Roff, Jason T. *UML: A Beginner's Guide.* Berkeley, CA: McGraw-Hill Education, 2003.

Tutorials Point. "UML Tutorial." *https://www.tutorialspoint.com/uml/.*

6

UML CLASS DIAGRAMS

This chapter describes *class diagrams*, one of the more important diagramming tools in UML. Class diagrams are the basis for defining data types, data structures, and operations on that data in programs. In turn, they're the basis for *object-oriented analysis (OOA)* and *object-oriented design (OOD)*.

6.1 Object-Oriented Analysis and Design in UML

The creators of UML wanted a formal system for designing object-oriented software to replace the structured programming formalisms available at the time (1990s). Here we'll discuss how to represent classes (data types) and objects (instance variables of data types) in UML.

The most complete form of a class diagram in UML is shown in Figure 6-1.

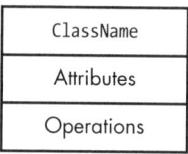

Figure 6-1: A complete class diagram

Attributes correspond to data field members of a class (that is, variables and constants); they represent information internal to the class.

Operations correspond to the activities that represent the class's behavior. Operations include methods, functions, procedures, and other things we normally identify as code.

Sometimes, you don't need to list all the attributes and operations when referencing a class diagram (or there might not even be any attributes or operations). In such situations, you can instead draw a partial class diagram, shown in Figure 6-2.

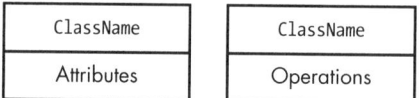

Figure 6-2: Partial class diagrams

The fact that attributes or operations are missing from a partial class diagram doesn't imply that they don't exist; it just means that it's not necessary in the current context to add them to the diagram. The designer might be leaving it up to the coder to fill them in during coding; or perhaps the complete class diagram appears elsewhere, and the current diagram contains only information of interest.

In its simplest form, UML represents classes with a simple rectangle containing the name of the class, as shown in Figure 6-3.

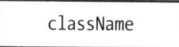

Figure 6-3: A simple class diagram

Again, this doesn't imply that the class contains no attributes or operations (which wouldn't make sense); it just means that those items are not of interest in the current diagram.

6.2　Visibility in a Class Diagram

UML defines four types of class member *visibility* (all taken from C++ and Java, although other languages, such as Swift, also support them): public, private, protected, and package. We'll discuss each in turn.

6.2.1　Public Class Visibility

A public class member is visible to all classes and code, inside and outside the class containing the public item. In well-designed object-oriented systems, public items are almost always operations (methods, functions, procedures, and so forth) and form the class's interface to the world outside the class. Although you can also make attributes public, doing so often defeats one of the primary benefits of object-oriented programming: *encapsulation*, or the ability to hide values and activities inside a class from the outside world.

In UML we preface public attributes and operations with the plus sign (+), as shown in Figure 6-4. The set of public attributes and operations provides the class's *public interface*.

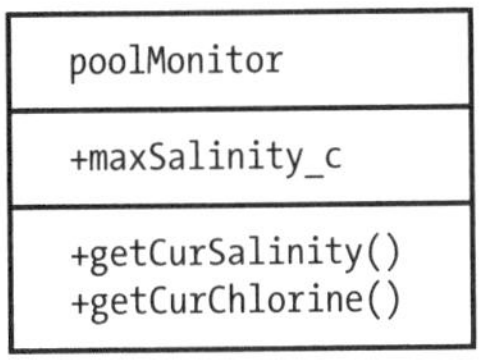

```
| poolMonitor        |
|--------------------|
| +maxSalinity_c     |
|--------------------|
| +getCurSalinity()  |
| +getCurChlorine()  |
```

Figure 6-4: Public attributes and operations

This figure has a single public attribute, maxSalinity_c. The _c suffix is a convention I use to indicate that the field is a *constant* rather than a variable.[1] In good designs constants are usually the only public attributes in a class, because external code cannot change the value of a constant: it's still visible (that is, not hidden or encapsulated), but it's unchangeable. One of the main reasons for encapsulation is to prevent side effects that can occur when some external code changes an internal class attribute. Because external code cannot change a constant's value, this immutability achieves the same result as encapsulation; therefore, object-oriented designers are willing to make certain class constants visible.[2]

---

1. The standard convention in C-derived languages is to use all uppercase characters to denote constants, but this is an absolutely terrible convention that I refuse to use for my own constants because ALL UPPERCASE IDENTIFIERS ARE MUCH HARDER TO READ THAN MIXED-CASE IDENTIFIERS. I modified the Unix convention of using _t to specify a type identifier to include _c for constants. Also, this convention is applicable across multiple languages and is not specific to C++.

2. This is not to imply that you should never make a variable attribute public. As with any other convention or rule, there are always exceptions where it makes sense to violate the convention. However, violations should be rare.

6.2.2 Private Class Visibility

At the other end of the spectrum lies private visibility. Private attributes and operations are accessible only within that class: they're hidden from other classes and code. Private attributes and operations are the embodiment of encapsulation.

We use the minus sign (-) to denote private entities within a class diagram, as shown in Figure 6-5.

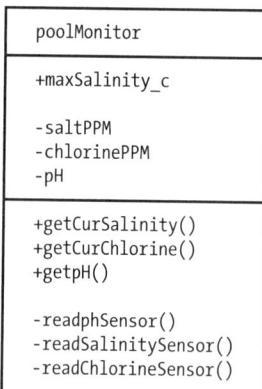

Figure 6-5: Private attributes and operations

You should use private visibility for any attribute or operation that doesn't absolutely require some other form of visibility, and strive to ensure that all attributes (data fields in the class) are private members of the class. If outside code needs to access a data field, you can use public *accessor* functions (getters and setters) to provide access to the private class member. A *getter* function returns the value of a private field. A *setter* function stores a value into a private field.

If you're wondering why you should even bother using accessor functions (after all, it's a whole lot easier to simply access the data field directly[3]), consider this: a setter function can check the value you're storing in an attribute to ensure it's within range. Also, not all fields are independent of all other attributes in a class. For example, in a saltwater pool, the salinity, chlorine, and pH levels aren't completely independent of one another: the pool contains an electrolysis cell that converts water and sodium chloride (salt) into sodium hydroxide and chlorine. This conversion reduces the salinity and increases the chlorine and pH levels. So rather than allowing some external code to arbitrarily change the salinity level, you might want to pass the change through a setter function that can decide whether to adjust other levels at the same time.

---

3. Some modern languages, like Apple's Swift, provide syntax options that let you invoke getter and setter functions using standard assignment operations. Therefore, there's no syntactical overhead associated with using getters and setters (other than, of course, writing the getter or setter methods in the first place).

6.2.3 Protected Class Visibility

Although public and private visibility covers a large percentage of the visibility requirements, in some special situations, like inheritance, you'll need to use something in between: protected visibility.

Inheritance, along with encapsulation and polymorphism, is one of the "big three" features of object-oriented programming. Inheritance allows one class to receive all the features from another class.

One problem with private visibility is that *you cannot access private fields within classes that inherit them.* Protected visibility, however, relaxes these restrictions to allow access by inheriting classes, but it doesn't allow access to private fields outside the original class or its inheriting classes.

UML notation uses the hash symbol (#) to denote protected visibility, as shown in Figure 6-6.

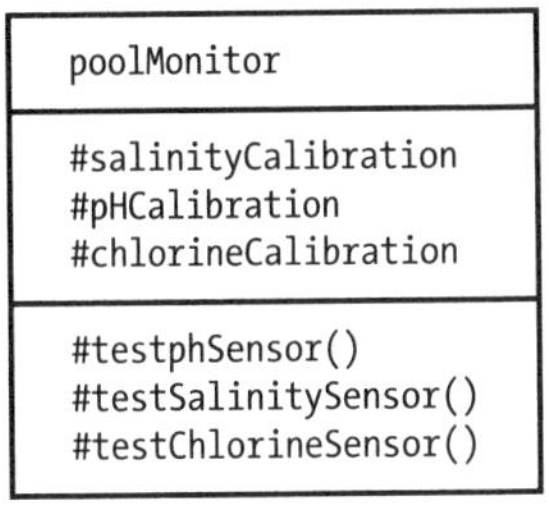

```
poolMonitor
#salinityCalibration
#pHCalibration
#chlorineCalibration
#testphSensor()
#testSalinitySensor()
#testChlorineSensor()
```

Figure 6-6: Protected attributes and operations

6.2.4 Package Class Visibility

Package visibility sits between private and protected and is largely a Java concept. Other languages have something similar, including Swift, C++, and C#, in which you can use namespaces to simulate package visibility, although the semantics aren't quite the same.

Package-protected fields are visible among all classes in the same package. Classes outside the package (even if they inherit from the class containing the package-protected fields) cannot access items with package visibility.

We use the tilde (~) to denote package visibility, as shown in Figure 6-7. Chapter 8 discusses UML package notation (that is, how to place several classes in the same package).

```
poolMonitor
~powerSupplyVoltage_c
~readCurPwrSupplyV()
```

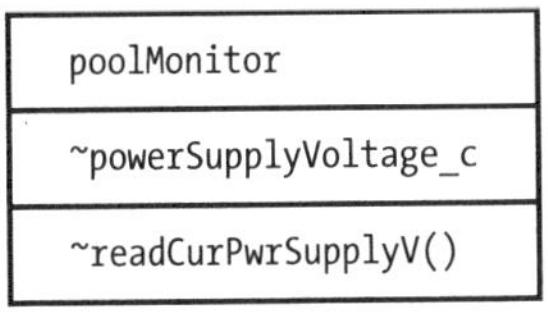

Figure 6-7: Package attributes and operations

6.2.5 Unsupported Visibility Types

What happens if your programming language of choice doesn't support the same visibility types that UML specifies? Well, the good news is that UML visibility is largely a spectrum, as shown in Figure 6-8.[4]

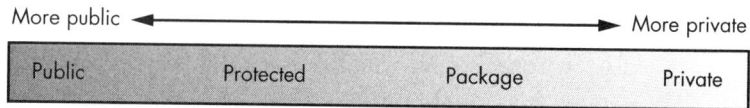

Figure 6-8: Visibility spectrum

You can always substitute a more public visibility for a more private visibility if your programming language doesn't support a specific visibility. For example, the High-Level Assembly (HLA) language supports only public fields; C++ only partially supports package visibility (using friend declarations or *namespaces*); and Swift supports an offshoot of package visibility—all private fields within an object are automatically visible to all classes declared in the same source file. One way to avoid abusing the extra visibility is to add some sort of visibility notation to the attribute or operation's name in the class—for example, by prefacing protected names with prot_ and then declaring them as public objects, as shown in Figure 6-9.

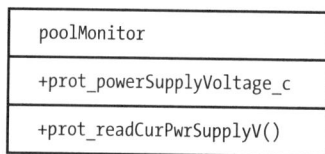

Figure 6-9: Faking visibility restriction

6.3 Class Attributes

Attributes in a UML class (also known as *data fields* or simply *fields*) hold the data associated with an object. An attribute has a visibility and a name; it can also have a data type and an initial value, as shown in Figure 6-10.

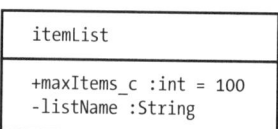

Figure 6-10: Attributes

---

4. Package and protected visibility might vary in this diagram depending on your choice of programming language, but the basic idea of a spectrum applies nonetheless.

6.3.1 Attribute Visibility

As discussed earlier, you specify the visibility of an attribute by prefixing its name with the +, -, #, or ~ symbols, which specify public, private, protected, and package visibility, respectively. See "Visibility in a Class Diagram" on page 105 for more details.

6.3.2 Attribute Derived Values

Most of the time, a class stores the value of an attribute as a variable or constant data field (a *base* value). However, some fields contain *derived* values rather than base values. The class calculates a derived value whenever some expression references that attribute. Some languages, like Swift, provide syntax for directly defining declared values; in other languages (such as C++), you'll typically write getter and setter accessor functions to implement a derived value.

To create a derived attribute in UML, you immediately precede the attribute name (after the visibility symbol) with a forward slash (/), as shown in Figure 6-11.

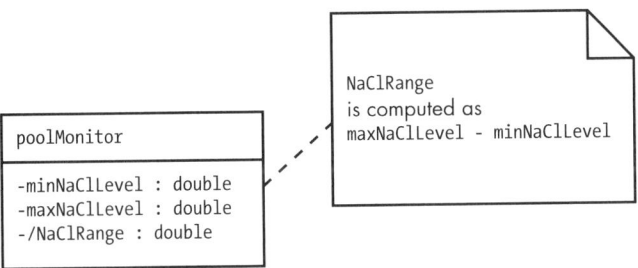

Figure 6-11: A derived attribute

Whenever you use a derived attribute, somewhere you must define how to calculate it. Figure 6-11 uses a comment for this purpose, although you could also use a *property string* (see "Property Strings" on page 112).

6.3.3 Attribute Names

The attribute name should work in whichever programming language(s) you use to implement the design. As much as possible, you should refrain from naming syntax or conventions that are specific to a programming language unless you're requiring implementation in that language. As a general rule, the following conventions work well for UML attribute names:

- All names should begin with an (ASCII) alphabetic character (a–z or A–Z).
- After the first character, names should contain only ASCII alphabetic characters (a–z, A–Z), numeric digits (0–9), or underscores (_).

- All names should be unique within the first six to eight characters (some compilers allow arbitrary-length names but keep only a prefix of them in the internal symbol table during compilation).
- Names should be shorter than some arbitrary length (we'll use 32 characters here).
- All names should be *case neutral*; that is, two separate names must contain at least one distinct character rather than just a difference in case. Also, all occurrences of a given name should be consistent with respect to alphabetic case.[5]

6.3.4 Attribute Data Types

A UML object can optionally have an associated data type (see the examples in Figure 6-10). UML doesn't require you to explicitly state the data type; if it's absent, the assumption is that the reader can infer it from the attribute's name or usage, or that the programmer will decide on a type while implementing the design.

You can use any type names you want for primitive data types and leave it up to the programmer to choose the appropriate or closest matching data type when writing the code. That being said, when working with generic data types most people choose C++ or Java type names (which makes sense, because UML's design was largely based on these two languages). Common data types you'll find attached to UML attributes include:

- `int, long, unsigned, unsigned long, short, unsigned short`
- `float, double`
- `char, wchar`
- `string, wstring`

Of course, any user-defined type names are perfectly valid as well. For example, if you've defined `uint16_t` to mean the same thing as `unsigned short` in your design, then using `uint16_t` as an attribute type is perfectly acceptable. In addition, any class objects you define in UML also make perfectly good data type names.

6.3.5 Operation Data Types (Return Values)

You can also associate a data type with an operation. Functions, for example, can return a value having some data type. To specify a return data type, follow the operation name (and parameter list) with a colon and the data type, as shown in Figure 6-12.

---

5. Case neutrality guarantees that the names you choose will be valid in both case-sensitive and case-insensitive languages. For example, `hello` and `Hello` would be considered different names in a case-sensitive language like C++, but the same in a case-insensitive language like Pascal. Neither is case neutral, so you should consistently use only one or the other in UML diagrams.

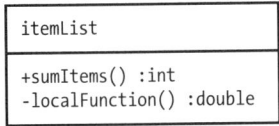

Figure 6-12: Return types

We'll discuss operations more in "Class Operations" on page 112.

6.3.6 Attribute Multiplicity

Some attributes could contain a collection (array or list) of data objects. In UML we denote multiplicity using square brackets [ ], similar to array declarations in many high-level languages; see Figure 6-13.

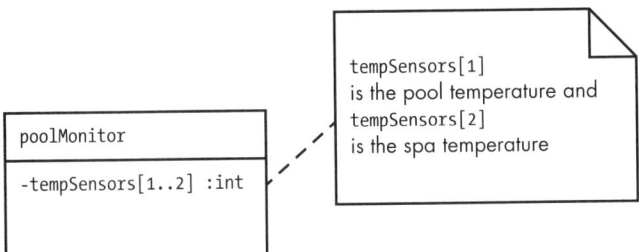

Figure 6-13: Multiplicity

Within the brackets, you specify an expression, which can be any of the following:

- A numeric value (for example, 5) indicating the number of elements in the collection
- A numeric range (for example, 1..5 or 0..7) indicating the number of elements and valid suffix range for the collection of elements
- An asterisk (*) representing an arbitrary number of elements
- An asterisk-terminated range (for example, 0..* or 1..*) indicating an open-ended range of array elements

If this notation is absent, the multiplicity defaults to [1] (that is, a single data object).

6.3.7 Default Attribute Values

To specify an initial value for an attribute, you use an equal sign (=) followed by an expression (with a type appropriate for the attribute). This typically follows the attribute's multiplicity (if present) and/or type. But if the type can be inferred from the initial value, you can omit both it and the multiplicity. If the multiplicity is something other than 1, you enclose a comma-separated list of initial values, one for each element, within a pair of braces. See Figure 6-14.

```
poolMonitor
-numTempSensors = 2
-tempSensorOffset[2] : double = {32.0, 32.0}
-tempSensorSpan = {100.0, 100.0}
```

Figure 6-14: Initial values

In this example, the `numTempSensors` attribute is an `integer` type (which can be inferred by the initial value 2), and `tempSensorSpan` is an array of `doubles` with two elements (inferred by the number and types of values in the braces).

6.3.8 Property Strings

UML's attribute syntax probably doesn't cover every possible case for your attributes. UML provides the *property string* to handle outlier situations. To create a property string, you add text within braces at the end of the attribute that describes it, as shown in Figure 6-15.

```
poolMonitor
-minNaClLevel : double
-maxNaClLevel : double
-/NaClRange : double {maxNaClLevel - minNaClLevel}
```

Figure 6-15: Property strings

You can also use property strings to define other property types. Common examples include {readOnly}, {unique}, and {static}.[6] Keep in mind that a property string is a catch-all field in the attribute. You can define any syntax you want inside the braces.

6.3.9 Attribute Syntax

The formal syntax for an attribute looks as follows (note that optional items appear in braces, except quoted braces, which represent literal brace characters):

{*visibility*}{"/"} *name* { ":" *type* }{*multiplicity*}{"=" *initial*}{"{"*property string*"}"}

6.4 Class Operations

Class operations are items within a class that perform actions. Generally, the operations represent the code in a class (but there can also be code associated with derived attributes, so having code is not exclusive to operations in a UML class).

---

6. Underlining the attribute is the standard way to specify static objects in UML, but using a property string is probably clearer.

UML class diagrams place attributes and operations into separate rectangles, though this is not what differentiates one from the other. (Consider Figure 6-2: the partial class diagrams are ambiguous with respect to which class diagram contains only attributes and which contains only operations.) In UML we explicitly specify operations within a class diagram by following the operation's name with a (possibly empty) parameter list surrounded by parentheses (refer to Figure 6-4 for an example).

As noted in "Operation Data Types (Return Values)" on page 110, you can also specify a return type for an operation by following the parameter list with a colon and a data type name. If the type is present, you definitely have a function; if it's absent, you likely have a procedure (a *void function*).

What's been missing in all the operation examples thus far is parameters. To specify parameters, you insert a comma-separated list of attributes within the parentheses immediately following the operation name, as shown in Figure 6-16.

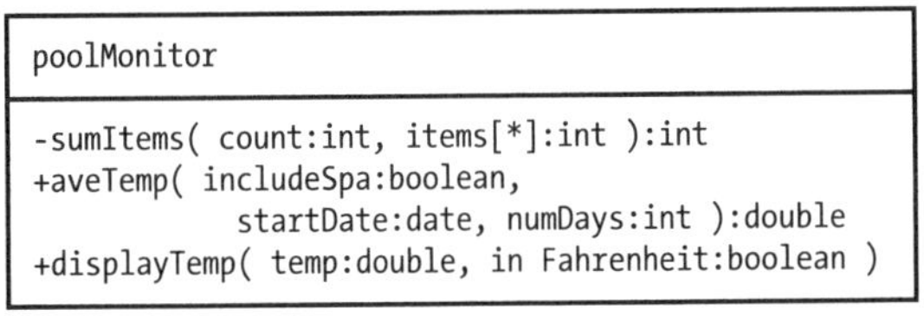

```
poolMonitor
-sumItems( count:int, items[*]:int ):int
+aveTemp( includeSpa:boolean,
          startDate:date, numDays:int ):double
+displayTemp( temp:double, in Fahrenheit:boolean )
```

Figure 6-16: Operation parameters

By default, parameters in a UML operation are *value* parameters, meaning they're passed to the operation as an argument, and changes an operation makes to a value parameter do not affect the actual parameter the caller passes to the function. A value parameter is an *input parameter*.

UML also supports *output* parameters and *input/output* parameters. As their names suggest, output parameters return information from the operation to the calling code; input/output parameters pass information to and return data from an operation. UML uses the following syntax to denote input, output, and input/output parameters:

- Input parameters: in *paramName:paramType*
- Output parameters: out *paramName:paramType*
- Input/output parameters: inout *paramName:paramType*

The default parameter-passing mechanism is input. If there's nothing specified before the parameter name, UML assumes that it is an in parameter. Figure 6-17 shows a simple example of an inout parameter.

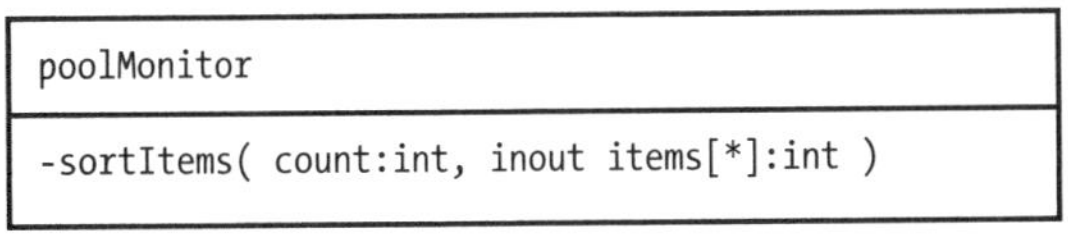

```
poolMonitor
-sortItems( count:int, inout items[*]:int )
```

Figure 6-17: Parameter inout example

In this figure, the list of items to sort is an input *and* an output parameter. On input, the `items` array contains the data to be sorted; on output, it contains the sorted items (an in-place sort).

UML tries to be as generic as possible. The `in`, `out`, and `inout` parameter-passing specifiers don't necessarily imply pass by value or pass by reference. This implementation detail is left to, well, the actual implementation. From a design point of view, UML is specifying only the direction in which, not how, the data is transferred.

6.5   UML Class Relationships

In this section, we'll explore five different types of relationships between classes: dependency, association, aggregation, composition, and inheritance.

Like visibility, class relationships fall along a spectrum (see Figure 6-18). This range is based on their *strength*, or the level and type of intercommunication between two classes.

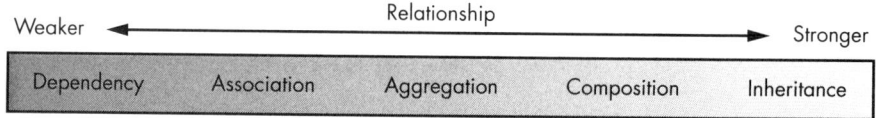

Figure 6-18: Class relationship spectrum

Strength ranges from *loosely coupled* to *tightly coupled*. When two classes are tightly coupled, any modifications to one class will likely affect the state of the other class. Loosely coupled classes are mostly independent of each other; changes to one are unlikely to affect the other.

We'll discuss each type of class relationship in turn, from weakest to strongest.

6.5.1   Class Dependency Relationships

Two classes are dependent on each other when objects of one class need to *briefly* work with objects of another class. In UML we use a dashed open-ended arrow to denote a dependency relationship, as shown in Figure 6-19.

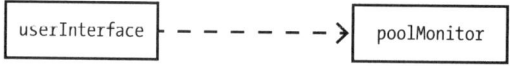

Figure 6-19: Dependency relationship

In this example, the `userInterface` and `poolMonitor` classes work together whenever a `userInterface` object wants to retrieve data to display (for example, when you pass a `poolMonitor` object to a `userInterface` method as a parameter). Other than that, the two classes (and objects of those classes) operate independently of each other.

6.5.2 Class Association Relationships

An association relationship occurs when one class contains an attribute whose type is a second class. There are two ways to draw an association relationship in UML: inline attributes and association links. You've already seen inline attributes—they're the normal attribute definitions you saw in "Attribute Syntax" on page 112). The only requirement is that the type name must be some other class.

The second way to specify a class association relationship is with an association *line* or *link*, as shown in Figure 6-20.

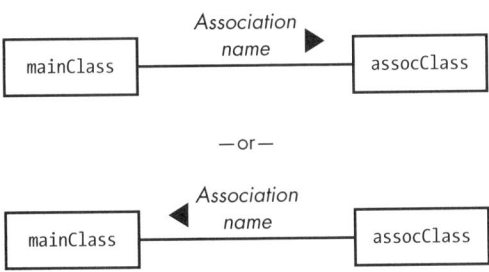

Figure 6-20: Association relationship

The *association name* is typically a verb phrase that describes the association, such as *has, owns, controls, is owned by*, and *is controlled by* (see Figure 6-21).

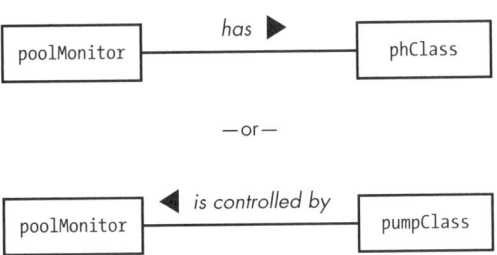

Figure 6-21: Association names

How can we tell from an association diagram which class is an attribute of the other? Notice the arrowhead immediately to the left or right of the association name. This provides the direction of the association; here, it shows that the `poolMonitor` has a `phClass`, rather than the reverse.

But while a meaningful association name and arrowhead verb phrase can give you a clue, there's no guarantee that your intuition will be correct. Although it might seem counterintuitive, `pumpClass` in Figure 6-21 could contain the `poolMonitor` object as an attribute, even though the `poolMonitor` class controls the `pumpClass` object. The UML solution is to apply *navigability* (see "Navigability" on page 123) by placing an open-ended arrow pointing at the class that is an attribute of the other class, as shown in Figure 6-22.

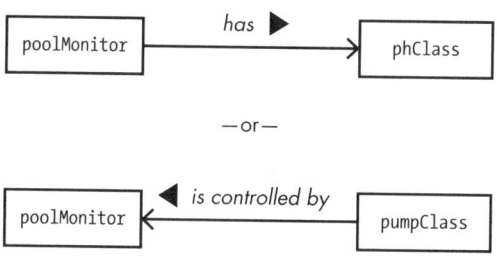

Figure 6-22: Association navigability

6.5.3 Class Aggregation Relationships

An aggregation, a slightly more tightly coupled version of association, exists as a class that could be stand-alone but is part of a larger class. Most of the time, an aggregation relationship is a *controls* relationship; that is, a controlling class (the *aggregate* or *whole* class) controls a set of subservient objects or attributes (the *parts* classes). The aggregate class cannot exist without the parts classes; however, the parts classes can exist outside the context of the aggregate class (for example, a parts class could be associated with both the aggregate class and an additional class).

Aggregates act as *gatekeepers* to their parts attributes, ensuring that the parts' methods are being called with appropriate (for example, range-checked) parameters and that the operating environment for those parts is consistent. The aggregate class can also check return values for consistency and handle exceptions and other issues raised by the parts.

For example, you could have a pHSensor class that works well with a stand-alone pH meter and a salinitySensor class that works well with a stand-alone salinity (or conductivity) sensor. The poolMonitor class is not a stand-alone class: it needs both of these classes to do its job, even though they don't need poolMonitor to do theirs. We model this relationship using an empty diamond symbol on the aggregate class (poolMonitor) and an association line leading to the parts classes (pHSensor and salinitySensor), as shown in Figure 6-23.

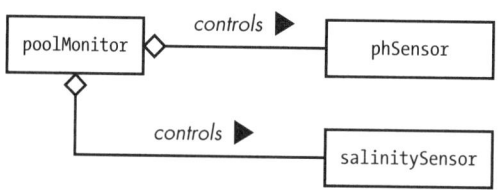

Figure 6-23: Aggregation relationship

The class with the open diamond end of the association line (that is, the aggregated class) always contains the attribute-associated class (the parts class) at the other end of the line.

The lifetimes of an aggregate object and its associated parts objects are not necessarily the same. You could create several parts objects and then attach them to an aggregate object. When the aggregate object finishes its task, it can be deallocated while the parts objects continue to solve other problems. In other words, from a low-level programming perspective, the system stores pointers to the parts objects in the aggregate object. When the system deallocates the storage for the aggregate object, the pointers might go away, but the objects they reference might persist (and could be pointed at by other aggregate objects in the system).

Why use an aggregate diagram? The code produced for an association and an aggregation will be identical. The difference is one of intent. In an aggregation diagram, the designer is saying that the parts objects or classes are under the control of the aggregate class or object. To return to our poolMonitor example, in the aggregation relationship, the poolMonitor is in complete charge—the salinitySensor and pHSensor objects are being controlled by it, and never the other way around. In an association relationship, however, the associated classes are *peers* rather than having a master/slave relationship; that is, both the pHSensor and salinitySensor could operate independently of the poolMonitor—and vice versa—sharing information only as necessary.

6.5.4   Class Composition Relationships

In composition relationships, the smaller classes contained by the larger class are not stand-alone classes: they exist strictly to support the containing, or *composing*, class. Unlike with aggregates, composition parts can belong only to a single composition.

The lifetimes of the composing object and the parts objects are the same. When you destroy the composing object, you also destroy the parts objects it contains. The composing object is responsible for allocating and deallocating storage associated with the parts.

We use a solid diamond to denote a composition relationship, as shown in Figure 6-24.

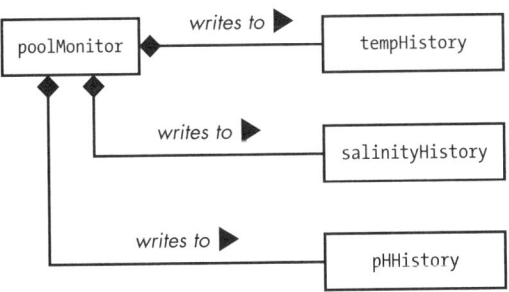

Figure 6-24: Composition relationship

6.5.5   Relationship Features

For dependency, association, aggregation, and composition relationships, UML supports these 10 features, some of which you've already seen:

- Attribute names
- Roles

- Interface specifiers
- Visibility
- Multiplicity
- Ordering
- Constraints
- Qualifiers
- Navigability
- Changeability

These features don't apply to the inheritance relationship, which is why I haven't yet described it. We'll get to inheritance shortly in the section "Class Inheritance Relationships" on page 125, but first we'll cover each of these relationship features.

NOTE *For simplicity's sake I use* association *to discuss each feature, but* dependency, aggregate, *and* composition *all equally apply.*

6.5.5.1 Association and Attribute Names

The association name attached to a link can tell you the type or ownership of the interaction, but it doesn't tell you how the two classes refer to each other. The association link only provides a connection between the two class objects. Classes refer to each other using attribute and operation fields in the class definition.

As you read in "Class Association Relationships" on page 115, the association diagram is effectively an alternative to the inline syntax for incorporating an attribute or operation name within a class. The two diagrams in Figure 6-25 are equivalent.

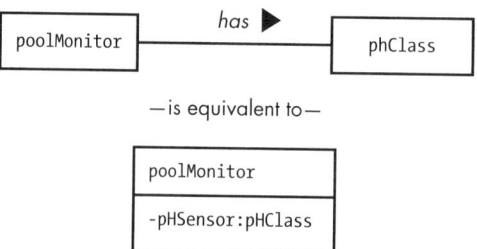

Figure 6-25: Shorthand (top) and longhand (bottom) association relationship diagrams

In Figure 6-25, the shorthand version is missing the attribute or operation name (pHSensor in this example) and the visibility (-, or private), but you can supply these missing pieces by attaching the attribute name to the association link nearest the object that will hold the object reference data field, as shown in Figure 6-26.

Like the inline syntax, an attribute name consists of an attribute or operation name with a visibility symbol prefix (-, ~, #, or +). The visibility symbol must be present because it differentiates an attribute name from a role (described next).

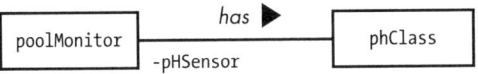

Figure 6-26: Attribute name

Another option is to combine the association and attribute names, as shown in Figure 6-27.

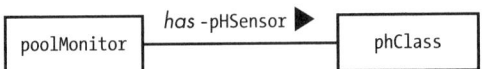

Figure 6-27: Combining association and attribute names

6.5.5.2 Roles

In Figure 6-27, it isn't entirely clear what the two classes are doing. The `pool Monitor` class has a `pHSensor` field that connects to the `pHClass`, but otherwise the diagram doesn't explain what's going on. *Roles*, which typically appear at both ends of the association link, provide this missing description.

In this example, the `poolMonitor` class or object generally reads the pH value from a pH sensor device (encapsulated in `pHClass`). Conversely, the `pHClass` class or object can supply pH readings. You can describe these two activities (reading pH and supplying a pH value) using roles in UML. Figure 6-28 shows an example of these roles.

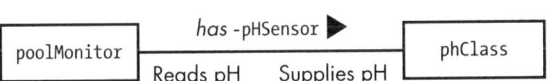

Figure 6-28: Roles

6.5.5.3 Interface Specifiers

An *interface* is a set of operations expected from certain classes. It's similar to a class except there are no objects instantiated from it. Classes that adhere to an interface are guaranteed to provide all the operations present in it (and provide methods for those operations). If you're a C++ programmer, you can think of an interface as an abstract base class containing only abstract member functions. Java, C#, and Swift have their own special syntax for defining interfaces (also known as *protocols*).

NOTE *Interface specifiers are supported in UML 1.x but have been dropped from UML 2.0. I describe them in this chapter because you might encounter them, but you shouldn't use them in new UML documents because they're deprecated.*

If a class implements an interface, it's effectively inheriting all the operations from that interface. That is, if an interface provides operations A, B, and C, and some class implements that interface, that class must also provide operations A, B, and C (and provide concrete implementations of these operations). There are two distinct ways to specify an interface—with *stereotype* or *ball* notation, as shown in Figure 6-29.

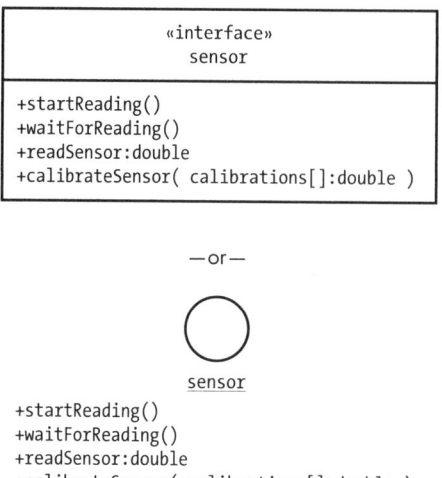

Figure 6-29: Interface syntax: stereotype (top) and ball (bottom) notation

To show that a class implements a given interface, you draw a dashed line with a hollow arrowhead from the class to the interface diagram, as shown in Figure 6-30.

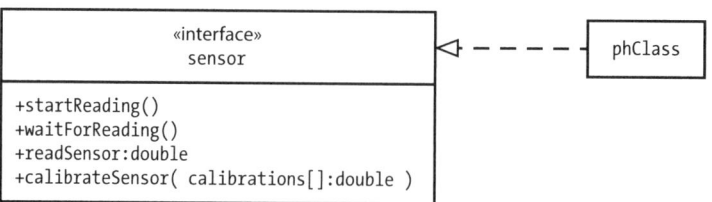

Figure 6-30: Interface implementation diagram

6.5.5.4 Visibility

Visibility applies to attribute names in an association link. As noted earlier, all attribute names must be prefixed with a symbol (-, ~, #, or +) that specifies their visibility (private, package, protected, or public, respectively).

6.5.5.5 Multiplicity

The section "Attribute Multiplicity" on page 111 described multiplicity for inline attributes. You can also include multiplicity in association diagrams by specifying multiplicity values at either or both ends of an association link (see Figure 6-31). Place multiplicity values above or below the link and closest to the class or object to which they apply. If a multiplicity value is not provided, it defaults to 1.

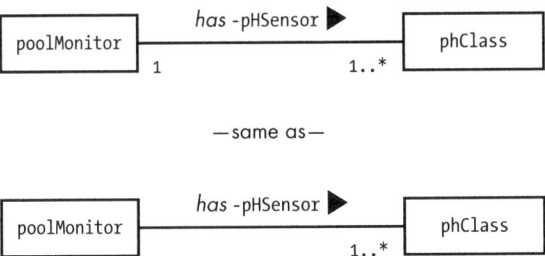

Figure 6-31: Multiplicity on an association link

Figure 6-31 indicates that there is a single `poolMonitor` object, and it can have one or more associated `pHSensors` (there could be, for example, separate pH sensors in the spa and in the swimming pool proper).

This example shows a *one-to-many* relationship. It's also possible to have *many-to-one* and even *many-to-many* relationships in these diagrams. For example, Figure 6-32 shows a many-to-many relationship between `poolMonitor` and `pHClass` classes or objects (if you're having a hard time visualizing how this would work, consider a water park that has multiple pools with multiple pH meters).

Figure 6-32: Many-to-many relationship

6.5.5.6 Ordering

UML provides the {ordered} constraint, which you can attach to any association that has a multiplicity other than 1 (see Figure 6-33).

Figure 6-33: An ordered association

When appearing by itself, the {ordered} constraint doesn't specify how to order the list of items, only that they *are* ordered. The type of ordering must be handled by the implementation.

6.5.5.7 Constraints

A constraint is application-specific text within braces that you attach to an association link. Although UML has some predefined constraints (like the {ordered} constraint just mentioned), you usually create your own to provide some application-defined control over the association link. You can even specify multiple constraints by separating them with commas within the braces. For example, the singular {ordered} constraint in Figure 6-33 doesn't describe how to sort the temperature history information. You can specify the ordering by adding another constraint to the diagram, such as sorted by date/time, as shown in Figure 6-34.

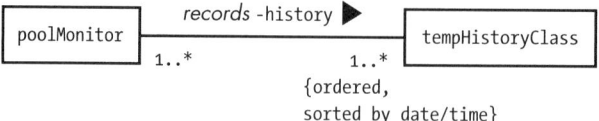

Figure 6-34: A custom constraint

6.5.5.8 Qualifiers

A qualifier informs the implementer that a specified association requires fast access, typically using a key or index value. For example, suppose the temperature recording mechanism in Figure 6-34 records the pool temperature every minute. Over the span of a week, the history object will accumulate 10,080 readings; over a year, it will accumulate more than 3.6 million readings. To extract one reading per day (say, the temperature at noon) over the past year, you have to scan through nearly 4 million readings to produce 365 or 366 readings. That could be computationally intensive and create some performance issues, particularly for real-time systems (which the pool monitor system is likely to be). We could instead give each reading a unique index value so we can extract only those we need.

To create a UML qualifier, you place some qualification (usually an attribute name in the qualifying class or object) in a rectangle at one end of the association link, as shown in Figure 6-35.

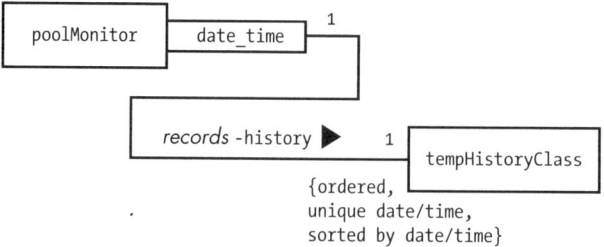

Figure 6-35: A qualifier example

The unique qualifier requires all tempHistoryClass objects to have unique dates and times; that is, no two readings can have the same date and time value.

Figure 6-35 suggests that the system will maintain a special mechanism that lets us directly select a single tempHistoryClass object based on its date_time value. This is similar to a key in a database table.[7]

In this example, the multiplicity values are both 1 because the dates and times are all unique, and the date_time qualifier will pick a specific

---

7. Similar to a key but not identical. A database maintains records and keys as disk files; qualifiers generally assume an in-memory data structure, such as an associative array, hash table, or map, to provide access to the specific record of interest.

date, for which there can be only one associated record. (Technically, there could be zero matches; however, the diagram doesn't allow for that, so there must be a matching object.)

The multiplicity could be something other than 1 if the date_time key is not unique among the history objects. For example, if you want to generate a report with all the temperatures recorded at noon, you could specify that as shown in Figure 6-36.

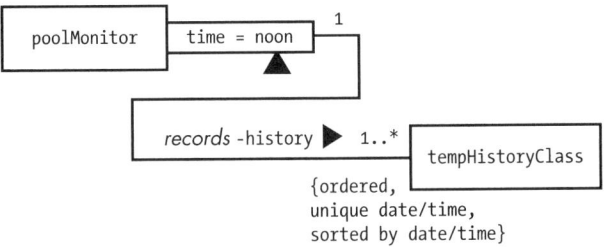

Figure 6-36: A qualifier set example

Assuming you have a year's worth of readings in the tempHistoryClass object, you'll get a set of 365/366 readings, all on different dates but at the same time (noon in this example).

One detail to keep in mind is that you can have multiple association diagrams that describe variants of the same association. For example, it's not unreasonable to find Figures 6-34, 6-35, and 6-36 in the same set of UML documents. Figure 6-34 describes the generic association between the poolMonitor class or object and the tempHistoryClass object. Figure 6-35 might describe a search operation where you're searching for a specific temperature; this operation might be so common that you want to generate some sort of associative array (that is, a hash table) to improve its performance. Likewise, Figure 6-36 suggests that you want another fast lookup table to speed up collecting a set of readings recorded at noon. Each diagram exists in its own context; they don't conflict with one another.

6.5.5.9 Navigability

In "Attribute Names" on page 109, I introduced the concept of adding attribute names to an association link. The suggestion was to place the name close to the class or object that contains the attribute (that is, that refers to the other class or object at the end of the association link). Although implicitly specifying the communication direction and attribute ownership this way works well for most simple diagrams, it can become confusing as your UML diagrams become more complex. The UML navigability feature remedies this problem.

Navigability specifies the direction of information flow in a diagram (that is, how the data navigates through the system). By default, association links are navigable in both directions. This means that a class/object at one end of the link can access data fields or methods at the other end. It's possible, however, to specify that information flows in only one direction along the association link.

To indicate navigability, place an arrowhead at the end of an association link to specify the direction of communication flow (you don't need to place arrowheads on both ends of an association link to specify bidirectional communication). For example, in Figure 6-37, the communication flows from the poolMonitor class or object to the phClass class or object. This direction tells you two things: the pHSensor attribute is a member of the poolMonitor class or object, and the phClass has no attributes that let it reference anything inside poolMonitor.

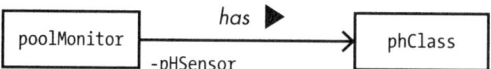

Figure 6-37: Navigability

UML 2.*x* added a new symbol to explicitly indicate that communication doesn't occur in a given direction: you place a small × on the association link near the side forbidding communication (see Figure 6-38).

Figure 6-38: Explicit non-navigability

I think this clutters the diagram and makes it harder to read, so I stick with the default specification. You can decide for yourself which option to use.

6.5.5.10 Changeability

The UML changeability feature allows you to specify whether a particular data set can be modified after its creation. In the history recording example from Figure 6-34, once a temperature is recorded in the history database, you don't want the system or a user to edit or delete that value. You can achieve this by adding the {frozen} constraint to the association link, as shown in Figure 6-39.

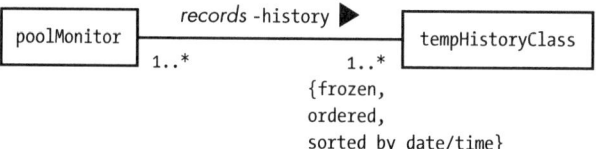

Figure 6-39: A {frozen} example

Now that you have a better understanding of the features of the first four relationship types, let's turn to the final type: inheritance.

6.5.6 Class Inheritance Relationships

The inheritance relationship (also known as the *generalization relationship* in UML) is the strongest, or most tightly coupled, form of class relationships. Any change you make to a base class's fields will have an immediate and dramatic effect on the child (inheriting) classes or objects.[8] Inheritance is a considerably different relationship than dependency, association, aggregation, or composition. These other relationships describe how one class or object uses another class or object; inheritance describes how one class *includes* everything from another class.

For inheritance we use a line with a hollow arrowhead at one end. The arrowhead points at the base class (the general item), and the other end of the line connects to the inheriting (derived) class, as shown in Figure 6-40.

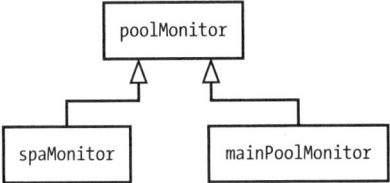

Figure 6-40: Inheritance

In this example, `spaMonitor` and `mainPoolMonitor` are *derived classes* that inherit all the fields of the base (ancestor) class `poolMonitor` (likely, these derived classes add new attributes and operations as well).

The inheritance relationship is not like dependency, association, aggregation, or composition in that features such as multiplicity, roles, and navigability don't apply.

6.6 Objects

You've seen two types of participants in all the diagrams thus far: *actors* and *classes*. Specifically, most items have been classes. However, from an object-oriented programming point of view, classes are merely data types, not actual data items that software can manipulate. An object is an instantiation of a class—the actual data object that maintains state within an application. In UML, you represent an object using a rectangle, just as you represent classes. The difference is that you specify an object name with its associated class name, and you underline the pair in the object diagram, as shown in Figure 6-41.

Figure 6-41: An object

---

8. The base class is also known as the *ancestor* class.

6.7 For More Information

Bremer, Michael. *The User Manual Manual: How to Research, Write, Test, Edit, and Produce a Software Manual.* Grass Valley, CA: UnTechnical Press, 1999. A sample chapter is available at *http://www.untechnicalpress.com/Downloads/UMM%20sample%20doc.pdf.*

Larman, Craig. *Applying UML and Patterns: An Introduction to Object-Oriented Analysis and Design and Iterative Development.* 3rd ed. Upper Saddle River, NJ: Prentice Hall, 2004.

Miles, Russ, and Kim Hamilton. *Learning UML 2.0: A Pragmatic Introduction to UML.* Sebastopol, CA: O'Reilly Media, 2003.

Pender, Tom. *UML Bible.* Indianapolis: Wiley, 2003.

Pilone, Dan, and Neil Pitman. *UML 2.0 in a Nutshell: A Desktop Quick Reference.* 2nd ed. Sebastopol, CA: O'Reilly Media, 2005.

Roff, Jason T. *UML: A Beginner's Guide.* Berkeley, CA: McGraw-Hill Education, 2003.

Tutorials Point. "UML Tutorial." *https://www.tutorialspoint.com/uml/.*

7

UML INTERACTION DIAGRAMS

Interaction diagrams model the operations that occur between different objects (participants) in a system. There are three main types of interaction diagrams in UML: sequence, collaboration (communication), and timing. The majority of this chapter will focus on sequence diagrams, followed by a very brief discussion of collaboration diagrams.

7.1 Sequence Diagrams

Sequence diagrams show the interaction between participants (actors, objects) in the order in which it takes place. Whereas activity diagrams describe the particulars of one operation on an object, sequence diagrams tie activity diagrams together to show the order in which multiple operations occur. From a design perspective, sequence diagrams are more informative than activity diagrams as they illustrate the overall architecture of the system; at the (lower) level of an activity diagram, however, a system architect can usually safely assume that the software engineer implementing the system can figure out the activities required by the design.

7.1.1 Lifelines

At the top of a sequence diagram you draw the set of participants, using rectangles or stick figures (see Figure 7-1), and then draw a dashed line from each participant to the bottom of the diagram to indicate that object's lifeline. *Lifelines* show the flow of time from the earliest (topmost) point of execution to the latest (bottommost) point. However, lifelines by themselves do not indicate the *amount* of time that passes, only the passage of time from the top to the bottom of the diagram, and equal line lengths need not correspond to the same amount of time—a 1 cm section at one point could be days, while a 1 cm section elsewhere could be microseconds.

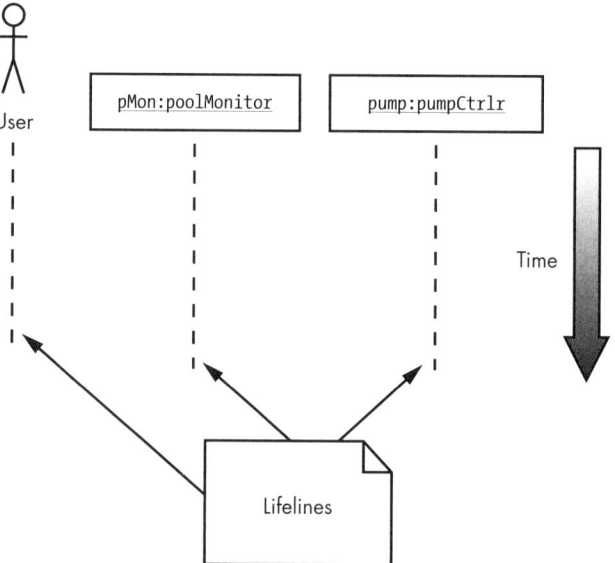

Figure 7-1: A basic sequence diagram

7.1.2 Message Types

Communication between participants takes the form of *messages* (which I will sometimes call *operations*), which consist of an arrow drawn between lifelines, or even from one lifeline to itself.

There are four types of message arrows you can use, as shown in Figure 7-2.

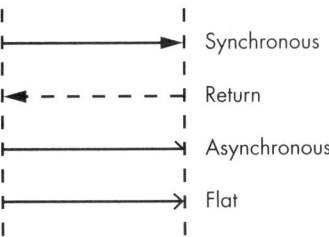

Figure 7-2: Message types in sequence diagrams

Synchronous messages are the typical call/return operation that most programs use (to execute object methods, functions, and procedures). The sender suspends execution until the receiver returns control.

Return messages indicate that control returns from a synchronous message back to the message sender, but they are purely optional in a sequence diagram. An object cannot continue execution until a synchronous message completes, so the presence of some other message (received or sent) on the same timeline inherently implies a return operation. Because a large number of return arrows can obfuscate a sequence diagram, it's best to leave them off if the diagram starts to get cluttered. If the sequence diagram is relatively clean, however, a return arrow can help show exactly what is happening.

Asynchronous messages trigger an invocation of some code in the receiver, but the message sender does not have to wait for a return message before continuing execution. For this reason, there's no need to draw an explicit return arrow for an asynchronous call in your sequence diagrams.

Flat messages can be either synchronous or asynchronous. Use a flat message when the type doesn't matter for the design and you want to leave the choice up to the engineer implementing the code. As a general rule, you do not draw return arrows for flat messages because that would imply that the implementer must use a synchronous call.

NOTE *Flat messages are UML 1.x entities only. In UML 2.0, asynchronous messages use the full open arrowhead instead.*

7.1.3 Message Labels

When you draw a message, you must attach a label to the message's arrow. This label could simply be a description of the message, as in Figure 7-3.

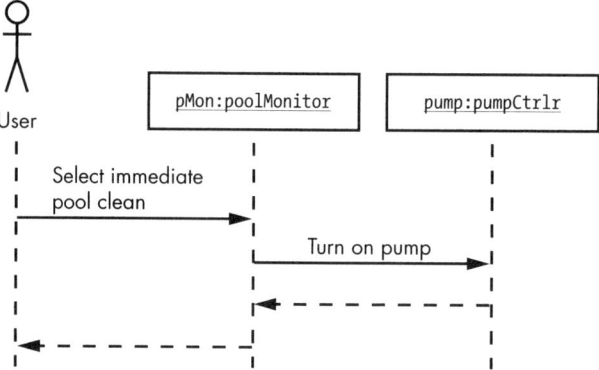

Figure 7-3: Message labels

The sequence of messages is indicated by their vertical placement. In Figure 7-3, the "Select immediate pool clean" label is the first message line in the diagram, meaning it is the first operation to execute. Moving downward, "Turn on pump" is the second message line, so it executes next. The return from "Turn on pump" is the third operation and the return from "Select immediate pool clean" is the fourth.

7.1.4 Message Numbers

As your sequence diagrams become more complex, it may be difficult to determine the execution order from the message position alone, so it can be helpful to attach additional indicators like numbers to each message label. Figure 7-4 uses sequential integers, though UML doesn't require this. You could use numbers like 3.2.4 or even non-numeric indicators (for example, A, B, C). However, the goal is to make it easy to determine the message sequence, so if you get too carried away here you might defeat that purpose.

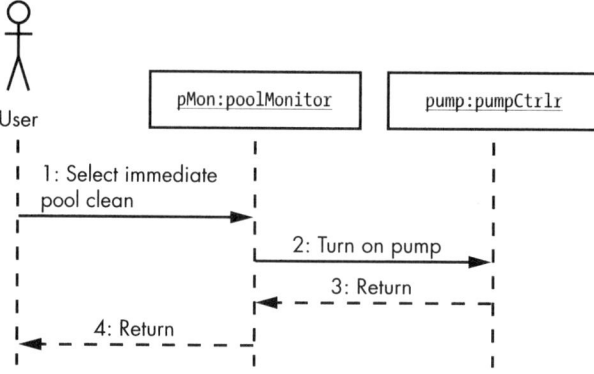

Figure 7-4: Message numbers

Although the message labels you've seen thus far are relatively straightforward descriptions, it's not uncommon to use the actual operation names, parameters, and return values as labels on message arrows, as in Figure 7-5.

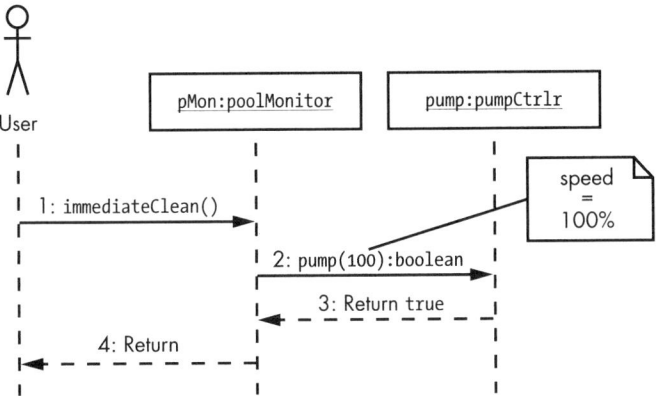

Figure 7-5: Message arguments and return values

7.1.5   Guard Conditions

Your message labels can also include guard conditions: Boolean expressions enclosed in brackets (see Figure 7-6). If the guard expression evaluates to true, the system sends the message; if it evaluates to false, the system does not send the message.

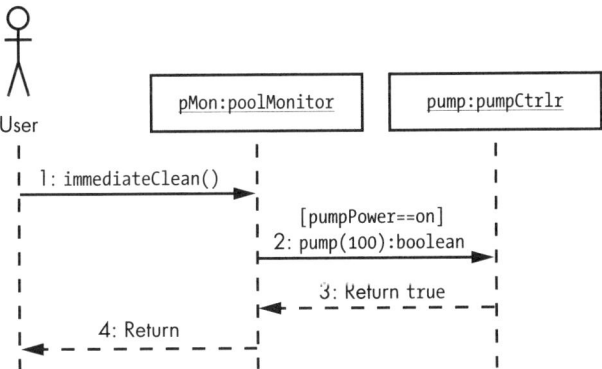

Figure 7-6: Message guard conditions

In Figure 7-6, the pMon object sends a pump(100) message to pump only if pumpPower is on (true). If pumpPower is off (false) and the pump(100) message does not execute, the corresponding return operation (sequence item 3) will not execute either, and control will move to the next outgoing arrow item in the pMon lifeline (sequence item 4, returning control to the user object).

7.1.6 Iterations

You can also specify the number of times a message executes by providing an iteration count in a sequence diagram. To specify an iteration, you use an asterisk symbol (*) followed by a guard condition or for loop iteration count (see Figure 7-7). The system will repeatedly send the message as long as the guard condition is true.

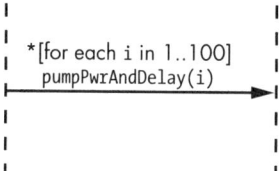

Figure 7-7: Partial sequence diagram with iteration

In Figure 7-7, the message executes 100 times, with the variable i taking on the value 1 through 100, incrementing on each iteration. If the pumpPwrAndDelay function applies the percent power specified as the argument and delays for 1 second, then in about 1 minute, 40 seconds, the pump will be running at full speed (increasing by 1 percent of the total speed each second).

7.1.7 Long Delays and Time Constraints

Sequence diagrams typically describe only the order of messages, not the amount of time each message takes to execute. Sometimes, however, a designer might want to indicate that a particular operation might take a long time relative to others. This is particularly common when one object sends a message to another object located outside the bounds of the current system (for example, when a software component sends a message to some object on a remote server across the internet), which we'll discuss shortly. You indicate that an operation will take longer by pointing the message arrow slightly downward. In Figure 7-8, for example, you would expect the scheduledClean() operation to take more time than a typical operation.

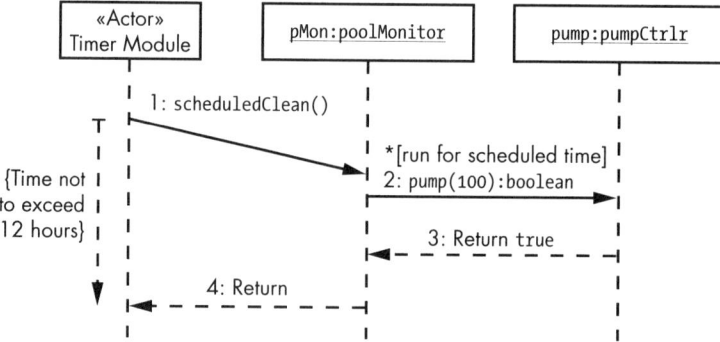

Figure 7-8: Timed messages with timing constraints

You must also specify the expected amount of time for each message by adding some sort of constraint to the diagram. Figure 7-8 demonstrates this with a dashed vertical arrow from the start of the `scheduledClean()` operation to the point on the lifeline where the system returns control to the Timer Module actor (probably the physical timer on the pool monitor system). The required time constraint appears inside braces next to the dashed arrow.

7.1.8   External Objects

Occasionally a component of a sequence diagram must communicate with some object *external* to the system. For example, some code in the pool monitor might check the salinity level and send an SMS message to the owner's cell phone if it drops too low. The code to actually transmit the SMS message is probably handled by an Internet of Things (IoT) device and thus outside the scope of the pool monitor software; hence, the SMS code is an external object.

You draw a heavy border around external objects and use a solid line for their lifelines rather than a dashed line (see Figure 7-9).

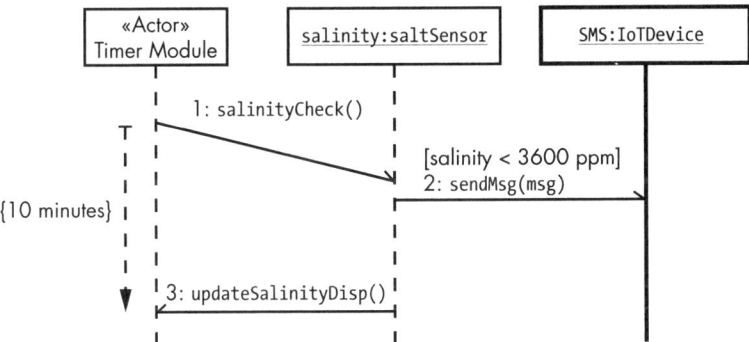

Figure 7-9: External objects in a sequence diagram

In Figure 7-9, the Timer Module makes an asynchronous call to the salinity object, and there is no return from the `salinityCheck()` operation. After that call, the Timer Module can perform other tasks (not shown in this simple diagram). Ten minutes later, as noted by the time constraint, the salinity object makes an asynchronous call to the Timer Module actor and has it update the salinity value on the display.

Because there isn't an explicit time constraint on the `sendMsg()` operation, it could occur any time after the `salinityCheck()` operation and before the `updateSalinityDisp()` operation; this is indicated by the `sendMsg()` message arrow's position between the other two messages.

7.1.9   Activation Bars

Activation bars indicate that an object is instantiated and active, and appear as open rectangles across a lifeline (see Figure 7-10). They are optional, as you can generally infer the lifetime of an object simply by looking at the messages traveling to and from it.

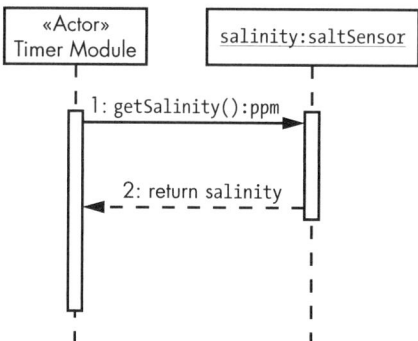

Figure 7-10: Activation bars

> **NOTE** *For the most part, activation bars clutter up sequence diagrams, so this book will not use them. They're described here just in case you encounter them in sequence diagrams from other sources.*

7.1.10 Branching

As noted in "Guard Conditions" on page 131, you can apply guard conditions to a message that say, effectively, "if true, then execute message; else, continue along this lifeline." Another handy tool is branching—the equivalent of the C-style switch/case statement where you can select one of several messages to execute based on a set of guard conditions, one guard for each message. In order to execute different messages based on whether a pool uses chlorine or bromine as a sanitizer, you might be tempted to draw branching logic as shown in Figure 7-11.

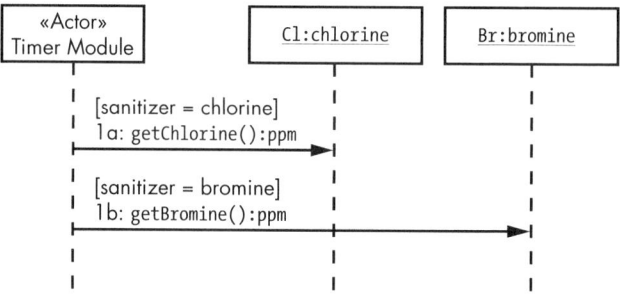

Figure 7-11: Bad implementation of branching logic

In one aspect, this diagram makes perfect sense. If the sanitizer for this particular pool is bromine rather than chlorine, the first message does not execute and control flows down to the second message, which does execute. The problem with this diagram is that the two messages appear at different points on the lifeline and, therefore, could execute at completely different times. Particularly as your sequence diagrams get more complex, some other message invocation could wind up between these two—and thus would execute prior to the getBromine() message. Instead, if the sanitizer is not chlorine you'd want to immediately check to see if it is bromine, with no possibility of intervening messages. Figure 7-12 shows the proper way to draw this logic.

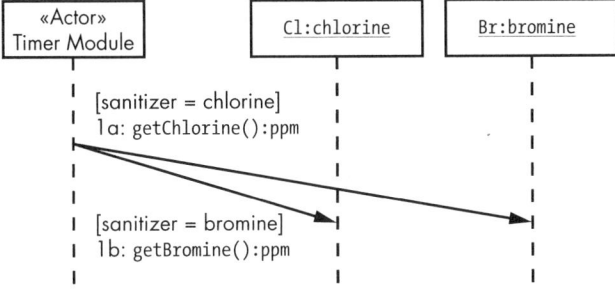

Figure 7-12: Good implementation of branching logic

Drawing branching logic with the arrow tails that start from the same vertical position and the arrowheads that end at the same vertical position avoids any ambiguity with the sequence of execution (assuming that the guard conditions are mutually exclusive—that is, it is not possible for both conditions to be simultaneously true).

Branching uses slanted message arrows similar to long delays, but a long delay item will have an associated time constraint.[1]

7.1.11   Alternative Flows

There's another potential issue with branching: what happens when you need to send one of two different messages to the same destination object? Because the arrow tails and heads must start and end, respectively, at the same vertical positions for both arrows, the two arrows would overlay each other and there would be no indication that branching takes place at all. The solution to this problem is to use an *alternative flow*.

In an alternative flow, a single lifeline splits into two separate lifelines at some point (see Figure 7-13).

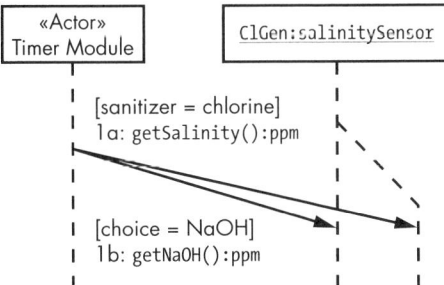

Figure 7-13: Alternative flows

---

1. If you're thinking this is a bad design element in the UML language, you're correct. Given its history and design-by-(political)-committee approach, it's understandable why UML isn't a little cleaner.

UML Interaction Diagrams   **135**

In this example, the Timer Module has to choose between retrieving the current level of salinity (NaCl) or sodium hydroxide (NaOH). The getSalinity() and getNaOH() operations are methods within the same class; therefore, their message arrows will both point at the same spot in the ClGen lifeline. To avoid overlapping the message arrows, Figure 7-13 splits the ClGen lifeline into two lifelines: the original and an alternative flow.

After the message invocation, you can merge the two flows back together if desired.

7.1.12 Object Creation and Destruction

So far in the examples, the objects have existed throughout the lifetime of the sequence diagram; that is, all objects existed prior to the execution of the first message (operation) and persist after the execution of the last message. In real-world designs, you'll need to create and destroy objects that don't exist for the full duration of the program's execution.

Object creation and destruction are messages just like any other. The common convention in UML is to use the special messages «create» and «destroy» (see Figure 7-14) to show object lifetimes within the sequence diagram; however, you can use any message name you like. The X at the end of the cleanProcess lifeline, immediately below the «destroy» operation, denotes the end of the lifeline, because the object no longer exists.

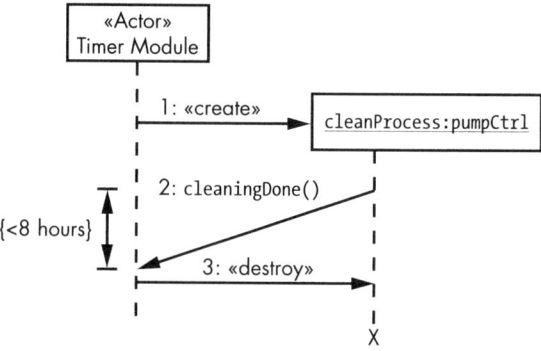

Figure 7-14: Object creation and destruction

This example uses a *dropped title box* to indicate the beginning of the lifeline for a newly created object. As Russ Miles and Kim Hamilton point out in *Learning UML 2.0* (O'Reilly, 2003), many standardized UML tools don't support using dropped title boxes, allowing you to place the object title boxes only at the top of the diagram. There are a couple of solutions to this problem that should work with most standard UML tools.

You can put the object at the top of the diagram and add a comment to explicitly indicate object creation and destruction at the points where they occur (see Figure 7-15).

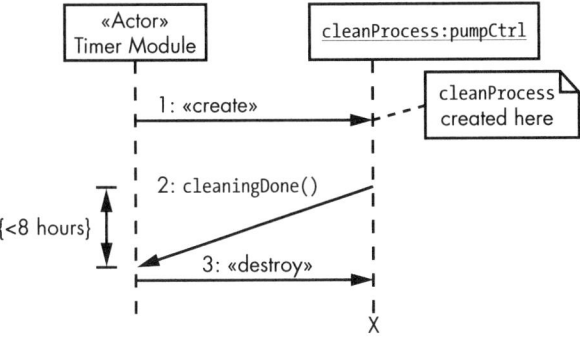

Figure 7-15: Using notes to indicate object lifetime

You can also use an alternative flow to indicate the lifetime of the object (see Figure 7-16).

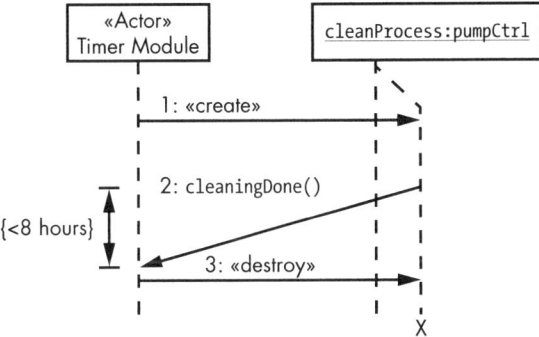

Figure 7-16: Using alternative flows to indicate object lifetime

Activation bars provide a third alternative that might be clearer here.

7.1.13 Sequence Fragments

UML 2.0 added *sequence fragments* to show loops, branches, and other alternatives, enabling you to better manage sequence diagrams. UML defines several standard sequence fragment types you can use, defined briefly in Table 7-1 (full descriptions appear later in this section).

Table 7-1: Brief Descriptions of Sequence Fragment Types

alt	Executes only the alternative fragment that is true (think of an if/else or switch statement).
assert	Notes that operations within the fragment are valid if a guard condition is true.
break	Exits a loop fragment (based on some guard condition).
consider	Provides a list of valid messages in a sequence fragment.
ignore	Provides a list of invalid messages in a sequence fragment.
loop	Runs multiple times and the guard condition determines whether the fragment repeats.
neg	Never executes.
opt	Executes only if the associated condition is true. Comparable to alt with only one alternative fragment.
par	Runs multiple fragments in parallel.
ref	Indicates a call to another sequence diagram.
region	(Also known as critical.) Defines a critical region in which only one thread of execution is possible.
seq	Indicates that operations (in a multitasking environment) must occur in a specific sequence.
strict	A stricter version of seq.

In general, you draw sequence fragments as a rectangle surrounding the messages, with a special penta-rectangle symbol (a rectangle with the lower-right corner cropped) in its upper-left corner that contains the UML fragment name/type (see Figure 7-17; substitute any actual fragment type for *typ* in this diagram).

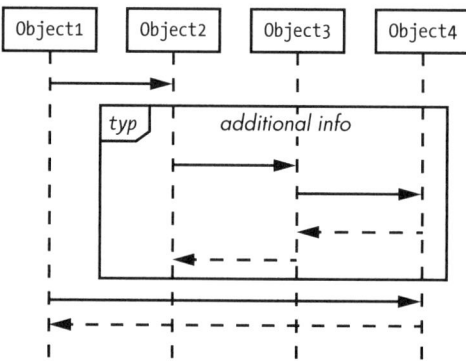

Figure 7-17: Generic sequence fragment form

For example, if you wanted to repeat a sequence of messages several times, you would enclose those messages in a loop sequence fragment. This tells the engineer implementing the program to repeat those messages the number of times specified by the loop fragment.

You can also include an optional *additional info* item, which is typically a guard condition or iteration count. The following subsections describe the sequence fragment types from Table 7-1 in detail, as well as any additional information they may require.

7.1.13.1   ref

There are two components to a ref sequence fragment: the UML interaction occurrence and the reference itself. An *interaction occurrence* is a stand-alone sequence diagram corresponding to a subroutine (procedure or function) in code. It is surrounded by a sequence fragment box. The penta-rectangle in the upper-left corner of the box contains sd (for *sequence diagram*) followed by the name of the ref fragment and any arguments you want to assign to it (see Figure 7-18).

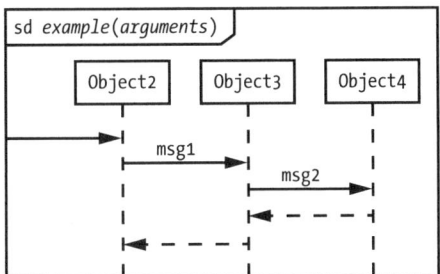

Figure 7-18: An interaction occurrence example

The leftmost incoming arrow corresponds to the *subroutine entry point*. If this isn't present, you can assume that control flows to the leftmost participant at the top of its lifeline.

Now we come to the second component of the ref sequence fragment: referencing the interaction occurrence within a different sequence diagram (see Figure 7-19).

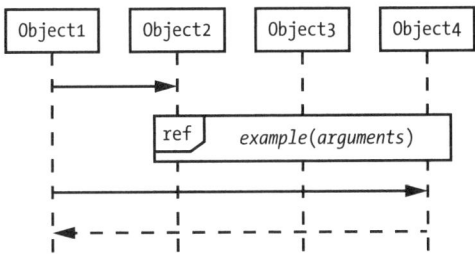

Figure 7-19: A ref sequence fragment example

This corresponds to a call to a subroutine (procedure or function) in code.

7.1.13.2 consider and ignore

The consider sequence fragment lists all messages that are valid within a section of the sequence diagram; all other messages/operators are illegal. The ignore operator lists names of messages that are invalid within a section of the sequence diagram; all other operators/messages are legal.

consider and ignore work either as operators in conjunction with an existing sequence fragment or as sequence fragments by themselves. A consider or ignore operator takes the following form:

```
consider{ comma-separated-list-of-operators }
ignore{ comma-separated-list-of-operators }
```

The consider and ignore operators may appear after the sd *name* title in an interaction occurrence (see Figure 7-20), in which case they apply to the entire diagram.

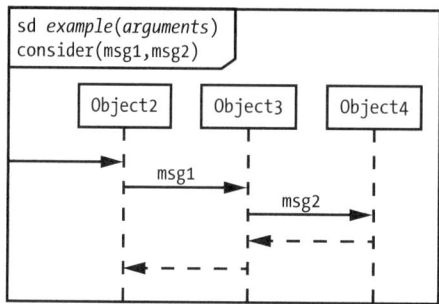

Figure 7-20: A consider operator example

You may also create a sequence fragment within another sequence diagram and label that fragment with a consider or ignore operation. In that case, consider or ignore applies only to the messages within the specific sequence fragment (see Figure 7-21).

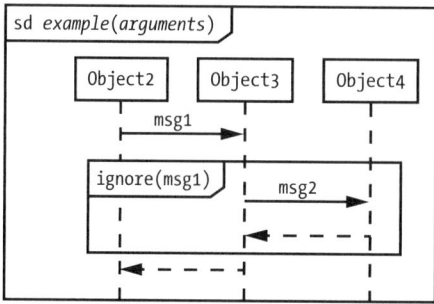

Figure 7-21: An ignore sequence fragment example

If these fragment types seem strange, consider creating a very generic ref fragment that handles only certain messages, but then referencing that ref from several different places that might pass along unhandled messages along with the handled ones. By adding a consider or ignore operator to the ref, you can have the fragment simply ignore the messages it doesn't explicitly handle, which allows you to use that ref without having to add any extra design to the system.

7.1.13.3 assert

The assert sequence fragment tells the system implementer that the messages within it are valid only if some guard condition evaluates to true. At the end of the assert fragment, you typically provide some sort of Boolean condition (the guard condition) that must be true once the sequence is complete (see Figure 7-22). If the condition isn't true after the assert fragment has finished executing, the design can't guarantee correct results. The assert reminds the engineer to verify that this condition is indeed true by, for example, using a C++ assert macro invocation (or something similar in other languages, or even just an if statement).

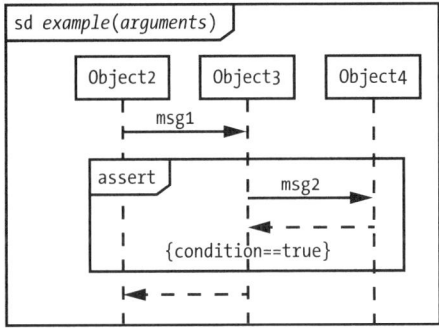

Figure 7-22: An assert sequence fragment example

In C/C++ you'd probably implement the sequence in Figure 7-22 using code like this:

```
Object3->msg1();            // Inside example
Object4->msg2();            // Inside Object3::msg1
assert( condition == TRUE ); // Inside Object3::msg1
```

7.1.13.4 loop

The loop sequence fragment indicates iteration. You place the loop operator in the penta-rectangle associated with the sequence fragment, and may also include a guard condition enclosed in brackets at the top of the sequence fragment. The combination of the loop operator and guard condition controls the number of iterations.

The simplest form of this sequence fragment is the *infinite* loop, consisting of the loop operator without any arguments and without a guard condition (see Figure 7-23). Most "infinite" loops actually aren't infinite, but terminate with a break sequence fragment when some condition is true (we'll discuss the break sequence in the next section).

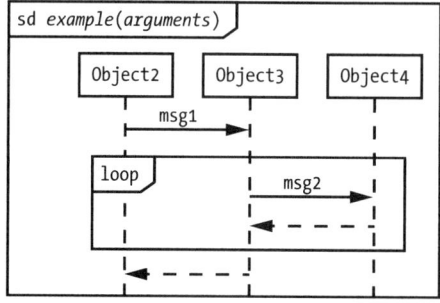

Figure 7-23: An infinite loop

The loop in Figure 7-23 is roughly equivalent to the following C/C++ code:

```
// This loop appears inside Object3::msg1
for(;;)
{
    Object4->msg2();
} // endfor
```

Or, alternatively:

```
while(1)
{
    Object4->msg2()
} // end while
```

NOTE *Personally, I prefer the following:*

```
#define ever ;;
    .
    .
    .
for(ever)
{
    Object4->msg2();
} // endfor
```

I feel this is the most readable solution. Of course, if you're "anti-macro at all costs," you would probably disagree with my choice for an infinite loop!

Definite loops execute a fixed number of times and can appear in two forms. The first is loop(*integer*), which is shorthand for loop(0, *integer*); that is, it will execute a minimum of zero times and a maximum of *integer* times. The second is loop(*minInt, maxInt*), which indicates that the loop will execute a minimum of *minInt* times and a maximum of *maxInt* times. Without a guard condition, the minimum count is irrelevant; the loop will always execute *maxInt* times. Therefore, most definite loops use the form loop(*integer*) where *integer* is the number of iterations to perform (see Figure 7-24).

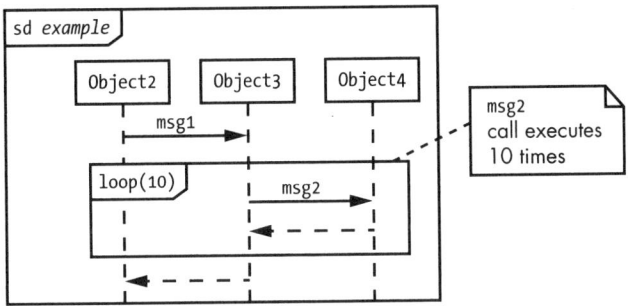

Figure 7-24: A definite loop

The loop in Figure 7-24 is roughly equivalent to the following C/C++ code:

```
// This code appears inside Object3::msg1
for( i = 1; i<=10; ++i )
{
     Object4->msg2();
} // end for
```

You can also use the multiplicity symbol * to denote infinity. Therefore, loop(*) is equivalent to loop(0, *) which is equivalent to loop (in other words, you get an infinite loop).

An *indefinite* loop executes an indeterminate[2] number of times (corresponding to while, do/while, repeat/until, and other loop forms in programming languages). Indefinite loops include a guard condition as part of the loop sequence fragment,[3] meaning the loop sequence fragment will always execute the loop *minInt* times (zero times if *minInt* is not present). After *minInt* iterations, the loop sequence fragment will begin testing the guard condition and continue iterating only while the guard condition is true. The loop sequence fragment will execute at most *maxInt* iterations (total, not in addition to the *minInt* iterations). Figure 7-25 shows a traditional while-type loop that executes a minimum of zero times and a maximum of infinity times, as long as the guard condition ([cond == true]) evaluates to true.

---

2. Indeterminate upon encountering the beginning of the loop on the first iteration.

3. Arguably, an infinite loop with a break sequence fragment is also an indefinite loop, not an infinite loop.

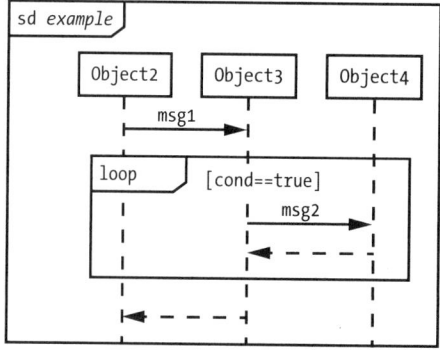

Figure 7-25: An indefinite while loop

The loop in Figure 7-25 is roughly equivalent to the following C/C++ code:

```
// This code appears inside Object3::msg1
while( cond == TRUE )
{
    Object4->msg2();
} // end while
```

You can create a do..while loop by setting the *minInt* value to 1 and the *maxInt* value to *, and then specifying the Boolean expression to continue loop execution (see Figure 7-26).

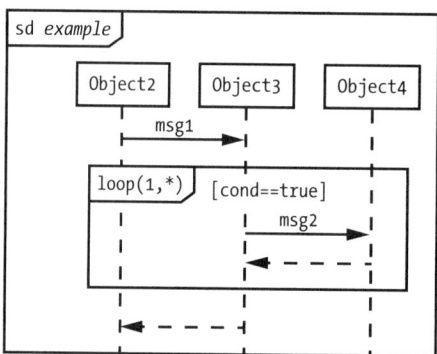

Figure 7-26: An indefinite do..while loop

The loop in Figure 7-26 is roughly equivalent to the following C/C++ code:

```
// This code appears inside Object3::msg1
do
{
    Object4->msg2();
} while( cond == TRUE );
```

It's possible to create many other complex loop types, but I'll leave that as an exercise for interested readers.

7.1.13.5 break

The break sequence fragment consists of the word break in a penta-rectangle along with a guard condition. If the guard condition evaluates to true, then the system executes the sequence inside the break sequence fragment, after which control immediately exits the enclosing sequence fragment. If the enclosing sequence fragment is a loop, control immediately executes to the first message past the loop (like a break statement in languages like Swift, C/C++, and Java). Figure 7-27 provides an example of such a loop.

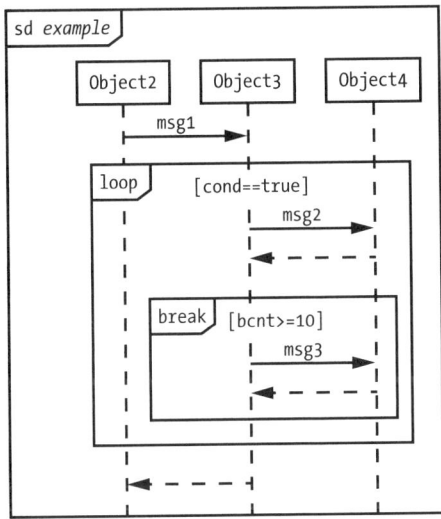

Figure 7-27: An example of the break sequence fragment

The loop in Figure 7-27 is roughly equivalent to the following C++ code fragment:

```
// This code appears inside Object3::msg1
while( cond == TRUE )
{
    Object4->msg2();
    if( bcnt >= 10 )
    {
        Object4->msg3();
        break;
    } // end if
    Object4->msg4();
} // end while loop
```

If the most recent break-compatible enclosing sequence is a subroutine, not a loop, the break sequence fragment behaves like a return from a subroutine operation.

7.1.13.6 opt and alt

The opt and alt sequence fragments allow you to control the execution of a set of messages with a single guard condition—particularly if the values of the components making up the guard condition could change over the execution of the sequence.

The opt sequence fragment is like a simple if statement without an else clause. You attach a guard condition and the system will execute the sequence contained within the opt fragment only if the guard condition evaluates to true (see Figure 7-28).

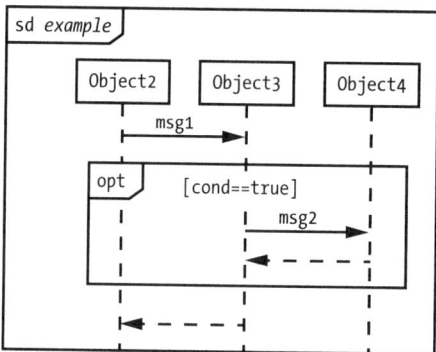

Figure 7-28: An example of the opt sequence fragment

The example in Figure 7-28 is roughly equivalent to the following C/C++ code:

```
// Assumption: Class2 is Object2's data type. Because control
// transfers into the Object2 sequence at the top of its
// lifeline, example must be a member function of Object2/Class2

void Class2::example( void )
{
     Object3->msg1();
} // end example
--snip--
//     This code appears in Object3::msg1
if( cond == TRUE )
{
     Object4->msg2();
} // end if
```

For more complex logic, use the alt sequence fragment, which acts like an if/else or switch/case. To create an alt sequence fragment, you combine several rectangles, each with its own guard condition and an optional else, to form a multiway decision (see Figure 7-29).

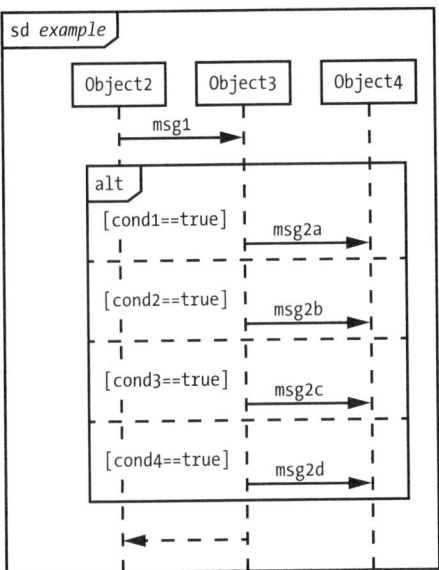

Figure 7-29: An alt sequence fragment

The interaction occurrence in Figure 7-29 is roughly equivalent to the following code:

```
// Assumption: Class2 is Object2's data type. Because control
// transfers into the Object2 sequence at the top of its
// lifeline, example must be a member function of Object2/Class2

void Class2::example( void )
{
    Object3->msg1();
} // end example

--snip--
//    This code appears in Object3::msg1
if( cond1 == TRUE )
{
    Object4->msg2a();
}
else if( cond2 == TRUE )
{
    Object4->msg2b();
}
else if( cond3 == TRUE )
{
    Object3->msg2c();
}
else
{
    Object4->msg2d();
} // end if
```

7.1.13.7 neg

You use a neg sequence fragment to enclose a sequence that will not be part of the final design. Effectively, using neg comments out the enclosed sequence. Why even include a sequence if it's not going to be part of the design? There are at least two good reasons: code generation and future features.

Although, for the most part, UML is a diagramming language intended to help with system design prior to implementation in a programming language like Java or Swift, there are certain UML tools that will convert UML diagrams directly into code. During development, you might want to include some diagrams that illustrate something but are not yet complete (certainly not to the point of producing executable code). In this scenario, you could use the neg sequence fragment to turn off the code generation for those sequences that aren't quite yet ready for prime time.

Even if you don't intend to generate code directly from a UML diagram, you might want to use the neg for future features. When you hand your UML diagrams off to an engineer to implement the design, they represent a contract that says, "This is how the code is to be written." Sometimes, though, you'll want your diagrams to show features that you plan to include in a future version of the software, but not in the first (or current) version. The neg sequence fragment is a clean way to tell the engineer to ignore that part of the design. Figure 7-30 shows a simple example of the neg sequence fragment.

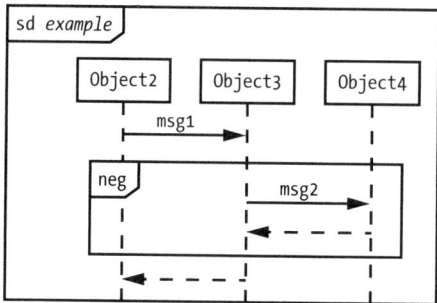

Figure 7-30: An example of the neg sequence fragment

The example in Figure 7-30 is roughly equivalent to the following C/C++ code:

```
// Assumption: Class2 is Object2's data type. Because control
// transfers into the Object2 sequence at the top of its
// lifeline, example must be a member function of Object2/Class2

void Class2::example( void )
{
    Object3->msg1();
} // end example
```

7.1.13.8 par

The par sequence fragment, an example of which is shown in Figure 7-31, states that the enclosed sequences[4] (operations) can be executed in parallel with each other.

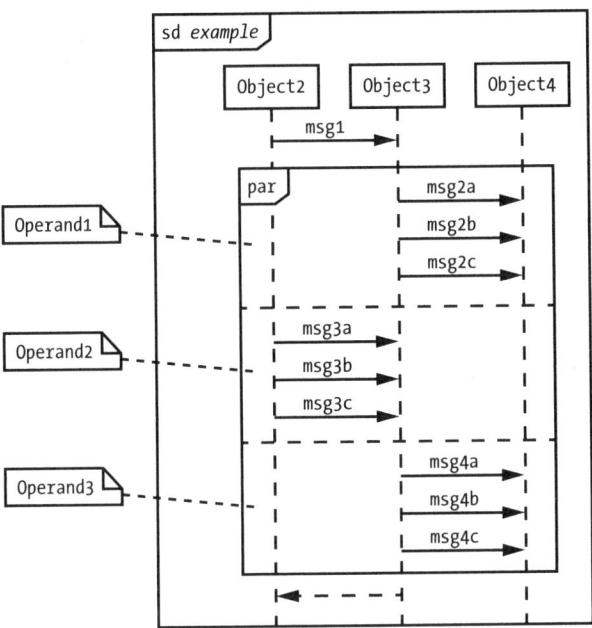

Figure 7-31: An example of the par sequence fragment

Figure 7-31 shows three operands: the sequence with {msg2a, msg2b, msg2c}, the sequence with {msg3a, msg3b, msg3c}, and the sequence with {msg4a, msg4b, msg4c}. The par sequence fragment requires that the operations within a given sequence must execute in the order in which they appear (for example, msg2a, then msg2b, then msg2c). However, the system is free to interleave operations from different operands as long as it maintains the internal order of those operands. So, in Figure 7-31, the order {msg2a, msg3a, msg3b, msg4a, msg2b, msg2c, msg4b, msg4c, msg3c} is legitimate, as is {msg4a, msg4b, msg4c, msg3a, msg3b, msg3c, msg2a, msg2b, msg2c}, because the ordering of the enclosed sequences matches. However, {msg2a, msg2c, msg4a, msg4b, msg4c, msg3a, msg3b, msg3c, msg2b} is not legitimate because msg2c occurs before msg2b (which is contrary to the ordering specified in Figure 7-31).

---

4. There will be two or more, separated by dashed lines, similar in syntax to the alt sequence fragment.

7.1.13.9 seq

The par sequence fragment enforces the following restrictions:

- The system maintains the ordering of the operations within an operand.
- The system allows operations on different lifelines from different operands to execute in any order.

And the seq sequence adds another:

- Operations on the same lifeline in different operands must execute in the order in which they appear in the diagram (from top to bottom).

In Figure 7-32, for example, Operand1 and Operand3 have messages that are sent to the same object (lifeline). Therefore, in a seq sequence fragment, msg2a, msg2b, and msg2c must all execute before msg4a.

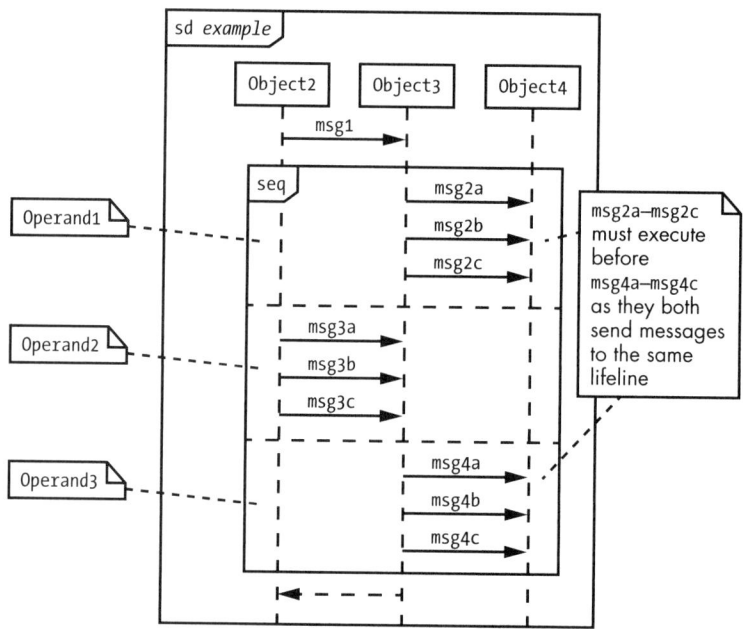

Figure 7-32: An example of the seq sequence fragment

Figure 7-32 shows a stand-alone seq sequence fragment. In typical usage, however, a seq sequence fragment will appear inside a par to control the execution sequence of a portion of the par's operands.

7.1.13.10 strict

The strict sequence fragment forces the operations to occur in the sequence they appear in each operand; interleaving of operations between operands is not allowed. The format for a strict sequence fragment is similar to that of par and seq (see Figure 7-33).

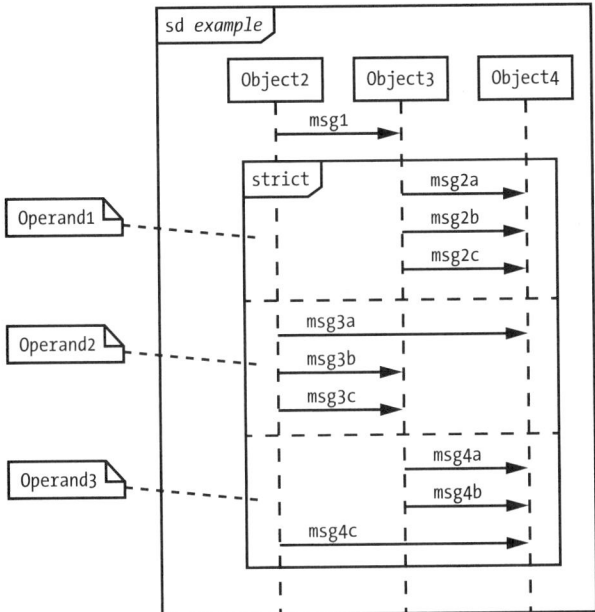

Figure 7-33: An example of the strict *sequence fragment*

The strict parallel operation allows the operands to execute in any order, but once a given operand begins execution, all the operations within it must complete in the sequence specified before any other operand can begin executing.

In Figure 7-33, there are six different operation sequences possible: {Operand1, Operand2, Operand3}; {Operand1, Operand3, Operand2}; {Operand2, Operand1, Operand3}; {Operand2, Operand3, Operand1}; {Operand3, Operand1, Operand2}; and {Operand3, Operand2, Operand1}.

However, operations internal to the operands cannot interleave, and must execute from top to bottom.

7.1.13.11   region

In the section "Extending UML Activity Diagrams" on page 99, I used the example of a home-brew critical section in an activity diagram to demonstrate how to extend UML for your own purposes. I pointed out why this is a bad idea (reread that section for the details), and mentioned there is another way to achieve what you want to do using standard UML: the region sequence fragment. UML activity diagrams don't support critical sections, but sequence diagrams do.

The region sequence fragment specifies that once execution enters the region, no other operations in the same parallel execution context can be interleaved until it completes execution. The region sequence fragment must always appear within some other parallel sequence fragment (generally par or seq; technically it could appear inside strict, though ultimately this would serve no purpose).

As an example, consider Figure 7-34—the system is free to interleave the execution of any operand's messages, subject to the rules given for the par sequence fragment, but once the system enters the critical region (with the execution of the msg4a operation), no other threads in the par sequence fragment can execute.

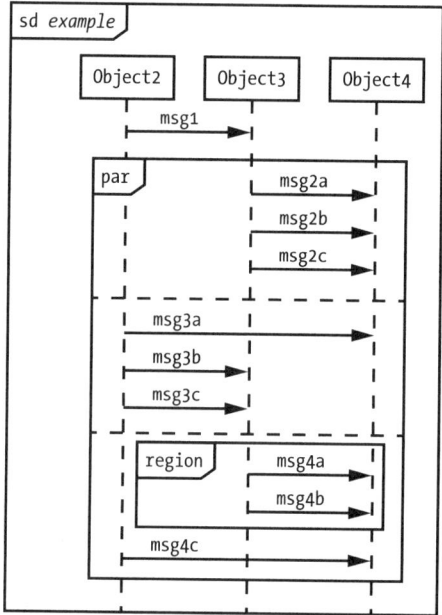

Figure 7-34: The region *sequence fragment*

7.2 Collaboration Diagrams

Collaboration (or communication) diagrams provide the same information as sequence diagrams but in a slightly more compact form. Rather than drawing arrows between lifelines, in collaboration diagrams we draw message arrows directly between objects, and attach numbers to each message to indicate the sequence (see Figure 7-35).

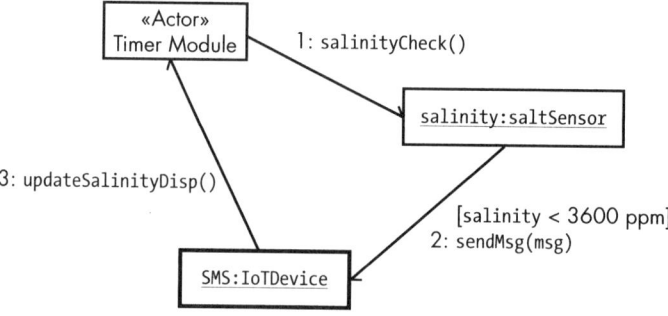

Figure 7-35: A collaboration diagram

The diagram in Figure 7-35 is roughly equivalent to the sequence diagram in Figure 7-9 (without the time constraint of 10 minutes). In Figure 7-35 the salinityCheck message executes first, sendMsg executes second, and updateSalinityDisplay executes last.

Figure 7-36 shows a more complex collaboration diagram that better demonstrates the compactness of this option. The six messages sent in this example would require six lines in a sequence diagram but here require only three communication links.

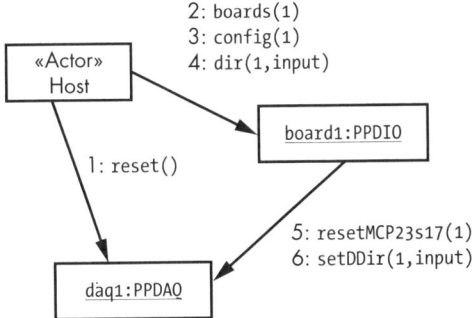

Figure 7-36: A more complex collaboration diagram

NOTE *Having both collaboration and sequence diagrams is probably an artifact of merging different systems together when UML was created. Which one you use is really just a matter of personal preference. Keep in mind, however, that as the diagrams become more complex, collaboration diagrams become harder to follow.*

7.3 For More Information

Bremer, Michael. *The User Manual Manual: How to Research, Write, Test, Edit, and Produce a Software Manual.* Grass Valley, CA: UnTechnical Press, 1999. A sample chapter is available at *http://www.untechnicalpress.com /Downloads/UMM%20sample%20doc.pdf.*

Larman, Craig. *Applying UML and Patterns: An Introduction to Object-Oriented Analysis and Design and Iterative Development.* 3rd ed. Upper Saddle River, NJ: Prentice Hall, 2004.

Miles, Russ, and Kim Hamilton. *Learning UML 2.0: A Pragmatic Introduction to UML.* Sebastopol, CA: O'Reilly Media, 2003.

Pender, Tom. *UML Bible.* Indianapolis: Wiley, 2003.

Pilone, Dan, and Neil Pitman. *UML 2.0 in a Nutshell: A Desktop Quick Reference.* 2nd ed. Sebastopol, CA: O'Reilly Media, 2005.

Roff, Jason T. *UML: A Beginner's Guide.* Berkeley, CA: McGraw-Hill Education, 2003.

Tutorials Point. "UML Tutorial." *https://www.tutorialspoint.com/uml/.*

8

MISCELLANEOUS UML DIAGRAMS

This chapter finishes up the book's discussion of UML by describing five additional diagrams that are useful for UML documentation: component, package, deployment, composite structure, and statechart diagrams.

8.1 Component Diagrams

UML uses *component diagrams* to encapsulate reusable components such as libraries and frameworks. Though components are generally larger and have more responsibilities than classes, they support much of the same functionality as classes, including:

- Generalization and association with other classes and components
- Operations
- Interfaces

UML defines components using a rectangle with the «component» stereotype (see Figure 8-1). Some users (and CASE tools) also use the stereotype «subsystem» to denote components.

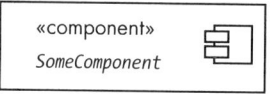

Figure 8-1: A UML component

Components use interfaces (or protocols) to encourage encapsulation and loose coupling. This improves the usability of a component by making its design independent of external objects. The component and the rest of the system communicate via two types of predefined interfaces: provided and required. A *provided* interface is one that the component provides and that external code can use. A *required* interface must be provided for the component by external code. This could be an external function that the component invokes.

As you would expect from UML by now, there's more than one way to draw components: using *stereotype notation* (of which there are two versions) or *ball and socket notation*.

The most compact way to represent a UML component with interfaces is probably the simple form of stereotype notation shown in Figure 8-2, which lists the interfaces inside the component.

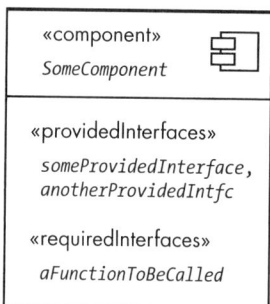

Figure 8-2: A simple form of stereotype notation

Figure 8-3 shows a more complete (though bulkier) version of stereotype notation with individual interface objects in the diagram. This option is better when you want to list the individual attributes of the interfaces.

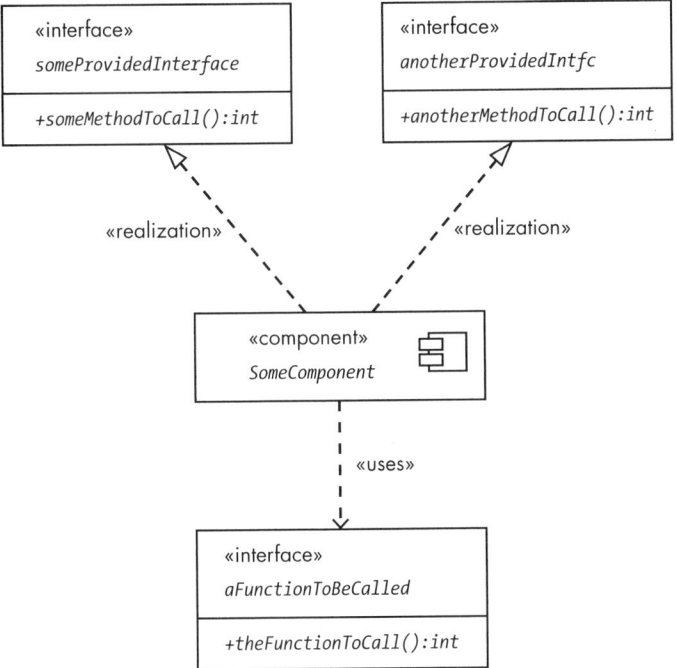

Figure 8-3: A more complete form of stereotype notation

Ball and socket notation provides an alternative to the stereotype notation, using a circle icon (the *ball*) to represent a provided interface and a half-circle (the *socket*) to represent required interfaces (see Figure 8-4).

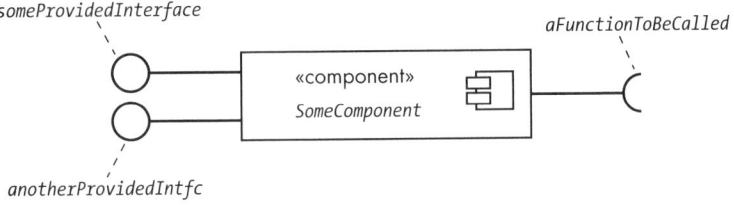

Figure 8-4: Ball and socket notation

The nice thing about ball and socket notation is that connecting components can be visually appealing (see Figure 8-5).

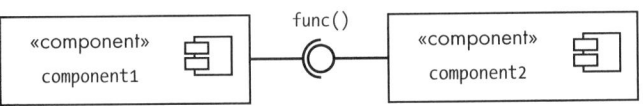

Figure 8-5: Connecting two ball and socket components

As you can see, the required interface of component1 connects nicely with the provided interface of component2 in this diagram. But while ball and socket notation can be more compact and attractive than the stereotype notation, it doesn't scale well beyond a few interfaces. As you add more provided and required interfaces, the stereotyped notation is often a better solution.

8.2   Package Diagrams

A UML package is a container for other UML items (including other packages). A UML package is the equivalent of a subdirectory in a filesystem, a namespace in C++ and C#, or packages in Java and Swift. To define a package in UML, you use a file folder icon with the package name attached (see Figure 8-6).

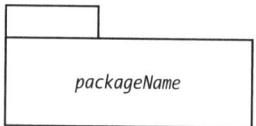

Figure 8-6: A UML package

For a more concrete example, let's return to the pool monitor application. One useful package might be sensors, to contain classes/objects associated with, say, pH and salinity sensors. Figure 8-7 shows what this package might look like in UML. The + prefix on the phSensors and saltSensor objects indicates that these are public objects accessible outside the package.[1]

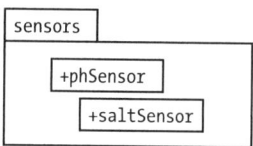

Figure 8-7: The sensors package

To reference (public) objects outside of a package, you use a name of the form *packageName::objectName*. For example, outside the sensors package you would use sensors::pHSensor and sensors::saltSensor to access the internal objects. If you have one package nested inside another, you could access objects in the innermost package using a sequence like *outsidePackage ::internalPackage::object*. For example, suppose you have two nuclear power channels named NP and NPP (from the use case examples in Chapter 4). You could create a package named instruments to hold the two packages NP and NPP. The NP and NPP packages could contain the objects directly associated with the NP and NPP instruments (see Figure 8-8).

---

1. The protected, private, and package visibility prefixes are also valid here with the appropriate meanings.

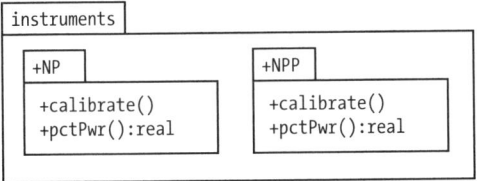

Figure 8-8: Nested packages

Note that the `NP` and `NPP` packages both contain functions named `calibrate()` and `pctPwr()`. There is no ambiguity about which function you're calling because outside these individual packages you have to use *qualified names* to access these functions. For example, outside the `instruments` package you'd have to use names like `instruments::NP::calibrate` and `instruments::NPP::calibrate` so that there is no confusion.

8.3 Deployment Diagrams

Deployment diagrams present a physical view of a system. Physical objects include PCs, peripherals like printers and scanners, servers, plug-in interface boards, and displays.

To represent physical objects, UML uses *nodes*, a 3D box image. Inside the box you place the stereotype «device» plus the name of the node. Figure 8-9 provides a simple example from the DAQ data acquisition system. It shows a host PC connected to a DAQ_IF and a Plantation Productions' PPDIO96 96-channel digital I/O board.

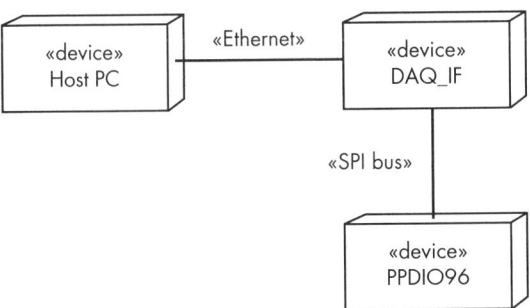

Figure 8-9: A deployment diagram

One thing missing from this figure is the actual software installed on the system. In this system, there are likely to be at least two application programs running: a program running on the host PC that communicates with the DAQ_IF module (let's call it *daqtest.exe*) and the firmware program (*frmwr.hex*) running on the DAQ_IF board (which is likely the true software system the deployment diagram describes). Figure 8-10 shows an expanded version with small icons denoting the software installed on the machines. Deployment diagrams use the stereotype «artifact» to denote binary machine code.

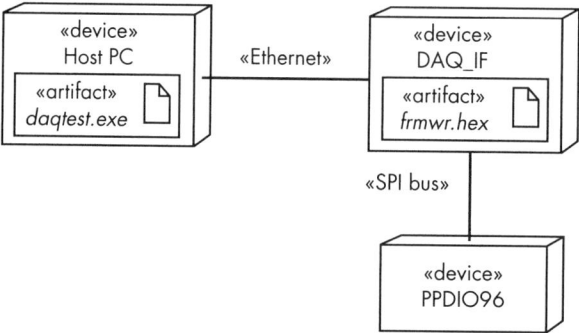

Figure 8-10: An expanded deployment diagram

Note that the PPDIO96 board is directly controlled by the DAQ_IF board: there is no CPU on the PPDIO96 board and, therefore, there is no software loaded onto the PPDIO96.

There is actually quite a bit more to deployment diagrams, but this discussion will suffice for those we'll need in this book. If you're interested, see "For More Information" on page 165 for references that explain deployment diagrams in more detail.

8.4 Composite Structure Diagrams

In some instances, class and sequence diagrams cannot accurately depict the relationships and actions between components in some classes. Consider Figure 8-11, which illustrates a class for the PPDIO96.

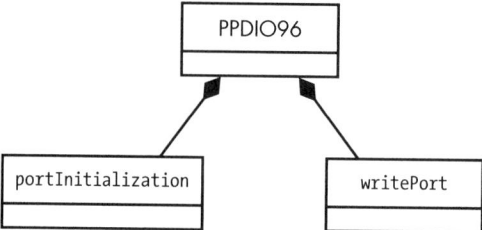

Figure 8-11: PPDIO96 class composition

This class composition diagram tells us that the PPDIO96 class contains (is composed of) two subclasses: portInitialization and writePort. What it does *not* tell us is how these two subclasses of PPDIO96 interact with each other. For example, when you initialize a port via the portInitialization class, perhaps the portInitialization class also invokes a method in writePort to initialize that port with some default value (such as 0). The bare class diagrams don't show this, nor should they. Having portIntialization write a default value via a writePort invocation is probably only one of many different operations that could arise within PPDIO96. Any attempt to show allowed and possible internal communications within PPDIO96 would produce a very messy, illegible diagram.

Composite structure diagrams provide a solution by focusing only on those communication links of interest (it could be just one communication link, or a few, but generally not so many that the diagram becomes incomprehensible).

A first (but problematic) attempt at a composite structure diagram is shown in Figure 8-12.

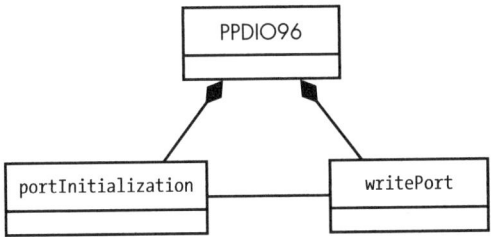

Figure 8-12: Attempted composite structure diagram

The problem with this diagram is that it doesn't explicitly state which writePort object portInitialization is communicating with. Remember, classes are just generic *types*, whereas the actual communication takes place between explicitly instantiated *objects*. In an actual system the intent of Figure 8-12 is probably better conveyed by Figure 8-13.

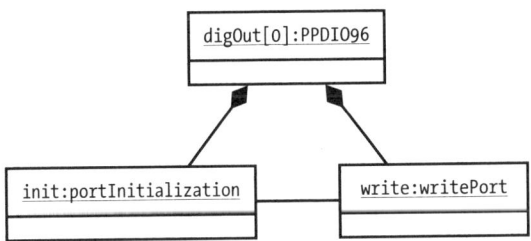

Figure 8-13: Instantiated composite structure diagram

However, neither Figure 8-12 nor Figure 8-13 implies that the portInitialization and writePort instantiated objects belong specifically to the PPDIO96 object. For example, if there are two sets of PPDIO96, portInitialization, and writePort objects, the topology in Figure 8-14 is perfectly valid based on the class diagram in Figure 8-12.

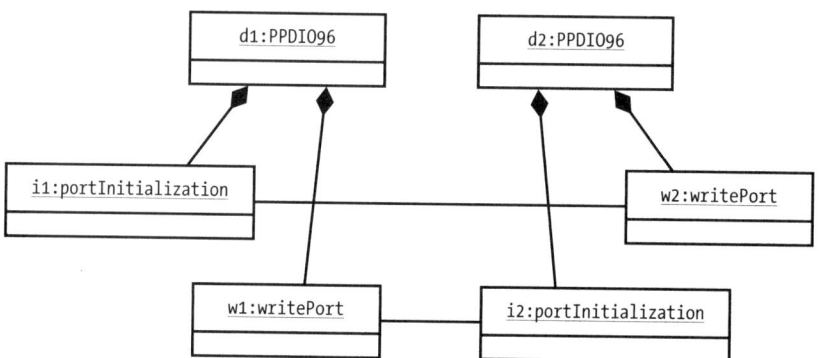

Figure 8-14: Weird, but legal, communication links

In this example, i1 (which belongs to object d1) calls w2 (which belongs to object d2) to write the digital value to its port; i2 (which belongs to d2) calls w1 to write its initial value to its port. This probably isn't what the original designer had in mind, even though the generic composition structure diagram in Figure 8-12 technically allows it. Although any reasonable programmer would immediately realize that i1 should be invoking w1 and i2 should be invoking w2, the composite structure diagram doesn't make this clear. Obviously, we want to eliminate as much ambiguity as possible in our designs.

To correct this shortcoming, UML 2.0 provides (true) composite structure diagrams that incorporate the member attributes directly within the encapsulating class diagram, as shown in Figure 8-15.

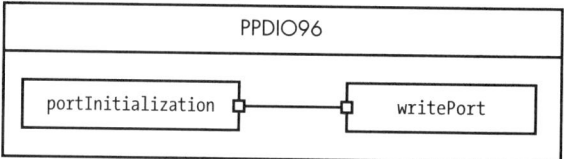

Figure 8-15: Composite structure diagram

This diagram makes it clear that an instantiated object of PPDIO96 will constrain the communication between the portInitialization and writePort classes to objects associated with that same instance.

The small squares on the sides of the portInitialization and writePort are *ports*. This term is unrelated to the writePort object or hardware ports on the PPDIO96 in general; this is a UML concept referring to an interaction point between two objects in UML. Ports can appear in composite structure diagrams and in component diagrams (see "Component Diagrams" on page 155) to specify required or provided interfaces to an object. In Figure 8-15 the port on the portInitialization side is (probably) a required interface and the port on the writePort side of the connection is (probably) a provided interface.

> **NOTE** *On either side of a connection, one port will generally be a required interface and the other will be a provided interface.*

In Figure 8-15 the ports are *anonymous*. However, in many diagrams (particularly where you are listing the interfaces to a system) you can attach names to the ports (see Figure 8-16).

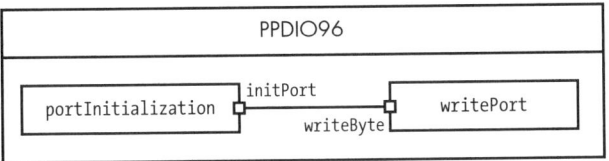

Figure 8-16: Named ports

You can also use the ball and socket notation to indicate which side of a communication link is the provider and which side has the required interface (remember, the socket side denotes the required interface; the ball side denotes the provided interface). You can even name the communication link if you so desire (see Figure 8-17). A typical communication link takes the form *name:type* where *name* is a unique name (within the component) and *type* is the type of the communication link.

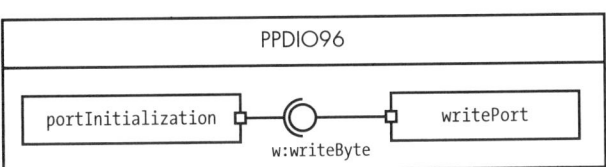

Figure 8-17: Indicating provided and required interfaces

8.5 Statechart Diagrams

UML statechart (or state machine) diagrams are very similar to activity diagrams in that they show the flow of control through a system. The main difference is that a statechart diagram simply shows the various states possible for a system and how the system transitions from one state to the next.

Statechart diagrams do not introduce any new diagramming symbols; they use existing elements from activity diagrams—specifically the start state, end state, state transitions, state symbols, and (optionally) decision symbols, as shown in Figure 8-18.

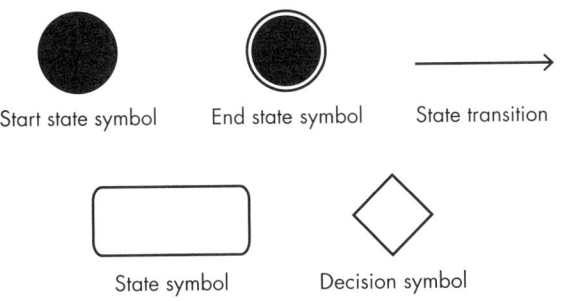

Figure 8-18: Elements of a statechart diagram

A given statechart diagram will have exactly one *start state* symbol; this is where activity begins. The state symbols in a statechart diagram always have an associated state name (which, obviously, indicates the current state). A statechart diagram can have more than one *end state* symbol, which is a special state that marks the end of activity (entry into any end state symbol stops the state machine). Transition arrows show the flow between states in the machine (see Figure 8-19).

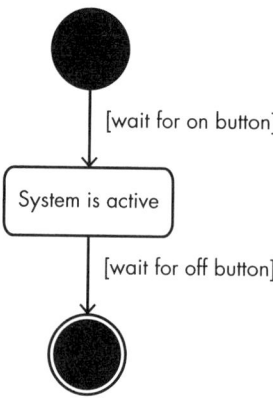

Figure 8-19: A simple statechart diagram

Transitions usually occur in response to some external events, or triggers, in the system. *Triggers* are stimuli that cause the transition from one state to another in the system. You attach guard conditions to a transition, as shown in Figure 8-19, to indicate the trigger that causes the transition to take place.

Transition arrows have a head and a tail. When activity occurs in a statechart diagram, transitions always occur from the state attached to the arrow tail to the state pointed at by the arrowhead.

If you are in a particular state and some event occurs for which there is no transition out of that state, the state machine ignores that event.[2] For example, in Figure 8-19, if you're already in the "System is active" state and an on button event occurs, the system remains in the "System is active" state.

If two transitions out of a state have the same guard condition, then the state machine is *nondeterministic*. This means that the choice of transition arrow is arbitrary (and could be randomly chosen). Nondeterminism is a bad thing in UML statechart diagrams, as it introduces ambiguity. When creating UML statechart diagrams, you should always strive to keep them deterministic by ensuring that the transitions all have mutually exclusive guard conditions. In theory, you should have exactly one exiting transition from a state for every possible event that could occur; however, most system

---

2. Technically, we should put a transition arrow from a state back to that same state labeled else to handle this situation; however, the else condition is implied in UML statechart diagrams.

designers assume that, as mentioned before, if an event occurs for which there is no exit transition, then the state ignores that event.

It is possible to have a transition from one state to another without a guard condition attached; this implies that the system can arbitrarily move from the first state (at the transition's tail) to the second state (at the head). This is useful when you're using decision symbols in a state machine (see Figure 8-20). Decision symbols aren't necessary in a statechart diagram—just as for activity diagrams, you could have multiple transitions directly out of a state (such as the "System is active" state in Figure 8-20)—but you can sometimes clean up your diagrams by using them.

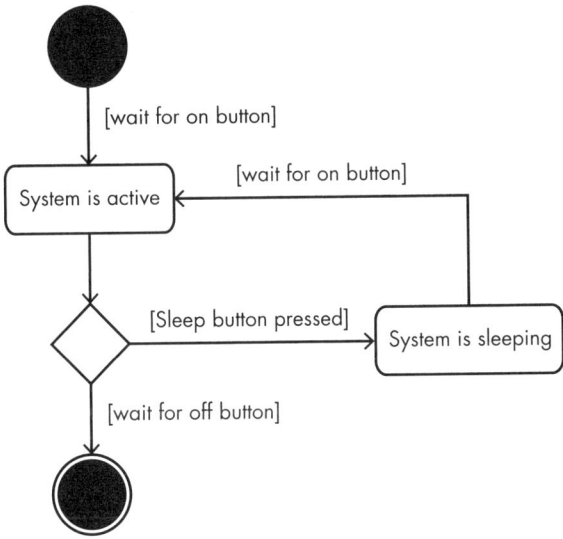

Figure 8-20: A decision symbol in a statechart

8.6   More UML

As has been a constant theme, this is but a brief introduction to UML. There are more diagrams and other features, such as the *Object Constraint Language (OCL)*, that this book won't use, so this chapter doesn't discuss them. However, if you're interested in using UML to document your software projects, you should spend more time learning about it. See the next section for recommended reading.

8.7   For More Information

Bremer, Michael. *The User Manual Manual: How to Research, Write, Test, Edit, and Produce a Software Manual.* Grass Valley, CA: UnTechnical Press, 1999. A sample chapter is available at *http://www.untechnicalpress.com /Downloads/UMM%20sample%20doc.pdf.*

Larman, Craig. *Applying UML and Patterns: An Introduction to Object-Oriented Analysis and Design and Iterative Development.* 3rd ed. Upper Saddle River, NJ: Prentice Hall, 2004.

Miles, Russ, and Kim Hamilton. *Learning UML 2.0: A Pragmatic Introduction to UML.* Sebastopol, CA: O'Reilly Media, 2003.

Pender, Tom. *UML Bible.* Indianapolis: Wiley, 2003.

Pilone, Dan, and Neil Pitman. *UML 2.0 in a Nutshell: A Desktop Quick Reference.* 2nd ed. Sebastopol, CA: O'Reilly Media, 2005.

Roff, Jason T. *UML: A Beginner's Guide.* Berkeley, CA: McGraw-Hill Education, 2003.

Tutorials Point. "UML Tutorial." *https://www.tutorialspoint.com/uml/.*

PART III

DOCUMENTATION

9

SYSTEM DOCUMENTATION

System documentation specifies system requirements, design, test cases, and test procedures. In a large software system, the system documentation is often the most expensive part; the Waterfall software development model, for example, often produces more documentation than code. In addition, typically you must maintain system documentation manually, so if you change a description (such as a requirement) in one document, you'll need to search through the system documentation and update every other document that references that description for consistency. This is a difficult and costly process.

In this chapter, we'll look at the common types of system documents, ways to enforce consistency within them, and documentation strategies to reduce some of the costs associated with development.

NOTE *This chapter discusses* system *documentation, not* user *documentation. To learn about user documentation in detail, check out "For More Information" on page 184.*

9.1 System Documentation Types

Traditional software engineering generally uses the following system documentation types:

System Requirements Specification (SyRS) document
   The SyRS (see "The System Requirements Specification Document" on page 193) is a *system-level* requirements document. In addition to software requirements, it might include hardware, business, procedural, manual, and other non-software-related requirements. The SyRS is a customer/management/stakeholder-level document that eschews detail to present a "big picture" view of the requirements.

Software Requirements Specification (SRS) document
   The SRS (see "The Software Requirements Specification Document" on page 194) extracts the software requirements[1] from the SyRS and drills down on the high-level requirements to introduce new requirements at a much finer level of detail (suitable for software engineers).

> **NOTE** *The SyRS and SRS are* requirements *documents whose content may differ in scope and detail. Many organizations produce a single document rather than two separate ones, but this book treats them separately because the SyRS deals with a wider range of requirements (for example, hardware and business requirements) than the SRS.*

Software Design Description (SDD) document
   The SDD (see Chapter 11) discusses *how* the system will be constructed (versus the SyRS and SRS, which describe *what* the system will do). In theory, any programmer should be able to use the SDD and write the corresponding code to implement the software system.

Software Test Cases (STC) document
   The STC (see "Software Test Case Documentation" on page 274) describes the various test values needed to verify that the system incorporates all the requirements, and functions correctly beyond the requirements list.

Software Test Procedures (STP) document
   The STP (see "Software Test Procedure Documentation" on page 288) describes the procedures to efficiently execute the software test cases (from the STC) to verify correct system operation.

Requirements (or Reverse) Traceability Matrix (RTM) document
   The RTM (see "The Requirements/Reverse Traceability Matrix" on page 178) links the requirements against the design, test cases, and

---

1. Hardware requirements might be extracted to a Hardware Requirements Specification (HRS), and other requirement types might be likewise extracted to their own specialized documents. Those documents are beyond the scope of this book.

code. Using an RTM, a stakeholder can verify that a requirement is implemented in the design and the code, and that the test cases and procedures properly check that requirement's implementation.

NOTE *Some organizations might also have a* Functional Requirements Specification *document; this often refers to the requirements that an external customer provides, or it can simply be a synonym for the SRS or SyRS. This book won't use this term further.*

There are many additional types of documents, but these are the basic ones you'd expect for any (non-XP, at least) project, and they correspond to the various stages of the Waterfall model (see "The Waterfall Model" on page 44), as shown in Figure 9-1.

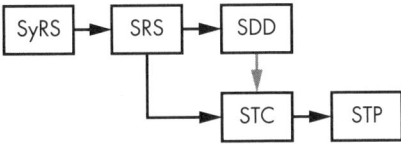

Figure 9-1: System documentation dependencies

As you can see, the SRS is constructed from the SyRS. The SDD is constructed from the SRS, as is the STC (which, in some cases, is also influenced by the SDD, as indicated by the gray arrow[2]). The STP is constructed from the STC.

9.2 Traceability

Perhaps the greatest logistical issue with system documentation is consistency. A requirement typically generates some design item and a test case (which is part of a test procedure in the STP). This is an intuitive and natural progression when you're following a strict Waterfall model—writing the SRS first, followed by the SDD, the STC, and the SDD. However, problems arise when you have to make corrections to documents earlier in this chain. For example, when you change a requirement, you might need to change entries in the SDD, STC, and STP documents. Best practice is therefore to use *traceability*, which allows you to easily trace items from one document to all the other system documents. If you can trace your requirements to design elements, test cases, and test procedures, you can rapidly locate and change those elements whenever you modify a requirement.

Reverse traceability allows you to trace a test procedure back to the corresponding test cases, and test cases and design items back to their corresponding requirements. For example, you might encounter problems with a test that require changes to the test procedure, in which case you can locate the corresponding test cases and requirements to ensure that your changes

---

2. While the STC can be *influenced* by the SDD, it's *generated* from the SRS, because you create test cases from the requirements, not from the design. Any test cases constructed from the SDD will come from design entities originating from requirements.

to the test procedure still handle all of them. In this way, reverse traceability also helps you determine whether you need to make changes to the test cases or requirements.

9.2.1 Ways to Build Traceability into Your Documentation

There are a couple of ways to accomplish traceability and reverse traceability. One approach is to build the traceability into an *identifier*, or *tag*, associated with the requirement, design element, test case, or test procedure documentation. This tag could be a paragraph (or item) number, a descriptive word, or some other set of symbols that uniquely identify the text to reference. Software documents that use tags avoid wasting space by directly quoting other documents.

Often authors use paragraph numbers as tags, which is really easy to do in a word processing system. However, many word processors don't support cross-referencing across multiple document types. Also, the tagging mechanism or format you want to use might not match what the word processor provides.

Although it's possible to write custom software, or use a database application to extract and maintain cross-reference information, the most common solution is to maintain tags manually. This might sound as though it would require considerable effort, but with a little planning, it isn't very difficult.

Perhaps the best solution is to create an RTM (see "The Requirements/Reverse Traceability Matrix" on page 178), which tracks the links between the items in your system documentation. Although the RTM is yet another document you'll have to maintain, it provides a complete and easy-to-use mechanism for tracking all the components in your system.

We'll first talk through common tag formats, and then we'll look into building an RTM.

9.2.2 Tag Formats

There is no particular standard for tag syntax; tags can take any form you like as long as the syntax is consistent and each tag is unique. For my own purposes (and for this book), I've created a syntax that incorporates elements of traceability directly into the tag. The tag formats that follow are organized by document type.

9.2.2.1 SyRS Tags

For the SyRS, a tag takes the form [*productID*_SYRS_*xxx*] where:

> ***productID***   Refers to the product or project. For example, for a swimming pool monitor application, *productID* might be "POOL." You don't want to use a long ID (four to five characters should be the maximum length) because it will be typed frequently.
>
> **SYRS**   States that this is a tag from the SyRS document (this is probably a system requirements tag).

xxx   Represents one or more numbers, separated by periods if more than one integer is used. This numeric sequence uniquely identifies the tag within the SyRS.

In a perfect world, all the SyRS requirements (and other items requiring a tag) would be numbered sequentially from 1 with no correlation between the integers and the meanings of the text blocks to which they refer.

Consider the following two requirements in an SyRS document:

[POOL_SYRS_001]: Pool temperature monitoring

The system shall monitor the pool temperature.

[POOL_SYRS_002]: Maximum pool temperature

The system shall turn on the "High Temp" LED if the pool temperature exceeds 86 degrees Fahrenheit.

Let's say that 150 additional requirements follow [POOL_SYRS_002].

Now suppose that someone suggests a requirement that the pool heater be turned on if the pool temperature drops below 70 degrees Fahrenheit. You could add the following requirements:

[POOL_SYRS_153]: Minimum pool temperature

The system shall turn on the pool heater if the pool temperature drops below 70 degrees Fahrenheit.

[POOL_SYRS_154]: Maximum heater on temperature

The system shall turn off the pool heater if the pool temperature exceeds 70 degrees Fahrenheit.

In the SyRS, it makes sense to arrange related requirements close to one another, so the reader can locate all the pertinent requirements for a given feature at one point in the document. You can see why you wouldn't want to sort the requirements by their tags—doing so would push the two new requirements for the pool heater to the end of the document, away from the other pool temperature requirements.

There's nothing stopping you from moving the requirements together; however, it's somewhat confusing to see a set of requirements like this:

[POOL_SYRS_001]: Pool temperature monitoring

The system shall monitor the pool temperature.

[POOL_SYRS_153]: Minimum pool temperature

The system shall turn on the pool heater if the pool temperature drops below 70 degrees Fahrenheit.

[POOL_SYRS_154]: Maximum heater on temperature

The system shall turn off the pool heater if the pool temperature exceeds 70 degrees Fahrenheit.

[POOL_SYRS_002]: Maximum pool temperature
　　The system shall turn on the "High Temp" LED if the pool temperature exceeds 86 degrees Fahrenheit.

　　A better solution is to renumber the tags using *dotted sequences* to expand the tag numbers. A dotted sequence consists of two or more integers separated by a dot. For example:

[POOL_SYRS_001]: Pool temperature monitoring
　　The system shall monitor the pool temperature.

[POOL_SYRS_001.1]: Minimum pool temperature
　　The system shall turn on the pool heater if the pool temperature drops below 70 degrees Fahrenheit.

[POOL_SYRS_001.2]: Maximum heater on temperature
　　The system shall turn off the pool heater if the pool temperature exceeds 70 degrees Fahrenheit.

[POOL_SYRS_002]: Maximum pool temperature
　　The system shall turn on the "High Temp" LED if the pool temperature exceeds 86 degrees Fahrenheit.

　　This allows you to flow in new requirements or changes anywhere. Note that 001.1 and 001.10 are not the same. These numbers are not floating-point numeric values; they're two integers separated by a period. The number 001.10 is probably the 10th value in the sequence 001.1 through 001.10. Likewise, 001 is not the same as 001.0.

　　If you need to insert a requirement between 001.1 and 001.2, you can simply add another period to the end of the sequence, such as 001.1.1. You can also leave gaps between your tag numbers if you expect to insert additional tags in the future, like so:

[POOL_SYRS_010]: Pool temperature monitoring
　　The system shall monitor the pool temperature.

[POOL_SYRS_020]: Maximum pool temperature
　　The system shall turn on the "High Temp" LED if the pool temperature exceeds 86 degrees Fahrenheit.

　　So when you decide to add the other two requirements, you have:

[POOL_SYRS_010]: Pool temperature monitoring
　　The system shall monitor the pool temperature.

[POOL_SYRS_013]: Minimum pool temperature
　　The system shall turn on the pool heater if the pool temperature drops below 70 degrees Fahrenheit.

[POOL_SYRS_017]: Maximum heater on temperature
The system shall turn off the pool heater if the pool temperature exceeds 70 degrees Fahrenheit.

[POOL_SYRS_020]: Maximum pool temperature
The system shall turn on the "High Temp" LED if the pool temperature exceeds 86 degrees Fahrenheit.

Keep in mind that it's important to make all the tags unique.

NOTE *Thus far in this section, tags have been part of a paragraph title, which is useful when people want to search for the tags within the document (particularly, if the document is not in electronic form). However, you can also place tags within paragraphs.*

9.2.2.2 SRS Tags

For system document sets that have only the SRS—not an SyRS—as the requirements document, "SRS" can simply replace "SYRS" in the tag: [POOL_SRS_010]: Pool temperature monitoring.

However, when a project's document set includes both an SyRS and an SRS, this book uses a convention that builds reverse traceability from the SRS to the SyRS directly into the SRS tag. Such SRS tags have the format [*productID*_SRS_*xxx*_*yyy*].

The *productID* is the same as for the SyRS tag: SRS denotes a Software Requirements Specification tag (versus a System Requirements Specification tag), and *xxx* and *yyy* are decimal numbers, where *xxx* is the number of a corresponding SyRS tag (see "SyRS Tags" on page 172).

Including the tag number of the parent SyRS requirement embeds reverse traceability information for an SRS requirement directly into its tag. Because almost all SRS requirements are derived from a corresponding SyRS tag, and there is a one-to-many relationship between SyRS requirements and SRS requirements, a single SyRS requirement can generate one or more SRS requirements, but each SRS requirement can be traced back to just one SyRS requirement, as shown in Figure 9-2.

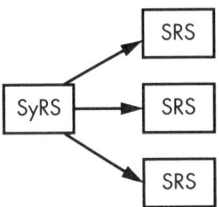

Figure 9-2: An SyRS-to-SRS relationship

The *yyy* component is the SRS tag value. As a general rule (and the convention this book follows), *yyy* doesn't have to be unique among all the SRS tags, but the combination *xxx_yyy* must be unique. The following are all valid (and unique) SRS tags:

[POOL_SRS_020_001]

[POOL_SRS_020_001.5]

[POOL_SRS_020_002]

[POOL_SRS_030.1_005]

[POOL_SRS_031_003]

This book also uses the convention of restarting the *yyy* numbering with each *xxx* value.

By constructing SRS tags this way, you build automatic reverse traceability from the SRS to the SyRS directly into the tag identifier. To locate the SyRS requirement associated with an SRS requirement, just extract the *xxx* value and search for the corresponding tag in your SyRS document. It's also easy to locate SRS tags associated with an SyRS tag in the SRS document. For example, to find all SRS requirements associated with POOL_SYRS_030, search for all instances of "SRS_030" in your SRS document.

It's possible that an SRS document might produce some brand-new requirements that are not based on a specific SyRS requirement. If so, there won't be an *xxx* number to use as part of the SRS tag. This book reserves SyRS tag number 000 (that is, there will never be an SyRS tag [*productID*_SYRS_000]), and any new SRS requirement that isn't based on an SyRS requirement will take the form [*productID*_SRS_000_*yyy*].

NOTE *Another convention this book uses is to substitute an asterisk (*) in place of the 000 value.*

It's a good idea to include all software-related requirements from the SyRS directly in the SRS.[3] This allows the SRS to serve as a stand-alone document for software developers to use. When copying SyRS requirements directly into the SRS, we'll use the syntax [*productID*_SRS_*xxx*_000] for the copied requirement tags. That is, a *yyy* value of 000 denotes a copied tag.

9.2.2.3 SDD Tags

Unfortunately, there is not a one-to-many relationship between SRS requirements and SDD design elements.[4] That makes it more difficult to build reverse traceability from an SDD tag to the corresponding SRS tag

---

3. Keep in mind that the SyRS might contain hardware and other non-software-related requirements that wouldn't be copied to the SRS; for more information, see "The Requirements/Reverse Traceability Matrix" on page 178, particularly the description of allocations.

4. In well-designed systems, there can be a many-to-one relationship between requirements and design items; in the worst case, there is a many-to-many relationship.

into the SDD tag syntax. You'll have to rely on an external RTM document to provide the links between the SRS and SDD documents.

Given that reverse traceability is not practical in the SDD tag, this book uses the simplified SDD tag format [*productID*_SDD_*ddd*], where *productID* has the usual meaning, and *ddd* is a unique identifier similar to *xxx* in the SyRS tag.

9.2.2.4 STC Tags

There should be a one-to-many relationship between SRS requirements and STC test cases, as shown in Figure 9-3.

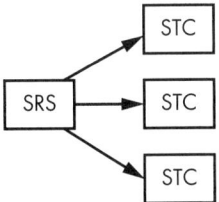

Figure 9-3: An SRS-to-STC tag relationship

This means you can build reverse traceability from the STC to the SRS into the tags, just as you did from the SRS to the SyRS. For STC tags, this book uses the syntax [*productID*_STC_*xxx*_*yyy*_*zzz*]. If all your *yyy* values were unique (rather than the *xxx*_*yyy* combination being unique), you could drop the *xxx* from the tag, but having both *xxx* and *yyy* does provide reverse traceability to both the SRS and SyRS, which can be convenient (at the expense of extra typing for your STC tags).

Although it rarely occurs, it's possible to create a unique test case that isn't based on any SRS requirement.[5] For example, the software engineers using the SDD to implement the code might create test cases based on the source code they write. In such situations, this book uses the scheme shown previously for SRS requirements that aren't based on an SyRS requirement: we reserve the *xxx*_*yyy* value of 000_000 or *_*, and any new STC tags that aren't based on a requirement tag will use 000 as the tag number suffix. An *xxx*_000 component means that the test case is based on an SyRS requirement but not any underlying SRS requirement (or perhaps it's based on the SRS tag copied from the SyRS using the syntax shown earlier); this is not a stand-alone test case.

---

5. Generally, if you need to test something, a requirement should be driving that test. However, you might derive some test cases from the SDD rather than directly from the SRS. For example, the requirements generally don't state details such as whether a coder should use an array or a dictionary (lookup table) to implement some operation. The SDD, on the other hand, might specify a particular data structure such as an array. This could lead to a test case that tests to ensure the program doesn't violate the bounds of the array when indexing into it.

STC tags that have the numeric form 000_000 don't contain any traceability information. In such cases, you'll need to explicitly provide link information to describe the origin of the test case. Here are a few suggestions:

- Use *:source* after the tag to describe the source of the test case (where *source* is the name of the file or other document containing the information producing the test case).
- Use an RTM to provide the source information (see the next section, "The Requirements/Reverse Traceability Matrix," for more details).
- Ensure that the document containing the source of the test case contains a comment or other link specifying the STC tag.

9.2.2.5 STP Tags

STC test cases have a many-to-one relationship with STP test procedures, as shown in Figure 9-4.

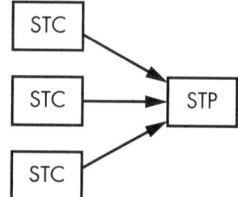

Figure 9-4: An STC-to-STP tag relationship

This means, as with the SDD, you can't encode reverse traceability information into the STP tags. Therefore, for STP tags this book uses the syntax [*productID*_STP_*ppp*], where *productID* has the usual meaning, and *ppp* is a unique STP tag value.

9.2.3 The Requirements/Reverse Traceability Matrix

As mentioned, it isn't possible to build reverse traceability into the SDD and STP tags, so you'll need the Requirements/Reverse Traceability Matrix (RTM).

As its name implies, an RTM is a two-dimensional matrix, or table, wherein:

- Each row specifies a link between requirements, design items, test cases, or test procedures.
- Each column specifies a particular document (SyRS, SRS, SDD, STC, or STP).
- Each cell contains the tag for the associated document type.

A typical row in the table might contain entries such as the following:

| POOL_SYRS_020 | POOL_SRS_020_001 | POOL_SDD_005 | POOL_STC_020_001_001 | POOL_STP_005 |

In general, the SyRS or SRS requirement tags drive the RTM, and you'd usually organize the table by sorting it via these columns.

Because there is a one-to-many relationship between SyRS requirements and SRS requirements, you might need to replicate the SyRS requirements across multiple rows, as in this example:

1	POOL_SYRS_020	POOL_SRS_020_001	POOL_SDD_005	POOL_STC_020_001_001	POOL_STP_005
2	POOL_SYRS_020	POOL_SRS_020_002	POOL_SDD_005	POOL_STC_020_002_001	POOL_STP_005
3	POOL_SYRS_020	POOL_SRS_020_003	POOL_SDD_005	POOL_STC_020_003_001	POOL_STP_004
4	POOL_SYRS_020	POOL_SRS_020_003	POOL_SDD_005	POOL_STC_020_003_002	POOL_STP_006
5	POOL_SYRS_030	POOL_SRS_030_001	POOL_SDD_006	POOL_STC_030_001_001	POOL_STP_010

Rows 1, 2, and 3 share the same SyRS tag with different SRS tags; rows 3 and 4 share the same SRS tags (and SyRS tags) with differing STC tags.

Sometimes, it might be cleaner to omit duplicate SyRS and SRS tags when they can be inferred from previous rows, like so:

1	POOL_SYRS_020	POOL_SRS_020_001	POOL_SDD_005	POOL_STC_020_001_001	POOL_STP_005
2		POOL_SRS_020_002	POOL_SDD_005	POOL_STC_020_002_001	POOL_STP_005
3		POOL_SRS_020_003	POOL_SDD_005	POOL_STC_020_003_001	POOL_STP_004
4			POOL_SDD_005	POOL_STC_020_003_002	POOL_STP_006
5	POOL_SYRS_030	POOL_SRS_030_001	POOL_SDD_006	POOL_STC_030_001_001	POOL_STP_010

Although you could create an RTM using a word processor (for example, Microsoft Word or Apple Pages), a far better solution is to use a spreadsheet program (for example, Microsoft Excel or Apple Numbers) or a database application, which allows you to easily sort the rows in the table based on your current requirements. This book assumes you're using a spreadsheet program.

9.2.3.1 Adding Extra Columns

At a bare minimum, you'll want one column in the RTM for each system document type—SyRS (if present), SRS, SDD, STC, and STP—but you might want to include other information in the RTM as well. For example, you might consider a "Description" column that can help make sense of all the tags.

Or, if you have an SyRS document, an "Allocations" column might be useful to specify whether an SyRS item is hardware, software, or other. Note that SRS, SDD, STP, and STC (by definition) are always software related, so the Allocations entry would be either "N/A" (not applicable) or always "software" for such tags.

Another useful column might be "Verification," which describes how a particular requirement might be tested (or verified) in the system. Examples of verification types might be test (as part of a software test procedure), by review, by inspection, by design, by analysis, other, or no test possible.

One last option is an additional column (or columns) containing some row numbers you can use to quickly sort data in different ways. For example, you might add a column numbered 1 through *n* (where *n* is the number of rows) that, when sorted, lists the rows in order of requirements (SyRS and SRS); another column numbered 1 through *n* that could order the rows by SDD tag values; and so on.

9.2.3.2 Sorting the RTM

Of course, if you fill in every cell in the matrix, you can sort by column values (or multiple column values). For example, suppose you're using Microsoft Excel and the columns are organized as follows:

- A: Description
- B: SyRS tags
- C: Allocations
- D: SRS tags
- E: Testing method
- F: SDD tags
- G: STC tags
- H: STP tags

Sorting by column B, then by D, then by G, will sort the document in requirements order. Sorting by column F, then by B, then by D, will sort the document in design element order. Sorting by column H, then by D, then by G, will sort the document in test procedure order.

To use the RTM to trace from an SyRS or SRS requirement to an SRS requirement, SDD design item, STC test case, or STP test procedure, simply sort the matrix by requirements order, find the SyRS or SRS tag you're interested in, and then pick out the corresponding tag(s) for the other document(s) from the same row as the requirement tag. You can use this same scheme to trace from STC tags to the corresponding test procedure (because the requirements sort will also sort the test case tags).

Reverse traceability from STC to SRS to SyRS is inherent in the tag syntax, so nothing special is needed for this operation. Reverse traceability from the SDD to the SRS (or SyRS) and from the STP to the STC/SRS/SyRS is a little more involved. First, sort the matrix by SDD tag order or STP tag order. This will give you a list of SDD or STP tags all collected together (and sorted in lexicographical order). Now all the tags on the rows containing a particular SDD or STP tag will be the tags of interest to you. The following example shows the previous RTM examples sorted by test procedure:

3	POOL_SYRS_020	POOL_SRS_020_003	POOL_SDD_005	POOL_STC_020_003_001	POOL_STP_004
1	POOL_SYRS_020	POOL_SRS_020_001	POOL_SDD_005	POOL_STC_020_001_001	POOL_STP_005
2	POOL_SYRS_020	POOL_SRS_020_002	POOL_SDD_005	POOL_STC_020_002_001	POOL_STP_005
4	POOL_SYRS_020	POOL_SRS_020_003	POOL_SDD_005	POOL_STC_020_003_002	POOL_STP_006
5	POOL_SYRS_030	POOL_SRS_030_001	POOL_SDD_006	POOL_STC_030_001_001	POOL_STP_010

In this table, you can easily see that test procedure 005 is associated with SyRS tag 020 and SRS tags 020_001 and 020_002. In this simple example, you wouldn't have to sort the data to determine these links. But with a more complex RTM (with dozens, hundreds, or even thousands of requirements), it would be significantly more work to manually search for these reverse links if the table wasn't sorted by STP tags.

9.3 Validation, Verification, and Reviews

Validation (see "The Iterative Model" on page 46) is the process of showing that the product meets the end users' needs (that is, "Are we building the right product?"), while verification is ensuring that you've built it to satisfy the project specifications (that is, "Are we building the product right?"). While validation takes place at the end of the requirements phase(s) and at the end of the entire development cycle (see "Reducing Costs via Validation" on page 182), verification typically occurs at the end of each phase in the software development process to ensure that the phase respects all the input requirements. For example, verification of the SDD would consist of ensuring that it covers all the requirements in the SRS document (the SRS requirements are the input to the SDD stage).

The verification steps for each phase are as follows:

SyRS/SRS Ensuring that the requirements in the document fully cover all the requirements provided by the customer—perhaps from UML use cases (see "The UML Use Case Model" on page 74) or the customer's functional specification.

SDD Ensuring that the design covers all requirements. The input is the requirements from the SRS.

STC Ensuring that at least one test case exists for each (testable) requirement. The inputs are the requirements from the SRS.

STP Ensuring that all the test cases are covered by the test procedures. The inputs are the test cases from the STC (and, indirectly, the requirements on which the test cases are based).

To verify each preceding phase, you'll need to review the document resulting from it. The RTM will prove useful during these reviews. For example, when reviewing the SDD, you'd search for each requirement in the SRS, look up the corresponding SDD tag, and then verify that the design element implements the specified requirement. You'd use the same process to verify that the STC document covers all the requirements with test cases.

When you're reviewing the code, the safest approach is to go through all the inputs to a phase (that is, requirements for the SDD and STC, and test cases for the STP) and physically check each input off after verifying that you properly handled it. This final list becomes part of the review document for that phase.

In the review process, you should also confirm the correctness of the outputs from the phase. For example, when reviewing the SRS, you should check each requirement to make sure it's useful (see "The Software Requirements Specification Document" on page 194); when reviewing the SDD, you should make sure each design item is correct (for example, you're using suitable algorithms and handling concurrent operations appropriately); when reviewing the STC documentation, you should ensure each test case properly tests the associated requirement; and when reviewing the STP, you should verify that each test procedure properly tests its associated test cases.

If at all possible, and for the best results, an engineer other than the document author should conduct the final, formal review, or a second engineer should participate in the review process. The document author is more likely to gloss over an omission, because they're too close to that portion of the project and could mentally fill in missing elements during the review. Of course, they should do their own review of the document prior to submitting it for formal review.

9.4 Reducing Development Costs Using Documentation

Documentation costs are often a major component of a project's overall cost. Part of the reason is that there is so *much* documentation. But another reason is that the documents are interdependent, which makes them difficult to update and maintain. In *Code Complete* (Microsoft Press, 2004), Steve McConnell reports that, compared to the requirements phase, correcting errors is 3 times more expensive during the design (architectural) phase, 5 to 10 times more expensive during coding, and 10 times more expensive during system testing. There a couple of reasons for this:

- If you fix a defect early in the development process, you don't waste time writing additional documentation, coding, and testing defective designs. For example, it takes time to write the SDD documentation for a requirement, to write code to implement that requirement, to write test cases and test procedures for the requirement, and to run those tests. If the requirement was wrong to begin with, you've wasted all that effort.
- If you discover a defective item in one phase of the system, you have to locate and edit anything associated with that defect throughout the rest of the system. This can be laborious work, and it's easy to miss changes, which creates inconsistencies and other problems down the line.

9.4.1 Reducing Costs via Validation

Nowhere is the validation activity more important than in the requirements phase (SyRS and SRS development). If you insist that the customer understands and approves all requirements before moving on to later phases, you can ensure there are no unwanted requirements and that you're solving the customer's problems. Few things are worse than spending several months documenting, coding, and testing a program's feature only to have the customer say, "This isn't what we were asking for." A good validation process can help reduce the likelihood of this scenario.

Validation, which should take place at the end of the requirements phase(s) and at the end of the development cycle, involves asking the following questions:

SyRS (if present)

1. Is each existing requirement important? Does the requirement describe some feature that the customer wants?
2. Is each requirement correct? Does it precisely state (without ambiguity) exactly what the customer wants?
3. Are there any missing requirements?

SRS

1. Are all software requirements listed in the SyRS (if present) also listed in the SRS?
2. Is each existing requirement important? Is this feature important to the system architect and agreed upon by the customer?
3. Is each requirement correct? Does it precisely state (without ambiguity) exactly what the software must do to be effective?
4. Are there any missing requirements?

During final acceptance testing, the test engineer(s) should have a list of all the requirements in the SRS in a checkbox form. They should check off each requirement as it's tested (perhaps when following the test procedures in the STP) to ensure that the software implements it correctly.

9.4.2 Reducing Costs via Verification

As mentioned in "Validation, Verification, and Reviews" on page 181, verification should occur after each phase of the software development process. In particular, there should be a verification step associated with each of the system documents after the SRS. Here are some questions you might ask after completing each document:

SDD

1. Do the design components completely cover all the requirements in the SRS?
2. Is there a many-to-one (or one-to-one) relationship between requirements (many) and software design elements (one)? Although a design item might satisfy multiple requirements, it should not take multiple design elements to satisfy a single requirement.
3. Does a software design element provide an accurate design that will implement the given requirement(s)?

STC

1. Is there a one-to-many (or one-to-one) relationship between requirements and test cases? (That is, a requirement can have multiple associated test cases, but you shouldn't have multiple requirements sharing the same test case.[6])
2. Does a particular test case accurately test the associated requirement?
3. Do all the test cases associated with a requirement completely test the correct implementation of that requirement?

STP

1. Is there a many-to-one relationship between test cases in the STC and test procedures in the STP? That is, does a test procedure implement one or more test cases while each test case is handled by exactly one test procedure?
2. Does a given test procedure accurately implement all its associated test cases?

9.5 For More Information

Bremer, Michael. *The User Manual Manual: How to Research, Write, Test, Edit, and Produce a Software Manual.* Grass Valley, CA: UnTechnical Press, 1999. A sample chapter is available at *http://www.untechnicalpress.com/Downloads/UMM%20sample%20doc.pdf*.

IEEE. "IEEE Standard 830-1998: IEEE Recommended Practice for Software Requirements Specifications." October 20, 1998. *https://doi.org/10.1109/IEEESTD.1998.88286*.

Leffingwell, Dean, and Don Widrig. *Managing Software Requirements.* Boston: Addison-Wesley Professional, 2003.

McConnell, Steve. *Code Complete.* 2nd ed. Redmond, WA: Microsoft Press, 2004.

Miles, Russ, and Kim Hamilton. *Learning UML 2.0: A Pragmatic Introduction to UML.* Sebastopol, CA: O'Reilly Media, 2003.

Pender, Tom. *UML Bible.* Indianapolis: Wiley, 2003.

Roff, Jason T. *UML: A Beginner's Guide.* Berkeley, CA: McGraw-Hill Education, 2003.

Wiegers, Karl E. *Software Requirements.* Redmond, WA: Microsoft Press, 2009.

———. "Writing Quality Requirements." *Software Development* 7, no. 5 (May 1999): 44–48.

---

6. It might turn out that a single test case would incidentally work for multiple requirements. However, you would still produce independent test cases. This redundancy is resolved when you create the test procedures.

10

REQUIREMENTS DOCUMENTATION

Requirements state what the software must do in order to satisfy the customer's needs, specifically:

- What functions the system must carry out (a *functional requirement*)
- How well the system must perform them (a *nonfunctional requirement*)
- The resource or design parameters in which the software must operate (*constraints*, which are also nonfunctional requirements)

If a piece of software does not fulfill a particular requirement, you cannot consider the software complete or correct. A set of software requirements, therefore, is the fundamental starting point for software development.

10.1 Requirement Origins and Traceability

Every software requirement must have an origin. This could be a higher-level requirements document (for example, a requirement in a Software Requirements Specification [SRS] might originate from a System Requirements Specification [SyRS], or a requirement in the SyRS might originate from a customer-supplied functional requirements document), a specific use case document, a customer "statement of work to be done," a customer's verbal communication, or a brainstorming meeting. You should be able to trace any requirement to its origin; if you can't, it probably isn't necessary and should be removed.

Reverse traceability is the ability to trace a requirement back to its origin. As discussed in Chapter 9, the Reverse Traceability Matrix (RTM) is a document or database that lists all requirements and their origins. With an RTM, you can easily identify the origin of a requirement to determine its importance (see "The Requirements/Reverse Traceability Matrix" on page 178 for an in-depth description of the RTM).

10.1.1 A Suggested Requirements Format

A written requirement should take one of the following forms:

- [*Trigger*] **Actor** shall **Action Object** [*Condition*]
- [*Trigger*] **Actor** must **Action Object** [*Condition*]

where the items inside the square brackets are optional. The word *shall* indicates a functional requirement; the word *must* indicates a nonfunctional requirement. Each item is described as follows, based on this sample requirement:

> When the pool temperature is in the range 40 degrees F to 65 degrees F the pool monitor shall turn off the "good" indication unless the atmospheric temperature is above 90 degrees F.

Trigger A trigger is a phrase indicating when the requirement applies. The absence of a trigger implies that the requirement always applies. In the example, the trigger is "When the pool temperature is in the range 40 degrees F to 65 degrees F."

Actor The actor is the person or thing that is performing the action—in this case, "the pool monitor."

Action The action is the activity that the requirement causes ("turn off").

Object The object is the thing being acted upon ("the 'good' indication").

Condition The condition is typically a negative contingency that stops the action (if a positive condition causes the action, it's a trigger). In the example, the condition is "unless the atmospheric temperature is above 90 degrees F."

Some authors allow the words *should* or *may* in place of *shall* or *must*; however, these terms suggest that the requirement is optional. This book subscribes to the view that all requirements are necessary and therefore should not include the words *should* or *may*.

10.1.2 Characteristics of Good Requirements

This section discusses the attributes that characterize good requirements.

10.1.2.1 Correct

That requirements must be correct should go without saying, but research shows that about 40 percent of a project's cost is due to errors in requirements. Therefore, taking time to review requirements and correct any mistakes is one of the most cost-efficient ways to ensure quality software.

10.1.2.2 Consistent

Requirements must be consistent with one another; that is, one requirement cannot contradict another. For example, if a pool temperature monitor states that an alarm must be triggered if the temperature falls below 70 degrees and another says that the same alarm must be triggered when the temperature falls below 65 degrees, the two requirements are inconsistent.

Note that consistency refers to requirements within the same document. If a requirement is not consistent with a requirement in a higher-level document, then that requirement is *incorrect*—never mind inconsistent.

10.1.2.3 Feasible

If you can't feasibly implement a software requirement, then you don't have a requirement. After all, requirements state what must be done in order to provide a satisfactory software solution; if the requirement is not viable, then it's likewise impossible to provide the software solution.

10.1.2.4 Necessary

By definition, if a software requirement is not necessary, it is not a requirement. Requirements are costly to implement—they require documentation, code, test procedures, and maintenance—so you do not want to include a requirement unless it is necessary. Unnecessary requirements are often the result of "gold plating," or adding features simply because somebody thought they would be cool, without regard to the costs involved in implementing them.

A requirement is necessary if it:

- makes the product market competitive;
- addresses a need expressed by a customer, end user, or other stakeholder;
- differentiates the product or usage model; or
- is dictated by a business strategy, roadmap, or a sustainability need.

10.1.2.5 Prioritized

Software requirements specify everything you must do to produce the desired application. However, given various constraints (time, budget, and so on), you may not be able to implement every requirement in the first release of the software. Furthermore, as time passes (and dollars are spent), some requirements may be abandoned because things change. Therefore, a good requirement will have an associated priority. This can help drive the schedule, as teams implement the most critical features first and relegate the less important ones to the end of the project development cycle. Typically, three or four levels of priority should be sufficient: critical/mandatory, important, desirable, and optional are good examples.

10.1.2.6 Complete

A good requirement will be complete; that is, it will not contain any *TBD* (to be determined) items.

10.1.2.7 Unambiguous

Requirements must not be open to interpretation (note that TBD is a special case of this). Unambiguous means that a requirement has exactly one interpretation.

Because most requirements are written in a natural language (such as English) and natural languages are ambiguous, you must take special care when writing requirements to avoid ambiguity.

Example of an ambiguous requirement:

> When the pool temperature is too cold the software shall signal an alarm.

An unambiguous example:

> When the pool temperature is below 65 degrees (F) the software shall signal an alarm.

Ambiguity results whenever the following natural language features appear in a requirement:

Vagueness Results when you use *weak words*—those without a precise meaning—in a requirement. This section will discuss weak words shortly.

Subjectivity Refers to the fact that different people will assign a different meaning for a term (a weak word) based on their own personal experiences or opinion.

Incompleteness Results from using TBD items, partial specifications, or unbounded lists in a requirement. Unbounded lists will be discussed in this section a little later.

Optionality Occurs when you use phrases that make a requirement optional rather than required (for example, *is caused by, use of, should, may, if possible, when appropriate, as desired*).

Underspecification Occurs when a requirement does not fully specify the requirement, often as a result of using weak words (such as *support, analyzed, respond,* and *based on*).

Consider this requirement:

> The pool monitor shall support Fahrenheit and Celsius scales.

What exactly does *support* mean in this context? One developer could interpret it to mean that the end user can select the input and output to be in degrees F or C (fixed), while another developer could interpret it to mean that both scales are used for output and that input allows either scale to be used. A better requirement might be:

> The pool monitor setup shall allow the user to select either the Fahrenheit or Celsius temperature scale.

Underreference   Refers to when a requirement provides an incomplete or missing reference to another document (such as a requirement's origin).

Overgeneralization   Occurs when a requirement contains universal qualifiers such as *any, all, always,* and *every*, or, in the negative sense, *none, never,* and *only*.

Nonintelligibility   Results from poor writing (grammar), undefined terms, convoluted logic (for example, double negation), and incompleteness.

Passive voice   Refers to when the requirement does not assign an actor to an action. For example, a bad requirement using the passive voice might be:

> An alarm shall be raised if the temperature drops below 65 degrees F.

Who is responsible for raising the alarm? Different people could interpret this differently. A better requirement might be:

> The pool monitor software shall raise an alarm if the temperature drops below 65 degrees F.

Using weak words in requirements often results in ambiguity. Examples of weak words include: *support, generally, kind of, mostly, pretty, slightly, somewhat, sort of, various, virtually, quickly, easy, timely, before, after, user-friendly, effective, multiple, as possible, appropriate, normal, capability, reliable, state-of-the-art, effortless,* and *multi*.

For example, a requirement such as "The pool monitor shall provide multiple sensors" is ambiguous because *multiple* is a weak word. What does it mean? Two? Three? A dozen?

Another way to create an ambiguous requirement is by using an unbounded list—a list missing a starting point, an ending point, or both. Typical examples include phrasing like *at least; including, but not limited to; or later; or more; such as; and so on;* and *etc.*

For example: "The pool monitor shall support three or more sensors." Does it have to support four sensors? Ten sensors? An infinite number of sensors? This requirement doesn't make it clear what the maximum number of supported sensors is. A better requirement might be:

> The pool monitor must support between three and six sensors.

Unbounded lists are impossible to design and test against (so they fail both the feasible and verifiable attributes).

10.1.2.8 Implementation-Independent

Requirements must be based solely on the inputs and outputs of a system. They should not delve into the implementation details of the application (that's the purpose of the Software Design Description [SDD] document). Requirements must view the system as a black box into which inputs are fed and from which outputs are produced.

For example, a requirement might state that an input to the system is a list of numbers that produce a sorted list as output. The requirement should not state something like "A quicksort algorithm shall be used." There may be good reasons why the software designer would want to use a different algorithm; the requirements should not force the software designer's or programmer's hand.

10.1.2.9 Verifiable

"If it isn't testable, it isn't a requirement" is the mantra by which a requirements author should live. If you can't create a test for it, you also can't verify that the requirement has been fulfilled in the final product. Indeed, the requirement might very well be impossible to implement if you can't come up with a way to test it.

If you can't create a physical test that can be run on the final software product, there's a good chance that your requirement is not based solely on system inputs and outputs. For example, if you have a requirement that states "The system shall use the quicksort algorithm to sort the data," how do you test for this? If you have to resort to "This requirement is tested by reviewing the code," then you may not have a good requirement. That's not to say that requirements can't be verified by inspection or analysis, but an actual test is always the best way to verify a requirement, especially if you can automate that test.

10.1.2.10 Atomic

A good requirement statement must not contain multiple requirements—that is, it must not be a compound requirement. Requirements should also be as independent as possible; their implementation should not rely on other requirements.

Some authors claim that the words *and* and *or* must never appear in a requirement. Strictly speaking, this isn't true. You simply want to avoid using the *fanboys* conjunctions (*for, and, nor, but, or, yet, so*) to combine separate requirements into a single statement. For example, the following is not a compound requirement:

> The pool monitor shall set the "good" indication when the temperature is between 70 degrees F *and* 85 degrees F.

This is a single requirement, not two. The presence of the word *and* does not produce two requirements. If you really want to be a stickler and eliminate the word *and*, you could rewrite the requirement thusly:

> The pool monitor shall set the "good" indication when the temperature is in the range from 70 degrees F to 85 degrees F.

However, there's really nothing wrong with the first version. Here's an example of a compound requirement:

> The pool monitor shall clear the "good" indication when the temperature is below 70 degrees F *or* above 85 degrees F.

This should be rewritten as two separate requirements:[1]

> The pool monitor shall clear the "good" indication when the temperature is below 70 degrees F.

> The pool monitor shall clear the "good" indication when the temperature is above 85 degrees F.

Note that compound requirements will create problems later when you're constructing traceability matrices, as this chapter will discuss in "Updating the Traceability Matrix with Requirement Information" on page 222. Compound requirements also create testing problems. The test for a requirement must produce a single answer: pass or fail. You cannot have part of a requirement pass and another part fail. That's a sure sign of a compound requirement.

10.1.2.11 Unique

A requirements specification must not contain any duplicate requirements. Duplication makes the document much more difficult to maintain, particularly if you ever modify requirements and forget to modify the duplicates.

10.1.2.12 Modifiable

It would be unreasonable to expect the requirements of a project to remain constant over its lifetime. Expectations change, technology changes, the market changes, and the competition changes. During product development, you'll likely want to revise some requirements to adapt to evolving

---

1. Arguably, this could be rewritten as the single requirement "The pool monitor shall clear the 'good' condition when the temperature is outside the range 70 to 85 degrees F."

conditions. In particular, you don't want to choose requirements that enforce certain system constraints that other requirements will be based on. For example, consider the following requirement:

> The pool monitor shall use an Arduino Mega 2560 single-board computer as the control module.

Based on this requirement, other requirements might be "The pool monitor shall use the A8 pin for the pool level indication" and "The pool monitor shall use the D0 pin as the low temperature output." The problem with such requirements, which are based on the use of the Mega 2560 board, is that if a new board comes along (say, a Teensy 4.0 module), then changing the first requirement necessitates also changing all the other requirements that depend on it. A better set of requirements might be:

> The pool monitor shall use a single-board computer that supports 8 analog inputs, 4 digital outputs, and 12 digital inputs.

> The pool monitor shall use one of the digital output pins as the low temperature alarm.

> The pool monitor shall use one of the analog input pins as the pool level input.

10.1.2.13 Traceable

All requirements must be forward- and reverse-traceable. *Reverse traceability* means that the requirement can be traced to its origin. To be traceable to some other object, the requirement must have a *tag* (a unique identifier, as introduced in Chapter 4).

Each requirement must include the origin as part of the requirement text or tag; otherwise, you must provide a separate RTM document (or database) that provides that information. In general, you should explicitly list a requirement's origin within the requirement itself.

Forward traceability provides a link to all documents based on (or spawned by) the requirements document. Most of the time, forward traceability is handled via an RTM document; it would be too much work to maintain this information in each requirements document (there would be too much duplicate information, which, as previously noted, makes document maintenance difficult).

10.1.2.14 Positively Stated

A requirement should state what must be true, not what must *not* happen. Most negatively stated requirements are impossible to verify. For example, the following is a bad requirement:

> The pool monitor shall not operate at atmospheric temperatures below freezing.

This requirement suggests that the pool monitor must stop operation once the temperature drops below freezing. Does this mean that the system will sense the temperature and shut down below freezing? Or does it simply mean that the system cannot be expected to produce reasonable values below freezing? Better requirements might be:

> The pool monitor shall automatically shut off if the temperature falls below freezing.

Hopefully, there is a requirement that discusses what should happen when the temperature rises back above freezing. If the pool monitor has been shut off, can it sense this change?

10.2   Design Goals

Although requirements can't be optional, it's sometimes beneficial to be able to list optional items in a requirements document. Such items are known as design goals.

Design goals violate many of the attributes of good requirements. Obviously, they are not necessary, but they can also be incomplete, be slightly ambiguous, specify implementation, or not be testable. For example, a design goal might be to use the C standard library's built-in sort() function (an implementation detail) in order to reduce development time. Another design goal might be something like:

> The pool monitor should support as many sensors as possible.

As you can see, this is both optional and open-ended. A design goal is a suggestion that a developer can use to guide development choices. It should not involve extra design work or testing that leads to further development expenses. It should simply help a developer make certain developmental choices when designing the system.

Like requirements, design goals can have tags, though there's little need to trace design goals through the documentation system. However, because they might be elevated to requirement status at some point, it's nice to have a tag associated with them so they can serve as an origin for a requirement in a spawned document.

10.3   The System Requirements Specification Document

The System Requirements Specification document collects all the requirements associated with a complete system. This may include business requirements, legislative/political requirements, hardware requirements, and software requirements. The SyRS is usually a very high-level document, though internal to an organization. Its purpose is to provide a *single-source* origin for all requirements appearing in an organization's subservient documents (such as the SRS).

The SyRS takes the same form as the SRS (described in the next section), so I won't further elaborate on its contents other than to point out that the SyRS spawns the SRS (and Hardware Requirements Specifications, or HRS, if appropriate). The SyRS is optional and typically absent in small software-only projects.

SyRS requirements typically state "The *system* shall" or "The *system* must." This is in contrast to requirements in the SRS that typically state "The *software* shall" or "The *software* must."

10.4 The Software Requirements Specification Document

The Software Requirements Specification is a document that contains all the requirements and design goals for a given software project. There are (literally) hundreds, if not thousands, of examples of SRS documents scattered across the internet. Many sites seem to have their own ideas about what constitutes an SRS. Rather than introduce yet another new template into the cacophony, this book will elect to use the template defined by the IEEE: the IEEE 830-1998 Recommended Practice for Software Requirements Specifications.

In this book, using the IEEE 830-1998 recommended practice is a safe decision, but note that the standard is by no means perfect. It was created by a committee and, as a result, it contains a lot of bloat (extraneous information). The problem with committee-designed standards is that the only way to get them approved is by letting everyone inject their own pet ideas into the document, even if those ideas conflict with others in the document. Nevertheless, the IEEE 830-1998 recommendation is a good starting point. You need not feel compelled to implement everything in it, but you should use it as a guideline when creating your SRS.

A typical SRS uses an outline similar to the following:

Table of Contents
1. Introduction
   - 1.1 Purpose
   - 1.2 Scope
   - 1.3 Definitions, Acronyms, and Abbreviations
   - 1.4 References
   - 1.5 Overview
2. Overall Description
   - 2.1 Product Perspective
     - 2.1.1 System Interfaces
     - 2.1.2 User Interfaces
     - 2.1.3 Hardware Interfaces
     - 2.1.4 Software Interfaces

- 2.1.5 Communication Interfaces
- 2.1.6 Memory Constraints
- 2.1.7 Operations
- 2.2 Site Adaptation Requirements
- 2.3 Product Functions
- 2.4 User Characteristics
- 2.5 Constraints
- 2.6 Assumptions and Dependencies
- 2.7 Apportioning of Requirements
3. Specific Requirements
   - 3.1 External Interfaces
   - 3.2 Functional Requirements
   - 3.3 Performance Requirements
   - 3.4 Logical Database Requirements
   - 3.5 Design Constraints
   - 3.6 Standards Compliance
   - 3.7 Software System Attributes
     - 3.7.1 Reliability
     - 3.7.2 Availability
     - 3.7.3 Security
     - 3.7.4 Maintainability
     - 3.7.5 Portability
   - 3.8 Design Goals
4. Appendixes
5. Index

Section 3 is the most important—this is where you will place all of your requirements as well as your design goals.

10.4.1 Introduction

The Introduction contains an overview of the entire SRS. The following subsections describe the suggested contents of the Introduction.

10.4.1.1 Purpose

In the Purpose section, you should state the purpose of the SRS and who the intended audience is. For an SRS, the intended audience is probably the customers who will need to validate the SRS and the developers/designers who will create the SDD, software test cases, and software test procedures, and will write the code.

10.4.1.2 Scope

The Scope section describes the software product by name (for example, Plantation Productions Pool Monitor), explains what the product will do, and, if necessary, states what it will *not* do. (Don't worry that this doesn't adhere to the "positively stated" rule, since this is a scope declaration, not a requirement statement.) The Scope section also outlines the objectives of the project, the benefits and goals of the product, and the application software being written for the product.

10.4.1.3 Definitions, Acronyms, and Abbreviations

The Definitions section provides a glossary of all terms, acronyms, and abbreviations the SRS uses.

10.4.1.4 References

The References section provides a link to all external documents that the SRS references. If your SRS relies on an external RTM document, you should reference that document here. If the documents are internal to the organization, you should provide their internal document numbers/references. If the SRS references a document that is external to the organization, the SRS should list the document's title, author, publisher, and date as well as information on how to obtain the document.

10.4.1.5 Overview

The Overview section describes the format of the rest of the SRS and the information it contains (this section is particularly important if you've omitted items from the IEEE recommendation).

10.4.2 Overall Description

The Overall Description section specifies the requirements of the following aspects:

10.4.2.1 Product Perspective

The Product Perspective section contextualizes the product with respect to other (possibly competing) products. If this product is part of a larger system, the product perspective should point this out (and describe how the requirements in this document relate to the larger system). This section might also describe various constraints on the product, such as:

10.4.2.1.1 System Interfaces

This section describes how the software will interface with the rest of the system. This would typically include any APIs, such as how the software interfaces with a Wi-Fi adapter in order to view pool readings remotely.

10.4.2.1.2 User Interfaces

This section lists all user interface (UI) elements needed to meet the requirements. For example, in the pool monitor scenario, this section could describe how the user interacts with the device via an LCD display and various push buttons on the device.

10.4.2.1.3 Hardware Interfaces

This section could describe how the software interacts with the underlying hardware. For example, the pool monitor SRS could state that the software will be running on an Arduino Mega 2560, using the A8 through A15 analog inputs to connect to the sensors and the D0 through D7 digital lines as inputs connected to buttons.

10.4.2.1.4 Software Interfaces

This section describes any additional/external software needed to implement the system. This might include operating systems, third-party libraries, database management systems, or other application systems. For example, the pool monitor SRS might describe the use of vendor-supplied libraries needed to read data from various sensors. For each software item, you should include the following information in this section:

- Name
- Specification number (a vendor-supplied value, if any)
- Version number
- Source
- Purpose
- Reference to pertinent documentation

10.4.2.1.5 Communication Interfaces

This section lists any communication interfaces, such as Ethernet, Wi-Fi, Bluetooth, and RS-232 serial that the product will use. For example, the pool monitor SRS might describe the Wi-Fi interface in this section.

10.4.2.1.6 Memory Constraints

This section describes all the constraints on memory and data storage. For the pool monitor running on an Arduino Mega 2560, SRS might state that there is a limitation in program storage of 1K EEPROM and 8K RAM plus 64K to 128K Flash.

10.4.2.1.7 Operations

This section (often folded into the UI section) describes various operations on the product. It might detail the various modes of operation—such as normal, reduced power, maintenance, or installation modes—and describe interactive sessions, unattended sessions, and communication features.

10.4.2.2 Site Adaptation Requirements

This section describes any site-specific adaptations. For example, the pool monitor SRS might describe optional sensors for pools with spas in this section.

10.4.2.3 Product Functions

The Product Functions section describes the software's (major) functionality. For example, the pool monitor SRS might use this section to describe how the software monitors pool levels, pool temperatures, atmospheric temperature, water conductivity (for saltwater pools), water flow though the filtration system, and filtration time since the last filter cleaning.

10.4.2.4 User Characteristics

The User Characteristics section describes the people that will use the product. For example, the pool monitor SRS might define a factory test technician (responsible for testing and repairing the unit), a field installation technician, an advanced end user, and an average end user. There may be different requirements for the software that apply only to certain types of users.

10.4.2.5 Constraints

The Constraints section describes any limitations that may affect the developer's choices when designing and implementing the software, such as:

- Regulatory policies
- Hardware limitations (for example, signal timing requirements)
- Interfaces to other applications
- Parallel operation
- Audit functions
- Control functions
- High-level language requirements
- Signal handshake protocols (for example, XON-XOFF)
- Reliability requirements
- Criticality of the application
- Safety and security considerations

10.4.2.6 Assumptions and Dependencies

The items listed in the Assumptions and Dependencies section apply only to the requirements; they do not present constraints on the design. If an assumption were to change, it would require changing requirements rather than the design (though changing requirements will likely affect the design as well). For example, in the pool monitor SRS an assumption might be that the Arduino Mega 2560 will provide sufficient computing power, ports, and memory to complete the task. If this assumption is incorrect, it may affect some requirements with respect to port usage, available memory, and the like.

10.4.2.7 Apportioning of Requirements

The Apportioning of Requirements section divides the requirements and features into two or more groups: those to be implemented in the current release, and those planned for future versions of the software.

10.4.3 Specific Requirements

The Specific Requirements section should list all the requirements and supporting documentation. This documentation should be written such that a system designer can construct a design for the software from the requirements documented.

All requirements should possess the characteristics discussed earlier in this chapter. They should also have a tag and a cross-reference (trace) to their origin. Because the requirements documentation will be read far more times than it is written, you should take special care to make this document as readable as possible.

10.4.3.1 External Interfaces

The External Interfaces section should describe all the inputs and outputs of the software system in great detail but without replicating the information in the interface subsections of the Product Perspective section. Each listing should contain the following information (as appropriate for the system):

- Tag
- Description
- Input source or output destination
- Valid range of values plus necessary accuracy/precision/tolerance
- Measurement units
- Timing and tolerances
- Relationship to other input/output items
- Screen/window formats (but list only screen requirements that are actual requirements—don't design the user interface here)
- Data formats
- Command formats, protocols, and any necessary sentinel messages

Many SRS authors will pull this section out of the Specific Requirements section and place it in the Product Perspective section in order to avoid redundancy, though the IEEE 830-1998 standard suggests that this section be part of the Specific Requirements section. However, the IEEE document is only a *recommended* practice, so the choice is really yours. What matters most is that the information appears in the SRS.

10.4.3.2 Functional Requirements

The Functional Requirements section contains those items that most people immediately recognize as requirements. This section lists the fundamental activities that take place on inputs and describes how the system uses the inputs to produce outputs. By convention, functional requirements always contain the auxiliary verb *shall*. For example, "The software *shall* raise an alarm when the pool low input is active."

Typical functional requirements include the following:

- Input validity checks and responses to invalid inputs
- Operation sequences
- Abnormal condition responses, including: overflow, underflow, arithmetic exceptions, communication failures, resource overruns, error handling and recovery, and protocol errors
- Persistence of data across executions of the software
- Effect of parameters
- Input/output relationships, including: legal and illegal input patterns, relationship of inputs to output, and how outputs are computed from inputs (but be careful not to incorporate software design into the requirements)

10.4.3.3 Performance Requirements

The Performance Requirements section lists nonfunctional requirements that specify either static or dynamic performance targets that the software must hit. Like most nonfunctional requirements, performance requirements usually contain the auxiliary verb *must*—for example, "The software *must* be able to control an internal display and a remote display."

Static performance requirements are those that are defined for the system as a whole and do not depend on the software's capabilities. A good example for the pool monitor is "The pool monitor must be able to read sensor input data from between 5 and 10 analog sensors." This is a static requirement because the number of sensors is static for a given installation (it isn't going to change because the software is written more efficiently, for example).

Dynamic performance requirements are those that the software must meet during execution. A good example might be "The software must read each sensor between 10 and 20 times per second."

10.4.3.4 Logical Database Requirements

The Logical Database Requirements section describes nonfunctional requirements that specify the record and field formats for databases that the application must access. Typically, these requirements deal with externally accessed databases. Databases internal to the application (that is, not visible to the outside world) are generally outside the domain of the software requirements, although the SDD might cover these.

10.4.3.5 Design Constraints

Standards compliance is an example of a *design constraint*. Any limitation that prevents the software designer from using an arbitrary implementation should be listed in the Design Constraints section. One example might be limiting readings from a 16-bit A/D converter to 13 bits because the A/D chip/circuit is noisy and the low-order 3 bits may not be reliable.

10.4.3.6 Standards Compliance

The Standards Compliance section should describe, and provide links to, all standards to which the software must adhere. Standards numbers and document descriptions should allow the reader to research the standards as necessary.

10.4.3.7 Software System Attributes

The Software System Attributes section lists characteristics for the software system, including:

10.4.3.7.1 Reliability

The Requirements section will specify the expected uptime requirements for the software system. Reliability is a nonfunctional requirement that describes, usually as a percentage, the amount of time that the system will operate without a failure. A typical example is "an expected reliability of 99.99 percent," meaning that the software will fail no more than 0.01 percent of the time. As with many nonfunctional requirements, it can be difficult to provide tests to ensure that reliability targets are met.

10.4.3.7.2 Availability

The availability attribute specifies the amount of *downtime* that is acceptable in the final application (actually, it specifies the *inverse* of downtime). Availability specifies the ability of the user to access the software system at any time. When the system is *down*, it is not available to the user. This nonfunctional requirement might differentiate between scheduled downtime and unscheduled downtime (for example, a hardware failure that forces a restart of the system).

10.4.3.7.3 Security

The security attribute is a nonfunctional requirement that specifies the expected system security, which could include items such as encryption expectations and network socket types.

10.4.3.7.4 Maintainability

Maintainability is another nonfunctional requirement that can be hard to specify and test. In most specifications, there is a nebulous statement like "the software shall be easy to maintain." This is unhelpful. Instead, this attribute should state, "It must take an experienced maintenance programmer no more than a week to come up to speed on this system and make changes to it."

REQUIREMENT ORGANIZATION

Any sufficiently complex system will have a large number of requirements, so the SRS can become unwieldy if it is not organized properly. There are many different application types, and an equally large number of ways to organize their requirements. No particular organization is correct; you'll have to choose one of the following options based on the audience for your SRS.

Organizing by system mode

Some systems operate in various modes—for example, an embedded system might have a low-power mode and a regular mode. In that case, you could organize the system requirements into those two groups.

Organizing by user class

Some systems support different classes of users (for example, beginners, power users, and system administrators). In a complex system, you might have normal users, power users, maintenance workers, and programmers accessing the system.

Organizing by object class

Objects are entities in the software system that correspond to real-world objects. You could organize your requirements based on the types or classes of these objects.

Organizing by feature

One of the more common ways to organize SRS requirements is by the features they implement. This is a particularly useful method of organization when the application provides a user interface for all the features in the system.

Organizing by input stimulus

If processing different inputs is a primary activity of the application, then you might consider organizing your SRS by the type of inputs the application processes.

Organizing by output response

Similarly, if producing a wide range of outputs is a primary activity of the application, then it might make sense to organize the requirements by output response.

Organizing by functional hierarchy

Another common SRS organization approach is by functionality. This is often the fallback position SRS authors use when no other organization seems appropriate. Grouping the requirements by common inputs, command outputs, common database operations, and data flow through the program are all reasonable ways to organize the SRS.

10.4.3.7.5 Portability

Portability describes what is involved in moving the software to a different environment. This section should include a discussion of portability across CPUs, operating systems, and programming language dialects.

10.4.3.8 Design Goals

Often it is tempting to put so-called optional requirements into an SRS. However, as noted earlier in this chapter, requirements by definition cannot be optional. Nevertheless, there will be times when you might wish to say, "If possible, add this feature." You can state such requests as design goals and leave it up to the designer or software engineer to decide if the feature is worth having. Place design goals in a separate section and clearly state "*As a design goal*, the software should . . . " in your SRS.

10.4.4 Supporting Information

Any good software requirements specification will contain supporting information such as a table of contents, appendixes, glossaries, and an index. There should also be a table of requirement tags (sorted numerically or lexicographically) that lists each tag, a short description of the requirement, and the page number where it appears in the document (this could also be placed in the RTM rather than in the SRS).

10.4.5 A Sample Software Requirements Specification

This section provides a sample SRS for a swimming pool monitor similar to the examples given thus far in this chapter. For space reasons, this swimming pool monitor SRS is greatly simplified; the purpose is not to provide a complete specification, but rather to provide an illustrative outline.

Table of Contents

1 **Introduction**

   1.1 **Purpose**

      The pool monitor device will track pool water levels and automatically refill the pool when levels are low.

   1.2 **Scope**

      The pool monitor software will be produced from this specification.

      The objectives of the hardware and software development are to provide functions, status information, monitor and control hardware, communications, and self-test functions per the requirements that have been allocated to the pool monitor system.

1.3 Definitions, Acronyms, and Abbreviations

Term	Definition
Accuracy	The degree of agreement with the true value of the measured input, expressed as percent of reading for digital readouts (ANSI N42.18-1980).
Anomaly	Anything observed in the documentation or operation of software that deviates from expectations. (Derived from IEEE Std 610.12-1990.)
Catastrophic event	An event without warning from which recovery is impossible. Catastrophic events include hardware or software failures resulting in computation and processing errors. The processor will halt or reset, based on a configuration item, after a catastrophic event.
Handled conditions	Conditions that the system is designed to handle and continue processing. These conditions include anomalies, faults, and failures.
SBC	Single-board computer
Software Requirements Specification (SRS)	Documentation of the essential requirements (functions, performance, design constraints, and attributes) of the software and its external interfaces (IEEE Std 610.12-1990).
SPM	Swimming pool monitor
System Requirements Specification (SyRS)	A structured collection of information that embodies the requirements of the system (IEEE Std 1233-1998). A specification that documents the requirements to establish a design basis and the conceptual design for a system or subsystem.

1.4 References
[None]

1.5 Overview

Section 2 provides an overall description of the swimming pool monitor (hardware and software).

Section 3 lists the specific requirements for the swimming pool monitor system.

Sections 4 and 5 provide any necessary appendixes and an index.

In section 3, requirements tags take the following form:

      <whitespace>   [POOL_SRS_*xxx*]
      <whitespace>   [POOL_SRS_*xxx.yy*]
      <whitespace>   [POOL_SRS_*xxx.yy.zz*]
      <and so on>.

where *xxx* is a three- or four-digit SRS requirement number.

Should the need arise to insert a new SRS requirement tag between two other values (for example, add a requirement between

POOL_SRS_040 and POOL_SRS_041), then a decimal fractional number shall be appended to the SRS tag number (for example, POOL_SRS_040.5). Any number of decimal point suffixes can be added, if needed (for example, POOL_SRS_40.05.02).

2 Overall Description

The purpose behind the swimming pool monitor (SPM) is to provide an automatic system for maintaining water level in the pool. This task is sufficiently simple to allow the creation of an SRS that is short enough to fit within this chapter.

2.1 Product Perspective

In the real world, an SPM would probably provide many additional features; adding those features here would only increase the size of the SRS without providing much additional educational benefit. This specification is intentionally simplified in order to fit within the editorial requirements of this book.

2.1.1 System Interfaces

The SPM design assumes the use of an Arduino-compatible SBC. Accordingly, the software will interface to the hardware using Arduino-compatible libraries.

2.1.2 User Interfaces

The user interface shall consist of a small four-line display (minimum 20 characters/line), six push buttons (up, down, left, right, cancel/back, and select/enter), and a rotary encoder (rotating knob).

2.1.3 Hardware Interfaces

This document doesn't specify a particular SBC to use. However, the SBC must provide at least the following:

- 16 digital inputs
- 1 analog input
- 2 digital outputs
- A small amount of nonvolatile, writable memory (for example, EEPROM) to store configuration values.
- A real-time clock (RTC; this can be an external module)
- A watchdog timer to monitor the system's software operation

The SPM provides pool sensors to determine when the pool level is high or low. It also provides a solenoid interface to a water valve, allowing the SPM to turn on or off a water source for the pool.

2.1.4 Software Interfaces

The SPM software is self-contained and provides no external interfaces, nor does it require any external software interfaces.

2.1.5 Communication Interfaces

The SPM is self-contained and does not communicate with the outside world.

2.1.6 Memory Constraints

As the SPM is running on an Arduino-compatible SBC, there will be (severe) memory constraints, depending on the exact model chosen (for example, an Arduino Mega 2560 SBC provides only 8KB of static RAM on board).

2.1.7 Operations

The SPM operates in an *always-on* mode, monitoring the pool 24/7/365. Therefore, the module itself should not consume excessive electrical power. It will, however, be connected to line voltage via a power supply, so extreme low-power operation is unnecessary. It will constantly monitor the pool's water level and automatically turn on a water source if the pool level is low. To avoid flooding if there is a sensor failure, the SPM will limit the amount of water introduced to the pool on a daily basis (time limit is user-selectable).

2.2 Site Adaptation Requirements

For this particular variant of the SPM, there is little in the way of site adaptation requirements. There are no optional sensors or operations and the only interfaces outside the SPM itself is a source of power for the system and a water source (interfaced via the solenoid valve).

2.3 Product Functions

The product shall use seven water-level sensors to determine the pool level: three digital sensors that provide a *low-pool* indication, three digital sensors that provide a *high-pool* indication, and an analog sensor that provides a pool level depth indication (perhaps only a couple inches or centimeters in range). The three low-pool digital sensors are active when the water level is at the level of the sensor. The system will begin filling the pool when there is a low-pool indication. To avoid flooding when a sensor fails, the three sensors operate in a *two out of three* configuration, meaning at least two sensors must indicate a low-pool condition before the SPM will attempt to fill the pool. The three high-pool sensors work in a likewise fashion when the SPM should stop filling the pool (water level is high). The analog sensor provides a small range of depth;

the SPM will use the analog sensor as a backup to verify that the pool level is low prior to filling the pool. The SPM will also use the analog sensor to determine that the pool is actually filling while the SPM has turned on the water source.

2.4 User Characteristics

There are two types of SPM users: technicians and end users. A technician is responsible for installing and adjusting the SPM. An end user is the pool's owner who uses the SPM on a day-to-day basis.

2.5 Constraints

The SPM should be carefully designed to prevent inadvertent flooding and excessive water use. In particular, the software must be robust enough to determine that the pool is not being properly filled and to cease attempting to fill the pool if the sensors do not indicate proper operation. Should any sensor fail, the software should be smart enough to avoid blindly keeping the water turned on (which could lead to flood damage). For example, if the SPM is attached to an aboveground pool and that pool has a leak, it might not ever be possible to fill the pool. The software should handle such situations.

The system should be fail-safe insofar as a power failure should automatically shut off the water valve. A watchdog timer of some sort should also check that the software is operating properly and turn off the water valve if a timeout occurs (for example, should the software hang up).

To avoid flooding because of a malfunctioning relay, the SPM should use two relays in series to open the water valve. Both relays must be actuated by the software in order to turn on the solenoid valve.

2.6 Assumptions and Dependencies

The requirements in this document assume that the SBC contains sufficient resources (computing power) to handle the task and that the device can reasonably operate in a 24/7/365 real-time environment.

2.7 Apportioning of Requirements

These requirements define a very simple swimming pool monitor for the purposes of demonstrating a complete SRS. As this is a minimal requirement set for a very small SPM, the assumption is that a product built around these requirements would implement all of them. A real product would probably include many additional features beyond those listed here, with a corresponding increase in the number of requirements appearing in this document.

3 Specific Requirements

3.1 External Interfaces

[POOL_SRS_001]
> The SPM shall provide a digital input for the navigation *up* button.

[POOL_SRS_002]
> The SPM shall provide a digital input for the navigation *down* button.

[POOL_SRS_003]
> The SPM shall provide a digital input for the navigation *left* button.

[POOL_SRS_004]
> The SPM shall provide a digital input for the navigation *right* button.

[POOL_SRS_005]
> The SPM shall provide a digital input for the *cancel/back* button.

[POOL_SRS_006]
> The SPM shall provide a digital input for the *select/enter* button.

[POOL_SRS_007]
> The SPM shall provide four digital inputs for the rotary encoder (quadrature) input.

[POOL_SRS_008.01]
> The SPM shall provide a digital input for the primary *water level low* sensor.

[POOL_SRS_008.02]
> The SPM shall provide a digital input for the secondary *water level low* sensor.

[POOL_SRS_008.03]
> The SPM shall provide a digital input for the tertiary *water level low* sensor.

[POOL_SRS_009.01]
> The SPM shall provide a digital input for the primary *water level high* sensor.

[POOL_SRS_009.02]
> The SPM shall provide a digital input for the secondary *water level high* sensor.

[POOL_SRS_009.03]
> The SPM shall provide a digital input for the tertiary *water level high* sensor.

[POOL_SRS_011]
  The SPM shall provide an analog input (minimum 8-bit resolution) for the water level sensor.

[POOL_SRS_012]
  The SPM shall provide two digital outputs to control the water source solenoid valve.

3.2 Functional Requirements

[POOL_SRS_013]
  The SPM shall allow the user to set the RTC date and time via the user interface.

[POOL_SRS_014]
  The SPM shall have a maximum fill time, specifying the maximum amount of time (hours:mins) that the water valve can be actuated during a 24-hour period.

[POOL_SRS_015]
  The user shall be able to set the maximum fill time from the SPM user interface (using the navigation and enter buttons).

[POOL_SRS_015.01]
  Once the user has selected the maximum fill time from the user interface, the user shall be able to select the hours or minutes fields using the navigation buttons.

[POOL_SRS_015.02]
  The user shall be able to independently set the maximum fill-time hours value using the rotary encoder after selecting the hours field.

[POOL_SRS_015.03]
  The user shall be able to independently set the maximum fill-time minutes value using the rotary encoder after selecting the minutes field.

[POOL_SRS_015.04]
  The software shall not allow a maximum fill time of greater than 12 hours.

[POOL_SRS_016]
  The SPM shall check the pool level once every 24 hours, at a specific time, to determine if it needs to add water to the pool.

[POOL_SRS_017]
  The user shall be able to set the time the SPM checks the pool level (and, therefore, when the SPM fills the pool) from the SPM user interface.

[POOL_SRS_017.01]
> Once the user has selected the pool-level check time from the user interface, the user shall be able to select the hours or minutes fields using the navigation buttons.

[POOL_SRS_017.02]
> The user shall be able to independently set the pool-level check-time hours value using the rotary encoder after selecting the hours field.

[POOL_SRS_017.03]
> The user shall be able to independently set the pool-level check-time minutes value using the rotary encoder after selecting the minutes field.

[POOL_SRS_017.04]
> The default (factory reset) pool check time shall be 1:00 AM.

[POOL_SRS_018]
> At the pool check time each day, the system shall read the three *pool level low* sensors and begin a pool fill operation if at least two of the three sensors indicate a pool low condition.

[POOL_SRS_018.01]
> During a pool fill operation the software shall accumulate a running *fill time*.

[POOL_SRS_018.02]
> During a pool fill operation if the running fill time exceeds the maximum fill time, the software shall cease the pool fill operation.

[POOL_SRS_018.03]
> During a pool fill operation the software shall read the *pool level high* sensors and cease the pool fill operation if at least two of the three sensors indicate a high pool level.

[POOL_SRS_018.04]
> During a pool fill operation the software shall read the analog pool-level sensor and shut off the water flow if the level isn't increasing after each half-hour of operation.

[POOL_SRS_019]
> The software shall allow the user to select a *manual pool* fill mode that turns on the water source to the pool.

[POOL_SRS_019.01]
> The software shall allow the user to select an *auto pool* fill mode that turns off the manual pool fill mode.

[POOL_SRS_019.02]
> In the manual pool fill mode, the software shall ignore the maximum fill time.

[POOL_SRS_019.03]
In the manual pool fill mode, the software shall ignore the *pool level high* and *pool level low* sensors (filling stops when the user turns off the manual fill mode).

[POOL_SRS_020]
The software shall update the system watchdog timer at least twice as frequently as the watchdog timeout period.

[POOL_SRS_020.01]
The watchdog timeout period shall be no less than 5 seconds and no greater than 60 seconds.

3.3 Performance Requirements
[POOL_SRS_001.00.01]
The SPM shall debounce all button inputs.

[POOL_SRS_007.00.01]
The SPM shall be capable of reading the rotary encoder inputs without losing any changes on the inputs.

[POOL_SRS_015.00.01]
The SPM shall maintain an accuracy of at least one minute for the maximum pool fill time.

[POOL_SRS_017.00.01]
The SPM shall maintain an accuracy of at least one minute for the pool level check time.

3.4 Logical Database Requirements
[POOL_SRS_014.00.01]
The SPM shall store the maximum fill time in nonvolatile memory.

[POOL_SRS_016.00.01]
The SPM shall store the pool check time in nonvolatile memory.

3.5 Design Constraints
[None]

3.6 Standards Compliance
[None]

3.7 Software System Attributes

3.7.1 Reliability
The software will run 24/7/365. Therefore, robustness is a critical factor in system design. In particular, the system should be fail-safe insofar as a software or other failure should result in the closure of the water valve.

3.7.2 Availability
The software should be running continuously (24/7/365). The software must not be subject to counter overflows or other problems associated with long-term execution. The end user should expect at least 99.99 percent uptime.

3.7.3 Security
There are no security requirements for the system (closed, disconnected, air-gapped system).

3.7.4 Maintainability
There are no maintainability requirements other than those customarily expected of a professional software engineering project.

That said, this is a bare-bones requirements document. Should someone actually build this system, one would expect future enhancements. Thus, the system should be designed and implemented with such expectations in mind.

3.7.5 Portability
The software is expected to run on an Arduino-class device. No portability requirements exist other than the possibility of selecting different Arduino-compatible modules (for example, Arduino Mega 2560 versus Teensy 4.0) during implementation.

3.8 Design Goals
None for this project.

4 Appendixes
[None]

5 Index
Given the (small) size of this SRS, no index appears here in order to reduce page count for this book.

10.5 Creating Requirements

Up to this point this chapter has defined requirements as well as requirements documentation. But you might be asking, "How does someone come up with the requirements in the first place?" This section will provide some insight into that question.

The modern approach to requirements creation involves use cases, which were introduced in Chapter 4. The system architect studies how an end user would use a system (the user story) and creates a set of scenarios (use cases) from that study. Each use case becomes the basis for a set of one or more requirements. This section departs from the swimming pool monitor scenario to consider an example from a real-world system, the Plantation Productions *digital data acquisition and control (DAQ) system*.[2]

The DAQ system consists of multiple interconnecting circuit boards, including analog I/O boards, digital I/O boards, digital output boards (relay boards), and an SBC, the Netburner MOD54415, that runs the system firmware. These components allow a system designer to read various analog and digital inputs, compute results and make decisions based on those inputs, and then control external devices by sending digital and analog output values to those devices. For example, the DAQ system was originally designed to control a TRIGA[3] research reactor.

The firmware requirements for the DAQ system are too large to duplicate here, so this chapter will limit the discussion to certain I/O initialization that must take place when the system first powers up. The Netburner MOD54415 includes a set of eight DIP switches, which the DAQ system uses to initialize various system components. These DIP switches do the following:

1. Enable/disable RS-232 port command processing.
2. Enable/disable USB port command processing.
3. Enable/disable Ethernet port command processing.
4. Specify one Ethernet connection or five simultaneous Ethernet connections.
5. Specify one of four different Ethernet addresses using two DIP switches; see Table 10-1.
6. Enable/disable test mode.
7. Enable/disable debug output.

Table 10-1: Ethernet Address Selection

DIP switch A	DIP switch A + 1	Ethernet address
0	0	192.168.2.70
1	0	192.168.2.71
0	1	192.168.2.72
1	1	192.168.2.73

One final thing to note about the DAQ software initialization: debug output uses the Netburner COM1: port. The Netburner shares this serial port hardware with the USB port. There is a conflict if the user enables both the debug output and the USB command ports. Therefore, to enable the debug port, two conditions must be met: debug output must be enabled and USB port command processing must be disabled.

---

2. For information on the Plantation Productions DAQ system, see *http://www.plantation-productions.com/Electronics/DAQ/DAQ.html*.

3. TRIGA™ is a registered trademark of General Atomics, Inc.

To enable commands from the RS-232 or USB ports, the software must read the switches. If the particular switch indicates that the command stream is active, then the software must create a new task[4] to handle input from that port. The newly created task is responsible for reading characters from the given port and sending entire lines of text to the system's command processor upon receiving a newline character. If the corresponding DIP switches are in the disabled position, the software won't create the RS-232 or USB tasks, and the system will ignore these ports.

Enabling Ethernet commands is slightly more complicated. There are four DIP switches associated with the Ethernet port. The Ethernet initialization operation must consider the settings for all four DIP switches.

One DIP switch controls the number of concurrent clients the DAQ software supports. In one position, the DAQ software supports only a single Ethernet client; in the other position, the software supports up to five Ethernet clients. In some environments, you might need to allow multiple host computers to access the data acquisition and control hardware; for example, while debugging you may want to have a test computer monitoring the operations. In some secure applications (after deployment), you may want to limit access to the DAQ system to a single computer.

The third and fourth Ethernet DIP switches allow an operator to select one of four separate IP/Ethernet addresses. This allows control of up to four separate Netburner modules in the same system. As noted in Table 10-1, the four selectable Ethernet addresses are 192.168.2.70 through 192.168.2.73 (the requirements could be changed to support different IP addresses, of course, but these were convenient addresses for the initial DAQ system that was built).

10.6 Use Cases

Given the preceding user story, the next step is to build a set of use cases that describe these operations. Remember, use cases are more than a few UML diagrams—they also include a descriptive narrative (see "Use Case Narratives" on page 80).

Actors There is a single actor in the following use cases, the *System User*.

Triggers In all of the following use cases, the trigger that activates each use case is system boot. The system reads the DIP switch settings at boot time and initializes based on those settings (see Figure 10-1).

Scenarios/Flow of Events These are the activities that occur for a given use case.

Associated Requirements The Associated Requirements provide cross-references to the DAQ System SRS. The requirements appear in

---

4. The Netburner runs a priority-based multitasking operating system called Micro-C/OS (or μC/OS). Tasks are the equivalent of threads in other operating systems.

the following sections (see "(Selected) DAQ Software Requirements (from SRS)" on page 219). You must create the requirements *before* filling in this section; otherwise, you'd simply be guessing at the requirements you'll need.

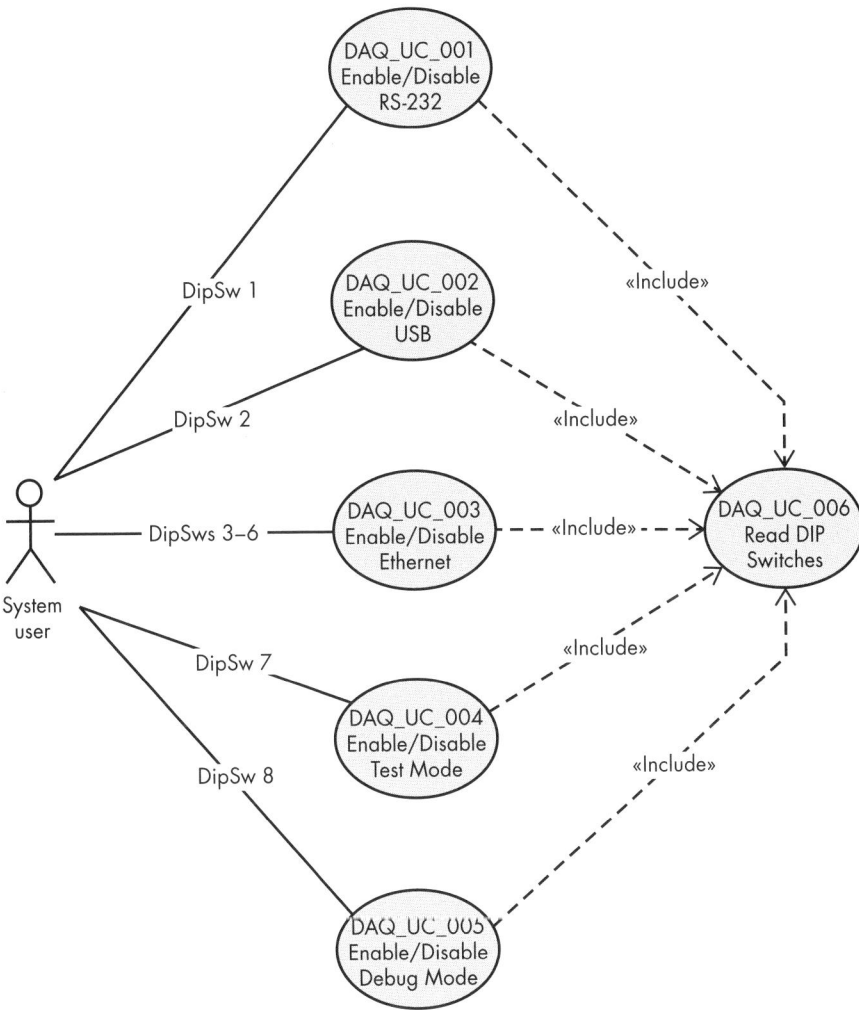

Figure 10-1: Read DIP switches use case

10.6.1 *Enable/Disable Debug Mode*

Goal   Enabling and disabling debug output on DAQ system.
Precondition   System has booted.
End condition   Debug mode is active or inactive, as appropriate.

10.6.1.1 Scenarios/Flow of Events

Enable/Disable Debug Mode

1. During system initialization, read DIP switches.
2. Save the value of DIP switch 8 (on = debug mode on, off = debug mode off).
3. Debug mode is enabled if DIP switch 8 is on and DIP switch 2 (USB mode) is off.
4. Start the maintPrintf task.

10.6.1.2 Associated Requirements

DAQ_SRS_721_001: PPDAQ Debug Mode Enabled

DAQ_SRS_721_002: PPDAQ Debug Mode Disabled

10.6.2 Enable/Disable Ethernet

Goal Enabling and disabling Ethernet command processing on DAQ system.

Precondition System has booted.

End condition Ethernet communication is active or inactive, as appropriate. If active, Ethernet input processing tasks are running.

10.6.2.1 Scenarios/Flow of Events

Enable/Disable Ethernet

1. During system initialization, read DIP switches.
2. Use the value of DIP switch 3 to determine if Ethernet is enabled (switch is on) or disabled (switch is off).
3. Save the value of DIP switch 4 to determine if the system supports one connection (switch is off) or five concurrent connections (switch is on).
4. Use the values of DIP switches 5 and 6 to determine the IP address.
5. If Ethernet is enabled (DIP switch 3 is on), then:
   5.1 Set the Ethernet address based on the value of DIP switches 5 and 6 as:
      5.1.1 192.168.2.70
      5.1.2 192.168.2.71
      5.1.3 192.168.2.72
      5.1.4 192.168.2.73
   5.2 Start the ethernetListenTask task with priority ETHL_PRIO.
6. Else (if Ethernet is not enabled):
   6.1 Do not start the ethernetListenTask.

ethernetListenTask

1. Initialize an array of five descriptors with zero elements (empty descriptor slots).
2. Wait for an external connection request on Ethernet socket 0x5050.
3. If a connection request is made:
    3.1 Search for an empty slot (array element containing zero) in the descriptor array.
    3.2 If there are no slots available:
        3.2.1 Refuse connection.
        3.2.2 Go to step 2.
    3.3 Else if a slot is available:
        3.3.1 Accept connection and store its file descriptor in the available slot.
        3.3.2 Create a new Ethernet command task associated with the new connection; the priority of the new task shall be ETH1_PRIO through ETH5_PRIO, selected by the index into the descriptor slot array; note that SER_PRIO < ETHL_PRIO < ETH1_PRIO to ETH5_PRIO < USB_PRIO (where smaller numbers mean the task has a higher priority in the task queue).
        3.3.3 Go to step 2.
4. Else if the listen connection is broken, terminate listen task.

10.6.2.2 Associated Requirements

DAQ_SRS_708_000: PPDAQ Ethernet IP Address
DAQ_SRS_709_000: PPDAQ Ethernet IP Address 192.168.2.70
DAQ_SRS_710_000: PPDAQ Ethernet IP Address 192.168.2.71
DAQ_SRS_711_000: PPDAQ Ethernet IP Address 192.168.2.72
DAQ_SRS_712_000: PPDAQ Ethernet IP Address 192.168.2.73
DAQ_SRS_716_000: PPDAQ Ethernet Enabled
DAQ_SRS_716.5_000: PDAQ Ethernet Disabled
DAQ_SRS_716_001: PPDAQ Ethernet Task
DAQ_SRS_716_002: PPDAQ Ethernet Task Priority
DAQ_SRS_717_000: PPDAQ Ethernet Port
DAQ_SRS_718_000: PPDAQ Ethernet Multiple Clients Enabled
DAQ_SRS_718_001: PPDAQ Ethernet Multiple Clients Disabled
DAQ_SRS_728_000: PPDAQ Command Source #3
DAQ_SRS_737_000: PPDAQ Maximum Ethernet Connections #1
DAQ_SRS_738_000: PPDAQ Maximum Ethernet Connections #2
DAQ_SRS_738_001: PPDAQ Ethernet Command Processing Tasks
DAQ_SRS_738_002: PPDAQ Ethernet Command Task Priorities

10.6.3 Enable/Disable RS-232

(Similar to the previous use cases; deleted for brevity.)

10.6.4 Enable/Disable Test Mode

(Similar to the previous use cases; deleted for brevity.)

10.6.5 Enable/Disable USB

(Similar to the previous use cases; deleted for brevity.)

10.6.6 Read DIP Switches

(Similar to the previous use cases; deleted for brevity.)

10.7 Creating DAQ Software Requirements from the Use Cases

Converting an informal use case to a formal requirement consists of extracting the information from a use case, filling in missing details, and structuring the result in the form of a requirement.

Consider the use case for "Enable/Disable Debug Mode." You might be tempted into thinking this use case generates a single requirement:

> The PPDAQ software shall operate in a special debug mode if the Netburner DIP switch 8 is set to the ON position and USB (DIP switch 2) is not enabled; it shall operate in a non-debug mode if switch 8 is in the OFF position or DIP switch 2 is enabled.

The problem is that this is actually two separate requirements—not because of the "and" and "or" components (you'll see why in a moment), but because of the semicolon separating the two clauses. The two separate requirements are:

> The PPDAQ software shall operate in a special debug mode if the Netburner DIP switch 8 is set to the ON position and USB (DIP switch 2) is not enabled.

and

> The PPDAQ software shall operate in a non-debug mode if switch 8 is in the OFF position or DIP switch 2 is enabled.

Note that the "and USB" and "or DIP switch 2" phrases do not imply that these requirements must be split into two separate requirements each. The clause "if the Netburner DIP switch 8 is set to the ON position and USB (DIP switch 2) is not enabled" is actually a logical phrase that is part of the *trigger* for this requirement. Technically, the requirement should probably be reworded.

If the Netburner DIP switch 8 is set to the ON position and USB (DIP switch 2) is not enabled, then the PPDAQ software shall operate in a special debug mode.

This moves the trigger clause to the beginning of the requirement, as suggested in section "A Suggested Requirements Format" on page 186. Note, however, that this is simply a suggested format; it's not unreasonable to place the trigger condition after the actor (PPDAQ software), action (operate), and object (debug mode).

The next section provides a listing of various requirements from the DAQ software system. It gives an example of how the DAQ requirements were generated from the use cases. You should be able to fill in the details for the remaining requirements on your own.

10.8 (Selected) DAQ Software Requirements (from SRS)

The actual DAQ SRS (not the POOL_SRS presented in "A Sample Software Requirements Specification" on page 203) contains hundreds of requirements; to keep the size of this chapter reasonable, I've selected the following requirements as they are representative of those needed to support the DIP switch use cases shown earlier. Note that the tags for these SRS requirements take the form [DAQ_SRS_xxx_yyy] because the actual DAQ system requirements have an SyRS as well as an SRS.

NOTE *The DAQ SRS document puts all requirements in section 3, as is the case for all SRSes. That is why the following section numbers revert to 3 rather than continuing the paragraph numbering of this chapter.*

3.1.1.1 PPDAQ Standard Software Platform

3.1.1.15 PPDAQ Ethernet IP Address

[DAQ_SRS_708_000]
The PPDAQ software shall set the Ethernet IP address to a value in the range 192.168.2.70–192.168.2.73 based on DIP switch 5–6 settings on the Netburner.

3.1.1.16 PPDAQ Ethernet IP Address 192.168.2.70

[DAQ_SRS_709_000]
The PPDAQ software shall set the Ethernet IP address to 192.168.2.70 if the Netburner DIP switches 5–6 are set to (OFF, OFF).

3.1.1.17 PPDAQ Ethernet IP Address 192.168.2.71

[DAQ_SRS_710_000]
The PPDAQ software shall set the Ethernet IP address to 192.168.2.71 if the Netburner DIP switches 5–6 are set to (ON, OFF).

3.1.1.18 PPDAQ Ethernet IP Address 192.168.2.72

[DAQ_SRS_711_000]

    The PPDAQ software shall set the Ethernet IP address to 192.168.2.72 if the Netburner DIP switches 5–6 are set to (OFF, ON).

3.1.1.19 PPDAQ Ethernet IP Address 192.168.2.73

[DAQ_SRS_712_000]

    The PPDAQ software shall set the Ethernet IP address to 192.168.2.73 if the Netburner DIP switches 5–6 are set to (ON, ON).

3.1.1.20 PPDAQ Ethernet Enabled

[DAQ_SRS_716_000]

    The PPDAQ software shall enable Ethernet operation if the Netburner DIP switch 3 is in the ON position.

3.1.1.21 PPDAQ Ethernet Disabled

[DAQ_SRS_716.5_000]

    The PPDAQ software shall disable Ethernet operation if the Netburner DIP switch 3 is in the OFF position.

3.1.1.22 PPDAQ Ethernet Task

[DAQ_SRS_716_001]

    The Ethernet listening task shall be started if Ethernet communications are enabled.

3.1.1.23 PPDAQ Ethernet Task Priority

[DAQ_SRS_716_002]

    The Ethernet listening task shall have a priority lower than the USB task but higher than the serial task.

3.1.1.24 PPDAQ Ethernet Port

[DAQ_SRS_717_000]

    The PPDAQ software shall communicate via Ethernet using socket port 0x5050 (decimal 20560, ASCII *PP*, for *Plantation Productions*).

3.1.1.25 PPDAQ Ethernet Multiple Clients Enabled

[DAQ_SRS_718_000]

    The PPDAQ software shall allow up to five Ethernet clients if the Netburner DIP switch 4 is set to the ON position.

3.1.1.26   PPDAQ Ethernet Multiple Clients Disabled

[DAQ_SRS_718_001]
   The PPDAQ software shall allow only a single Ethernet client if the Netburner DIP switch 4 is set to the OFF position.

3.1.1.29   PPDAQ Unit Test Mode I/O

[DAQ_SRS_721_000]
   The PPDAQ software shall utilize the UART0 serial port on the Netburner MOD54415 MOD-70 evaluation board for unit test communication unless USB commands are enabled (USB commands share the same serial port [UART0] as the test mode output).

3.1.1.30   PPDAQ Debug Mode Enabled

[DAQ_SRS_721_001]
   The PPDAQ software shall operate in a special *debug* mode if the Netburner DIP switch 8 is set to the ON position and USB (DIP switch 2) is not enabled.

3.1.1.31   PPDAQ Debug Mode Disabled

[DAQ_SRS_721_002]
   The PPDAQ software shall operate in the normal (nondebug) mode if the Netburner DIP switch 8 is set to the OFF position.

3.1.1.38   PPDAQ Command Source #3

[DAQ_SRS_728_000]
   The PPDAQ software shall accept commands from the Ethernet port on the Netburner MOD54415 MOD-70 evaluation board if Ethernet communications are enabled.

3.1.1.40   PPDAQ Maximum Ethernet Connections #1

[DAQ_SRS_737_000]
   The PPDAQ software shall only recognize a single connection on the Ethernet port if the Netburner DIP switch 4 is in the OFF position.

3.1.1.41   PPDAQ Maximum Ethernet Connections #2

[DAQ_SRS_738_000]
   The PPDAQ software shall only recognize up to five connections on the Ethernet port if the Netburner DIP switch 4 is in the ON position.

3.1.1.42   PPDAQ Ethernet Command Processing Tasks

[DAQ_SRS_738_001]
   The PPDAQ software shall start a new process to handle command processing for each connection.

3.1.1.43 PPDAQ Ethernet Command Task Priorities

[DAQ_SRS_738_002]

The PPDAQ command processing tasks shall each have a different priority that is higher than the priority of the Ethernet listening task and less than the priority of the USB command task.

10.9 Updating the Traceability Matrix with Requirement Information

The SyRS and SRS requirements typically add four to six columns to the RTM: Description, SyRS tag (if you have an SyRS), Allocations, SRS tag, and Test/verification type. The Description column provides a brief description of the requirement, such as *PPDAQ Standard Software Platform* from requirement DAQ_SRS_700_000 in the previous section. (Note that this does *not* refer to the POOL_SRS tag presented in "A Sample Software Requirements Specification" on page 203.)

The SyRS and SRS tag columns contain the actual SyRS (if present) and SRS tag identifiers. Generally, you would sort the rows in the RTM by SyRS (primary key) and then SRS (secondary key) unless there are no SyRS tags, in which case you'd simply sort the rows by the SRS tag.

The Allocations column specifies whether the requirement is hardware (*H*), software (*S*), other (*O*), or a combination of these. Typically, only SyRS requirements have hardware-only allocations; after all, SRS requirements are *software* requirements. It is possible, however, for an SRS requirement to have an *HS* allocation if it covers both software and hardware aspects of the system. The *other* designation is a catch-all to cover requirements that don't clearly fit into a hardware or software category (this could describe a manual process, for example).

Note that if you don't have an SyRS, or all of your requirement allocations are software allocations, you can eliminate the Allocations column; this can help reduce the size and complexity of the RTM.

The Verification type column in the RTM specifies how you will verify (test) this requirement in the system. Possible entries are: *by test* (*T*); *by review* (*R*); *by inspection* (*I*; the "by review" variant for hardware designs); *by design* (*D*; usually applies to hardware, not software); *by analysis* (*A*); *other* (*O*); and *no test, or no test possible* (*N*).

Clearly, requirements that have a *T* verification method will have some associated test to run to verify the requirement. This generally means that you will have a corresponding test case for this requirement and a test procedure to execute it.

It may be difficult, impractical, or dangerous to test certain requirements.[5] In these situations it may be much easier to carefully review the

---

5. For example, some requirements might state that it is preferable to damage the system hardware rather than allow the system to enter a state that might cause bodily harm or death. You would not want to test this by damaging the system.

code to verify that it will behave properly. For such requirements, the verification method would be *R*, by review.

The *by analysis* (*A*) verification method means that somewhere you are offering a formal (mathematical) proof that the software meets the formal requirement. This is a much more stringent process than *by review* and a subject that is well beyond the scope of this book. Nevertheless, this type of verification may be necessary for certain requirements whose failure could lead to catastrophic events (such as death). Consider the very first requirement from "(Selected) DAQ Software Requirements (from SRS)" on page 219:

[DAQ_SRS_700_000]
The PPDAQ software shall run on a Netburner MOD54415 MOD-70 evaluation board connected to a DAQ_IF interface board.

It would be somewhat difficult to come up with an actual test that proves this requirement is being met (other than installing the software on a Netburner MOD54415 and verifying that it actually runs). On the other hand, it's nearly trivial to look at the source code (and the build files) and verify that this code was written for the Netburner MOD54415. A *test by review* is easily the most appropriate way to handle this particular requirement.

The *other* verification method is a catch-all category that implies you're going to provide the documentation to justify either the lack of a testing method or the verification approach you plan to use.

The *no test* or *no test possible* verification requires you to justify why a test is not needed. If you are specifying *N* to represent *no test possible*, you should carefully consider whether the requirement is valid (is an actual requirement). Remember, if it can't be tested, it isn't a requirement.

These are the four column entries that [DAQ_SRS_700_000] would add to the RTM.

Description	SRS tag	Allocation	Verification
PPDAQ Standard Software Platform	DAQ_SRS_700_000	HS	R

Given the requirements in "(Selected) DAQ Software Requirements (from SRS)" on page 219, we can divide the requirements into two groups: those whose verification type should be *by test* and those whose verification type should be *by review* (because an actual test for them might be difficult to perform or awkward to create).

10.9.1   Requirements to Be Verified by Review

Table 10-2 shows a list of the requirements from "(Selected) DAQ Software Requirements (from SRS)" on page 219 that should be verified by review and should provide a justification for the choice that has been made.[6]

---

6. This is my opinion, so feel free to add or remove items from this list if your opinion differs. Note that I will use this list when creating a Software Review List later in this book.

Table 10-2: DAQ Software Requirement Justifications

Requirement	Justification
DAQ_SRS_700_000	Although you could argue that running the software on a Netburner verifies that it runs on a Netburner, reviewing the make/build files is an easier and more practical way to verify this requirement.
DAQ_SRS_700_000.01	Although you could argue that running the software on a μC/OS verifies that it runs under μC/OS, reviewing the make/build files is an easier and more practical way to verify this requirement.
DAQ_SRS_702_001	Writing a test to show that a separate process is running would be difficult without actually changing the code (i.e., to print some output to show this). However, reviewing the code to see that it is starting a new task to handle RS-232 communication isn't that difficult.
DAQ_SRS_702_002	Writing a test to show that the RS-232 process is running at a particular priority level would require modifying the code; reviewing the code is easier.
DAQ_SRS_703_001	Making this one by review is arguable. You could argue that if the system is accepting RS-232 commands, the task is running. However, this does not prove that a separate task is running or not running (the main task could be processing the commands). Hence, this should probably be a by review verification.
DAQ_SRS_705_001	The same argument applies as for DAQ_SRS_702_001 (just applied to the USB input task).
DAQ_SRS_705_002	Same justification as for DAQ_SRS_702_002.
DAQ_SRS_706_001	Same argument as for DAQ_SRS_705_001 (just the complement of that requirement).
DAQ_SRS_716_001	Same argument as for DAQ_SRS_702_001 (just applied to the Ethernet listen task).
DAQ_SRS_716_002	Same argument as for DAQ_SRS_702_002 (just applied to the Ethernet listen task priority).
DAQ_SRS_719_000	Currently, unit test mode is undefined on the DAQ system so there is no way to test that the system has entered this mode. Reviewing the code verifies that the internal variable is properly set up (the only effect the DIP switch will have).
DAQ_SRS_720_000	See DAQ_SRS_719_000.
DAQ_SRS_723_000	Another arguable case. The fact that the system is reading the DIP switches (to handle other tests) should be enough to show that the software is reading the Netburner switches. However, this requirement is sufficiently unimportant that the choice of review/test doesn't really matter.
DAQ_SRS_723_000.01	See DAQ_SRS_723_000.
DAQ_SRS_723_000.02	See DAQ_SRS_723_000.
DAQ_SRS_725_000	Checking to see that the DAQ responds to a command is no big deal (easily testable); however, this requirement states that the DAQ does not initiate communication on its own (that is, it's negatively stated, which, in general, is bad in a requirement). Reviewing code is the only proper way to handle negative requirements (which is why you want to avoid them).
DAQ_SRS_738_001	Similar justification to DAQ_SRS_702_001.
DAQ_SRS_738_002	Similar justification to DAQ_SRS_702_002.

10.9.2 Requirements to Be Verified by Testing

All requirements in "(Selected) DAQ Software Requirements (from SRS)" on page 219 that are not also listed in "Requirements to Be Verified by Review" on page 223 will be verified using test cases and test procedures.

10.10 For More Information

IEEE. "IEEE Standard 830-1998: IEEE Recommended Practice for Software Requirements Specifications." October 20, 1998. *https://doi.org/10.1109/IEEESTD.1998.88286*.

Leffingwell, Dean, and Don Widrig. *Managing Software Requirements*. Boston: Addison-Wesley Professional, 2003.

Wiegers, Karl E. *Software Requirements*. Redmond, WA: Microsoft Press, 2009.

———. "Writing Quality Requirements." *Software Development* 7, no. 5 (May 1999): 44–48.

11

SOFTWARE DESIGN DESCRIPTION DOCUMENTATION

The Software Design Description (SDD) document provides low-level implementation details for the design of the software. While it doesn't necessarily dive down to the level of actual code, it does provide the algorithms, data structures, and low-level flow control for the software implementation.

There are lots of different ideas about how to document software design. This chapter follows the guidelines proposed by IEEE Standard (Std) 1016-2009[1] and uses many of the concepts described in that standard.

IEEE Std 1016-2009 was written in an attempt to be language-independent. However, the Unified Modeling Language covers almost all of the requirements of the standard, which is why Chapter 4 introduced UML and why we'll use it in this chapter. If you're interested in the other software design

---

1. IEEE Std 1016 is a registered trademark of the IEEE. IEEE Std 1016-2009 is a revision of IEEE Std 1016-1998 that incorporates UML as the software modeling language.

modeling languages available, feel free to check out their descriptions in the IEEE Std 1016-2009 document.

11.1 IEEE Std 1016-1998 vs. IEEE Std 1016-2009

Finalized in 1998, the original IEEE SDD guidelines were based on structured programming software engineering concepts prevalent in the 1980s and 1990s. The recommendations were released just as the object-oriented programming revolution was under way and, as a result, immediately became outdated. It took 10 years to update, but the revision, Std 1016-2009, covered object-oriented analysis and design. The new guidelines maintained features of the 1016-1998 standard but in a somewhat deprecated form. Note, however, that some of them are still useful in modern design, so there's no reason to ignore the old standard if those features are appropriate in your context.

11.2 IEEE 1016-2009 Conceptual Model

The SDD does not live in a vacuum. The material in an SDD flows naturally from the Software Requirements Specification (SRS), and the Reverse Traceability Matrix (RTM) binds the two documents. Figure 11-1 shows this relationship.

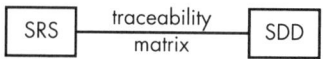

Figure 11-1: SRS relationship to SDD

11.2.1 Design Concerns and Design Stakeholders

Each requirement in the SRS ultimately relates to a design concern in the SDD (see Figure 11-2). A *design concern* is anything that is of interest to a stakeholder in the design of the system. A *stakeholder* is anyone who has a say in the system's design. A *requirement* refers to any individual requirement from the SRS, as explained in Chapter 10.

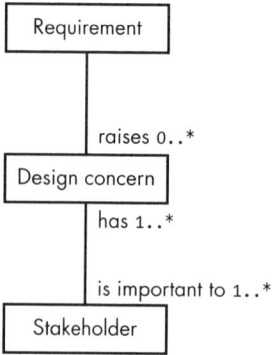

Figure 11-2: Mapping requirements to design concerns

Figure 11-2 maps requirements to design concerns as follows:

`0..*` Each requirement has zero or more associated design concerns.

`1..*` A single design concern is important to one or more design stakeholders.

`1...*` Each stakeholder has at least one (and possibly more) design concerns.

The IEEE conceptual model states that requirements raise zero or more design concerns. But in fact, requirements and design concerns should have a one-to-one relationship: for each design concern there is exactly one associated requirement. If a requirement doesn't raise any design concerns—that is, the requirement has no impact on the software design—then perhaps that requirement isn't necessary (and, therefore, is not a valid requirement). If a requirement maps to multiple design concerns, this probably suggests that you have a compound requirement that should be broken down into atomic requirements in your SRS (see "Atomic" on page 190).

Stakeholders and design concerns should have a many-to-many relationship. One stakeholder can (and usually does) have many design concerns. Likewise, a single design concern can be (and usually is) shared by many different stakeholders.

11.2.2 *Design Viewpoints and Design Elements*

Ultimately, the design concern (or just the requirement) is the interface point to the SDD. A *design viewpoint* logically groups a set of one or more design concerns. For example, *a logical viewpoint* (see "Logical Viewpoint" on page 235) would describe the static data structures in the design, so all the requirements associated with classes and data objects would be associated with that viewpoint. An *algorithmic viewpoint* (see "Algorithmic Viewpoint" on page 239) would describe certain algorithms that the design uses, so any requirements that specify certain algorithms to use (which, admittedly, should be rare) would be associated with that viewpoint.

IEEE Std 1016-2009 calls for specifying each design viewpoint by:

- A viewpoint name
- Design concerns associated with the viewpoint
- A list of design elements (types of design entities, attributes, and constraints) that the viewpoint uses
- A discussion of the analysis someone would use to construct a design view based on the viewpoint
- Criteria for interpreting and evaluating the design
- Author's name or a reference to the source material used for the viewpoint

Figure 11-3 shows the relationship between design concerns and design viewpoints. The multiplicity item 1..* indicates that a single viewpoint frames (or groups) one or more requirements.

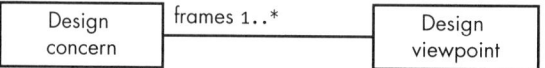

Figure 11-3: Mapping design concerns to design viewpoints

Design concerns and design viewpoints have a fundamental one-to-many relationship that provides traceability between the SDD and SRS. In the RTM, each requirement (design concern) will link to exactly one design viewpoint. Therefore, you would normally attach SDD tags to design viewpoints (or, as you'll see in a moment, you could also attach the tags to design views, as there is a one-to-one relationship between design views and design viewpoints).

Design viewpoints define a set of *design elements* (see Figure 11-4), examples of which include class diagrams, sequence diagrams, state diagrams, packages, use cases, and activity diagrams.

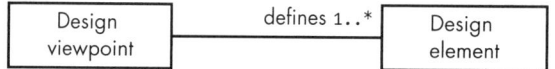

Figure 11-4: Mapping design viewpoints to design elements

A design element is anything that you would put in a design view, including design entities, attributes, relationships, and constraints:

- Design *entities* are objects that describe the major components of a design. Examples include systems, subsystems, libraries, frameworks, patterns, templates, components, classes, structures, types, data stores, modules, program units, programs, threads, and processes. IEEE Std 1016-2009 requires that each design entity in an SDD have a name and a purpose.
- Design elements have associated *attributes*: a name, a type, a purpose, and an author. When listing the design elements in your SDD viewpoint, you must provide these attributes.
- Design *relationships* have an associated name and type. IEEE Std 1016-2009 does not predefine any relationships; however, UML 2.0 defines several—such as association, aggregation, dependency, and generalization—that you would typically use in your SDDs. As per the IEEE requirements, you must describe all relationships you use in the design viewpoint specification.
- A design *constraint* is an element (the *source* element) that applies restrictions or rules to some other design element (the *target* element) of a design view. The IEEE requires that you list all design constraints by name and type (and source/target elements) in the viewpoint that defines them.

You define design elements using a formal design language (see Figure 11-5). As noted earlier, IEEE Std 1016-2009 tries to be language-agnostic, but the truth is that it was designed specifically around UML. Other (formal) design languages the IEEE suggests include IDEFO, IDEF1X, and Vienna Definition Method. However, for this book, you're probably better off using UML.

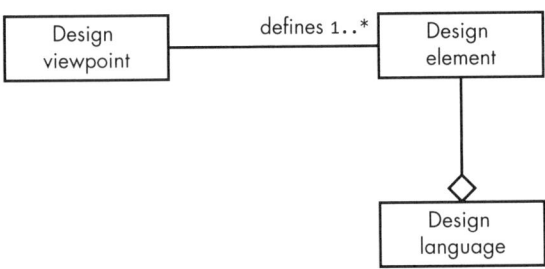

Figure 11-5: Relationship between design viewpoints, elements, and language

IEEE Std 1016-2009 defines a common set of design viewpoints. As the standard is a set of recommended practices, not absolute requirements, the list of viewpoints that follows here is neither exhaustive nor required. That is, in your SDD you can define and add further viewpoints as you see fit, and you don't need to include all of them (indeed, some of them are deprecated and included only for compatibility with the older IEEE Std 1016-1998).

11.2.2.1 Context Viewpoint

The design elements for which the context viewpoint collects requirements are actors (users, external systems, stakeholders), services the system provides, and their interactions (such as input and output). The context viewpoint also manages various design constraints, such as quality of service, reliability, and performance. In a sense, you begin this work while developing the requirements for the SRS (for example, while creating use cases to drive the requirements) and finish the work while developing the SDD.

The main purpose of the context viewpoint is to set the system boundary and define those considerations that are internal to the system and those that are external. This limits the scope of the design so that the designer and author(s) of the SDD can concentrate on the system design and not waste time considering external factors.

You typically represent context viewpoints in UML use case diagrams (see "Use Cases" on page 214). For a good example, refer back to Figure 10-1, which lists the initializations the user can set via DIP switches on the data acquisition (DAQ) system. As another example, Figure 11-6 shows an abbreviated set of use cases for DAQ commands between a host system (typically a PC) and the DAQ CPU interface board.

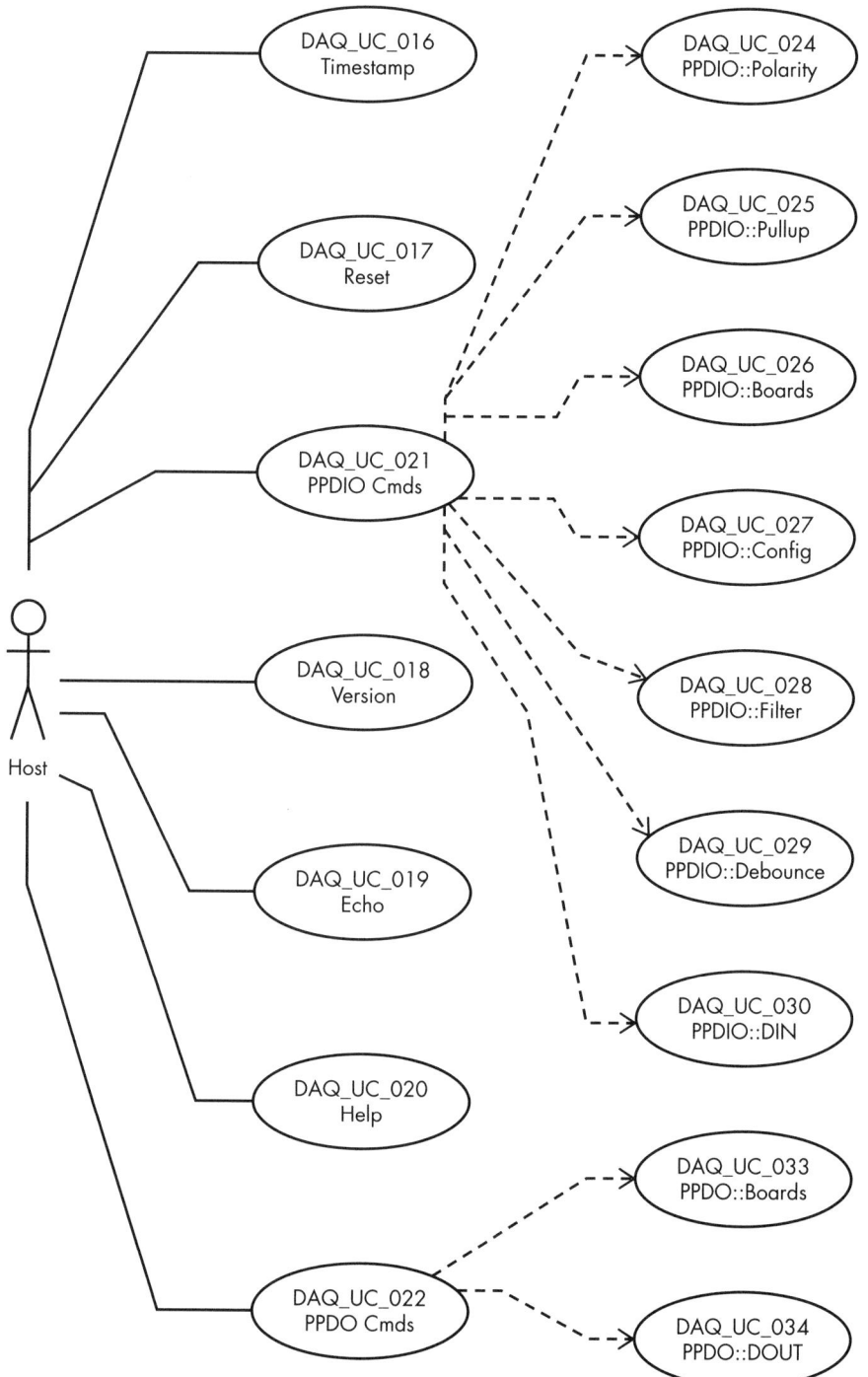

Figure 11-6: DAQ commands use case

This figure shows the command interface between the external system (the host actor) and the DAQ system. Note that each use case—in this example, there are 16—corresponds to requirements in the DAQ SRS.[2]

11.2.2.2 Composition Viewpoint

The composition viewpoint lists the major modules/components that make up the system. One of the main goals of this viewpoint is to foster code reuse by identifying, in the design, items that could come from existing libraries, or proprietary designs that could be reused in the system.

Design entities included in the composition viewpoint are—to name a few—composition (obviously), include, use, and generalization. The composition viewpoint states relationships between design entities using realization, dependency, aggregation, composition, and generalization as well as any other relationships between objects.

Note that this is an older viewpoint carried over from IEEE Std 1016-1998.[3] For the most part it is superseded by the structure viewpoint (see "Structure Viewpoint" on page 237) and, to a lesser extent, the logical viewpoint (see the next section). The composition viewpoint hails from the days when programs were composed largely of procedures and functions organized into libraries, long before the days of object-oriented analysis and design.

Modern designs, if they contain a composition viewpoint at all, largely relegate it to describing major components of a system, as recommended by IEEE Std 1016-2009. Figure 11-7 provides an example of such a composition viewpoint for the DAQ system, using watered-down component diagrams. In my opinion, component diagrams are not a good fit for composition viewpoint diagrams—they are too low-level for the task. Component diagrams typically include interfaces (required and provided) that don't make sense at the composition viewpoint level. However, apparently due to the similarity of the words *composition* and *component*, it's very common to use watered-down UML component diagrams to denote the composition viewpoint.

---

2. There are actually 29 use cases in the full use case diagram. See *http://www.plantation-productions.com/Electronics/DAQ/DAQ.html*.

3. The IEEE Std 1016-2009 includes many older viewpoints carried over from the 1016-1998 standard. You probably shouldn't use these older viewpoints in new designs. They are included only so that older SDD documents can still claim to be compliant with IEEE Std 1016.

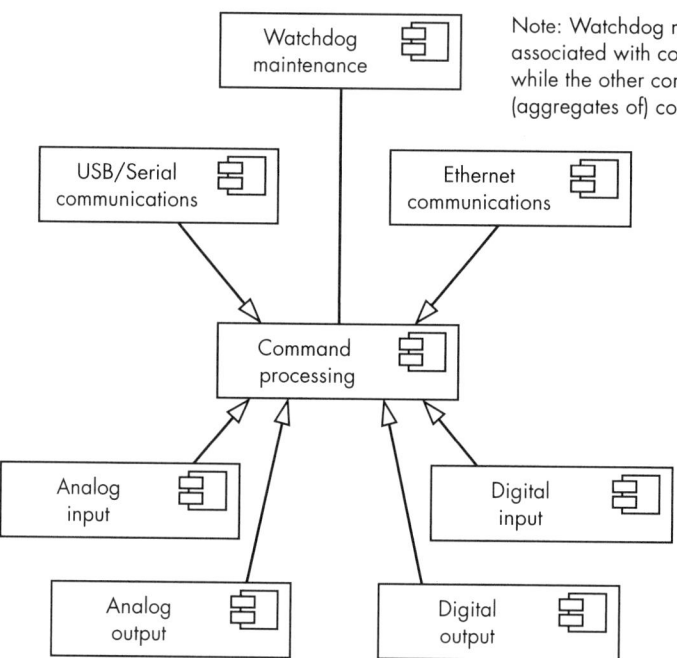

Figure 11-7: Composition viewpoint diagram

Some engineers use a combination of component and deployment diagrams (see "Deployment Diagrams" on page 159) to illustrate a composition viewpoint, as shown in Figure 11-8.

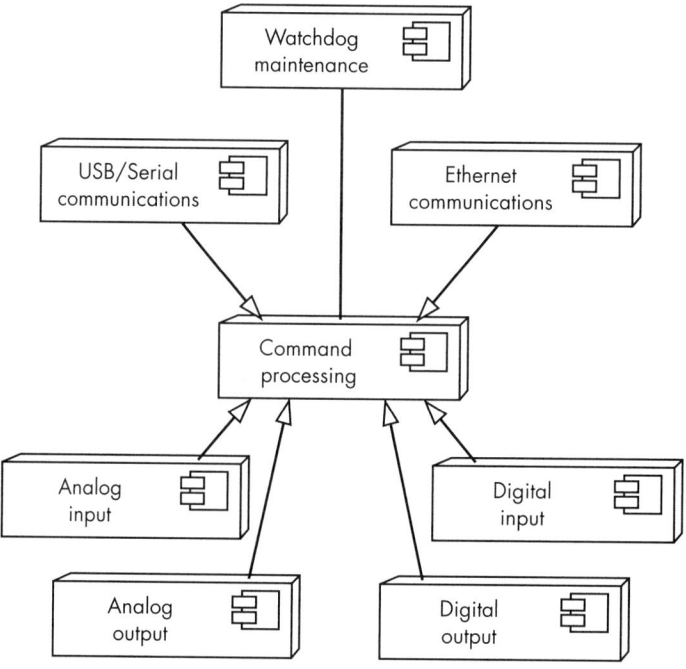

Figure 11-8: Deployment/component diagram

Note that the nodes in this diagram still include the component symbol to indicate that they are components forming a larger system, rather than hardware items. This is a nonstandard diagramming method for UML, but I've seen it in several example SDDs so I've included it here.

11.2.2.3 Logical Viewpoint

The logical viewpoint describes preexisting and new types used in the design, along with their class, interface/protocol, and structural definitions. The logical viewpoint also describes the objects (instances of the types) the design uses.

The logical viewpoint deals with classes, interfaces, data types, objects, attributes, methods, functions, procedures (subroutines), templates, macros, and namespaces. It also assigns attributes—such as names, visibility type, and values—and attaches appropriate constraints to these design entities.

Typically, you use UML class diagrams to implement a logical viewpoint. Figure 11-9 shows a class diagram for an `adcClass_t` class that might be appropriate for the analog input module in Figure 11-8. In addition to this basic class diagram, you'd probably want to include a *data dictionary*, or text describing the purpose of all the attributes for this class.

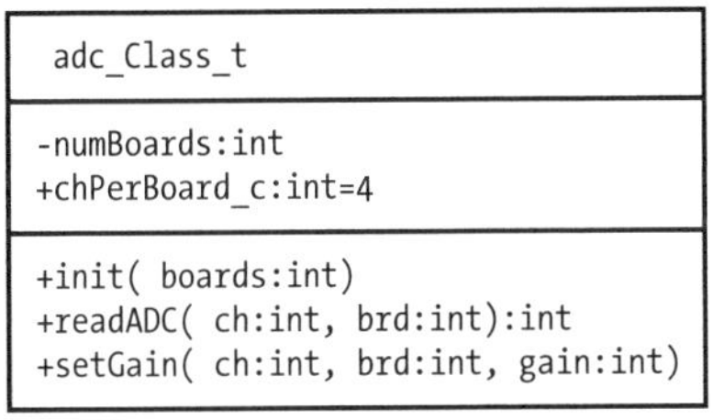

```
adc_Class_t
-numBoards:int
+chPerBoard_c:int=4
+init( boards:int)
+readADC( ch:int, brd:int):int
+setGain( ch:int, brd:int, gain:int)
```

Figure 11-9: adc class diagram

In addition to the bare class diagrams, a logical viewpoint should also include relationships between classes (such as dependency, association, aggregation, composition, and inheritance). See "UML Class Relationships" on page 114 for more details on these class relationships and how you can diagram them.

11.2.2.4 Dependency Viewpoint

Like the composition viewpoint, the dependency viewpoint is a deprecated viewpoint maintained for compatibility with IEEE Std 1016-1998; you generally wouldn't use this viewpoint in modern designs, as other options (such as the logical and resource viewpoints) can map dependencies in a more logical manner. However, there's nothing stopping you from using dependency viewpoints where appropriate, and it's also likely that you'll encounter them in SDDs, so you should know about them.

In an SDD, the dependency viewpoint illustrates design entity relationships and interconnections, including shared information, interface parameterization, and order of execution using terms such as *uses*, *provides*, and *requires.* Dependency viewpoints apply to subsystems, components, modules, and resources. IEEE Std 1016-2009 recommends using UML component diagrams and package diagrams to depict this viewpoint. Using a combined deployment/component diagram (as in Figure 11-8) is probably a good solution if you want to go the component diagram route (say, for dependencies between components or subsystems). Using package diagrams is a good idea if you are describing the dependency relationship between packages, as shown in Figure 11-10.

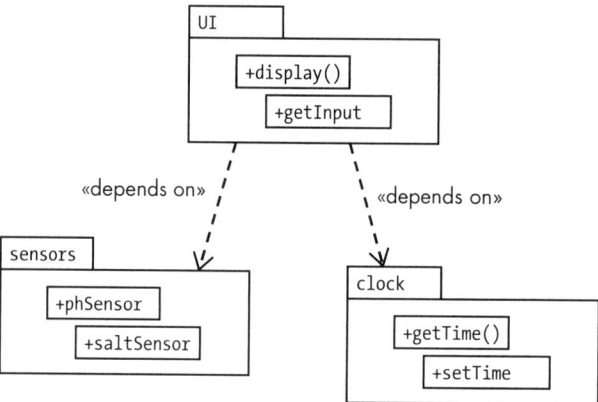

Figure 11-10: Package dependencies

11.2.2.5 Information/Database Viewpoint

The information/database viewpoint describes persistent data usage in your design. It is similar to the logical viewpoint in that you use class diagrams to show data structure, content, and metadata definitions. The information viewpoint would also describe data access schemes, data management strategies, and data storage mechanisms.

This is also a deprecated item included to maintain compatibility with IEEE Std 1016-1998. In modern designs, you would likely use the logical viewpoint or possibly the resource viewpoint instead.

11.2.2.6 Patterns Use Viewpoint

The patterns use viewpoint maps out the design patterns—and the reusable components implemented from them—that are used in the project. For more information about design patterns, see "For More Information" on page 260.

Patterns use viewpoint diagrams use a combination of UML composite structures, class diagrams, and package diagrams along with association, collaboration use, and connectors to indicate objects generated from the patterns. This viewpoint is loosely designed, so you have a lot of latitude in its creation should you choose to use it in your SDD.

11.2.2.7 Interface Viewpoint

The interface viewpoint describes the services (for example, APIs) provided by the design. Specifically, it includes a description of interfaces for which there are no requirements in the SRS, including interfaces to third-party libraries, other parts of the project, or other projects within the same organization. It is a road map that other programmers can use when interacting with the portion of the design covered by the interface viewpoint.

IEEE Std 1016-2009 recommends using UML component diagrams for the interface viewpoint. Figure 11-11 shows two components (possibly in the DAQ system) dealing with digital I/O and relay output (a specific form of digital output).

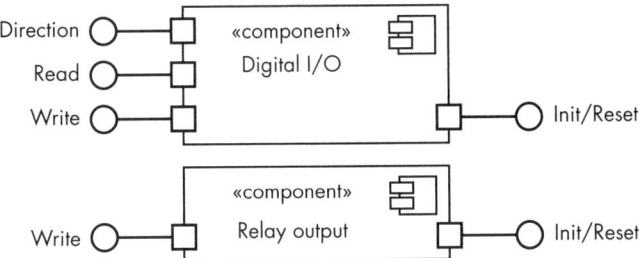

Figure 11-11: Interface viewpoint example

In addition to the component diagram, the interface viewpoint should include a description of how the system interacts with these interfaces, including data types, function calls, latencies, constraints on inputs, the range of outputs, and other important issues. For example, when discussing the Direction interface, you might include information such as:

Direction
Direction(ddir:int, port:int)

A call to Direction sets the specified digital I/O port (port = 0..95) to either an input port (if ddir = 0) or an output port (if ddir = 1).

For Read, you might use a description such as:

Read
Read(port:int):int

A call to Read returns the current value (0 or 1) of the specified digital input port (port = 0..95).

Again, the interface viewpoint is included in IEEE Std 1016-2009 only for compatibility with the older IEEE Std 1016-1998. In modern SDDs, consider placing interface items in the context and structure viewpoints instead.

11.2.2.8 Structure Viewpoint

The structure viewpoint describes the internal organization and construction of the objects in the design. It is the more modern version of the composition viewpoint, which describes how the design is (recursively) broken down into parts. You would use the structure viewpoint to break down larger objects into their smaller pieces for the purpose of determining how to reuse those smaller components throughout the design.

The diagramming methods typically used for the structure viewpoint are UML composite structure diagrams, UML package diagrams, and UML class diagrams. These diagrams are illustrated for the swimming pool monitor (SPM) in Figures 11-12, 11-13, and 11-14, respectively.

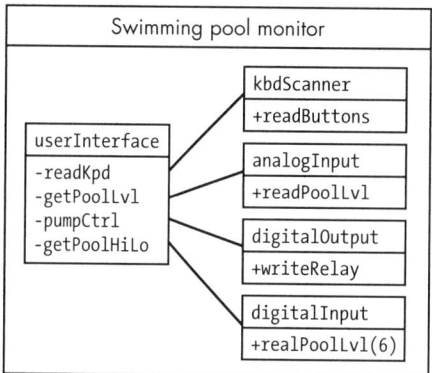

Figure 11-12: SPM composite structure diagram

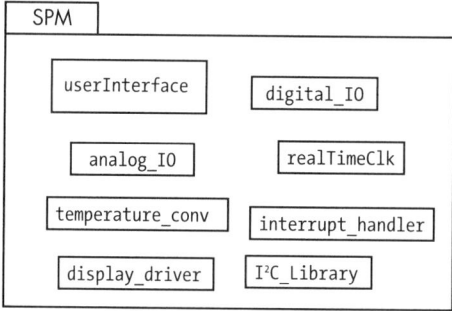

Figure 11-13: SPM package diagram

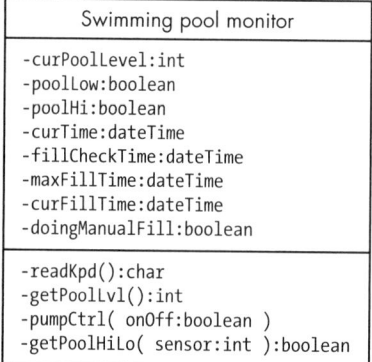

Figure 11-14: SPM class diagram

These examples illustrate that you'll typically have more than one diagram in a given viewpoint. Also note that a typical structure viewpoint will have multiple composite structure diagrams, (possibly) multiple package diagrams, and (certainly) multiple class diagrams.

11.2.2.9 Interaction Viewpoint

The interaction viewpoint is the main place where you define the activities that take place in the software. This is where you'll place most of your interaction diagrams—activity diagrams, sequence diagrams, collaboration diagrams, and the like—with the possible exception of state diagrams, because they normally appear in the state dynamics viewpoint (covered in the next section). In addition to interaction diagrams, you might also use composite structure and package diagrams in the interaction viewpoint.

A full example of the interaction viewpoint appears in "A Sample SDD" on page 247.

11.2.2.10 State Dynamics Viewpoint

The state dynamics viewpoint describes the internal operating state of a software system. For this viewpoint, you would typically use UML statechart diagrams (see "Statechart Diagrams" on page 163).

11.2.2.11 Algorithmic Viewpoint

The algorithmic viewpoint is another older viewpoint carried over from IEEE 1016-1998. Its purpose was to describe the algorithms (typically through flowcharts, Warnier/Orr diagrams, pseudocode, and the like) used in the system. This viewpoint largely has been replaced by the interaction viewpoint in the Std 1016-2009 document.

11.2.2.12 Resource Viewpoint

The resource viewpoint describes how the design uses various system resources. This includes CPU usage (including multicore usage), memory usage, storage, peripheral usage, shared libraries, and other security, performance, and cost issues associated with the design. Typically, resources are entities that are external to the design.

This is another Std 1016-1998 item included for compatibility reasons in Std 1016-2009. In new designs, you would typically use the context viewpoint to describe resource usage.

11.2.3 Design Views, Overlays, and Rationales

IEEE Std 1016-2009 states that an SDD is organized into one or more design views. Therefore, the design view is the fundamental unit of organization in an SDD. Design views provide (possibly) multiple perspectives on the system design to help clarify to stakeholders, designers, and programmers how the design fulfills the requirements as specified by an associated design viewpoint.

An SDD is *complete* when it covers every requirement (design concern) in at least one design view, covers all the entities and relationships in the associated design viewpoint, and lives within all the constraints applied to the design. In plain terms, this means that you've matched all the requirements to appropriate diagrams and textual discussions as outlined in "Design Viewpoints and Design Elements" on page 229.

An SDD is *consistent* if there is no conflict between any of the elements in the design views. For example, if a class diagram states that an attribute (field) named hasValue is a boolean, but an activity diagram treats that field as a string, you have an inconsistency.

11.2.3.1 Design Views vs. Design Viewpoints

There is a one-to-one relationship between design view and design viewpoints, as shown in Figure 11-15. The association link states that a design view conforms to exactly one design viewpoint and a design viewpoint is governed by exactly one design view.

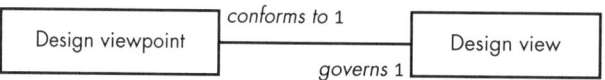

Figure 11-15: Design views and design viewpoints

So, what's the difference between a design view and a design viewpoint? A *design view* is the actual information (graphic and textual) that you would normally consider to be the "design." A design viewpoint is the *point of view* from which you create the design. In the IEEE recommendations, the design viewpoints would be something like the context viewpoint or interaction viewpoint. These are not the actual design views, but rather the format used to present the views. In terms of the organization of your SDD, the view/viewpoint section of the table of contents might look something like the following:[4]

1 Viewpoint #1

    1.1 Viewpoint #1 Specification (see "Design Viewpoints and Design Elements" on page 229)

    1.2 View #1

2 Viewpoint #2

    2.1 Viewpoint #2 Specification

    2.2 View #2

---

4. In almost every sample SDD I've found on the internet, the authors combine design viewpoints and design views into the same sections. When they differentiate them, the Design Views section is a brief introduction and the actual views are listed under the Viewpoint sections (which seems backward to me, but the IEEE Std 1016-2009 document is not very clear on this matter).

3   Viewpoint #3

  3.1   Viewpoint #3 Specification

  3.2   View #3

4   Etc.

The reason for organizing the views by viewpoints is simple: viewpoints represent the perspectives of different stakeholders, so this organization allows stakeholders to quickly locate the sections of the SDD of interest to them instead of having to read the whole document.

Note that each view in this outline does not necessarily correspond to a single diagram or textual description. A single view could consist of many separate UML diagrams and intervening textual descriptions. For example, in a logical viewpoint you'll probably have many different class diagrams (not just one) if for no other reason than that it's difficult to combine multiple classes into a single diagram. Even if you could, you might want to logically organize your class diagrams to make them easier to read. Furthermore, in addition to the class diagrams themselves, you'll need to provide some text describing the members (attributes) of those classes. Rather than having a huge class diagram (perhaps consuming dozens of pages) followed by a very long textual description (spanning additional dozens of pages), it's probably better to put a few class diagrams in one figure, immediately follow them with the textual information about the attributes, and then repeat this for the remaining classes you need to document.

11.2.3.2 Design Overlays

A design overlay is an "escape clause" for a view. Design views conform to design overlays or, conversely, design overlays govern design views, as shown in Figure 11-16. So, if you've created a logical viewpoint, for example, and you want to incorporate some interaction diagrams in that viewpoint for clarification, you would use a design overlay.

A design overlay modifies the view/viewpoint organization like so:

1   Viewpoint #1

  1.1   Viewpoint #1 Specification

  1.2   View #1

  1.3   Overlay #1

  1.4   Overlay #2

  1.5   Etc.

2   Etc.

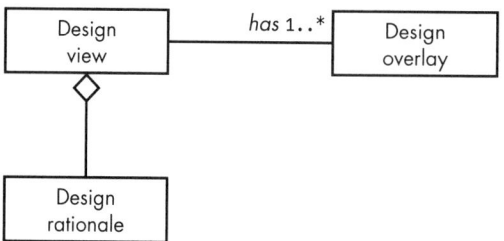

Figure 11-16: Design view/overlay/rationale relationship

Design overlays must be identified as such (to avoid confusion with the associated viewpoint), uniquely named, and associated with only a single viewpoint.

One benefit of a design overlay is that it lets you mix and match design languages or extend an existing design language when it isn't expressive enough to satisfy your needs. Design overlays also allow you to extend an existing view without having to create a whole new viewpoint (which can be a lot of extra work).

11.2.3.3   Design Rationale

The design rationale explains the purpose behind the design and justifies the design to other viewers. Generally, a design rationale consists of comments and annotations throughout the design. It may address (but certainly isn't limited to) potential concerns about the design, different options and tradeoffs considered during the design, arguments and justifications for why certain decisions were made, and even changes made during the prototyping or development phases (because the original design did not pan out). Figure 11-16 shows the relationship of design rationales to design views (the aggregation symbol implies that the design rationale comments are included, or are a part of, the design view).

11.2.4   The IEEE Std 1016-2009 Conceptual Model

Figures 11-17 and 11-18 provide conceptual model diagrams for the SDD and design elements, according to IEEE Std 1016-2009.[5]

---

5. With a few changes for clarity.

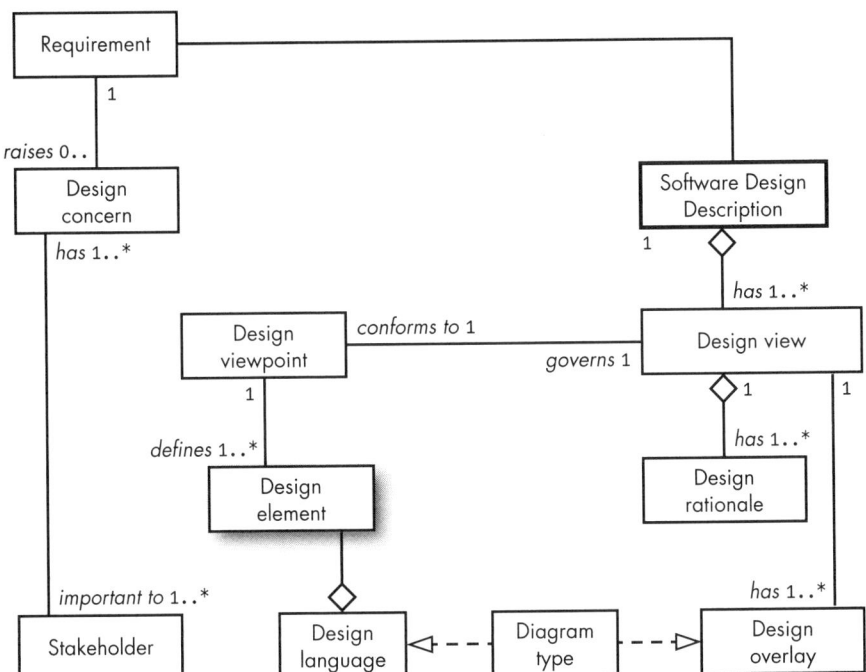

Figure 11-17: SDD conceptual model

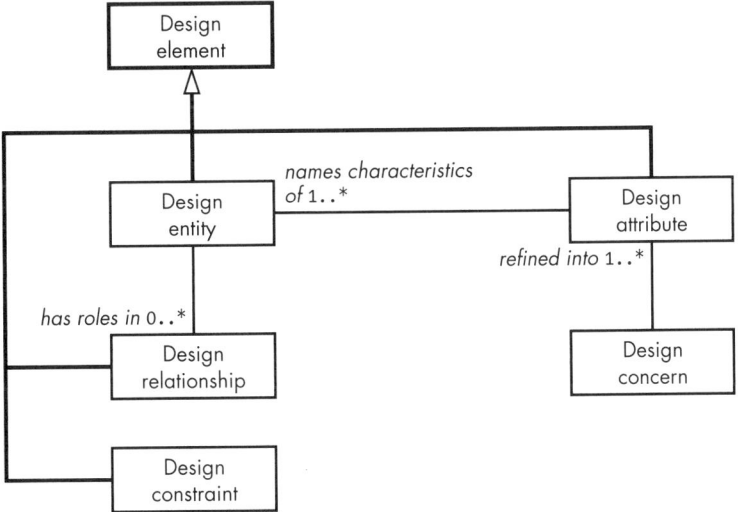

Figure 11-18: SDD design element conceptual model

11.3 SDD Required Contents

An SDD must have the following contents (according to IEEE Std 1016-2009):

- An SDD identification
- A list of the design stakeholders
- Design concerns (developed from the product requirements)
- A set of one or more design viewpoints (note that there's exactly one design viewpoint for each design view in an SDD)
- A set of one or more design views (roughly corresponding to the different types of UML diagrams, though a design viewpoint is not necessarily tied to a particular UML diagram type)
- Any needed design overlays
- Any necessary design rationales (IEEE requires at least a purpose)

11.3.1 SDD Identification

At the very least, an SDD should include the following identification information (not necessarily in this order):

- Creation date/date of issue
- Current status
- Purpose/scope
- Issuing organization
- Authors (including copyright information)
- References
- Context
- A description of the design languages used for design viewpoints
- Body
- Summary
- Glossary
- Change history

Most of this information is boilerplate (except for dates, you typically copy this information from an organization's generic SDD template). Obviously, some of this information changes from one SDD to another (like dates, authors, and change history), but for the most part very little intellectual activity is involved in the SDD identification. It exists primarily so that the SDD can stand as an independent document.

11.3.2 Design Stakeholders and Their Design Concerns

The SDD must list all the individuals who contributed requirements/design concerns to the project. This content is critical: if there is ever a question about the design rationale that is not addressed in the SDD, a reader should be able to determine which stakeholder to contact with questions about the design concerns.

11.3.3 Design Views, Viewpoints, Overlays, and Rationales

The design views, viewpoints, overlays, and rationales form the main body of the SDD.

11.4 SDD Traceability and Tags

We haven't yet discussed how to trace design elements in an SDD back to the SRS and other system documents via the RTM (see "Traceability" on page 171). As noted in Chapter 9, you use *tags* to trace elements of the design throughout the documentation. For SDDs, you use tags of the form *proj*_SDD_*xxx* where *proj* is some project-specific name or mnemonic and *xxx* is a numeric (possibly decimal) value (see "SDD Tags" on page 176). All you have to do, then, is ensure you have unique SDD tags (generally by verifying that *xxx* is unique among all the SDD tags) and define where exactly to attach the SDD tags.

Technically, the requirements from the SRS map directly to the design concerns (one-to-one usually), which might tempt you to think that you should attach SDD tags to the design concerns. However, as the design views form the main body of the SDD and design concerns map to them in a many-to-one fashion (through the design viewpoints, which have a one-to-one relationship to design views), it's best to attach SDD tags to the design views or viewpoints. It will make your life a whole lot easier when you're creating the RTM if the mapping from the requirements to the design elements is either one-to-many or many-to-one (in particular, you want to avoid many-to-many).

In practice, a given design view can be broken down into multiple images or descriptions. If you are careful to only ever connect a design concern to one of these images or descriptions, you can assign SDD tags to the individual components of a design view. However, you must exercise caution when doing this, because if a single design concern maps to a couple of different components in a single design view, you can wind up with a many-to-many relationship.[6]

11.5 A Suggested SDD Outline

IEEE Std 1016-2009, Annex C, provides one suggested outline to organize and format an SDD that conforms to the required contents (see "SDD

---

6. Note that a many-to-many relationship between design concerns and components in a design view isn't invalid, even if you attach tags to all of the components. However, the RTM can become unwieldy when this happens and, seeing as the RTM is messy enough as it is, you don't want to make it worse.

Required Contents" on page 244). Note that this outline is by no means a requirement; you can organize your SDD however you like and it will still be valid as long as it contains those required contents. The following is a slightly modified variant of the IEEE's suggestion:[7]

1. Frontispiece
    1.1 Table of Contents
    1.2 Date of Issue and Status
    1.3 Issuing Organization
    1.4 Authorship
    1.5 Change History
2. Introduction
    2.1 Purpose
    2.2 Scope
    2.3 Intended Audience
    2.4 Context
    2.5 Overview/Summary
3. Definitions, Acronyms, and Abbreviations
4. References
5. Glossary
6. Body
    6.1 Identified Stakeholders and Design Concerns
    6.2 Design Viewpoint 1
        6.2.1 Design View 1
        6.2.2 (Optional) Design Overlays 1
        6.2.3 (Optional) Design Rationales 1
    6.3 Design Viewpoint 2
        6.3.1 Design View 2
        6.3.2 (Optional) Design Overlays 2
        6.3.3 (Optional) Design Rationales 2
    6.4 Design Viewpoint n
        6.4.1 Design View n
        6.4.2 (Optional) Design Overlays n
        6.4.3 (Optional) Design Rationales n
7. (Optional) Index

---

7. These modifications are for clarity and consistency with the SRS guidelines (see "The System Requirements Specification Document" on page 193).

11.6 A Sample SDD

This section presents a complete (though highly simplified, for editorial reasons) SDD example. This SDD describes the design for the sample use case and requirements documentation appearing in the previous chapter (see "Use Cases" on page 214). Specifically, this SDD covers the design of the Plantation Productions digital data acquisition and control (DAQ) system components that process the DIP switches upon system initialization.

1 **Plantation Productions DAQ DIP Switch Control**

   1.1 **Table of Contents**
   [Omitted for editorial reasons]

   1.2 **Date of Issue and Status**
   First created on Mar 18, 2018

   Current status: complete

   1.3 **Issuing Organization**
   Plantation Productions, Inc.

   1.4 **Authorship**
   Randall L. Hyde

   Copyright 2019, Plantation Productions, Inc.

   1.5 **Change History**
   Mar 18, 2019: Initial SDD created.

2 **Introduction**

   2.1 **Purpose**
   The DAQ system from Plantation Productions, Inc., is a digital data acquisition and control system intended to provide analog and digital I/O for industrial and scientific systems.

   This Software Design Description (SDD) describes the DIP switch initialization component of the DAQ system. The intent is that a developer wishing to implement the functionality for the DIP switch control from the Software Requirement Specifications (SRS) can use this document to achieve that purpose.

   2.2 **Scope**
   This document describes only the DIP switch design in the DAQ system (for space/editorial reasons). For the full SDD, please see *http://www.plantation-productions.com/Electronics/DAQ/DAQ.html*.

   2.3 **Intended Audience**
   The intended audience *expected* for an SDD:

   This document is intended for use by software developers who will implement this design, by design stakeholders who wish to review the design prior to its implementation, and by the authors of the Software Test Cases (STC) and Software Test Procedures (STD) documents.

The true intended audience for *this* SDD:

This document is intended for readers of *Write Great Code, Volume 3*, as a means for providing a sample SDD.

2.4 Context

The Plantation Productions DAQ system fulfilled a need for a well-documented digital data acquisition and control system that engineers could design into safety-critical systems such as nuclear research reactors. Although there are many commercial off-the-shelf (COTS) systems that could be used, they suffer from a couple of major drawbacks including: they are usually proprietary (difficult to modify or repair after purchase), they are often obsolete within 5 to 10 years with no way to repair or replace them, and they rarely have full support documentation (for example, SRS, SDD, STC, and STP) that an engineer can use to validate and verify the system.

The DAQ system overcomes this problem by providing an open hardware and open source set of designs with full design documentation that is validated and verified for safety systems.

Although originally designed for a nuclear research reactor, the DAQ system is useful in any place where you need an Ethernet-based control system supporting digital (TTL-level) I/O, optically isolated digital inputs, mechanical or solid-state relay digital outputs (isolated and conditioned), analog inputs (for example, ±10v and 4–20mA), and (conditioned) analog outputs (±10v).

2.5 Overview/Summary

The remainder of this documentation is organized as follows.

Section 3 covers the software design, including:

    Section 3.1   Stakeholders and Design Concerns

    Section 3.2   Context Viewpoint and Overall Architecture

    Section 3.3   Logical Viewpoint and Data Dictionary

    Section 3.4   Interaction Viewpoint and Control Flow

Section 4 provides an index.[8]

---

8. The index is actually empty for editorial/space reasons. It is a placeholder in this sample to show that you should provide an index in your SDD.

3 Definitions, Acronyms, and Abbreviations

Term	Definition
DAQ	Data acquisition system
SBC	Single-board computer
Software Design Description (SDD)	Documentation of the design of the software system (IEEE Std 1016-2009)—that is, this document.
Software Requirements Specification (SRS)	Documentation of the essential requirements (functions, performance, design constraints, and attributes) of the software and its external interfaces (IEEE Std 610.12-1990).
System Requirements Specification (SyRS)	A structured collection of information that embodies the requirements of the system (IEEE Std 1233-1998). A specification that documents the requirements to establish a design basis and the conceptual design for a system or subsystem.

4 References

Reference	Discussion
IEEE Std 830-1998	SRS documentation standard
IEEE Std 829-2008	STP documentation standard
IEEE Std 1012-1998	Software verification and validation standard
IEEE Std 1016-2009	SDD documentation standard
IEEE Std 1233-1998	SyRS documentation standard

5 Glossary
DIP: Dual inline package

6 Software Design

6.1 Stakeholders and Design Concerns

The stakeholders for the DAQ DIP switch design are Plantation Productions, Inc., and Randall Hyde. One main design concern is to create a simplified SDD that fits within the editorial constraints of *Write Great Code, Volume 3*, while still providing a reasonable example of an SDD. The remaining design concerns are all the requirements for the DAQ DIP switch system as described in the SRS (see "(Selected) DAQ Software Requirements (from SRS)" on page 219).

6.2 Context Viewpoint and Overall Architecture

The DAQ context viewpoint shows the functionality that exists between the user and the system.

Name/tag: DAQ_SDD_001

Author: Randall Hyde

Design elements used: This viewpoint employs use cases, actors (host PC and end user), nodes, components, and packages to describe the system interface.

Requirements/design concerns:[9]

DAQ_SRS_700_000

DAQ_SRS_701_000

DAQ_SRS_704_000

DAQ_SRS_707_000

DAQ_SRS_723_000.1

6.2.1 Contextual View[10]

The DAQ system firmware runs on a Netburner MOD54415 SBC connected to a DAQ_IF (DAQ interface) board. An end user can set DIP switch settings to initialize the way the DAQ interfaces to a host PC. The host PC can communicate with the DAQ system using RS-232 Serial, USB, or Ethernet connections (see Figure 11-19). This design expects existing library routines for maintPrintf, serialTask Init, usbTaskInit, ethernetTaskInit, and readDIPSwitches.

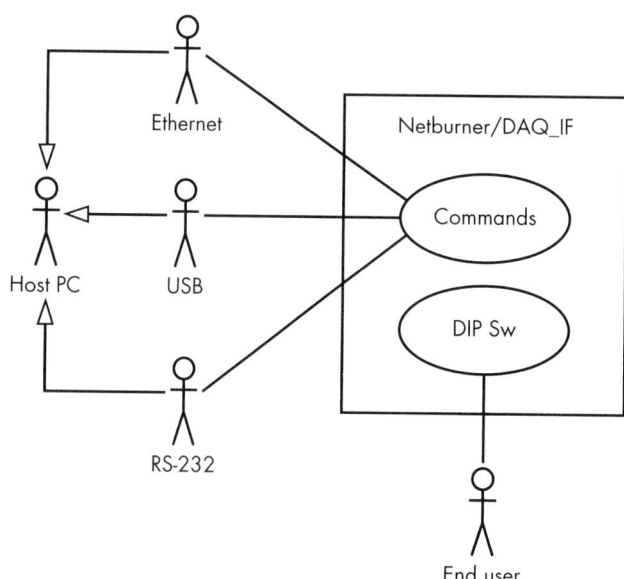

Figure 11-19: Sample contextual view

---

9. The requirements listing also provides a means for evaluating/verifying the design to see that it meets the specifications defined in the SRS. A reviewer will compare each of the listed requirements in the SRS against the contextual view to see that the view meets the requirements.

10. As the contextual view is provided here, there's no need to discuss the analysis needed to create the design view; that's trivial, because the design view is already present.

6.2.2 Component/Deployment Overlay

The following design overlay provides a different look at the contextual view using a combination deployment/component diagram. Figure 11-20 shows the physical components of the system[11] and their interconnections.

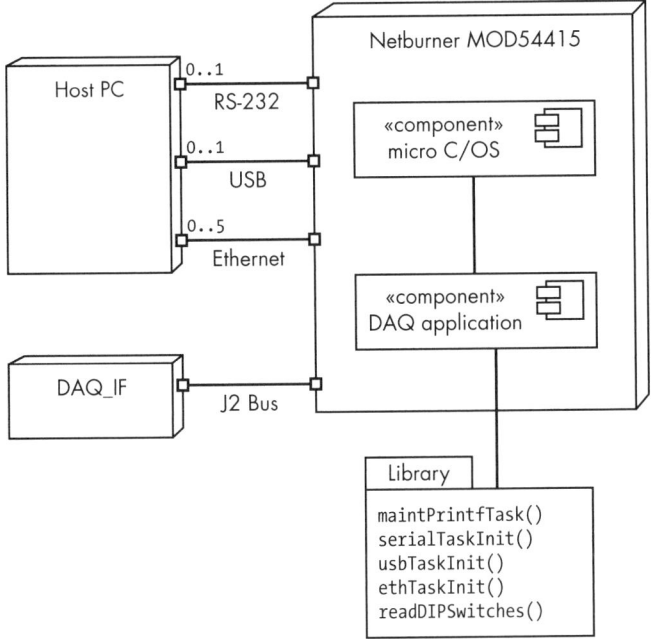

Figure 11-20: Sample design overlay diagram

6.2.3 (Optional) Design Rationales

The purpose of this viewpoint is to show how the user controls the way in which the host PC communicates with the DAQ system.

6.3 Logical Viewpoint and Data Dictionary

Name/tag: DAQ_SDD_002

Author: Randall Hyde

Design elements used: This viewpoint employs a single class diagram to describe the data storage for this application.

---

11. At least those components important to this SDD.

NOTE *In the real application, it would probably be better to use global variables to hold the DIP switch settings rather than an actual class.*

Requirements/Design Concerns:

DAQ_SRS_723_000.2

6.3.1 DIP Switch Variables

The data storage requirement for the DAQ (DIP switch) application is very simple. A set of 12 global variables in Figure 11-21 (which this SDD groups together under *globals*) is all that is really needed.

Name	Description
dipsw_g	Eight-bit array (in a byte) containing DIP switch values
serialEnable_g	true if RS-232 communication is enabled
USBEnabled_g	true if USB communications is enabled
ethEnabled_g	true if Ethernet communications is enabled
ethMultClients_g	Allow only a single Ethernet client if false; allow five clients if true
ethernetDipSw_g	Hold dipsw_g[5] in bit 0 and dipsw_g[6] in bit 1 (0..3)
unitTestMode_g	true if operating in unit test mode
debugMode_g	true if maintPrintf() function sends output to COM1:, false if maintPrintf() is disabled
ethernetAdrs_g	Holds IP address (192.168.2.70–192.168.2.73)
maxSockets_g	Either 0, 1, or 5 based on ethEnabled_g and ethMultClients_g values
slots_g	Holds file descriptors for up to five active Ethernet sockets
slot_g	Used to index into slots_g
maintPrintfTask()	External function that starts the maintPrintf() task (to handle debug output)
serialTaskInit()	External function that starts the RS-232 command receipt task
usbTaskInit()	External function that starts the USB command receipt task
ethTaskInit()	External function that starts an Ethernet command receipt task (up to five of these threads can be running concurrently)

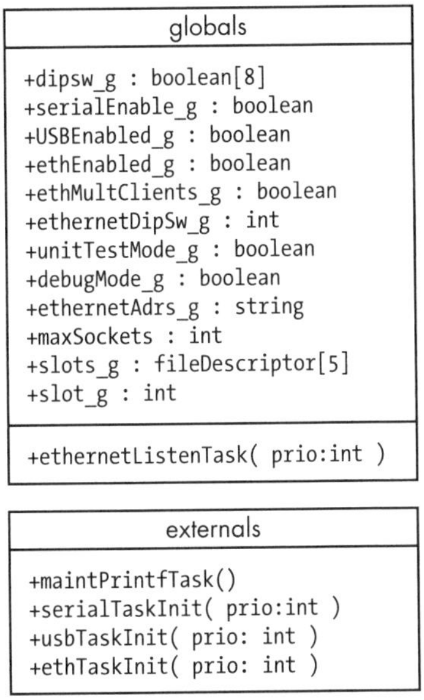

```
┌─────────────────────────────────────┐
│              globals                │
├─────────────────────────────────────┤
│ +dipsw_g : boolean[8]               │
│ +serialEnable_g : boolean           │
│ +USBEnabled_g : boolean             │
│ +ethEnabled_g : boolean             │
│ +ethMultClients_g : boolean         │
│ +ethernetDipSw_g : int              │
│ +unitTestMode_g : boolean           │
│ +debugMode_g : boolean              │
│ +ethernetAdrs_g : string            │
│ +maxSockets : int                   │
│ +slots_g : fileDescriptor[5]        │
│ +slot_g : int                       │
├─────────────────────────────────────┤
│ +ethernetListenTask( prio:int )     │
└─────────────────────────────────────┘

┌─────────────────────────────────────┐
│             externals               │
├─────────────────────────────────────┤
│ +maintPrintfTask()                  │
│ +serialTaskInit( prio:int )         │
│ +usbTaskInit( prio: int )           │
│ +ethTaskInit( prio: int )           │
└─────────────────────────────────────┘
```

Figure 11-21: DAQ global entities

6.3.2 Design Overlays
[None]

6.3.3 Design Rationales

This logical view used a class diagram rather than a set of global variables simply because a typical read dipswitches function for the Netburner returns all eight readings in a single 8-bit byte (that is, as a bit array). For that reason, it makes sense to treat all eight values as fields of a class, as these attributes would normally be derived anyway—that is, computed by masking out the specific bit.

6.4 Interaction Viewpoint and Control Flow
Name/tag: DAQ_SDD_003

Author: Randall Hyde

Design elements used: This viewpoint employs a couple of activity diagrams to show the control flow (and the value calculations) through the program.

Requirements/design concerns:

DAQ_SRS_702_000

DAQ_SRS_702_001

DAQ_SRS_702_002

DAQ_SRS_703_000

DAQ_SRS_703_001

DAQ_SRS_705_000

DAQ_SRS_705_001

DAQ_SRS_705_002

DAQ_SRS_706_000

DAQ_SRS_706_001

DAQ_SRS_708_000

DAQ_SRS_709_000

DAQ_SRS_710_000

DAQ_SRS_711_000

DAQ_SRS_712_000

DAQ_SRS_716_000

DAQ_SRS_716_001

DAQ_SRS_716_002

DAQ_SRS_716.5_000

DAQ_SRS_717_000

DAQ_SRS_718_000

DAQ_SRS_718_001

DAQ_SRS_719_000

DAQ_SRS_720_000

DAQ_SRS_721_001

DAQ_SRS_721_002

DAQ_SRS_723_000

DAQ_SRS_723_000

DAQ_SRS_723_000

DAQ_SRS_723_000.2

DAQ_SRS_726_000

DAQ_SRS_727_000

DAQ_SRS_728_000

DAQ_SRS_737_000

DAQ_SRS_738_000

DAQ_SRS_738_001

DAQ_SRS_738_002

6.4.1 Design View

The design view for the interaction viewpoint uses UML activity diagrams (flowcharts) to show the control flow through the application. See Figures 11-22, 11-23, and 11-24.

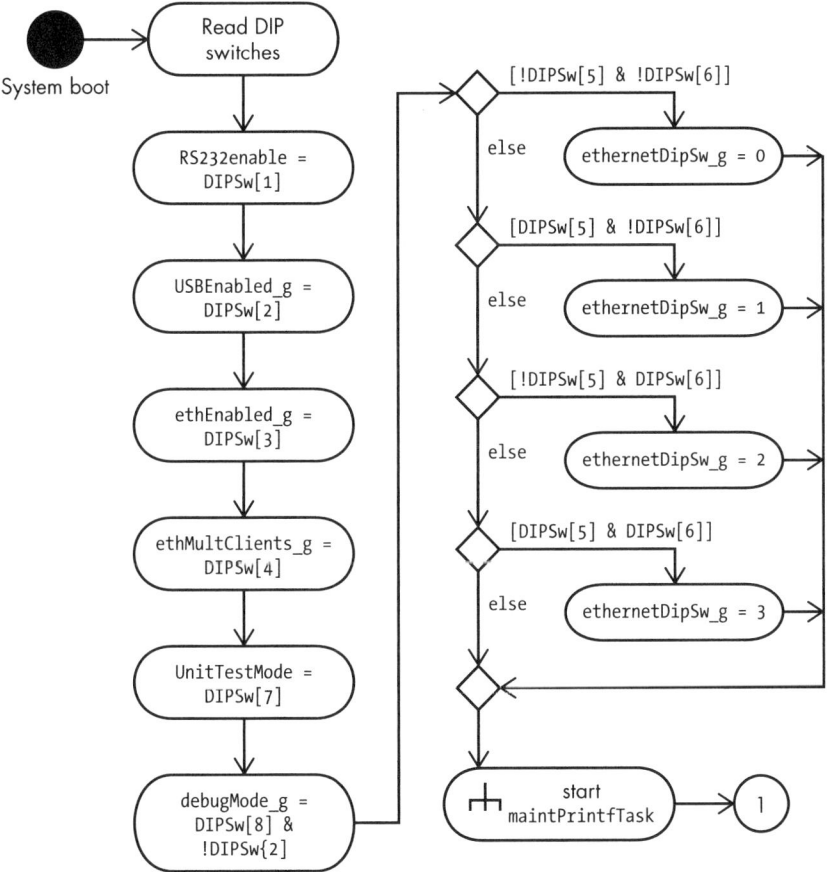

Figure 11-22: Activity diagram: reading DIP switches

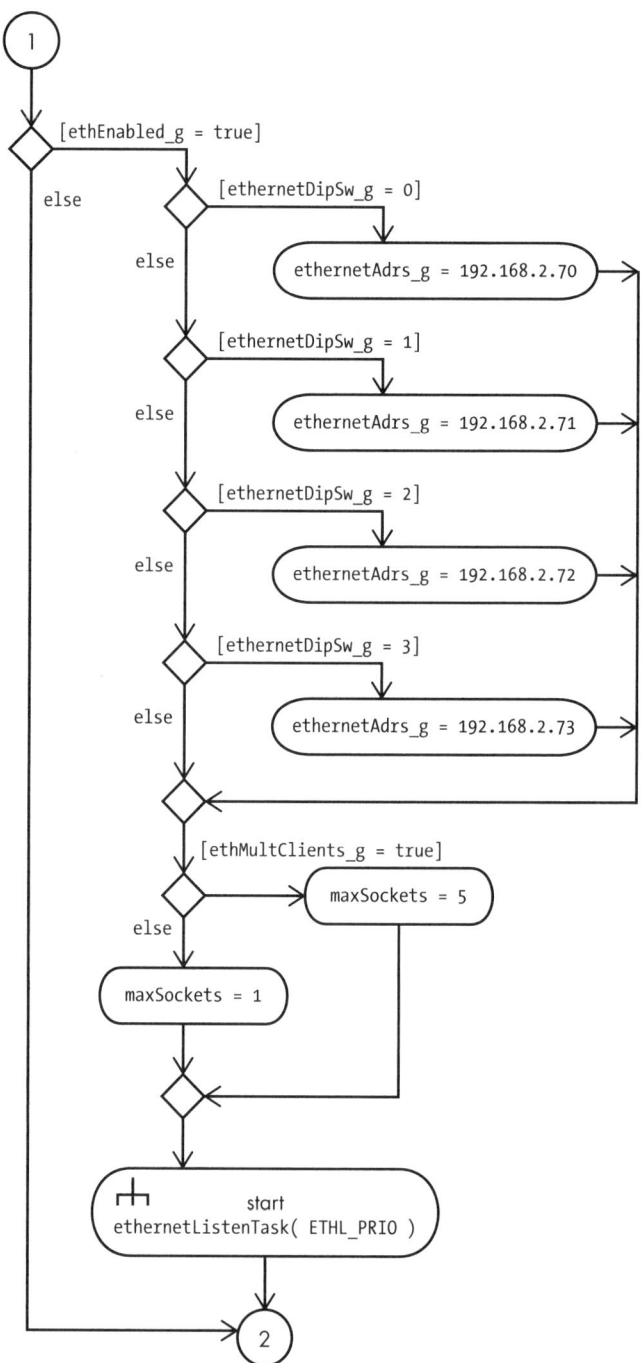

Figure 11-23: Activity diagram continuation #1

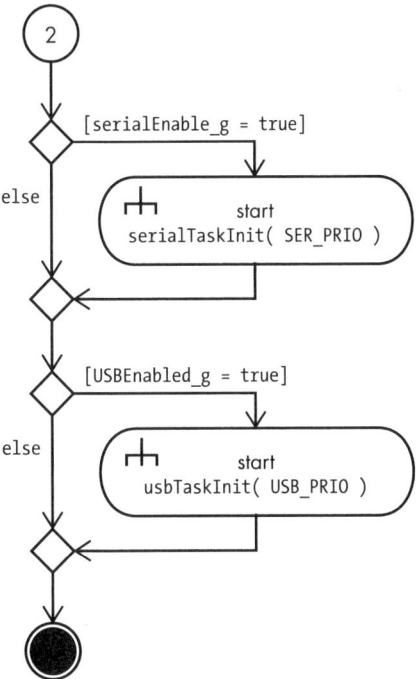

Figure 11-24: Activity diagram continuation #2

The serialTaskInit() and usbTaskInit() functions are library code that is external to this design. These functions start a task, ethernetListenTask, to handle RS-232 and USB communications as shown in Figure 11-25.

The ethTaskInit() function (provided in a library external to this design) runs until the connecting host terminates the Ethernet connection. At that time, the ethernetListenTask task will set the entry of the corresponding slots to 0 and terminate the task (thread). Should the listen connection become broken, ethernetListenTask terminates.

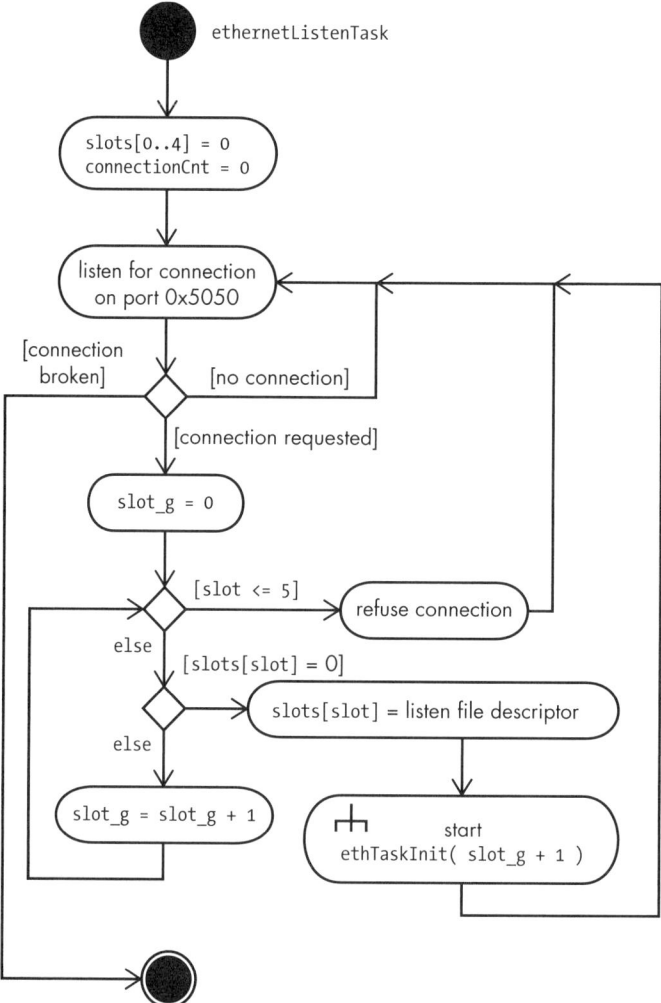

Figure 11-25: Activity diagram: `ethernetListenTask`

6.4.2 Sequence Diagram Overlay

The sequence diagram in Figure 11-26 shows another way of looking at the initialization of the threads in the DAQ application.

6.4.3 Design Rationale

The DAQ DIP switches project is relatively simple (purposely, so that the SDD example wouldn't be too large to fit into this book). Accordingly, the design is an old-fashioned procedural/imperative programming model (as opposed to an object-oriented design).

7 Index

[Omitted for editorial reasons]

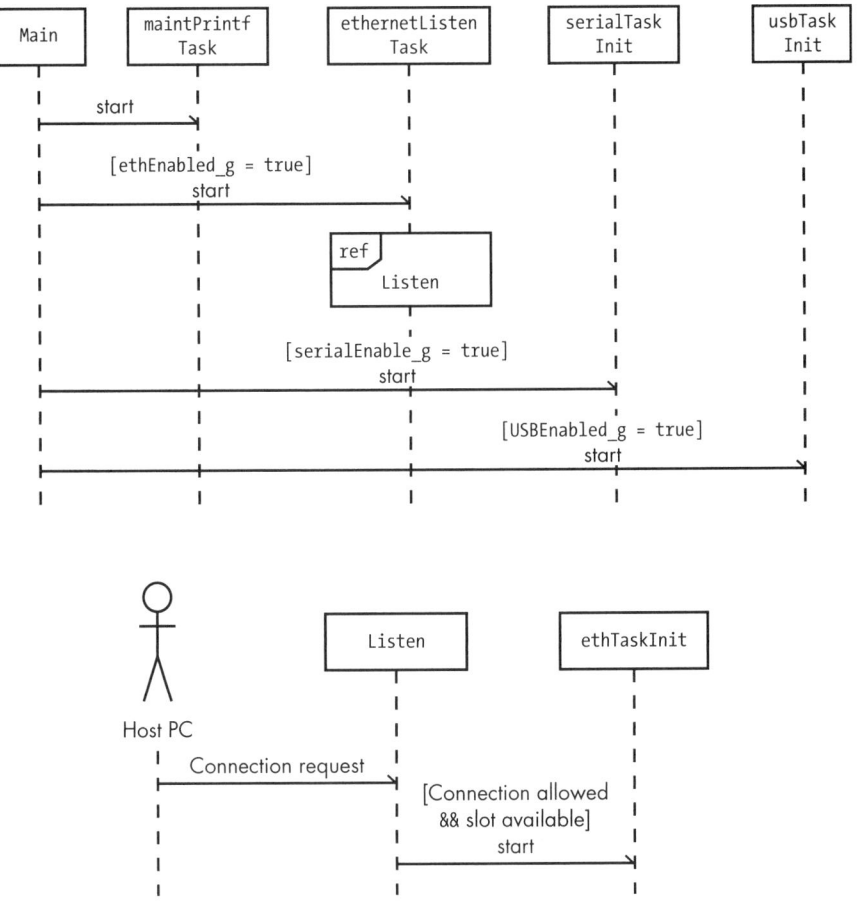

Figure 11-26: Sequence diagram: initializing tasks

11.7   Updating the Traceability Matrix with Design Information

The SDD adds a single column to the RTM: the SDD tag column. However, the SDD tag does not directly embed any traceability information, so you'll have to extract that information from the SDD to determine where to place your SDD tags in the RTM.

As noted in "Design Views vs. Design Viewpoints" on page 240, each viewpoint in an SDD must include design concerns and requirements information. In this chapter (see "A Sample SDD" on page 247), I've strongly suggested supplying all the SRS requirement tags as the list of design concerns in the viewpoint documentation. If you've done that, you've already created the reverse traceability back to the requirements. As a result, filling in the SDD tags in the RTM is easy: just locate each requirement tag (listed in the current viewpoint) and copy the viewpoint's SDD tag into the SDD tag column in the RTM. Of course, considering that you can have multiple requirements associated with a single viewpoint, you'll also have several copies of the same SDD tag spread throughout the RTM (one per associated requirement).

Should you ever want to trace your SDD tags back to all the requirements in the RTM (without looking up the list in the SDD), simply sort the RTM by the SDD tag column. This will collect all the requirements (and everything else linked to that SDD tag) into a contiguous group in the matrix and make it easy to identify everything associated with that tag.

If you choose some other method of specifying design concerns in the viewpoint that doesn't involve incorporating the SRS tags within them, then determining the placement of the SDD tags in the RTM becomes a manual (even laborious) process. That's why I strongly recommend using SRS tags when generating your viewpoints. Since you have to consider all the requirements when generating the viewpoint anyway, it makes sense to collect that information into the SDD at the same time.

11.8   Creating a Software Design

This chapter has spent considerable time discussing how to create a Software Design Description. In the examples you've seen, it might seem that the actual designs were plucked out of thin air. Where did these designs originate from? If you're creating a new system design, how do you come up with that design in the first place? Well, that's the subject of the next volume in this series, *Write Great Code, Volume 4: Designing Great Code*. This chapter has laid the groundwork for that book.

11.9   For More Information

Freeman, Eric, and Elizabeth Robson. *Head First Design Patterns: A Brain-Friendly Guide*. Sebastopol, CA: O'Reilly Media, 2004.

Gamma, Erich, et al. *Design Patterns: Elements of Reusable Object-Oriented Software*. Upper Saddle River, NJ: Addison-Wesley Professional, 1994.

IEEE. "IEEE Std 1016-2009: IEEE Standard for Information Technology—Systems Design—Software Design Descriptions." July 20, 2009. *https://ieeexplore.ieee.org/document/5167255/*. (It's not cheap—about $100—and it's worded in a way that only a lawyer can appreciate, but this is the gold standard for SDDs.)

12

SOFTWARE TEST DOCUMENTATION

This chapter covers software test documentation, focusing primarily on the Software Test Case (STC) and Software Test Procedure (STP) documents. As has been the case for the previous chapters, this discussion is based on IEEE Standards, specifically the IEEE Standard for Software and System Test Documentation (IEEE Std 829-2008, hereafter *Std 829*[1]).

---

1. IEEE Std 829-2008 is a registered trademark of the IEEE.

12.1 The Software Test Documents in Std 829

Std 829 actually describes many additional documents above and beyond the STC and STP, including:

- Master Test Plan (MTP)
- *Level* Test Plan (LTP)
- *Level* Test Design (LTD)
- *Level* Test Case (LTC)
- *Level* Test Procedure (LTPr)
- *Level* Test Log (LTL)
- Anomaly Report (AR)
- *Level* Interim Test Status Report (LITSR)
- *Level* Test Report (LTR)
- Master Test Report (MTR)

Note that these are not actual document names—the word *level* is a placeholder for the scope or extent of software testing being documented. The scope could be at the level of *components* or *component integration*, apply to the entire *system*, or focus on *acceptance*. For example, *Level* Test Plan could refer to a Component (or Unit) Test Plan, Component Integration (or simply Integration) Test Plan, System (or System Integration) Test Plan, or an Acceptance Test Plan.

NOTE *Test levels are explained further in "Software Development Testing Levels" on page 265.*

In all, Std 829 defines 31 different document types, but these are the main ones. The majority of these documents exist to support software management activities. Because this is a book on personal software engineering rather than software project management, this chapter won't go into detail on most of them. Instead, we'll concentrate on those *level* test documents that pertain to actual software testing—specifically, the *Level* Test Case, *Level* Test Procedure, *Level* Test Log, and Anomaly Report document types. We will cover all four *level* classifications—component, component integration, system, and acceptance—though the latter two are the main test documents used in this chapter. The differences between the *level* test documents are relatively minor, so this chapter applies the umbrella names mentioned earlier: Software Test Cases and Software Test Procedures. Keep in mind, however, that while these are common software engineering terms, Std 829 refers only to the *level* test documents.

12.1.1 Process Support

Although this chapter focuses on software testing, Std 829 describes the testing process in far more general terms. In particular, the testing process also handles the verification and validation of each document step in the development process. Specifically, this means that the testing process tests the documentation as well as the actual software.

For the SyRS and SRS, the verification step ensures that the requirements actually satisfy customer needs (and *only* satisfy customer needs, without gold plating). For the SDD, the verification step ensures that the SDD covers all the requirements. For the STC, the verification step ensures that each requirement has one or more test cases that test the requirement. For the STP, the verification ensures that the set of test procedures fully covers all the test cases.

In addition to documentation, Std 829 discusses test procedures for verifying acquisitions (such as purchases of third-party libraries and computing hardware), administering RFPs (Requests for Proposals), and many other activities. These testing activities are very important. As noted previously, though, these are largely management activities rather than software development activities, so they're mentioned only briefly here.

Std 829 states that testing needs to support the processes of management, acquisition, supply, development, operation, and maintenance. This chapter will concentrate on the development and operation processes (and, to a limited extent, the maintenance processes, which are largely an iteration of the development and operation processes). For more details on the other processes, see Std 829, IEEE/EIA Std 12207.0-1996 [B21], and ISO-IEC-IEEE-29148-2011.

Note that Std 829 allows you to combine and omit some of the testing documents. This means that you could have only a single document and still conform to Std 829. In reality, the final number of documents you create depends on the size of the project (large projects will require more documentation) and the turnaround you expect (fast projects will have fewer documents).

12.1.2 Integrity Levels and Risk Assessment

Std 829 defines four *integrity levels* that describe the importance or sensitivity to risk for a piece of software:

> **Catastrophic (level 4)** This level means that the software must execute properly, or something disastrous could occur (such as death, irreparable harm to the system, environmental damage, or a huge financial loss). There are no workarounds for catastrophic system failures. An example is a braking failure in a software-controlled self-driving vehicle.
>
> **Critical (level 3)** This level means that software must execute properly, or there could be serious problems including permanent injury, major performance degradation, environmental damage, or financial loss. A partial workaround may be possible for a critical system failure. An example is the transmission-controlling software in the self-driving vehicle being unable to shift out of second gear.
>
> **Marginal (level 2)** This level means that the software must execute properly, or there may be (minor) incorrect results produced and some

functionality lost. Workarounds to solve the problem are possible. Continuing with the self-driving-vehicle example, a software failure that prevents the infotainment center from operating is a marginal problem.

Negligible (level 1) This level means that the software must execute properly, or else some minor functionality might not exist in the system (or the software might not be as "polished" as it should be). Negligible issues generally don't require a workaround and can be safely ignored until an update comes along. An example is a spelling mistake on the touchscreen of the infotainment center in the self-driving vehicle.

The higher the level, the greater the importance of the testing process; that is, level 4 (catastrophic) items demand higher-quality and more intensive testing than level 1 (negligible) items. Integrity levels, then, become the basis for determining the number, quality, and depth of test cases you create. For a feature in the program that could have catastrophic results in the event of a failure, you want a fair number of test cases that exercise that feature with considerable depth. For features that have negligible potential consequences, you might not have any test cases or only very shallow tests (such as a cursory review).[2]

Risk assessment is an attempt to determine where in your system failures are likely to occur, their expected frequency, and the associated costs. While risk assessment is predictive by its very nature (which means it won't be perfect), you can often identify those parts of the program that are more likely to exhibit problems (such as complex sections of code, code produced by less experienced engineers, code from questionable sources like open source libraries found on the internet, and code using poorly understood algorithms). If you can categorize the likelihood of a problem as *likely*, *probable*, *occasional*, or *unlikely*, you can help identify the code that warrants more stringent testing (and, conversely, code that requires minimal testing).

You can combine the integrity level and risk assessment levels in a matrix to produce a risk assessment scheme, as shown in Table 12-1. In this example, a value of 4 denotes extreme importance, and a value of 1 indicates little importance.

Table 12-1: Risk Assessment Scheme

Consequence	Likelihood			
	Likely	Probable	Occasional	Unlikely
Catastrophic	4	4	3.5	3
Critical	4	3.5	3	2.5
Marginal	3	2.5	1.5	1
Negligible	2	1.5	1	1

---

2. It might seem strange to not have any test cases at all. However, keep in mind that having too many trivial test cases will make the testing process lengthy and more expensive, resulting in too little time spent testing the really important features of the system.

Std 829 does not mandate using an integrity level or risk assessment scheme in your test documentation, though it does consider this to be best practice. If you do use an integrity level, Std 829 does not require that you use the IEEE-recommended scheme (you could, for example, use a finer-grained integrity level with values from 1 to 10). However, if you "roll your own" integrity level, the IEEE recommends that you document a mapping from your integrity levels to those suggested by the IEEE so that readers can easily compare them.

12.1.3 Software Development Testing Levels

In addition—and in contrast—to the integrity levels just described, the IEEE defines four testing levels, each of which generally describes the scope or extent of software testing being documented:

Component (also known as *unit*)[3] This level deals with subroutines, functions, modules, and subprograms at the lowest code level. *Unit testing*, for example, consists of testing individual functions and other small program units independent of the rest of the program.

Component integration (also known as simply *integration*) This level is the point at which you begin combining individual units together to form a larger portion of the system, though not necessarily the whole system. Integration testing, for example, occurs when you combine (pretested) units to see if they play well together (that is, pass appropriate parameters, return appropriate function results, and so on).

System (also known as *system integration*) This level of testing is the ultimate form of integration testing—you've integrated all the program units together and formed the complete system. Unit testing, integration testing, and system integration testing are typically tests the developers perform before releasing a complete system outside the development group.

Acceptance (variants include *factory acceptance* and *site acceptance*) *Acceptance testing (AT)* is post-development. As its name implies, it refers to how the customer determines whether the system is acceptable. Depending on the system, there may be a couple of acceptance testing variants. *Factory acceptance testing (FAT)* occurs on systems prior to leaving the manufacturer (typically on the factory floor, hence the name). Even if a product is pure software, it can have a factory acceptance test where the customer's representatives come to test the software under the watchful eye of the software development team. This allows the team to make quick changes to the system if the customer discovers minor errors during the FAT.

A *site acceptance test (SAT)* is performed at the customer's site after the system is installed. For hardware-based systems, this ensures that

---

3. The names in parentheses are not part of the IEEE Std 829-2008. However, they are common industry names.

the hardware is installed properly and the software is functioning as intended. For pure software systems, the SAT provides a final check (after a possible AT or FAT) that the software is usable by the system's end users.

12.2 Test Plans

A software test plan is a document that describes the scope, organization, and activities associated with the testing process. This is largely a managerial overview of how the testing will take place, the resources testing will require, schedules, necessary tools, and objectives. This chapter won't consider test plans in detail, as they are beyond the scope of this book; however, the following sections will present outlines provided in IEEE Std 829-2008 as a reference. For more details on these test plans, consult Std 829.

12.2.1 Master Test Plan

The *Master Test Plan (MTP)* is an organization-wide top-level management document that tracks the testing process across a whole project (or set of projects). Software engineers are rarely involved directly with the MTP, which is largely an umbrella document that the QA (Quality Assurance) department uses to track quality aspects of a project. A project manager or project lead might be aware of the MTP—and might contribute to it during schedule and resource development—but the development team rarely sees the MTP except in passing.

The following outline comes from Section 8 of IEEE Std 829-2008 (and uses the IEEE section numbers):

1 Introduction
   1.1 Document Identifier
   1.2 Scope
   1.3 References
   1.4 System Overview and Key Features
   1.5 Test Overview
      1.5.1 Organization
      1.5.2 Master Test Schedule
      1.5.3 Integrity Level Schema
      1.5.4 Resources Summary
      1.5.5 Responsibilities
      1.5.6 Tools, Techniques, Methods, and Metrics
2 Details of the Master Test Plan
   2.1 Test Processes Including Definition of Test Levels
      2.1.1 Process: Management
          2.1.1.1 Activity: Management of Test Effort

2.1.2　Process: Acquisition
　　　　　2.1.2.1　Activity: Acquisition Support Test
　　　2.1.3　Process: Supply
　　　　　2.1.3.1　Activity: Planning Test
　　　2.1.4　Process: Development
　　　　　2.1.4.1　Activity: Concept
　　　　　2.1.4.2　Activity: Requirements
　　　　　2.1.4.3　Activity: Design
　　　　　2.1.4.4　Activity: Implementation
　　　　　2.1.4.5　Activity: Test
　　　　　2.1.4.6　Activity: Install/Checkout
　　　2.1.5　Process: Operation
　　　　　2.1.5.1　Activity: Operational Test
　　　2.1.6　Process: Maintenance
　　　　　2.1.6.1　Activity: Maintenance Test
　　2.2　Test Documentation Requirements
　　2.3　Test Administration Requirements
　　2.4　Test Reporting Requirements
3　General
　　3.1　Glossary
　　3.2　Document Change Procedures and History

Many of these sections contain information common to IEEE documents (for example, see the SRS and SDD samples in previous chapters). As the MTP is beyond the scope of this chapter, please consult Std 829 for specific descriptions of each section in this outline.

12.2.2　Level *Test Plan*

A Level *Test Plan (LTP)* refers to a set of test plans based on the development state. As this chapter noted earlier, each document in the set generally describes the scope or extent of software test being documented: Component Test Plan (aka Unit Test Plan, or UTP), Component Integration Test Plan (aka Integration Test Plan, or ITP), System Test Plan (aka System Integration Test Plan, or SITP), and Acceptance Test Plan (ATP; may include a Factory Acceptance Test Plan [FATP] or Site Acceptance Test Plan [SATP]).[4]

LTPs are also managerial/QA documents, but the development team (even to the level of individual software engineers) often has input on their creation and use, because these documents reference detailed features of the software design. These test plans are not guiding documents—that is,

---

4. The parenthetical names are common names for these test plans; these names do not come from Std 829.

a software engineer wouldn't necessarily reference these documents while actually testing the software—but they can't be created without development team feedback. Like the MTP, LTPs provide a road map for the creation of the test case and test procedure documents (of primary interest to the development and testing teams) and outline how to perform the tests. LTPs provide a good high-level view of the testing process, especially for external organizations interested in its quality.[5]

Here is the LTP outline from Std 829:

1 Introduction
    1.1 Document Identifier
    1.2 Scope
    1.3 References
    1.4 Level in the Overall Sequence
    1.5 Test Classes and Overall Test Conditions

2 Details for This Level of Test Plan
    2.1 Test Items and Their Identifiers
    2.2 Test Traceability Matrix
    2.3 Features to Be Tested
    2.4 Features Not to Be Tested
    2.5 Approach
    2.6 Item Pass/Fail Criteria
    2.7 Suspension Criteria and Resumption Requirements
    2.8 Test Deliverables

3 Test Management
    3.1 Planned Activities and Tasks; Test Progression
    3.2 Environmental/Infrastructure
    3.3 Responsibilities and Authority
    3.4 Interfaces Among the Parties Involved
    3.5 Resources and Their Allocation
    3.6 Training
    3.7 Schedules, Estimates, and Costs
    3.8 Risk(s) and Contingency(s)

4 General
    4.1 Quality Assurance Procedures
    4.2 Metrics
    4.3 Test Coverage

---

5. A good example of such an external organization is the Nuclear Regulatory Commission (NRC), a US-based governmental organization tasked with licensing commercial nuclear reactors.

4.4 Glossary

4.5 Document Change Procedures and History

You might notice that there is considerable overlap between the LTPs and the MTP. Std 829 states that if you are replicating information in a test plan that exists elsewhere, you can simply provide a reference to the containing document rather than duplicating the information in your LTP (or MTP). For example, you're likely to have an overall Reverse Traceability Matrix (RTM) that includes traceability for all the tests. Rather than replicating that traceability information in section 2.2 of an LTP, you would simply reference the RTM document that contains this information.

12.2.3 Level *Test Design Documentation*

The Level *Test Design (LTD)* documentation, as its name suggests, describes the design of the tests. Once again, there are four types of LTD documents, each generally describing the scope or extent of software testing being documented: Component Test Design (aka Unit Test Design, or UTD), Component Integration Test Design (aka Integration Test Design, or ITD), System Test Design (aka System Integration Test Design, or SITD), and Acceptance Test Design (ATD; this may include a Factory Acceptance Test Design [FATD] or a Site Acceptance Test Design [SATD]).

The main purpose of the LTD is to collect common information in one place that would be replicated throughout the test procedures. That means that this document could very easily be merged with your test procedures document (at the cost of some repetition in that document). This book will take that approach, merging pertinent items from the test design directly into the test cases and test procedures documents.[6] For that reason this section will present the IEEE recommended outline without additional commentary and save the details for the STC and STP documents.

1 Introduction
    1.1 Document Identifier
    1.2 Scope
    1.3 References

2 Details of the Level Test Design
    2.1 Features to Be Tested
    2.2 Approach Refinements
    2.3 Test Identification
    2.4 Feature Pass/Fail Criteria
    2.5 Test Deliverables

---

6. I personally prefer this approach, even at the cost of maintaining duplicate information (and potentially introducing inconsistencies), because it keeps those documents self-contained (especially the test procedure documents). During the testing process, I don't want to have to keep referring to different documents, which can slow down the testing and lead to errors in the testing process.

3   General
    3.1   Glossary
    3.2   Document Change Procedures and History

12.3 Software Review List Documentation

When you build the RTM starting with your requirements, one of the columns you usually create is the test/verification type column. Typically, a software requirement will have one of two associated verification types: *T* (for *test*) and *R* (for *review*).[7] Requirements marked *T* will have associated test cases and test procedures (see "Updating the Traceability Matrix with Requirement Information" on page 222 for details on creating test cases). Items marked *R* will need to be reviewed. This section describes how to create a Software Review List (SRL) document to track the review of the system (usually the source code) to verify those requirements.

The SRL is relatively straightforward. The core of the document is simply a list of items, each of which you check off after you review it and are confident that the software properly supports the associated requirement.

In theory, you could create *level* review list documentation at four separate levels: component, component integration, system, and acceptance (as is the case for other Std 829 *level* documents). In reality, however, a single SRL that is suitable for both system (integration) and acceptance use will suffice.

NOTE   *The SRL document is not a part of Std 829 (or any other IEEE standards document, for that matter). Std 829 certainly allows you to use this document as part of your verification package, but the format presented in this section is not from the IEEE.*

12.3.1 Sample SRL Outline

Although the SRL is not a standard IEEE document, the following outline for it is somewhat similar to the SRS, STC, and STP recommended formats from the IEEE:

1   Introduction (once per document)
    1.1   Document Identifier
    1.2   Document Change Procedures and History
    1.3   Scope
    1.4   Intended Audience
    1.5   Definitions, Acronyms, and Abbreviations

---

7. There are other verification types, but we'll ignore those here. If you ever use those types (typically for hardware, although *analysis*, *other*, and *no test* are possible software options), you'll have to create an appropriate document that justifies or describes how you will verify the associated requirement.

        1.6 References
        1.7 Notation for Description
    2   General System Description
    3   Checklist (one per review item)
        3.1 Review Identifier (Tag)
        3.2 Discussion of Item to Review

12.3.2 Sample SRL

This sample SRL continues to use the DAQ DIP switch project from the previous chapters. Specifically, this SRL is based on the requirements from "(Selected) DAQ Software Requirements (from SRS)" on page 219 and the verification types detailed in "Requirements to Be Verified by Review" on page 223.

1   Introduction
This Software Review List provides a software review checklist for those DAQ system requirements that are to be verified by review.

   1.1   Document Identifier
DAQ_SRL v1.0

   1.2   Document Change Procedures and History
All revisions should be noted here, by date and version number.

Mar 23, 2018—Version 1.0

   1.3   Scope
This SRL deals with those requirements in the DAQ DIP switch initialization project for which creating a formal test procedure would be difficult (or otherwise economically unviable) but whose correctness can be easily verified by reviewing the source code and the build system for the source code.

   1.4   Intended Audience
The *normal* audience for an SRL:

This document is intended primarily for those individuals who will be testing/reviewing the DAQ DIP switch project. Project management and the development team may also wish to review this document.

The *real* audience for this SRL:

This SRL is intended for readers of *Write Great Code, Volume 3*. It provides an example SRL that can serve as a template for SRLs they may need to create.

1.5 Definitions, Acronyms, and Abbreviations

DAQ: Data acquisition system

DIP: Dual inline package

SDD: Software Design Document

SRL: Software Review List

SRS: Software Requirements Specification

1.6 References
SDD: IEEE Std 1016-2009

SRS: IEEE Std 830-1998

STC/STP: IEEE Std 829-2008

1.7 Notation for Description
Review identifiers (*tags*) in this document shall take the form:

DAQ_SR_*xxx_yyy*_*zzz*

where *xxx_yyy* is a string of (possibly decimal) numbers taken from the corresponding requirement (for example, DAQ_SRS_*xxx_yyy*) and *zzz* is a (possibly decimal) numeric sequence that creates a unique identifier out of the whole sequence. Note that *zzz* values in SRL tags are usually numbered from 000 or 001 and usually increment by 1 for each additional review item sharing the same *xxx_yyy* string.

2 General System Description
The purpose behind the DAQ DIP switch system is to initialize the DAQ system upon power-up. The DAQ DIP switch system is a small subset of the larger Plantation Productions DAQ system that is useful as an example within this book.

3 Checklist
Check off each of the following items as it is verified during the review process.

3.1 DAQ_SR_700_000_000
Verify code is written for a Netburner MOD54415 evaluation board.

3.2 DAQ_SR_700_000.01_000.1
Verify code is written for μC/OS.

3.3 DAQ_SR_702_001_000
Verify that software creates a separate task to handle serial port command processing.

3.4 **DAQ_SR_702_002_000**
Verify that serial task priority is lower than USB and Ethernet task priorities (note that the higher the priority number, the lower the priority).

3.5 **DAQ_SR_703_001_000**
Same as DAQ_SRS_702_001, but doesn't start an RS-232 task if DIP switch 1 is in the OFF position.

3.6 **DAQ_SR_705_001_000**
Verify that software creates a separate task to handle USB port command processing.

3.7 **DAQ_SR_705_002_000**
Verify that a USB task has a higher priority than the Ethernet and serial protocol tasks.

3.8 **DAQ_SR_706_001_000**
Verify that software does not start the USB task if DIP switch 2 is in the OFF position.

3.9 **DAQ_SR_716_001_000**
Verify that the Ethernet listening task is started only if Ethernet communications are enabled.

3.10 **DAQ_SR_716_002_000**
Verify that the Ethernet listening task has a priority lower than the USB task but higher than the serial task.

3.11 **DAQ_SR_719_000_000**
Verify that software sets the unit test mode value to ON based on the DIP switch 7 setting.

3.12 **DAQ_SR_720_000_000**
Verify that software sets the unit test mode value to OFF based on the DIP switch 7 setting.

3.13 **DAQ_SR_723_000_000**
Verify that the software provides a function to read the DIP switches.

3.14 **DAQ_SR_723_000.01_000**
Verify that the system uses the DIP switch reading to initialize RS-232 (serial), USB, Ethernet, unit test mode, and debug mode on startup.

3.15 **DAQ_SR_723_000.02_000**
Verify that the startup code stores the DIP switch reading for later use by the software.

3.16 **DAQ_SR_725_000_000**
Verify that the command processor responds to a command when a complete line of text is received from the USB, RS-232, and Ethernet ports.

3.17 **DAQ_SR_738_001_000**
Verify that the system starts a new process (task) to handle command processing for each new Ethernet connection.

3.18 **DAQ_SR_738_002_000**
Verify that the Ethernet command processing tasks have a priority between the Ethernet listening task and the USB command task.

12.3.3 Adding SRL Items to the Traceability Matrix

Once you've created an SRL, you'll want to add all the *SR* tags to the RTM so you can trace the reviewed items back to the requirements, as well as to everything else in the RTM. To do so, just locate the requirement associated with each review item tag (this is trivial if you're using the tag numbering this chapter recommends; the SRS tag number is incorporated into the SRL tag number) and add the SRL tag to the appropriate column in the same row of the RTM containing the requirement.

When you've got both SRL and STC documents, there's really no need to create separate columns in the RTM for both types, as they are mutually exclusive and the tag will differentiate them. (See "A Sample Software Requirements Specification" on page 203 for some additional commentary on this.)

12.4 Software Test Case Documentation

For each item in the RTM whose requirement verification type is *T*, you'll need to create a software test case. The *Software Test Case (STC)* document is where you'll put the actual test cases.

As with all the 829 Std *level* documents, there are four levels in the *Level* Test Case documentation. The term *Software Test Case* generically refers to any one of these. As this chapter noted earlier, this is actually a set of test cases, where each document in the set type generally describes the scope or extent of software testing being documented: Component Test Cases (aka Unit Test Cases, or UTC), Component Integration Test Cases (aka Integration Test Cases, or ITC), System Test Cases (aka System Integration Test Cases, or SITC), and Acceptance Test Cases (ATC; may include Factory Acceptance Test Cases [FATC] and Site Acceptance Test Cases [SATC]).[8]

---

8. As usual, I've included some common (non-IEEE) names in parentheses.

The STC document lists all the individual test cases (tests) for a project. Here is the Std 829 outline for the *Level* Test Case documentation:

1. Introduction (once per document)
    1.1 Document Identifier
    1.2 Scope
    1.3 References
    1.4 Context
    1.5 Notation for Description
2. Details (once per test case)
    2.1 Test Case Identifier
    2.2 Objective
    2.3 Inputs
    2.4 Outcome(s)
    2.5 Environmental Needs
    2.6 Special Procedural Requirements
    2.7 Intercase Dependencies
3. Global (once per document)
    3.1 Glossary
    3.2 Document Change Procedures and History

In common practice, the Unit Test Cases and the Integration Test Cases are often combined into the same document (the differentiation between the two usually occurs at the level of test procedures). You will typically develop UTCs and ITCs from your source code and from the SDD (see Figure 12-1, which is an extension of Figure 9-1).

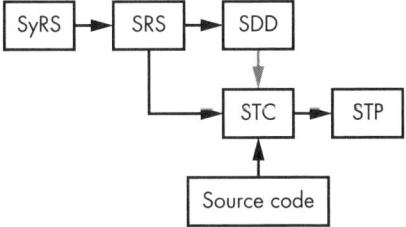

Figure 12-1: Unit and Integration Test Case sources

Often, the UTC and ITC (and test procedure) documents exist as software rather than as natural-language documents. Using an *automated test procedure*, a piece of software that runs all the unit and integration tests, is a software engineering best practice. By doing so, you can dramatically reduce the time it takes to run tests as well as the errors introduced in manually performed test procedures.[9]

Unfortunately, it isn't possible to create automated tests for every test case, so you'll usually have a UTC/ITC document covering (at least) the test cases you must perform manually.

Many organizations—particularly those that embrace Agile development models and test-driven development (TDD)—forgo formal UTC and ITC documents. Informally written procedures and automated test procedures are far more common in these situations because the cost of creating and (especially) maintaining the documentation quickly gets out of hand. As long as the development team can provide *some* documentation that they are performing a fixed set of unit/integration tests (that is, they're not doing ad hoc, "by the seat of the pants" tests that could differ on every test run), larger organizations tend to leave them be.

Regardless of whether it's formal, informal, or automated, having a repeatable test procedure is key. *Regression tests*, which check to see if anything has broken, or regressed, since you've made changes to the code, require a repeatable testing process. Therefore, you need some kind of test case to ensure repeatability.

For unit/integration testing, the test data you generate will be a combination of black-box-generated test data and white-box-generated test data. *Black-box test data* generally comes from the system requirements (SyRS and SRS); you consider only the functionality of the system (which the requirements provide) when you create its input test data. When you generate *white-box test data*, on the other hand, you analyze the software's source code. For example, ensuring that you execute every statement in the program at least once during testing—that is, achieving complete code coverage—requires careful analysis of the source code and, therefore, is a white-box test-data-generation technique.

NOTE *Write Great Code, Volume 6: Testing, Debugging, and Quality Assurance* will *consider the techniques for generating white-box and black-box test data in greater detail.*

Once you get to the level of a system integration test or (even more importantly) an acceptance test, formal documentation for your test cases becomes mandatory. If you're creating a custom system for a customer, or your software is subject to regulatory or legal restrictions (such as life-threatening environments in an autonomous vehicle), you'll likely have to convince some overseer organization that you've put in your best effort during testing and prove that the system meets its requirements. This is where it's essential to have formal documentation like that recommended

---

9. Do keep in mind, however, that creating the automated test procedure can be expensive and you have to validate the resulting code to ensure that it properly executes all the tests. In the long run, automated test procedures tend to be cost-effective because on all but the smallest of projects, you wind up rerunning test procedures many times during development.

by Std 829.[10] For this reason, most SITC and (most certainly) ATC documents derive their cases directly from the requirements (see Figure 12-2). So, with this motivation in hand, let's return to the discussion of the *Level* Test Case document (see the outline at the beginning of this section).

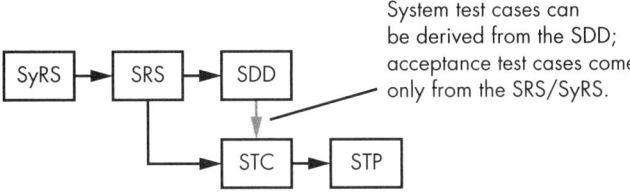

Figure 12-2: SITC and ATC derivation

More often than not, the (F)ATC document is simply a subset of the SITC document. (If you have FATC documentation and SATC documentation, the site variant is often a subset of the FATC document.) The SITC document will contain test cases for every requirement. In the ATC documents, system architects may merge or eliminate test cases that are nearly or entirely redundant, or are of little interest to customers and end users.

12.4.1 Introduction in the STC Document

The introductory section of an STC (or any *Level* Test Case) document should include the following information.

12.4.1.1 Document Identifier

The document identifier should be some unique name/number and should include the issuing date, author identification, status (for example, draft or final), approval signatures, and possibly a version number. A single ID name/number is imperative so you can reference the test case documentation in other documents (such as the STP and RTM).

12.4.1.2 Scope

This section summarizes the software system and features to test.

12.4.1.3 References

This section should provide a list of all reference documents, internal and external, associated with the STC. Internal references would normally include documents such as the SyRS, SRS, SDD, RTM, and (if it exists) the MTP. External references would include standards like IEEE Std 829-2008 and any regulatory or legal documents that might apply.

---

10. Even if your system is not life-threatening or doesn't exhibit catastrophic consequences if it misbehaves, having formal SITC and ATC documentation can help prevent you from delivering a shoddy product. At the very least, great code is going to run through a formal test process with formal test case/test procedure documentation.

12.4.1.4 Context

In this section you provide any context for the test cases that doesn't appear in any other documentation. Examples might include naming automated test-generation software or internet-based tools used to generate or evaluate test cases.

12.4.1.5 Notation for Description

This section should describe the tags (identifiers) you'll apply to the test cases. For example, this chapter uses tags of the form *proj_STC_xxx_yyy_zzz*, so this section of the STC would explain what this means and how to generate STC tags.

12.4.2 Details

You repeat the subsections contained herein for each test case in the STC.

12.4.2.1 Test Case Identifier

The test case identifier is the tag associated with this particular test case. For example, this book uses tags of the form *DAQ_STC_002_000_001* where *DAQ* is the project ID (for the DAQ DIP switch project), *002_000* is from the SRS requirement tag, and *001* is a test-case-specific value to make this tag unique among all the others. The Swimming Pool Monitor (SPM) project from previous chapters might use tags like *POOL_STC_002_001* within the STC. Std 829 doesn't require the use of this tag format, only that all test case tags be unique.

12.4.2.2 Objective

This is a brief description of the focus or goal of this particular test case. (Note that a set of test cases can have the same objective, in which case this field could simply reference the objectives in a different test case.) This field is a good place to put risk assessment and integrity level information, if relevant.

12.4.2.3 Input(s)

This section lists all inputs and their relationships (in terms of timing, ordering, and the like) that a tester needs in order to perform this test case. Some inputs might be exact, and some may be approximate, in which case you must provide tolerances for the input data. If the input set is large, this section might simply reference an input file, database, or some other input stream that will provide the test data.[11]

---

11. Note that test runs must be reproducible outputs. Therefore, random input data is rarely appropriate as an input data stream unless you're testing average responses to inputs that don't depend on any particular input data set.

12.4.2.4 Outcome(s)

This section lists all expected output data values and behaviors such as response time, timing relationships, and order of output data. The test case should provide exact output data values if possible; if you can provide only approximate data values, the test case must also supply tolerances. If an output stream is large, then this section can reference externally supplied files or databases.

If the test is successful by virtue of the fact that it runs without crashing—that is, self-validating—then this section is unnecessary in the test case.

12.4.2.5 Environmental Needs

This section describes any preexisting software or data such as a known database that is needed for the test. It could also describe any internet sites referenced by their URLs that must be active in order to execute the test case. This could also include any special power requirements, such as requiring a UPS to be fully charged before testing power failures, or it could include other conditions such as the swimming pool being filled with water before running tests on the SPM system.

12.4.2.5.1 Hardware Environmental Needs

This section lists any hardware needed to run the test and specifies its configuration settings. It could also specify any special hardware such as a test fixture for the test operation. For example, a test fixture for the SPM might be a five-gallon bucket filled with water and a hose connected to the water feed valve that is part of the SPM.

12.4.2.5.2 Software Environmental Needs

This section lists all software (and its versions/configurations) that would be needed to run the test. This could include operating systems/device drivers, dynamically linked libraries, simulators, code scaffolding (as in code drivers),[12] and test tools.

12.4.2.5.3 Other Environmental Needs

This is a catch-all section that lets you add information such as configuration specifics or anything else you feel the need to document. For example, for tests at a specific date or time, you'd need to consider Daylight Saving Time changes where a daily report may have 23 or 25 hours to report on, and so on.

12.4.2.6 Special Procedural Requirements

This section lists any exceptional conditions or constraints on the test case. This could also include any special preconditions or postconditions. For example, one precondition on the SPM when testing to see if the software properly responds to a low pool condition is that the water level is

---

12. *Write Great Code, Volume 6*, will go into details concerning code scaffolding and drivers.

below all three low-pool sensors. This should also list any postconditions, such as the bucket must not have overfilled. If you're using an automated test procedure, this is a good place to specify the particular tool to use and how to employ it for the test.

Note that this section should not duplicate steps that appear in the test procedure. Instead, it should provide guidance for properly writing the steps in the test procedure that will perform this test case.

12.4.2.7 Intercase Dependencies

This section should list (by tag identifier) any test cases that must be executed immediately prior to the current one, so that appropriate system state conditions are in place before the current test is executed. Std 829 suggests that by sequencing the test cases in the order in which they must execute, you can reduce the need to state intercase dependencies. (Obviously, such dependencies should be clearly documented.) In general, however, you shouldn't rely on such implicit dependency organization and should explicitly document any dependencies. In the STP, though, you *can* rely on the ordering of test steps. Having already clearly delineated the execution order in the STC will help reduce errors when you create the STP.

12.4.2.8 Pass/Fail Criteria

In Std 829, the IEEE recommends putting the pass/fail criteria in the *Level Test Design* documentation; they are not part of the Std 829 STC. However, it's not a bad idea, especially in cases where you don't have an LTD in your documentation set, to include pass/fail criteria for each test case.

Note that if the pass/fail criterion is simply "All system outputs must match that specified by the Outcome(s) section," then you can probably dispense with this section, but it wouldn't hurt to explicitly state this default condition in the introduction section.

12.4.3 General

This section provides a brief introduction and discussion of the Glossary and Document Change Procedures and History sections.

12.4.3.1 Glossary

The Glossary section provides an alphabetical list of all terms used in the STC. It should include all acronyms along with their definitions. Although Std 829 lists the glossary at the end of the outline, it usually appears near the beginning of the document, close to the References section.

12.4.3.2 Document Change Procedures and History

This section describes the process for creating, implementing, and approving changes to the STC. This could be nothing more than a reference to a Configuration Management Plan document that describes the document change procedures for all project documents or for all documents within an organization. The change history should contain a chronological list of the following information:

- Document ID (each revision should have a unique ID, which can simply be a date affixed to the document ID)
- Version number (which you should number sequentially, starting with the first approved version of the STC)
- A description of the changes made to the STC for the current version
- Authorship and role

Often, the change history appears in the STC near the beginning of the document, or just after the cover page and near the document identifier.

12.4.4 A Sample Software Test Case Document

Continuing with the theme of the past couple of chapters, this chapter will provide a sample STC for the Plantation Productions DAQ system DIP switch initialization design. This STC will serve as an acceptance test (pure functional test cases) built exclusively from the project SRS (see "(Selected) DAQ Software Requirements (from SRS)" on page 219). The test cases appearing in this sample STC are all the requirements from this project SRS that have not been included in "Requirements to Be Verified by Review" on page 223 where the "verify by review" requirements are listed. Note, however, that for editorial/space reasons, this example will not provide test cases for every "verify by review" test requirement in that project SRS.[13]

Term	Definition
DAQ	Data acquisition system
SBC	Single-board computer
Software Design Description (SDD)	Documentation of the design of the software system (IEEE Std 1016-2009)—that is, this document.
Software Requirements Specification (SRS)	Documentation of the essential requirements (functions, performance, design constraints, and attributes) of the software and its external interfaces (IEEE Std 610.12-1990).
System Requirements Specification (SyRS)	A structured collection of information that embodies the requirements of the system (IEEE Std 1233-1998). A specification that documents the requirements to establish a design basis and the conceptual design for a system or subsystem.
Software Test Cases (STC)	Documentation that describes test cases (inputs and outcomes) to verify correct operation of the software based on various design concerns/requirements (IEEE Std 829-2009).
Software Test Procedures (STP)	Documentation that describes the step-by-step procedure to execute a set of test cases to verify correct operation of the software based on various design concerns/requirements (IEEE Std 829-2009).

---

13. Once you've seen a half-dozen sample test cases or so, you'll learn the basic idea of how to write them. Explicitly providing all the test cases for a phantom project like the DAQ DIP switches won't help you learn the material any better.

1 Introduction

Software Test Cases for DAQ DIP Switch Project

1.1 Document Identifier (and Change History)

Mar 22, 2018: DAQ_STC v1.0; Author: Randall Hyde

1.2 Scope

This document describes only the DIP switch test cases in the DAQ system (for space/editorial reasons). For the full software design description, please see *http://www.plantation-productions.com/Electronics/DAQ/DAQ.html*.

1.3 Glossary, Acronyms, and Abbreviations

NOTE *This is a very simple and short example to keep the book's page count down. Please don't use this as boilerplate; you should diligently pick out terms and abbreviations that your document uses and list them in this section.*

1.4 References

Reference	Discussion
DAQ STC	An example of a full STC for the Plantation Productions DAQ system can be found at http://www.plantation-productions.com/Electronics/DAQ/DAQ.html.
IEEE Std 830-1998	SRS documentation standard
IEEE Std 829-2008	STP documentation standard
IEEE Std 1012-1998	Software verification and validation standard
IEEE Std 1016-2009	SDD documentation standard
IEEE Std 1233-1998	SyRS documentation standard

1.5 Context

The DAQ system of Plantation Productions, Inc., fulfilled a need for a well-documented digital data acquisition and control system that engineers could design into safety-critical systems such as nuclear research reactors. Although there are many COTS systems[14] that could be used, they suffer from a couple of major drawbacks, including: they are usually proprietary, thus being difficult to modify or repair after purchase; they are often obsolete within 5 to 10 years without a way to repair or replace them; and they rarely have full support documentation (for example, SRS, SDD, STC, and STP) that an engineer can use to validate and verify the system.

---

14. Commercial off-the-shelf systems.

The DAQ system overcomes this problem by providing an open hardware and open source set of designs with full design documentation that is validated and verified for safety systems.

Although originally designed for a nuclear research reactor, the DAQ system is useful anywhere you need an Ethernet-based control system supporting digital (TTL-level) I/O, optically isolated digital inputs, mechanical or solid-state relay digital outputs, (isolated and conditioned) analog inputs (for example, ±10v and 4-20mA), and (conditioned) analog outputs (±10v).

1.6 Notation for Description

Test case identifiers (*tags*) in this document shall take the form:

DAQ_STC_*xxx_yyy_zzz*

where *xxx_yyy* is a string of (possibly decimal) numbers taken from the corresponding requirement (for example, DAQ_SRS_*xxx_yyy*) and *zzz* is a (possibly decimal) numeric sequence that creates a unique identifier out of the whole sequence. Note that *zzz* values in STC tags are usually numbered from 000 or 001 and usually increment by 1 for each additional test case item sharing the same *xxx_yyy* string.

2 Details (Test Cases)

2.1 DAQ_STC_701_000_000

Objective: Test command acceptance across RS-232.

Inputs:

1. DIP switch 1 set to ON position.
2. Type **help** command on serial terminal.

Outcome:

1. Screen displays help message.

Environmental Needs:

    Hardware   Functioning (booted) DAQ system, PC with RS-232 port connected to DAQ

    Software   Latest version of DAQ firmware installed

    External   Serial terminal emulator program running on PC

Special Procedural Requirements:

    [None]

Intercase Dependencies:

    [None]

2.2 DAQ_STC_702_000_000

Objective: Test command acceptance with DIP switch 1 ON.

Inputs:

1. DIP switch 1 set to ON position.
2. Type **help** command on serial terminal.

Outcome:

1. Screen displays **help** message.

Environmental Needs:

> **Hardware** Functioning (booted) DAQ system, PC with RS-232 port connected to DAQ
> **Software** Latest version of DAQ firmware installed
> **External** Serial terminal emulator program running on PC

Special Procedural Requirements:

> [None]

Intercase Dependencies:

> Same test as DAQ_STC_701_000_000

2.3 DAQ_STC_703_000_000

Objective: Test command rejection with DIP switch 1 OFF.

Inputs:

1. DIP switch 1 set to OFF position.
2. Type **help** command on serial terminal.

Outcome:

1. System ignores command, no response on terminal program.

Environmental Needs:

> **Hardware** Functioning (booted) DAQ system, PC with RS-232 port connected to DAQ
> **Software** Latest version of DAQ firmware installed
> **External** Serial terminal emulator program running on PC

Special Procedural Requirements:

> [None]

Intercase Dependencies:

> [None]

NOTE *For space/editorial reasons, this sample has deleted several test cases at this point because they are very similar in content to the previous test cases.*

2.4 DAQ_STC_709_000_000

Objective: Test Ethernet address with both DIP switches 5 and 6 OFF.

Inputs:

1. DIP switch 3 set to ON position (4 = don't care).
2. DIP switch 5 set to OFF position.
3. DIP switch 6 set to OFF position
4. Using an Ethernet terminal program, attempt connection to IP address 192.168.2.70, port 20560 (0x5050).
5. Issue **help** command.

Outcome:

1. Ethernet terminal connects to DAQ system.
2. Terminal program display DAQ help message.

Environmental Needs:

Hardware Functioning (booted) DAQ system, PC with Ethernet port connected to DAQ

Software Latest version of DAQ firmware installed

External Ethernet terminal emulator program running on PC

Special Procedural Requirements:

[None]

Intercase Dependencies:

Cases DAQ_STC_708_000_000 to DAQ_STC_718_001_000 are closely related and should be performed together.

NOTE *For space/editorial reasons, this sample has deleted several test cases at this point because they are very similar in content to the previous test cases.*

2.6 DAQ_STC_710_000_000

Objective: Test Ethernet address with DIP switches 5 ON and 6 OFF.

Inputs:

1. DIP switch 3 set to ON position (4 = don't care).
2. DIP switch 5 set to ON position.
3. DIP switch 6 set to OFF position.
4. Using an Ethernet terminal program, attempt connection to IP address 192.168.2.71, port 20560 (0x5050).
5. Issue **help** command.

Outcome:

1. Ethernet terminal connects to DAQ system.
2. Terminal program displays DAQ help message.

Environmental Needs:

Hardware Functioning (booted) DAQ system, PC with Ethernet port connected to DAQ

Software Latest version of DAQ firmware installed

External Ethernet terminal emulator program running on PC

Special Procedural Requirements:

[None]

Intercase Dependencies:

Cases DAQ_STC_708_000_000 to DAQ_STC_718_001_000 are closely related and should be performed together.

2.7 DAQ_STC_711_000_000

Objective: Test Ethernet address with DIP switch 5 OFF and 6 ON.

Inputs:

1. DIP switch 3 set to ON position (4 = don't care).
2. DIP switch 5 set to OFF position.
3. DIP switch 6 set to ON position.
4. Using an Ethernet terminal program, attempt connection to IP address 192.168.2.72, port 20560 (0x5050).
5. Issue `help` command.

Outcome:

1. Ethernet terminal connects to DAQ system.
2. Terminal program displays DAQ `help` message.

Environmental Needs:

Hardware Functioning (booted) DAQ system, PC with Ethernet port connected to DAQ

Software Latest version of DAQ firmware installed

External Ethernet terminal emulator program running on PC

Special Procedural Requirements:

[None]

Intercase Dependencies:

Cases DAQ_STC_708_000_000 to DAQ_STC_718_001_000 are closely related and should be performed together.

2.8 DAQ_STC_712_000_000

Objective: Test Ethernet address with both DIP switches 5 and 6 ON.

Inputs:

1. DIP switch 3 set to ON position (4 = don't care).
2. DIP switch 5 set to ON position.

3. DIP switch 6 set to ON position.
4. Using an Ethernet terminal program, attempt connection to IP address 192.168.2.73, port 20560 (0x5050).
5. Issue `help` command.

Outcome:

1. Ethernet terminal connects to DAQ system.
2. Terminal program displays DAQ `help` message.

Environmental Needs:

Hardware Functioning (booted) DAQ system, PC with Ethernet port connected to DAQ

Software Latest version of DAQ firmware installed

External Ethernet terminal emulator program running on PC

Special Procedural Requirements:

[None]

Intercase Dependencies:

Cases DAQ_STC_708_000_000 to DAQ_STC_718_001_000 are closely related and should be performed together.

> **NOTE** *For space/editorial reasons, this sample has deleted several test cases at this point because they are very similar in content to the previous test cases.*

2.9 DAQ_STC_726_000_000

Objective: Test command acceptance from RS-232 port.

Inputs:

1. DIP switch 1 set to ON position.
2. Type `help` command on serial terminal.

Outcome:

1. Screen displays `help` message.

Environmental Needs:

Hardware Functioning (booted) DAQ system, PC with RS-232 port connected to DAQ

Software Latest version of DAQ firmware installed

External Serial terminal emulator program running on PC

Special Procedural Requirements:

[None]

Intercase Dependencies:

Same test as DAQ_STC_701_000_000

3   **Test Case Document Change Procedure**

When making any modifications to this STC, the author of the change must make a new entry in section 1.1 of this STC document, listing (at a minimum) the date, document ID (DAQ_STC), version number, and authorship.

12.4.5   Updating the RTM with STC Information

Due to software review and software test case (and analysis/other) verification methods being mutually exclusive, you need only a single column in the RTM to associate the tags for these objects with other items in the RTM. In the RTM of the official DAQ system (which has only test cases and software review items), the label for this column is simply *Software Test/Review Cases*. When you add both DAQ_SR_*xxx_yyy_zzz* and DAQ_STC_*xxx_yyy_zzz* items to this column, there is never any ambiguity as the tag clearly identifies which verification type you're using. Of course, this assumes that you're using the tag identifier format that this chapter suggests. You could use your own tag format that also differentiates review and test case items in the tag name.

If you're using this chapter's STC tag format, locating the row in the RTM where you want to place the test case tag is very easy. Just locate the requirement with the tag DAQ_SRS_*xxx_yyy* and add the STC tag to the appropriate column in the same row. If you're using a different tag format that doesn't include requirement traceability directly in the tag name, you'll have to determine the association manually (hopefully it's contained within the test case).

12.5   Software Test Procedure Documentation

The *Software Test Procedure (STP)* specifies the steps for executing a collection of test cases, which, in turn, evaluate the quality of the software system. In one respect, the STP is an optional document; after all, if you execute all the test cases (in an appropriate order), you will fully test all the test cases. The purpose behind an STP is to streamline the testing process. More often than not, test cases overlap. Although they test different requirements, it may turn out that the inputs for multiple test cases are identical. In some cases, even the outcomes are identical. By merging such test cases into a single procedure, you can run a single test sequence that handles all test cases.

Another reason for merging test cases into a single STP is the convenience of a common setup. Many test cases require (possibly elaborate) setup to ensure certain environmental conditions prior to execution. More often than not, multiple test cases require the same setup prior to their execution. By merging those test cases into a single procedure, you can perform the setup once for the entire set rather than repeating it for each and every test case.

Finally, some test cases may have dependencies that require other test cases to execute prior to their execution. By putting these test cases in a test procedure, you can ensure that the test operation satisfies the dependencies.

Std 829 defines a set of Level *Test Procedures (LTPr)*. As with all of the *level* test documents in Std 829 there are four variants of the LTPr, each variant being a document generally describing the scope or extent of software testing being documented: Component Test Procedures (aka Unit Test Procedures, or UTP), Component Integration Test Procedures (aka Integration Test Procedures, or ITP), System Test Procedures (aka System Integration Test Procedures, or SITP), and Acceptance Test Procedures (ATP; may include Factory Acceptance Test Procedures [FATP] or Site Acceptance Test Procedures [SATP]).[15]

UTPs and ITPs are often automated test procedures or less formal documents, similar to their test case document counterparts; see "Software Test Case Documentation" on page 274 for an in-depth discussion.

If you look back at Figures 12-1 and 12-2, you can see that the STP (and all LTPrs) are derived directly from the STC (LTC) documentation. Figure 12-1 applies to UTPs and ITPs. Figure 12-2 applies to SITPs and ATPs (noting that ATPs derive from test cases that come strictly from SyRS/SRS requirements, not from SDD elements).

As is true for test case documentation, ATPs are usually a subset of the SITPs to the customer or end user. Likewise, if there are FATP and SATP documents, the SATP is often a subset of the FATP, with further refinement to end-user requirements.[16]

12.5.1 The IEEE Std 829-2009 Software Test Procedure

The outline for the Std 829 STP is as follows:

1 Introduction
   1.1 Document Identifier
   1.2 Scope
   1.3 References
   1.4 Relationship to Other Documents
2 Details
   2.1 Inputs, Outputs, and Special Requirements
   2.2 Ordered Description of the Steps to Be Taken to Execute the Test Cases
3 General
   3.1 Glossary
   3.2 Document Change Procedures and History

---

15. As usual, I've included some industry-standard names that are synonyms for the *Level* Test Procedure names in parentheses. Remember, *Software Test Procedure* is a generic term representing any one of these four levels of test procedure.

16. This is not always true. Sometimes the SATP has to include additional testing procedures to deal with site environmental issues that may not exist at the factory. For example, noise (electrical as well as acoustical) and the actual physical system installation may expose some defects that could not be caught on the factory floor.

12.5.2 Extended Outline for Software Test Procedure

As is typical for IEEE standards, you're allowed to augment this outline (adding, deleting, moving, and editing items, with appropriate justification). This flexibility is important in this particular case because there are a couple of things missing from this outline.

First of all, the introduction is missing Notation for Descriptions, which appears in the STC outline ("Software Test Case Documentation" on page 274).[17] Perhaps the authors of Std 829 were expecting very few test procedures to appear in Section 2 ("Details") of the document. In practice, however, it's common to have a large number of test procedures. There are some very good reasons for breaking a single large test procedure into a series of smaller ones:

- Testing can take place in parallel. By assigning (independent) test procedures to multiple test teams, you can complete the testing faster.
- Certain tests may tie up resources (for example, test equipment such as oscilloscopes, logic analyzers, test fixtures, and signal generators). By breaking up a large test procedure into smaller test procedures, you may be able to limit the time a testing team needs access to certain resources.
- It's nice to be able to complete a test procedure within a single working day (or even between breaks in the day) so testers don't lose focus when performing tests.
- Organizing test procedures by their related activities (and by required setup prior to those activities) can streamline test procedures, reducing steps and making them more efficient to run.
- Many organizations require a testing team to rerun a test procedure from the beginning (a regression test) if any part of that test fails. Breaking a test procedure into smaller pieces makes rerunning test procedures far less expensive.

To be able to trace these test procedures back to the STC, to the SRS, and to other documentation in the RTM, you're going to need test procedure identifiers (tags). Therefore, you should have a section to describe the notation you're using for these tags.

Of course, the second thing missing from the IEEE outline is an entry for the test procedure identification in the *Details* section. To make traceability easier, it would also be nice to have a section in each test procedure where you list the associated test cases it covers. Finally, for my own purposes, I like to include the following information with each test procedure:

- Brief description
- Tag/identification
- Purpose

---

17. It's also missing the *Context* field, but that's nearly irrelevant here. The context is implied by the *Context* field in the STC documentation.

- Traceability (test cases covered)
- Pass/fail criteria (as this may change with each procedure)
- Any special requirements (for example, environmental) required to run this test procedure; this could include input/output files that must exist, among other things
- All setup required prior to running the test procedure
- Software version number when executing the test procedure
- Procedure steps to execute the test procedure

Incorporating these items produces the following extended outline for an arbitrary STP suitable for an SIT, AT, FAT, or SAT:

1. Table of Contents
2. Introduction
   - 2.1 Document Identifier and Change History (moved)
   - 2.2 Scope
   - 2.3 Glossary, Acronyms, and Abbreviations (moved)
   - 2.4 References
   - 2.5 Notation for Descriptions
   - 2.6 Relationship to Other Documents (removed)
   - 2.7 Instructions for Running the Tests (added)
3. Test Procedures (name changed from *Details*)
   - 3.1 Brief Description (simple phrase), Procedure #1
     - 3.1.1 Procedure Identification (Tag)
     - 3.1.2 Purpose
     - 3.1.3 List of Test Cases Covered by This Procedure
     - 3.1.4 Special Requirements
     - 3.1.5 Setup Required Prior to Running Procedure
     - 3.1.6 Software Version Number for This Execution
     - 3.1.7 Detailed Steps to Run the Procedure
     - 3.1.8 Sign-off on Test Procedure
   - 3.2 Brief Description (simple phrase), Procedure #2
     - (Same subsections as previous section)
     - ...
   - 3.*n* Brief Description (simple phrase), Procedure #*n*
     - (Same subsections as previous sections)
4. General
   - 4.1 Document Change Procedures
   - 4.2 Attachments and Appendixes
5. Index

12.5.3 Introduction in the STP Document

The following subsections describe the components of the STP introduction.

12.5.3.1 Document Identifier and Change History

The document identifier should be some (organization-wide) unique name; this will typically include some project designation such as *DAQ_STP*, a creation/modification date, a version number, and authorship. A list of these identifiers (one for each revision to the document) would form the change history.

12.5.3.2 Scope

The scope here has largely the same definition as that used for the STC (see "Software Test Case Documentation" on page 274). Std 829 suggests describing the scope of the STP based on its focus and relationship to the STC and other test documentation. More often than not, you can get away with a simple reference to the Scope section in the STC.

12.5.3.3 References

As usual, provide a link to any external documents (such as the STC) that are relevant to the STP. Std 829 also suggests including links to the individual test cases covered by this procedure. That, however, would be meaningful only if the STP contained just a few test procedures. In this revised format, the STP will attach the test case links to the individual test procedures in Section 3 ("Test Procedures"). If you have a very large system consisting of multiple, independent applications, you will probably have separate STPs for each of those applications. You would want to provide links to those other STPs in this section of the STP document.

12.5.3.4 Notation for Descriptions

As in the STC, you would describe your STP tag format here. This book recommends using STP tags of the form *proj_STP_xxx*, where *proj* is some project-specific ID (such as *DAQ* or *POOL*) and *xxx* is some unique (possibly decimal) numeric sequence.

Note that there is a many-to-one relationship from STC test cases to STP test procedures. Therefore, you cannot easily embed traceability information into the STP tags (there's a similar situation with SDD tags; see "SDD Traceability and Tags" on page 245). This is why it's important to include the related STC tags with each test procedure, to facilitate traceability back to the corresponding test cases.

12.5.3.5 Relationship to Other Documents

In the modified variant of the STP, I've removed this section. Std 829 suggests using it to describe the relationship of this STP to other test procedure documents—specifically, which test procedures must be performed before or after other test procedures. However, in the modified form all test procedures appear in the same document. Therefore, a description of the relationship between tests should accompany each individual test procedure. (This information appears in the "Special Requirements" section.)

This is one reason for including this section in the modified form of the STP: very large systems may contain multiple (and relatively independent) software applications. There would probably be separate STP documents for each of these applications. This section of the modified STP could describe the relationship of this STP to those others, including the order in which tests must execute these STPs.

12.5.3.6 Instructions for Running Tests

This section should contain generic instructions to whomever will be running the tests. Usually the people running the tests are not the software developers.[18] This section can provide insights into the software to be tested for those who have not lived with it on a daily basis from its inception.

One important piece of information that should appear here is what to do if a test procedure fails. Should the tester attempt to continue that test procedure (if possible) in hopes of finding additional problems? Should the tester immediately suspend testing operations until the development team resolves the issue? If a test has been suspended, what is the process for resuming the test? For example, most QA teams require, at the very least, rerunning the test procedure from the beginning.[19] Some QA teams may also require a meeting with development to determine a set of regression tests to run before resuming the test procedure from the point of failure.

This section should also discuss how to log any problems/anomalies that occur during testing and to describe how to bring the system back into a stable state or shut it down should a critical or catastrophic event occur.

This is also where you'll describe how to log successful runs of a test procedure. A tester will usually log the date and time they begin a test, provide the name of the test engineer, and specify which test procedure they are executing. At the successful conclusion of a test, most test procedures require signatures by the test engineer, a possible QA or customer representative, and possibly other managerial or project-related personnel. This section should describe the process for obtaining these signatures and signing off on successful runs of a test procedure.

---

18. Indeed, QA guidelines claim that it is unacceptable and unethical for developers to run the formal system integration and acceptance tests for a product. Many companies won't even allow the developers to produce the executable code, instead relying on the QA department to construct the builds from the source code control system for testing.

19. Some might even require running the entire STP from the beginning, although this is usually too expensive and, therefore, impractical. The usual compromise is to rerun each test procedure that fails and then, at the end of the STP, rerun the whole STP to guarantee it runs in its entirety without failure.

12.5.4 Test Procedures

This section of the document repeats for each individual test procedure for the system under test. This is a modification of the Std 829 STP, which describes only a single (or maybe a few) test procedures in the document. Presumably, there would be multiple STP documents if your system requires a large number of test procedures.

12.5.4.1 Brief Description (for Test Procedure #1)

This is the title of the test procedure. It should be a short phrase, such as *DIP Switch #1 Test*, that provides a quick and perhaps informal procedure identification.

Procedure Identification

This is the unique identifier (tag) for this test procedure. Other documentation (such as the RTM) will reference this test procedure using its tag.

Purpose

This is an expanded description of this test procedure: why it exists, what it tests, and where it sits in the big picture.

List of Test Cases Covered by This Procedure

This section provides reverse traceability back to the STC document. It is simply a list of all the test cases that this test procedure covers. Note that this set of test cases should be mutually exclusive of the sets found in other test procedures—no test case tag should ever appear in more than one test procedure. You want to preserve the many-to-one relationship from test cases to test procedures. This will help keep the RTM clean, meaning that you won't have to attach multiple test procedures to the same row in the RTM.

Now, it is quite possible that multiple test procedures will provide inputs (and verify corresponding outcomes) that test the same test case. This isn't a problem; just pick one procedure that will take credit for covering that test case and assign the test case to that procedure. When someone is tracing through the requirements and verifying that the test procedures test a particular requirement, they're not going to care if the test procedures test that requirement multiple times; they'll be interested only in determining that the requirement has been tested at least once somewhere in the test procedures.

If you have a choice of test procedures with which to associate a given test case, it's best to include that test case in a test procedure that also handles related test cases. Of course, in general, this type of association, whereby related test cases are put into the same test procedure, happens automatically. That's because you don't arbitrarily create test procedures and then assign test cases to them. Instead, you pick a set of (related) test cases and use them to generate a test procedure.

Special Requirements

This section identifies anything external you'll need for the test procedure in order to successfully execute the test. This includes databases, input files, existing directory paths, online resources (such as web pages), dynamically linked libraries and other third-party tools, and automated test procedures.

Setup Required Prior to Running Procedure

This section describes any processes or procedures to execute before you can run the test procedure. For example, a test procedure for autonomous vehicle software might require an operator to drive the vehicle to a specified starting point on a test track before starting the test. Other examples might be ensuring an internet or server connection is available. With the SPM, an example of setup could include ensuring that the test fixture (five-gallon bucket of water) is filled to some specified level.

Software Version Number for This Execution

This is a "fill in the blank" field for the test procedure. It does not mandate a software version for running the test; rather, the tester enters the current software version number prior to the test's execution. Note that this field has to be filled in for each test procedure. You cannot simply write this value down once for the whole STP. The reason is quite simple: during testing you may encounter defects that require you to suspend the test. Once the development team corrects those defects, the testing can resume, usually from the beginning of the test procedure. Because different procedures in an STP could have been run on different versions of the software, you need to identify which version of the software you're using when running each procedure.[20]

Detailed Steps Required to Run This Procedure

This section contains steps that are necessary to execute the test procedure. There are two types of steps in a test procedure: actions and verifications. An *action* is a statement of work to be done, such as providing some input to the system. A *verification* involves checking some outcome/output and confirming that the system is operating correctly.

You must number all procedure steps sequentially—typically starting from 1, though you could also use section numbers like 3.2.1 through 3.2.40 for a test procedure that has 40 steps. At the very least, each verification step should be preceded by three or so underline characters (___) or a box symbol (see Figure 12-3) so that the tester can physically check off the step once they have successfully completed

---

20. As noted earlier, some QA teams will require running the entire LTP over again if there were any failures on individual test procedures (whose defects were presumably corrected and retested). This ensures that all test procedures in the LTP all have the same version number.

it. Some people prefer putting the checkbox on every item (that is, both actions and verifications) in the test procedure to ensure that the tester marks off each step as they complete it. Perhaps there should be lines on the actions and checkboxes on the verifications. However, this adds considerable menial work to the process, so consider carefully whether it's important enough to do.

3.1.25 ☐ Verify...

Figure 12-3: Using a checkbox on a verify statement

Note that the detailed steps should include information (in appropriate positions) such as the following:

- Any actions needed to start the procedure (obviously, these should appear in the first few steps of the procedure)
- A discussion of how to make measurements or observe outputs (don't assume the tester is as familiar with the software as the developers are)
- How to shut down the system at the conclusion of the test procedure to leave the system in a stable state (if this is necessary, it will obviously appear in the last steps of the procedure)
- Sign-off

At the end of the test procedure there should be blank lines for the tester, observers, customer representatives, and possibly management personnel to sign off on the successful conclusion of the test procedure. A signature and date are the minimum information that should appear here. Each organization may mandate which signatures are necessary. At the very least (such as in a one-person shop), whoever executes the test procedure should sign and date it to affirm that it was run.

12.5.5 General

The last section of an STP is a generic catch-all section where you can place information that doesn't fit anywhere else.

12.5.5.1 Document Change Procedures

Many organizations have set policies for changing test procedure documents. They could, for example, require customer approval before making official changes to an ATP. This section outlines the rules and necessary approval procedures and processes for making changes to the STP.

12.5.5.2 Attachments and Appendixes

It's often useful to attach large tables, images, and other documentation directly to the LTP so that it is always available to a reader, as opposed to providing a link to a document that the reader cannot access.

12.5.6 Index

If desired, you can add an index at the end of the STP.

12.5.7 A Sample STP

This section presents a shortened (for space/editorial purposes) example of an STP for the DAQ DIP switch project.

1 **Table of Contents**
[Omitted for space reasons]

2 **Introduction**

    2.1 Document Identifier
    Mar 22, 2018: DAQ_LTP, Version 1.0 Randall Hyde

    2.2 Scope
    This document describes some of the DIP switch test procedures in the DAQ system (shortened for space/editorial reasons).

    2.3 Glossary, Acronyms, and Abbreviations

> **NOTE** *This is a very simple and short example to keep this book smaller. Please don't use this as boilerplate; you should diligently pick out terms and abbreviations your document uses and list them in this section.*

Term	Definition
DAQ	Data acquisition system
SBC	Single-board computer
Software Design Description (SDD)	Documentation of the design of the software system (IEEE Std 1016-2009)—that is, this document.
Software Requirements Specification (SRS)	Documentation of the essential requirements (functions, performance, design constraints, and attributes) of the software and its external interfaces (IEEE Std 610.12-1990).
System Requirements Specification (SyRS)	A structured collection of information that embodies the requirements of the system (IEEE Std 1233-1998). A specification that documents the requirements to establish a design basis and the conceptual design for a system or subsystem.
Software Test Cases (STC)	Documentation that describes test cases (inputs and outcomes) to verify correct operation of the software based on various design concerns/requirements (IEEE Std 829-2009).
Software Test Procedures (STP)	Documentation that describes the step-by-step procedure to execute a set of test cases to verify correct operation of the software based on various design concerns/requirements (IEEE Std 829-2009).

2.4 References

Reference	Discussion
DAQ STC	See "A Sample Software Test Case Document" on page 281.
DAQ STP	An example of a full STP for the Plantation Productions DAQ system can be found at *http://www.plantation-productions.com/Electronics/DAQ/DAQ.html*.
IEEE Std 830-1998	SRS documentation standard
IEEE Std 829-2008	STP documentation standard
IEEE Std 1012-1998	Software verification and validation standard
IEEE Std 1016-2009	SDD documentation standard
IEEE Std 1233-1998	SyRS documentation standard

NOTE *An additional reference that might make sense (not included here because it doesn't exist for this simple project) is a link to any associated documentation for the DAQ system, such as programming manuals or schematics.*

2.5 Notation for Descriptions

Test procedure identifiers (*tags*) in this document shall take the form:

DAQ_STP_*xxx*

where *xxx* is a (possibly dotted decimal) numeric sequence that creates a unique identifier out of the whole sequence. Note that *xxx* values for STP tags are usually numbered from 000 or 001 and usually increment by 1 for each additional test case item sharing the same *xxx* string.

2.6 Instructions for Running the Tests

Execute each test procedure exactly as stated. If tester encounters an error or omission in the procedure, tester should redline (with red ink, which tester should use only for redlines) the procedure with the correct information and justify the redline in the test log (with date/timestamp and signature). All redlines within the test procedure(s) must be initialized by all signatories at the end of the test procedure.

If tester discovers a defect in the software itself (that is, not simply a defect in the test procedure), the tester shall note the anomaly in a test log and create an Anomaly Report for the defect. If the defect is marginal or negligible in nature, the tester may continue with the test procedure, if possible, and attempt to find any other defects in the system on the same test procedure run. If the defect is critical or catastrophic in nature, or the defect is such that it is impossible to continue the test procedure, the tester shall immediately suspend the test and shut off power to the system. Once the defect is corrected, tester must restart the test procedure from the beginning of the procedure.

A test procedure succeeds if and only if the tester completes all steps without any failures.

3 Test Procedures

3.1 RS-232 (Serial Port) Operation

3.1.1 DAQ_STP_001

3.1.2 Purpose
This test procedure tests the proper operation of DAQ commands sourced from the RS-232 port.

3.1.3 Test Cases
DAQ_STC_701_000_000

DAQ_STC_702_000_000

DAQ_STC_703_000_000

DAQ_STC_726_000_000

3.1.4 Special Requirements
This test procedure requires a serial terminal emulator program running on a PC (for example, the *MTTY.exe* program that comes as part of the Netburner SDK; you could even use Hyperterm if you are masochistic). There should be a NULL modem cable between the PC's serial port and the COM1 port on the Netburner.

3.1.5 Setup Required Prior to Running
Netburner powered up and running application software. Serial terminal program should be properly connected to the serial port on the PC that is wired to the Netburner.

3.1.6 Software Version Number
Version number: _____

Date: _____

3.1.7 Detailed Steps
1. Set DIP switch 1 to the ON position.

2. Reset the Netburner and wait several seconds for it to finish rebooting. Note: Rebooting Netburner may produce information on the serial terminal. You can ignore this.

3. Press ENTER on the line by itself into the terminal emulator.

4. ___ Verify that the DAQ system responds with a newline without any other output

5. Type **help**, then press ENTER on a line by itself.

6. ___ Verify that the DAQ software responds with a help message (contents unimportant as long as it is obviously a help response).

7. Set DIP switch 1 to the OFF position.

8. Reset the Netburner and wait several seconds for it to finish rebooting. Note: Rebooting Netburner may produce information on the serial terminal. You can ignore this.

9. Type the help command into the serial terminal.

10. ___Verify that the DAQ system ignores the help command.

3.1.8 Sign-off on Test Procedure
Tester: _____ Date: _____

QA: _____ Date: _____

NOTE *In a full STP document, there would probably be additional test procedures here; the following test procedure ignores that possibility and continues tag numbering with DAQ_STP_002.*

3.2 Ethernet Address Selection

3.2.1 DAQ_STP_002

3.2.2 Purpose
This test procedure tests the initialization of the Ethernet IP address based on DIP switches 5 and 6.

3.2.3 Test Cases
DAQ_STC_709_000_000

DAQ_STC_710_000_000

DAQ_STC_711_000_000

DAQ_STC_712_000_000

3.2.4 Special Requirements
This test procedure requires an Ethernet terminal emulator program running on a PC (*Hercules.exe* has been a good choice in the past). There should be an Ethernet (crossover or through a hub) cable between the PC's Ethernet port and the Ethernet port on the Netburner.

3.2.5 Setup Required Prior to Running
Netburner powered up and running application software. DIP switch 3 in the ON position. DIP switch 4 in the OFF position.

3.2.6 Software Version Number
Version number: _____

Date: _____

3.2.7 Detailed Steps
1. Set DIP switches 5 and 6 to the OFF position.

2. Reset the Netburner and wait several seconds for it to finish rebooting.

3. From the Ethernet terminal program, attempt to connect to the Netburner at IP address 192.168.2.70, port 20560 (0x5050).

4. Verify that the connection was successful.

5. Enter a **help** command and press the ENTER key.

6. ____ Verify that the DAQ system responds with an appropriate help message.

7. Set DIP switch 5 to the ON position and 6 to the OFF position.

8. Reset the Netburner and wait several seconds for it to finish rebooting.

9. From the Ethernet terminal program, attempt to connect to the Netburner at IP address 192.168.2.71, port 20560 (0x5050).

10. ____ Verify that the connection was successful.

11. Enter a **help** command and press the ENTER key.

12. ____ Verify that the DAQ system responds with an appropriate help message.

13. Set DIP switch 5 to the OFF position and 6 to the ON position.

14. Reset the Netburner and wait several seconds for it to finish rebooting.

15. From the Ethernet terminal program, attempt to connect to the Netburner at IP address 192.168.2.72, port 20560 (0x5050).

16. ____ Verify that the connection was successful.

17. Enter a **help** command and press the ENTER key.

18. ____Verify that the DAQ system responds with an appropriate help message.
19. Set DIP switches 5 and 6 to the ON position.
20. Reset the Netburner and wait several seconds for it to finish rebooting.
21. From the Ethernet terminal program, attempt to connect to the Netburner at IP address 192.168.2.73, port 20560 (0x5050).
22. ____Verify that the connection was successful.
23. Enter a **help** command and press the ENTER key.
24. ____Verify that the DAQ system responds with an appropriate help message.

3.2.8 Sign-off on Test Procedure
Tester: _____ Date: _____
QA: _____ Date: _____

NOTE *In a full STP document, there would probably be additional test procedures here.*

4 General

4.1 Document Change Procedures
Whenever making changes to this document, add a new line to Section 2.1 listing, at a minimum, the date, project name (*DAQ_STP*), version number, and authorship.

4.2 Attachments and Appendixes
[In the interests of space, none are provided here; in a real STP, putting the schematic of the DAQ system would be a good idea.]

5 Index
[Omitted for space reasons.]

12.5.8 Updating the RTM with STP Information

Because STP tags are very similar in nature to SDD tags, it should come as no surprise that the process for adding STP tags to the RTM is quite similar to that for adding SDD tags (see "Updating the Traceability Matrix with Design Information" on page 259).

The STP adds a single column to the RTM: the STP tag column. Unfortunately, the STP tag does not directly embed any traceability information, so you'll have to extract that information from the STP to determine where to place STP tags in the RTM.

As you may recall from "List of Test Cases Covered by This Procedure" on page 294, each test procedure in an STP must include the list of test cases it covers. Though Std 829 does not require this, I strongly suggest that you include this section. If you've done that, you've already created the reverse traceability back to the requirements, which makes it easy to fill in the STP tags in the RTM. To do so, just locate each test case tag (listed in the current test procedure) and copy the test procedure's STP tag into the STP tag column in the RTM (on the same row as the corresponding test case). Of course, because there are multiple test cases associated with a single test procedure, you'll also have several copies of the same STP tag spread throughout the RTM (one per associated test case).

Should you ever want to easily trace your STP tags back to all the requirements in the RTM, particularly without having to look up the list in the STP, simply sort the RTM by the STP tag column. This will collect all the requirements (and everything else linked to that STP tag) into a contiguous group in the matrix and make it easy to identify everything associated with that tag.

If you choose some other method of specifying test cases in the test procedure that doesn't involve incorporating the STC tags within the test procedures, then determining the placement of the STP tags in the RTM becomes a manual—and often laborious—process. That's why I strongly recommend including STC tag numbers in a test procedure when you first create it.

12.6 *Level* Test Logs

Although each test procedure contains a signature section where the tester (and any other desired personnel) can sign off on a successful test completion, a separate test log is needed to handle anomalies that occur during testing or to simply hold comments and concerns that the tester may have while running the test procedure.

Perhaps the most important job of this Level *Test Log (LTL)* is to present a chronological view of the testing process. Whenever a tester begins running a test procedure, they should first log an entry stating the date, time, test procedure they are executing, and their name. Throughout the test's execution, the tester can add entries to the test log (as necessary) indicating:

- Start of a test procedure (date/time)
- End of a test procedure (date/time)
- Anomalies/defects found (and whether the test was continued or suspended)
- Redlines/changes needed to the test procedure because of errors found in the procedure itself (for example, the test procedure could list an incorrect outcome; if the tester can show that the program output was correct even if it differs from the test procedure, they would redline the test procedure and add an appropriate justification to the test log)
- Concerns about outcomes the program produces that the tester finds questionable (perhaps the test procedure doesn't list any outcome, or the test procedure's outcomes are questionable)

- Personnel changes (for example, if a tester changes in the middle of a test due to a break, shift change, or different experience needed)
- Any break period during the test procedure (for example, lunch break or end of the workday)

Technically, all you need for a test log is a sheet of (preferably lined) paper. More often than not, STP creators add several sheets of lined paper to the end of the STP specifically for this test log. Some organizations simply maintain the test log electronically using a word processor or text editor (or even a specially written application). Of course, Std 829 outlines a formal recommendation for test logs:

1 Introduction
   1.1 Document Identifier
   1.2 Scope
   1.3 References
2 Details
   2.1 Description
   2.2 Activity and Event Entries
3 General
   3.1 Glossary

12.6.1 Introduction in the Level *Test Logs* Document

In addition to introducing the subsections that follow, this section might also identify the organization that created the document and the current status.

12.6.1.1 Document Identifier

A unique identifier for this document; as with all Std 829 documents this should include, at the very least, the date, some descriptive name, a version number, and authorship. A change history (of the outline/format, not the specific log) might appear here as well.

12.6.1.2 Scope

The Scope section summarizes the system and features that the associated test procedure tested. Generally, this would be a reference to the test procedure's Scope section unless there was something special about this particular test run.

12.6.1.3 References

At the very least, this section should refer to the STP (and in particular, the specific test) document for which this test log was created.

12.6.2 Details

This section introduces the following subsections and is what most people would consider the actual "test log."

12.6.2.1 Description

This section (only one occurrence per test log) describes items that will apply to all test log entries. This could include the following:

- Identification of the test subject (for example, by version number)
- Identification of any changes made to the test procedure (for example, redlines) prior to this test
- Date and time of the start of the test
- Date and time of the stop of the test
- Name of the tester running the test
- Explanation for why testing was halted (if this should happen)

12.6.2.2 Activities and Event Entries

This section of the test log records each event during the execution of the test procedure. This section (containing multiple entries) typically documents the following:

- Description of the test procedure execution (procedure ID/tag)
- All personnel observing/involved in the test run—including testers, support personnel, and observers—and the role of each participant
- The result of each test procedure execution (pass, fail, commentary)
- A record of any deviations from the test procedure (for example, redlines)
- A record of any defects or anomalies discovered during the test procedure (along with a reference to an associated Anomaly Report if one is generated)

12.6.3 Glossary

This section of the LTL documentation contains the usual glossary associated with all Std 829 documents.

12.6.4 A Few Comments on Test Logs

To be honest, the Std 829 outline is way too much effort for such a simple task. There are a few tips for managing the effort involved in this document.

12.6.4.1 Overhead Management

Almost all of the effort that would go into creating an Std 829 LTL outline-compliant document can be eliminated by simply attaching the test log directly to the end of the STP. The test log then inherits all the preface information from the STP, so all you need to document is the information that appears at the very beginning of "*Level* Test Logs" on page 303.

Note that LTLs have four variants, as typical for all Std 829 level documents: Component Test Logs (aka Unit Test Logs), Component Integration Test Logs (aka Integration Test Logs), System Test Logs (aka System Integration Test Logs), and Acceptance Test Logs (possibly including Factory Acceptance Test Logs or Site Acceptance Test Logs).[21]

In reality, it's rare for there to be much in the way of Component or Component Integration Test Logs. Most frequently, the corresponding test procedures are automated tests. Even when they're not, the development team usually runs these tests and immediately corrects any defects they find. Because these tests run frequently (often multiple times per day, particularly in teams using Agile-based methodologies), the overhead with documenting these test runs is far too much.

System Test Logs and Acceptance Test Logs are the variants of the LTL that testers (independent of the development team) run, and hence the ones that require the creation of actual test logs.

12.6.4.2 Recordkeeping

The test logs are different from the other Std 829 documents in a very fundamental sense. Most Std 829 documents are static documents; about the only thing you do with them is fill in details like software version numbers and check off verification steps. The basic structure of the document doesn't change if you run the procedure over and over again. Ultimately, there is no reason to keep any old copies of the test procedure around (like runs of the test procedure that failed in the middle of execution). All you really need to show the customer is the last run of the test procedure where you successfully executed all steps and passed the entire procedure.

The test logs, unlike the other documents you've seen in this chapter thus far, are *dynamic* documents. They will differ radically from test run to test run (even if nothing else changes, at least all the dates and timestamps will change). Furthermore, a test log isn't a boilerplate document where you simply fill in a few blanks and check off some checkboxes. It's essentially a blank slate that you create while actually running the test. If there are failures, or redlines, or commentary, the test log maintains the history of these events. Therefore, it is important to keep all your test logs, even the ones that recorded failed tests. It is highly improbable that any system will be perfect; there will be mistakes and defects you discover during testing. The test logs provide proof that you've found, corrected, and retested for these defects.

If you throw away all the old test logs that document all the defects discovered along the way and present only perfect test logs, any reasonable customer is going to question what you're hiding. Mistakes and defects are a normal part of the process. If you don't show that you've found and corrected these mistakes, your customers will assume that you haven't tested the system well enough to find the defects or that you've faked the test logs.

---

21. As usual, I've included some common names (non–Std 829) in parentheses.

Keep the old test logs! This proves you've done your QA due diligence for your product.

You could argue that keeping old test procedures to show redlines or interruptions in the test process is also important. However, any redline or interruption that appears on a test procedure document had better show up in the corresponding test log, so you don't need to keep old test procedures that you've actually rerun.

Note that this does not imply that all test procedures you've run should be perfect. If you have properly documented and justified redlines on a test procedure, yet the test execution ran successfully to its conclusion, there is no need to *rewrite* the test procedure and refill all the checkboxes to include a clean test procedure in your final documentation. If it was successful, even with redlines, leave it alone.[22] Redlines don't indicate a failure of the software system; they are a defect, of course, but in the test procedure itself rather than the software. The goal of the test procedure is to test the software, not the test procedure. If minor changes to the test procedure are all you have, redline them and move on.

In many organizations, as I've said before, if any verification step in a test procedure fails, then after any defects are corrected, the entire procedure must be run from the beginning (a full regression test). For some test procedures or in some organizations, there may be a process in place to temporarily suspend a test procedure, update the software, and then resume the test procedure upon resolving the defect. In such cases, you can treat the verification failure step as though it were a redline: document the original failure in the test log, document the fact that the development team repaired the defect, and then document the correct operation of the software (at the failed verification step) with the new version of the software.[23]

12.6.4.3 Paper vs. Electronic Logs

Some people prefer creating electronic test logs; some organizations or customers demand paper test logs (filled in with pens, not pencils). The problem with electronic logs (especially if you create them using a word processor rather than an application program specifically designed to log test procedure runs) is that they are easily faked. Of course, no great programmer would ever fake a test log. However, there are less-than-great programmers in this world who have faked a test log. Unfortunately, the actions of those few have sullied the reputations of all software engineers. Therefore, it's best to create test logs that are not easily faked, which often means using paper.

Someone *could* fake paper logs; however, it's a lot more work and usually more obvious. Ultimately, customers are probably going to want hard copies

---

22. You should, of course, update the electronic version of the document so you don't have to re-redline the test procedure if you ever have to run it again.

23. Personally, I would have a big problem with this approach. However, if you have a particularly large test procedure, it could be very expensive to restart that procedure every time testers find a defect.

of the test logs; when they want them in electronic form, they'll probably want scanned images of the hardcopy logs. They will be expecting you to maintain those paper logs in storage for legal reasons.

Perhaps the best solution is to use a software application specifically designed for creating test logs, one that automatically logs the entries to a database (making it a bit more difficult to fake the data). For the customer, you would print a report from the database to provide a hardcopy (or generate a PDF report if they wanted an electronic copy).

Regardless of how testers generate the original test log, most organizations will require them to eventually create a paper test log, and then the testers, observers, and other personnel associated with the test run will have to sign and date it to certify that the information is correct and accurate. This is a legal document at this point; someone attempting to fake any data could land in serious legal jeopardy.

12.6.4.4 Inclusion in the RTM

Normally, test logs don't appear in the traceability matrix. However, there is no reason you couldn't include them there. There is a one-to-many relationship between test procedures (and, therefore, STPs) and test logs. Thus, if you assign a unique identifier (tag) to each test report, you can add that identifier to an appropriate column in the RTM.

Because test logs have a many-to-one relationship to test procedures, it wouldn't be a bad idea to model the tag ID on the others that this book presents. For example, use something such as: proj_TL_*xxx*_*yyy* where *xxx* comes from the test procedure tag (for example, *005* from *DAQ_STP_005*) and *yyy* is a (possibly decimal) numeric sequence that creates a unique tag for the test log.

12.7 Anomaly Reports

When a tester, a development team member, a customer, or anyone else using the system discovers a software defect, the proper way to document it is with an *Anomaly Report (AR)*, also known as a *Bug Report* or *Defect Report*. All too often an AR consists of someone telling a programmer, "Hey, I found a problem in your code." The programmer then runs off to their machine to correct the problem and there's no documentation to track the anomaly. This is very unfortunate, because tracking defects in a system is very important to maintaining the quality of that system.

The AR is the formal way to track system defects. Among other things, it captures the following information:

- Date and time of defect occurrence
- The person who discovered the defect (or at least, who recorded the defect report in response to some user's complaint)
- A description of the defect
- A procedure for reproducing the defect in the system (assuming the issue is deterministic and is easy enough to reproduce)

- The impact the defect has on the system (for example, catastrophic, critical, marginal, negligible)
- The importance of the defect to end users (economic and social impact) so management can assign a priority to correcting it
- Any possible workarounds to the defect (so users can continue using the system while the development team works on correcting the defect)
- A discussion of what it might take to correct the defect (including recommendations and conclusions concerning the defect)
- Current status of the anomaly (for example, "new anomaly," "development team is working on correction," "in testing," "corrected in software version *xxx.xxx*")

Naturally, Std 829 has a suggested outline for Anomaly Reports. However, most organizations use defect-tracking software to record defects or anomalies. If you aren't willing to spend the money on a commercial product, there are many open source products freely available, such as Bugzilla. Most of these products use a database organization that is reasonably compatible with the recommendations from Std 829:

1 Introduction
    1.1 Document Identifier
    1.2 Scope
    1.3 References
2 Details
    2.1 Summary
    2.2 Date Anomaly Discovered
    2.3 Context
    2.4 Description of Anomaly
    2.5 Impact
    2.6 Originator's Assessment of Urgency (see IEEE 1044-1993 [B13])
    2.7 Description of Corrective Action
    2.8 Status of the Anomaly
    2.9 Conclusions and Recommendations
3 General
    3.1 Document Change Procedures and History

12.7.1 *Introduction in the Anomaly Reports Document*

The following subsections describe the components of the AR introduction.

12.7.1.1 Document Identifier

This is a unique name that other reports can reference (such as test logs and test reports).

12.7.1.2 Scope

The Scope section gives a brief description of anything that doesn't appear elsewhere in the AR.

12.7.1.3 References

References include links to other relevant documents, such as test logs and test procedures.

12.7.2 Details

This section introduces the subsections that follow.

12.7.2.1 Summary

Here you give a brief description of the anomaly.

12.7.2.2 Date Anomaly Discovered

List the date (and time, if possible/appropriate) when the anomaly was discovered.

12.7.2.3 Context

Software version and installation/configuration information goes in the Context section. This section should also refer to relevant test procedures and test logs, if appropriate, which should help to identify this anomaly. If no such test procedure exists for this anomaly, consider suggesting an addition to some test procedure that would catch it.

12.7.2.4 Description of Anomaly

Provide an in-depth description of the defect including (if possible) how to reproduce it. The description might include the following information:

- Inputs
- Actual results
- Outcome(s) (particularly, the outcomes that vary from the test procedure)
- Procedure step of failure
- Environment
- Was the defect repeatable?
- Any tests executed immediately prior to failure than might have affected results
- Tester(s)
- Observer(s)

12.7.2.5 Impact

Describe the impact this defect will have on system users. Describe any possible workarounds, such as changing the documentation or modifying the use of the system. If possible, estimate cost and time to repair this defect and the risk associated with leaving it in place. Estimate the risk associated with fixing it, which could impact other system features.

12.7.2.6 Originator's Assessment of Urgency

State the level of urgency for a speedy repair. The integrity levels and risk assessment scale from "Integrity Levels and Risk Assessment" on page 263 are probably a good minimum mechanism for stating the urgency of repair.

12.7.2.7 Description of Corrective Action

This section describes the time needed to determine the reason for the defect; an estimate of the time, cost, and risk associated with repairing it; and an estimate of the effort required to retest the system. Include any necessary regression tests to ensure that nothing else is broken by the fix.

12.7.2.8 Status of the Anomaly

List the status of the current defect. Std 829 recommends statuses such as "open," "approved for resolution," "assigned for resolution," "fixed," and "tested with the fix confirmed."

12.7.2.9 Conclusions and Recommendations

This section should provide commentary as to why the defect occurred and recommend possible changes to the development process to prevent similar defects in the future. This section might also suggest additional requirements, test cases, and (modifications to) test procedures to catch the anomaly in the future; this is particularly important if testing discovered the anomaly by accident rather than by running specific test procedure steps to catch this particular defect.

12.7.2.10 General

This is the usual end-of-document section in Std 829 documents providing a change history (to the AR format, not to a specific AR) and change procedures. Std 829 does not recommend a glossary.

12.7.3 A Few Comments on Anomaly Reports

It is worthwhile to bear the following points in mind when dealing with Anomaly Reports.

12.7.3.1 ARs Don't Go in the RTM

The purpose of the traceability matrix is to be able to trace requirements of designs and tests to ensure that the system successfully meets all requirements. While one could argue that test logs belong in the RTM, most people don't bother to put them there because they normally attach test logs directly to the completed test procedures.

Anomalies, on the other hand, aren't something whose existence you're trying to prove; indeed, in a perfect world you're trying to *disprove* the existence of anomalies. This doesn't mean you discard ARs. Just as with test logs, it's very important to keep all the old ARs around—they provide valuable proof that you've done your due diligence when testing the system. More importantly, you want to keep ARs for regression purposes. Sometimes long after a defect has been discovered and corrected, it finds its way into the system again. Having a historical record of ARs makes it possible to go back and examine the original cause and its solution.

12.7.3.2 Electronic vs. Paper ARs

As this chapter noted earlier, most organizations use a defect-tracking system to capture and track ARs. Although Std 829 doesn't specifically suggest or require paper documents (indeed, Std 829 points out that you can use software to track anomalies), the outline form tends to suggest a hardcopy format. But given that most organizations use defect-tracking software, why bother with hardcopy ARs? The main reason is portability in the "you can carry it with you" sense. While using the defect-tracking system makes a lot of sense for system integration, factory acceptance tests, and other tests done at the development site where there is easy access to the tracker, in some cases it may not be available or accessible at an installation during a site acceptance test.[24] In such situations, creating ARs on paper and then entering them into the defect-tracking system when possible is probably the best approach.

12.8 Test Reports

When testing is completed, a test report summarizes the results. As for many of the other test documents, Std 829 describes a wide variety of test reports you can produce. Std 829 defines *Level* Interim Test Status Reports (LITSR), *Level* Test Reports (LTR), and Master Test Reports (MTR). Of course, you can substitute *Component, Component Integration, System,* and *Acceptance* in place of *Level* (with the usual common names as well).

A very large organization might need to produce interim test reports so management can figure out what's going on in an equally large system. For more information on LITSRs, refer to IEEE Std 829-2008; they are, quite

---

24. Many defect-tracking systems are accessible via a web page interface. So as long as you have internet access and your tracking system is available online, you can fill out bug reports remotely.

frankly, documentation for documentation's sake for most projects, but large governmental contracts might explicitly require them.

Level and Master Test Reports vary according to the size of the project. Most small to medium-sized systems with (typically) a single software application and, therefore, a single STP, will have a single test report, if any at all.

Once a system grows to the size that it contains several major software applications, there will usually be a test report for each major application and then an MTR as a summary of the results from the individual test reports. The MTR, then, provides an *executive-level review* of all the tests.

12.8.1 Brief Mention of the Master Test Report

As the MTR is generally not a document that individual developers will deal with, this section will simply present the Std 829-suggested outline without further comment and then concentrate on LTRs.

1. Introduction
    1.1 Document Identifier
    1.2 Scope
    1.3 References
2. Details of the Master Test Report
    2.1 Overview of All Aggregate Test Results
    2.2 Rationale for Decisions
    2.3 Conclusions and Recommendations
3. General
    3.1 Glossary
    3.2 Document Change Procedures and History

For more information on the MTR, see IEEE Std 829-2008.

12.8.2 Level *Test Reports*

Although you could have component/unit test reports and component integration test reports, most organizations leave unit and integration testing to the development department, as upper management generally doesn't care about the low-level details. Thus, the most common Level *Test Reports (LTRs)* you'll see will be System (Integration) Test Reports and Acceptance Test Reports, typically Factory Acceptance Test Reports and Site Acceptance Test Reports. Std 829 outlines LTRs as follows:

1. Introduction
    1.1 Document Identifier
    1.2 Scope
    1.3 References

2   Details
      2.1   Overview of Test Results
      2.2   Detailed Test Results
      2.3   Rationale for Decisions
      2.4   Conclusions and Recommendations
   3   General
      3.1   Glossary
      3.2   Document Change Procedures and History

Sections 1 ("Introduction") and 3 ("General") are the same as for most other Std 829 test documents in this chapter. The core of the test report is in Section 2 ("Details"). The following subsections describe its contents.

12.8.2.1   Overview of the Test Results

This section is a summary of the test activities. It would briefly describe the features covered by the tests, testing environment, software/hardware version numbers, and any other general information about the test. The overview should also mention if there was anything special about the testing environment that would yield different results if the test were conducted in a different environment, like a factory.

12.8.2.2   Detailed Test Result

Summarize all the results in this section. List all anomalies discovered and their resolution. If the resolution to a defect has been deferred, be sure to provide justification and discuss the impact that defect will have on the system.

If there were any deviations from the test procedure, explain and justify those deviations. Describe any changes (redlines) to the test procedures.

This section should also provide a confidence level in the testing process. For example, if the testing process focuses on code coverage, this section should describe the estimated percentage of code coverage that the testing processing achieved.

12.8.2.3   Rationale for Decisions

If the team had to make any decisions during the testing process such as deviations from test procedures or failure to correct known anomalies, this section should provide the rationale for those decisions. This section might also justify any conclusions reached (in the next section).

12.8.2.4   Conclusions and Recommendations

This section should state any conclusions emanating from the test processing. This section should discuss the product's fitness for release/production use, and recommend possibilities such as disabling certain, possibly known, anomalous features to allow early release of the system. This section could also recommend stalling the release pending further development and possible debugging.

12.9   Do You Really Need All of This?

IEEE Std 829-2008 describes a huge volume of documentation. Do you really need to create all this documentation for the next "killer app" you're developing by yourself in your home office? Of course not. Except for the largest (government-sponsored) applications, the vast majority of the documentation described in Std 829 is complete overkill. For normal projects, you'll probably want to have the STC, SRL, and STP documents.[25] Test logs will simply be an appendix to the STP. Anomaly Reports would be entries in your defect-tracking system (from which you can produce hardcopy reports).

You can also reduce the size of your STC and STP documents by using automated testing. You probably can't eliminate all manual tests, but you can get rid of many of them.

Test reports are easy enough to eliminate in smaller projects. The test log at the end of the STP will likely serve as a reasonable alternative unless you have multiple levels of management demanding full documentation.

Agile development methodologies might seem like a good alternative for reducing the cost of all this documentation. However, keep in mind that developing, validating, verifying, and maintaining all those automated test procedures also has an associated—and often equivalent—cost.

12.10   For More Information

Dingeldein, Tirena. "5 Best Free and Open Source Bug Tracking Software for Cutting IT Costs." September 6, 2019. *https://blog.capterra.com/top-free-bug-tracking-software/*.

IEEE. "IEEE Std 829-2008: IEEE Standard for Software and System Test Documentation." July 18, 2008. *http://standards.ieee.org/findstds/standard/829-2008.html*. This is expensive ($160 US when I last checked), but this is the gold standard. It's more readable than the SDD standard, but still heavy reading.

Peham, Thomas. "7 Excellent Open Source Bug Tracking Tools Unveiled by Usersnap." May 8, 2016. *https://usersnap.com/blog/open-source-bug-tracking/*.

---

25. With careful requirements design, you can probably eliminate the SRL if all your requirements are testable. If you are really brave, you could combine the STC and LTP into a single document; however, it's almost always a better idea to keep them separate.

Plantation Productions, Inc. "Open Source/Open Hardware: Digital Data Acquisition & Control System." n.d. *http://www.plantation-productions.com/Electronics/DAQ/DAQ.html*. This is where you'll find the DAQ Data Acquisition Software Review, Software Test Case, Software Test Procedures, and Reverse Traceability Matrix.

Software Testing Help. "15 Best Bug Tracking Software: Top Defect/Issue Tracking Tools of 2019." November 14, 2019. *http://www.softwaretestinghelp.com/popular-bug-tracking-software/*.

Wikipedia. "Bug Tracking System." Last modified April 4, 2020. *https://en.wikipedia.org/wiki/Bug_tracking_system*.

AFTERWORD: DESIGNING GREAT CODE

In the introduction, I explained how there wasn't space in this book for many of the topics that Volume 2 promised would be included here. Expect to see those topics in Volumes 4, 5, and 6:

- *Volume 4: Designing Great Code*
- *Volume 5: Great Coding*
- *Volume 6: Testing, Debugging, and Quality Assurance*

Assuming I'm still alive to finish this series, I might add a book on user documentation to the list. About the only thing I can promise is that there won't be as large a gap between Volumes 3 and 4 as there was between Volumes 2 and 3!

Volume 4, *Designing Great Code*, will pick up where the second half of this book left off. In this volume you've learned how to document the software development process; in Volume 4 you'll learn more about the design process and how to apply the knowledge you've gained to design great code.

GLOSSARY

A

Accessor function A function whose sole purpose is to provide read or write access to an otherwise private member of some object.

ACM Association for Computing Machinery

Activity diagram A UML flowcharting scheme that graphically indicates the flow of control through some design.

Actor External entity that interacts with or otherwise controls a system.

Aggregation A relationship where one class (the whole class) controls another class (the parts class). The parts class could be stand-alone (used by itself or other classes), but the whole class cannot exist without the parts class.

Alternative flow A condition section in a Flow of Events scenario—typically, where error or exceptional conditions are handled.

Amateur programmer A novice or a programmer who lacks formal training, who engages in programming without talent or skill, or who prioritizes writing clever code to impress others over making code more readable and maintainable.

Anomaly Report A formal document (electronic or hard copy) reporting an instance of a defect in a software system.

Apprentice A person learning by practical experience under skilled workers.

AR Anomaly Report

ASD Adaptive Software Development

AT Acceptance Test

B

Backdoor An exploit that a computer programmer preprograms into a system to allow anyone with knowledge of the backdoor to bypass system security.

Best practices A set of well-known procedures or processes that have proved to produce successful and efficient results.

Black-box test data Input data for tests that is generated by considering only the system's functionality, without looking at the source code.

BSCS Bachelor of Science in Computer Science

Bug Report See *Anomaly Report*.

C

CACM *Communications of the ACM* (journal)

CASE Computer-Aided Software Engineering

Case-neutral An identifier is case-neutral if it would be accepted by a compiler that is either case-insensitive or case-sensitive (that is, the compiler would not permit two identifiers that differ only by alphabetic case).

Catastrophic integrity level A definition for software such that the consequences of failure are disastrous (including death, system destruction, environmental damage, or huge financial loss).

Change-driven process A development process that anticipates changes in requirements, resources, technology, and performance as the project progresses, and is focused on delivering value incrementally.

Coarse-grained Low level of detail.

Code coverage The percentage of the source code that executes based on a set of input (test) data. Code coverage of 100 percent implies that every statement in the program executes at least once given the corresponding set of inputs.

Code drivers Temporary testing code used to simulate a function when the real function doesn't yet exist.

Code monkey Derogatory term for an amateur programmer. Also see *Cowboy coder*.

Code refactoring Restructuring code to improve the source without changing the external behavior of the software.

Code scaffolding Temporary testing code used to call functions that are part of a system (when the system doesn't yet contain code to call those functions or the system code isn't stable or able to call the function code).

Code spike A brief coding activity by a single person to test a theory or to prototype some code (usually throwaway code).

Coder An engineer responsible for writing computer code.

Conceptual complexity Complexity resulting from a system whose components are difficult to understand.

Constraint A restriction on the domain or range of some value or function.

COTS Commercial Off-the-Shelf. Basically, any system you can purchase on the open market that is not custom-designed.

Cowboy coder Generally, a synonym for an amateur programmer—one who writes code without formal processes or consideration for others.

Cowboy coding Software development where programmers have autonomy over the development process. This includes control of the project's schedule, languages, algorithms, tools, frameworks, and coding style. (Source: Wikipedia.)

CPM Critical Path Method

CPU Central Processing Unit

Cracker A criminal who illegally accesses computer systems or computer data by stealing passwords or employing other system exploits.

Craftsman One who creates or performs with skill or dexterity.

Critical integrity level A level of performance where software must execute properly or there could be serious problems including permanent injury, major performance degradation, environmental damage, or financial loss.

Critical section A section of code that cannot support concurrent execution by multiple threads.

D

DAQ Shortened name for the Plantation Productions Digital Data Acquisition system. See *http://www.plantation-productions.com/Electronics/DAQ/DAQ.html*.

DAQ_IF DAQ interface board. A circuit board containing level shifters, a watchdog timer, I2C multiplexer, and other SBC support circuitry for the Plantation Productions DAQ system.

Defect Report See *Anomaly Report*.

Delphi An object-oriented programming language based on (Object) Pascal. Originally created by Borland International, currently marketed by Embarcadero, Inc.

Derived value An attribute (data field of a class) is derived if its value is computed on each access rather than retrieved from memory.

Design attribute Anything in a design that is a characteristic of a design entity, relationship, or constraint.

Design constraint Any restriction or rule that applies to a design element, attribute, or relationship.

Design element Any item occurring in a design that is structurally or functional distinct from other items in the design. Any item that is part of a design including design entities, relationships, attributes, or constraints.

Design entity A major component of a design, such as a library, component, or program unit.

Design patterns Generic templates for common programming tasks.

Design relationship A design element that names a connection or correspondence between design entities.

Deterministic In a deterministic system, the same series of inputs produces the same flow of activity with the same outcomes.

DRY Don't repeat yourself. Duplicate code is complex code. See also *OAOO*.

Due diligence (in software development) Research and quality assurance tasks that a development team does to prepare for the release of a software system.

E

Elitism The belief that belonging to a select group makes an individual better than others outside that group.

Empirical Originating in or being based on observation or experience, as opposed to being based on theory alone.

Encapsulation Hiding information inside an object so that external entities cannot access it. Also known as *information hiding*.

Ethics A system or set of moral principles.

Event External stimulus to a system that often causes a transition from one state to another or initiates the execution of some activity.

F

FAT Factory Acceptance Test

FDD Feature-Driven Development

Feature creep Constantly adding new features to the system.

Fine-grained Highly detailed.

Flow of Events (UML) Step-by-step description of how an external actor interacts with a system during the execution of a use case.

Flowchart A graphical representation of control flow through a program.

FPA See *Function Point Analysis*.

Framework A software library containing a skeletal component of an application into which a programmer injects application-specific code.

Functional Requirements Specification (FRS)   External requirements provided by a customer for a software system.

Function Point Analysis   A software metric that considers the number of inputs, outputs, and basic computations a program requires.

G

Gantt charts   Resource scheduling charts that specify resource usage over time.

Getter   An accessor function that returns the value of a private member of some object.

GMP   Grand Master Programmer

Gold plating   Padding a system with unnecessary or unrequested features.

Grand Master Programmer   A programmer who is approximately 10 times (or better) more productive than the least productive programmer.

Guards (UML)   A conditional expression attached to a transition in a UML activity diagram. The transition occurs only if the expression evaluates as true.

H

Hacking   Writing code without any formal development process in place. Also see *cowboy coding*.

HLL   High-level language

HRS   Hardware Requirements Specification

HTML   HyperText Markup Language. An early standard language for creating web pages.

I

IDE   Integrated Development Environment. Usually a software tool that combines an editor, compiler, linker, debugger, and other software tools into the same package.

IEEE   The Institute of Electrical and Electronics Engineers. This is an umbrella organization that also covers computer and software engineers.

In the zone   Mentally focused on the current task.

Incremental model   A software development model that is similar to the iterative model, but involves putting more work into the initial design with only minor (incremental) improvements after the initial implementation.

Information hiding   See *encapsulation*.

Integration testing   Combining (usually independently pretested) program units together and testing them to see if the units communicate properly with each other.

Integrity level   An ordinality assigned to a piece of software describing its importance and risk to stakeholders. IEEE Std 829-2008 defines four integrity levels: Catastrophic, Critical, Marginal, and Negligible.

IoT   Internet of Things

IP   Intellectual property (also: internet protocol)

Iterative model   A software model that runs through multiple cycles of requirements, coding, testing, demonstration, and feedback in order to validate the design (that is, to ensure it properly satisfies the end users of the software).

J

JBGE Just barely good enough

Journeyman A worker who has learned a trade and works for another person.

K

K&R Kernighan and Ritchie (authors of *The C Programming Language*).

Killer app A genre-defining, massively selling, popular application.

KLOC Thousands of lines of code

L

Large-scale project A software project that requires a large team (more than 5 to 10 people) to create.

Lead programmer The engineer directly in charge of a particular software project.

Learning curve The graph of the time it takes a programmer to learn a concept versus their productivity with respect to that concept. Specifically, this term describes the amount of time it takes to learn and become proficient in some subject.

Lightweight process A process that requires little overhead. In software development, reducing documentation and managing overhead is the hallmark of a lightweight process.

LITSR *Level* Interim Status Report (document)

LOC Lines of code

LTC *Level* Test Case (document)

LTD *Level* Test Design (document)

LTL *Level* Test Log (document)

LTP *Level* Test Plan (document)

LTPr *Level* Test Procedure (document)

LTR *Level* Test Report (document)

M

Man-hour A unit of one hour of work performed by one person. Used for accounting purposes.

Marginal integrity level A level of performance where software must execute properly, or there may be (minor) incorrect results and some program functionality lost.

MBA Master of Business Administration

Medium-sized projects Projects that require a small team (typically five people or fewer) to accomplish in a reasonable amount of time.

Metaphor A figurative representation of a real situation, often used as an analogy. For example, "It's like shooting fish in a barrel" is a metaphor meaning something is very easy to do.

Milestone A significant (and often articulated) point in development.

Mnemonic A memory aid.

MSCS Master of Science in Computer Science

MTP Master Test Plan (document)

MTR Master Test Report (document)

Multiplicity An expression denoting a counting relationship between two objects (or the number of elements associated with a single object). Can also represent one-to-many, many-to-one, and other unbounded relationships.

N

Negligible integrity level A software performance level below which some expected functionality might not be present in the system but no serious consequences will result.

NRC Nuclear Regulatory Commission (a US-based governmental agency that oversees many of the nuclear reactors in the United States).

O

OAOO Once and only once (see also *DRY*).

Overhead Activities that add time and money to a project's cost but don't directly contribute to getting the work done.

P

Penta-rectangle A rectangle with the lower right-hand corner folded in (which actually makes it a pentagon).

Personal software engineering Processes and methodologies that apply to a single programmer working on a small project or on their portion of a larger project.

PERT Program Evaluation Review Technique

Polymorphism The ability to take on different forms (types) based on context.

Productivity The number of unit tasks completed in a unit amount of time or for a given cost.

Project head The engineer or manager directly in charge of a project (or portion of a project).

PSP Personal Software Process (see Watts S. Humphrey's *A Discipline for Software Engineering*).

Q

QA Quality Assurance

R

R&D Research and development

Rapid Application Development (RAD) A lightweight version of the Spiral development model emphasizing prototypes and VHLLs.

Real hours The amount of real time ("wall clock time" or "calendar time") consumed by a project regardless of the number of people working on it (see also *man-hour*).

Regression test A test to ensure that something that was previously working hasn't broken (regressed) in the current version of the software.

Requirement A mandatory goal associated with a software system.

Requirement gap Features (and associated tests) that should be in a program to satisfy user needs, but do not appear as actual, documented requirements for the software.

Reverse Traceability Matrix (RTM) A document/database that allows the reader to trace features in documentation (such as the STP, STC, and SDD) back to their original requirements.

RFP Request for Proposal, a request for a bid from vendors to supply products or services.

Risk assessment Evaluation of the risks associated with a project and attempting to quantify those risks, allowing for mitigating them.

RTM Reverse Traceability Matrix. Also known as the *Requirements Traceability Matrix*.

S

SAT Site Acceptance Test

SBC Single-board computer

Scaffolding See *code scaffolding*.

Scale down Modifying a process that works for a large project so it will work for a smaller project.

Scaling up Modifying a process that works for a small project so it will work for a larger project.

Scenario (UML) A single path through a use case.

Scope complexity Complexity resulting when the size of a system becomes too large for a single person to completely understand the whole system.

SDD Software Design Description

SDLC Software Development Life Cycle

Self-validating A test is self-validating if the simple execution of that test runs properly (that is, without crashing the system or indicating errors).

Setter A function that allows a caller to write a value to a private member of some object.

Small-scale projects Software systems than can be easily produced by a single engineer in a reasonable amount of time.

SMS Short Message Service, a text message on a cell phone.

Software crisis A situation in which the need for software is expanding faster than the supply of programmers who can write that software.

Software development model An abstraction of the software development process that helps engineers understand how to compare different approaches to software development.

Software engineering The study of the development and management of large software systems.

Software IC A standardized software module that can be plugged into arbitrary applications, much like how an integrated circuit (IC) could be plugged into an electronic circuit.

Software methodology A system of principles—as well as a set of ideas, concepts, methods, techniques, and tools—that defines the style of software development.

Spiral model An iterative software development model that repeats four phases: planning, design, risk analysis/evaluation, and construction.

SPM Swimming pool monitor, a software system example used throughout this book.

Sprint A short amount of time, typically one to four weeks, allotted to complete a software development task.

SRL Software Review List (document)

SRS Software Requirements Specification (document)

Stakeholder An individual or other party that has an interest in the design and development of a system.

Standard library A set of standardized functions and subroutines, often tied to a specific programming language or framework, to achieve common tasks.

Stand-up meeting A meeting where every (capable) person remains standing. This forces the meeting to be short and focused, as people don't want to stand for more than a few minutes.

State diagram A graphical representation showing how a system transitions from one state to another.

STC Software Test Cases

Stereotype An extension mechanism for UML to create new elements.

STP Software Test Procedures

SyRS System Requirements Specification (document)

T

TBD To be determined

TDD Test-driven development

Test-driven development (TDD) A software development process in which you develop tests first and then write the code that satisfies these tests.

Throwaway programs Small programs that are written once, used once or only a few times, and then discarded and never used again.

Time to market The time between the initial conceptualization of a product and its first delivery to customers.

Traceability matrix See *Reverse Traceability Matrix*.

Trigger (UML) External event that causes the execution of a use case.

U

UML Unified Modeling Language

Unit testing Testing small program units (such as functions) independently of the rest of the system.

UPS Uninterruptible Power Supply

URL Uniform Resource Locator, a protocol for addressing objects on the internet (for instance, a web address).

Use case A list of actions or event steps defining the interactions between an (external) actor and a system to achieve some goal.

User stories Requirements, features, and use case documentation.

V

V model A software development process based on the Waterfall model (see also *Waterfall model*).

Validation The process of showing that a product meets the needs of its end users.

Verification The process of ensuring that a product meets requirements.

VHLL Very high-level language

W

Waterfall model A software development process whereby software occurs in distinct and serial steps (for example, system documentation, coding, testing, deployment, maintenance, and retirement).

Weak words Imprecise words, generally adjectives, that attempt to make something sound better or worse without any quantification.

White-box test data Input test data generated by looking at the source code for a system. For example, to achieve code coverage you need to look at the source code to create test data that exercises all statements in a program.

X

XP Extreme Programming

Y

Y2K Year 2000. Specifically relating to computer software maintaining only the last two digits of a year (for example, "99" for "1999") and being unable to handle dates from 2000 and beyond.

YAGNI You aren't gonna need it. Avoid speculative coding.

INDEX

Symbols

+ (UML class visibility operator), 105
~ (UML package class visibility operator), 107
* (iteration specification in UML sequence diagrams), 132
- (UML private class visibility operator), 106
(UML protected class visibility operator), 107
«component» stereotype (UML), 156
«create» message in a UML sequence diagram, 136–137
«destroy» message in a UML sequence diagram, 136–137
«extend» keyword, 79
{frozen} UML constraint, 124
{ordered} UML constraint, 121
{readOnly} UML property, 112
{static} UML property, 112
{unique} UML property, 112

A

Acceptance Test Cases, 274
Acceptance Test Design, 269
Acceptance Test Plan, 267
acceptance testing (AT), 42, 265
accessor functions, 106, 109
actions
    in a requirement, 186
    in a test procedure, 295
activation bars (sequence diagrams, UML), 133
activity diagrams, UML, 89–101, 239–251
    call symbols, 96
    expression coverage, 92
    partitions, 96, 97
    states, 91
    state symbols, 89

actor
    in a requirement, 186
    use case element, 74
Adaptive Software Development (ASD), 53
adding SRL items to the traceability matrix, 274
aggregration relationships, UML, 116
Agile Manifesto, 53
Agile software methodology
    heavyweight documentation, 54–55
    JBGE (Just Barely Good Enough) documentation, 55
    pair programming, 54
    regression testing, 53
    sprints, 53–54
    stand-up meetings, 54
algorithmic viewpoint (SDD), 229, 239
Allocations column (RTM), 222
alternative flows in UML sequence diagrams, 81, 135
alt sequence fragment (UML), 146
amateur (programmer classification), xxii
ambiguity
    in requirements, 188
    in state machines, 164
analysis phase, software development, 40
analysis verification method (RTM), 222
analysts (programmers), 6
annotations and comments (UML), 98
anomaly logging during tests, 293
Anomaly Reports (AR), 262, 308–311
    assessment of urgency, 311
    conclusions and recommendations, 311
    Context section, 310
    correcting defects, 309
    date and time of defect occurrence, 308
    Description of Anomaly section, 310
    Description of Corrective Action section, 311

Anomaly Reports (*continued*)
   Details section, 310
   document identifier, 309
   electronic versus paper, 312
   Impact section, 311
   information to include, 308–309
   Introduction section, 309
   References section, 310
   reproducing defects, 308
   Scope section, 310
   summary, 310
   workarounds to a defect, 309
anomaly status, 309
anonymous ports (UML), 163
applying engineering principles to software development, 12
Apportioning of Requirements section (SRS), 199
apprenticeship, 7, 13
architects
   computer programmers as, 6
   contribution to software development, 8
AR. *See* Anomaly Reports
artists
   computer programmers as, 5
   contribution to software development, 8
assert sequence fragment, 141
assessment of urgency (AR), 311
associating test cases with a test procedure, 294
associations, UML
   links, 115
   names, 115, 118
   relationships, 114
Assumptions and Dependencies section (SRS), 198
asynchronous messages in UML sequence diagrams, 129
AT (acceptance testing), 42, 265
atomic requirements, 190
ATP (Acceptance Test Procedure), 289
attributes, UML
   data types, 110
   derived values, 109
   multiplicity, 111
   names, 109
   syntax, 112
   visibility, 109
audit functions in an SRS, 198
automated test procedures, 275–276
automated unit testing
   Agile, 53
   XP, 57
availability (SRS), 201

B

ball and socket notation (UML), 156, 163
base values in a class (UML), 109
BASIC programming language, xxi
best practices, 14, 265
   Agile, 53
   lack of in Scrum, 66
   in software development, 15
binary numbering system, xxi
black-box-generated test data, 276
break sequence fragment (UML), 138, 145
Brief Description section (STP), 294–296
build by feature (FDD), 68
burn-down chart in Scrum, 66

C

C and C++ programming languages, xxi
C, C++, and C# programming languages, xxi
calling a UML subroutine, 96
CASE (computer-aided software engineering), 50
case neutrality in identifiers, 110
casual narratives, 81
catch-all transition in a UML activity diagram, 92
changeability, 124
change-driven process in XP, 57
change history
   STC, 280
   STP, 292
change procedures
   STC, 280
characteristics of good requirements, 187–193
class aggregation relationships (UML), 116
class association relationships (UML), 115
class attributes (UML), 108–112
class composition relationships (UML), 117

class dependency relationships
(UML), 114
class diagrams, UML, 104, 235, 236, 238
class inheritance relationships
(UML), 125
class interface, 105
class operators, UML, 112
class relationships, UML, 114–125
cleaning up UML sequence
diagrams, 129
coach on XP team, 56
coder (programmer classification), xxii
coding in XP, 57
coding standards in XP, 60
collaboration diagrams (UML), 152, 239
collective ownership in XP, 60
collocation in XP, 64
comments and annotations (UML), 98
common setup for test cases, 288
communication diagrams.
See collaboration
diagrams (UML)
Communication Interfaces section
(SRS), 197
communication links, UML, 74
communication in XP, 58
completeness of an SDD, 240
complete programmer (programmer
classification), xxiii
component diagrams, UML, 155–158,
236, 237
Component Integration Test Cases, 274
Component Integration Test Design, 269
Component Integration Test Plan, 267
«component» stereotype (UML), 156
Component Test Cases, 274
Component Test Design, 269
Component Test Plan, 267
Component Test Procedures, 289
composite structure diagrams (UML),
160–163, 236, 238
composition relationships, UML, 117
composition viewpoint (SDD), 233–235
compound requirement, 190
computer-aided software engineering
(CASE), 50
computer programmers as musicians, 5
conceptual model diagrams (SDD), 44
concurrent processing (UML), 96
conditionals (UML)
decision points, 92–93
transition guards, 91–92

condition for a requirement, 186
Configuration Management Plan, 280
connectors (UML), 98
`consider` sequence fragment (UML), 138
consistency in requirements, 187
consistency in an SDD, 240
consistency in system
documentation, 171
constraints in requirements, 185
Constraints section (SRS), 198
constraints, UML, 121
{frozen}, 124
{ordered}, 121
timing in sequence diagrams, 133
construction phase in Rapid
Application Development
model, 50
Context section
in an AR, 310
in an STC document, 278
context viewpoint (SDD), 231–233
continuous integration in XP, 63
control functions in an SRS, 198
correcting defects, 309
courage in XP, 55
craftsmen
computer programmers as, 7
contribution to software
development, 8
«create» message in a UML sequence
diagram, 136–137
creating requirements, 212–214
criticality of an application in an
SRS, 198
critical requirements, 188
critical section of UML activity
diagram, 99
customer representative in XP, 56
cutover phase in RAD model, 50

D

dangerous-to-test requirements, 222
database viewpoint (SDD), 236
data dictionary
in a class diagram, 235
in an SDD, 41
data fields. *See* class attributes (UML)
debriefings in XP, 64
decision points, 92–93
decision symbols (UML), 163–165
default attribute values (UML), 111–112

Defect Reports. *See* Anomaly Reports
defining software systems, 12
definite loops, UML, 142
Definitions section (SRS), 196
dcpcndency relationships, UML, 114, 117
dependency viewpoint (SDD), 235–236
deployment diagrams, UML, 159–160
deployment phase, 42
derived attributes, 253
derived classes in UML, 125
derived use cases, 79
derived values in a class (UML), 109
Description of Anomaly section (AR), 310
Description of Corrective Action section (AR), 311
design by feature (FDD), 68
design concerns in a viewpoint (SDD), 229
Design Constraints section (SRS), 201
design elements (SDD), 230
design entities (SDD), 230
design goals (SRS), 193, 203
design guidelines, 62
designing in XP, 57
design language (SDD), 231
design overlay (SDD), 241–242
design patterns (SDD), 236
design phase
    in RAD, 50
    in SDD, 41
design quality obtained from pair programming, 61
design rationale (SDD), 242
design relationships (SDD), 230
design verification method (RTM), 222
design viewpoints (SDD), 229–239
design views (SDD), 239–240
desirable requirements, 188
«destroy» message in a UML sequence diagram, 136–137
Detailed Steps Required to Run This Test Procedure section (STP), 295
Details section (Anomaly Report), 310
deterministic defects, 308
deterministic state machines, 164
developing an overall model in FDD, 67
dialog (use case), 81

differentiating between branching and long delays in UML sequence diagrams, 135
difficult-to-test requirements, 222
document change procedures for a test procedure (STP), 296
documented code, xxi
document identifier
    in an AR, 309
    in an STP, 292
Don't repeat yourself (DRY) design principle, 62
downtime, 201
driver on pair programming team, 60
dropped title box (UML sequence diagrams), 136
DRY (Don't repeat yourself) design principle, 62
duplicate code, 62

E

economic benefits of pair programming, 61
education and training, xxiv–xxv, 13
efficiency and great code, xxi
electronic test logs, 307–308
electronic versus paper ARs, 312
elements, design (SDD), 230
empirical processes, 12
encapsulation, 105, 107
end conditions (UML), 81
end state (UML), 163
engineers
    computer programmers as, 7
    contribution to software development, 8
engineers, software, xxiv
enhanceable code, xxi
environmental condition requirement in test cases and test procedurcs, 288
environmental needs (STC), 279
event (state machine), 164
events (UML), 94–95
exceptions (use case), 81
expression coverage in a UML activity diagram, 92
«extend» keyword, 79
extension, use case, 79–80, 81, 85
External Interfaces section (SRS), 199

external objects in a UML sequence
    diagram, 133
Extreme Programming (XP)
    change-driven process, 57
    coding in, 57
    coding standards, 60
    collective ownership, 60
    continuous integration, 63
    debriefings, 64
    designing, 57
    feature creep, 65
    functional testing, 58
    implementation phase, 58
    iterations, 58
    listening, 57
    metaphors, 59
    No Big Design Up Front, 65
    onsite customer, 59
    open workspace and collocation, 64
    pair programming, 54, 60–63
    planning game, 58
    priorities (release planning), 56
    problems with, 64
    refactoring, 60
    release cycles, 58
    release planning, 58
    respect, 55
    retrospectives, 64
    roles, 56
    scalability, 65
    self-directed teams, 64
    simple design, 59, 60
    simplicity, 55
    small releases (building blocks), 7
    software development activities, 65
    steering phase, 184
    sustainable pace, 59, 63
    test-driven development, 57
    testers, 56
    testing, 57, 59, 60
    unit tests, 65
    user stories, 56, 59
    values of, 55
    whole team concept, 55

F

factory acceptance (software
    development level), 265
Factory Acceptance Test Cases, 274
Factory Acceptance Test Design, 269
Factory Acceptance Test Plan, 267
Factory Acceptance Test Procedures, 289
faking test logs, 307
fast code, xxi
feasible requirements, 187
feature creep in XP, 65
Feature-Driven Development (FDD), 66
    build by feature, 68
    design by feature, 68
    developing an overall model, 67
    iteration zero, 66
    plan by feature, 67
feedback in XP, 55
flat messages in UML sequence
    diagrams, 129
flowcharts. *See* activity diagrams, UML
Flow of Events (UML use cases), 81
fork operation (UML), 96
forward traceability (requirements), 192
{frozen} UML constraint, 124
fully dressed use case, 81
functional requirements, 185
Functional Requirements section
    (SRS), 200
Functional Requirements
    Specification, 171
functional tests in XP, 56, 58
function return type, 129

G

generalization relationship.
    See class inheritance
    relationships (UML)
generalization, use case, 77–79
getter functions, 106, 109
Glossary section (STC), 280
GNU toolset, 15
Golden Rule of Software
    Development, xxi
gold plating, 187
graduating from a software
    apprenticeship, 14
great programmers, characteristics
    of, xxiv
guard conditions in UML sequence
    diagram messages, 131, 134
guards (UML), 91
guidelines for simple design, 62

H

hacking, 43
hardware environmental needs (STC), 279
Hardware Interfaces section (SRS), 197
hardware limitations (SRS), 198
heavyweight documentation, 54–55
hexadecimal numbering system, xxi
high-level language requirements (SRS), 198

I

IEEE/EIA Std 12207.0-1996 [B21], 263
IEEE Standard for Software and System Test Documentation, 261
IEEE Std 829-2009 *Level* Test Procedure, 289
IEEE Std 1016-1998 versus IEEE Std 1016-2009, 228
IEEE Std 1016-2009, 227
if statements in use case descriptions, 84
ignore sequence fragment, 138
impact of a defect, 309
Impact section (AR), 311
imperative (procedural) programming languages, xxi
implementation-independent requirements, 190
implementation phase in XP, 58
importance of an apprenticeship, 13
important requirements, 188
impractical-to-test requirements, 222
including test logs in the RTM, 308
inclusion (use case), 77
incompleteness in requirements, 188
Incremental software development model, 51–52
    disadvantages of, 51
    "keep the code working" concept, 51
indefinite loops, 143
industry best practices, 14
information in an Anomaly Report, 308–309
information viewpoint (SDD), 236
inheritance, 107
input/output parameters (UML), 113
Input section (STC), 278
inspection verification method (RTM), 222
Instructions for Running Tests section (STP), 293
integration (software development level), 265
Integration Test Cases, 274
Integration Test Design, 269
Integration Test Plan, 267
Integration Test Procedures, 289
integration testing, 11, 41, 265
integrity levels, 263–265
intellectual property (IP), 61
interaction occurrence sequence diagram (UML), 139
interaction viewpoint (SDD), 239
intercase dependencies (STC), 280
interface specifiers, 119–120
interfaces to other applications (SRS), 198
interfaces (UML), 156
interface viewpoint (SDD), 237
Internet of Things, 133
intern (programmer classification), xxii
intern, software, 7
Introduction section
    in an AR, 309
    in an SRS, 195
    in an STC, 277
iterations in UML sequence diagrams, 132
iterations in XP, 58
iteration zero in FDD, 66
Iterative software development model, 46–47

J

Java programming language, xxi
JBGE (Just Barely Good Enough) documentation, 55
join operation (UML), 96
journeyman, software, 7
junior programmer (programmer classification), xxii
Just Barely Good Enough (JBGE) documentation, 55

K

keeping test logs, 306
killer app, 315
KLOC (thousands of lines of code), 10

L

large projects, 10, 12
lead programmer, 11
learning while pair programming, 61
legal jeopardy, test logs and, 308
Level Interim Test Status Reports, 262, 312
Level Test Case, 262
Level Test Design, 262
Level Test Design documentation, 269
Level Test Logs, 303
Level Test Plans, 267–269
Level Test Procedures, 262, 289, 290
Level Test Reports, 312
lifeline in UML sequence diagrams, 128
lifetime of an object in a UML sequence diagram, 136
lightweight software development models, 50
limiting APIs, 62
lines of code (LOC), 10
Linux, 15
listening in XP, 57
List of Test Cases Covered by This Procedure section (STP), 294
LOC (lines of code), 10
logging anomalies during tests (STP), 293
Logical Database Requirements section (SRS), 200
logical viewpoint (SDD), 229, 235
long delays in UML sequence diagrams, 132–133
looking for new software development tools and techniques, 14
loop sequence fragment (UML), 138, 141–145
loosely coupled classes (UML), 114

M

maintainability (SRS), 201
maintainable code, xxi
maintaining documentation, 54
maintenance phase of software development, 42
management complexity in Spiral model, 49
manager/tracker on XP team, 56
man-hours and real time, 19

master craftsman, 15
masterpieces, software, 15
Master Test Plan, 266–267
Master Test Reports, 312
medium-sized projects, 10, 11
Memory Constraints section (SRS), 197
memory usage of great code, xxi
merge points (UML), 93–94
merging test cases into a single test procedure, 288
messages in UML sequence diagrams, 129–130
metaphors, computer programming
  programmer as architect, 6
  programmer as artist, 5
  programmer as craftsman, 7
  programmer as engineer, 7
metaphors in XP, 59
minimal guarantees (use case), 81
minimum viable product (MVP), 47
modifiable requirements, 191
multiple merge/decision points (UML), 94
multiple requirements in one statement, 190
multiplicity, 120
musicians, computer programmers as, 5
MVP (minimum viable product), 47

N

namespaces (packages), UML, 76
naming a communication link (UML), 163
NATO and the creation of software engineering, 7
natural talents of a computer programmer, 5
navigability (UML), 115, 123
navigator on pair programming team, 60
neg sequence fragment (UML), 138, 148
Netburner MOD54415, 213
No Big Design Up Front (XP), 65
nodes (UML), 159
nondeterministic state machines, 164
nonfunctional requirements, 185
nonintelligibility in requirements, 189
Notation for Description section
  in STC, 278
  in STP, 290, 292
no test verification method (RTM), 222

O

object (in a requirement), 186
object-oriented analysis and design (UML), 103–104
object-oriented programming languages, xxi
Objective section (STC), 278
objects in UML, 125
old test logs, 306
Once and only once (OAOO) design principle, 62
onsite customer in XP, 59
open hardware, 283
open source, 283
open workspace in XP, 64
Operations section (SRS), 197
operator return type, 129
operators, UML, 112
opt sequence fragment (UML), 138, 146
optimization in Spiral-based software development model, 49
optionality (requirements), 188
{ordered} constraint (UML), 121
organizing test procedures by their related activities (STP), 290
other allocations in an RTM, 222
other verification method (RTM), 222
Outcome section (STC), 279
overgeneralization in requirements, 189
overlapping test cases, 288
Overview section (SRS), 196

P

package diagrams (UML), 236, 238
package visibility (UML), 107
packages (UML), 76
pair programming
   Agile, 54
   design quality, 61
   driver role, 60
   economic benefits of, 61
   learning during, 61
   navigator role, 60
   satisfaction, 61
   team building and communication, 61
   in XP, 59
parallel execution in UML diagrams, 149
parallel operations (SRS), 198
parameters in UML sequence diagram messages, 131
par sequence fragment (UML), 138, 149
partial class diagrams (UML), 104
Pascal programming language, xxi
pass/fail criteria, 280
   in an STP, 291
passive voice in requirements, 189
patterns use viewpoint (SDD), 236
penta-rectangle symbol in sequence diagram, 138
Performance Requirements section (SRS), 200
phases in software development
   coding, 41
   deployment, 42
   design, 41
   maintenance, 42
   product conceptualization, 40
   requirement development and analysis, 40
   retirement, 42
   testing, 41
plan by feature (FDD), 67
planning game in XP, 58
polymorphism, 107
portability (SRS), 203
ports, 162
positively stated requirements, 192
post conditions (UML), 81
predictive software development methodologies, 52
priorities (release planning) in XP, 56
private class visibility (UML), 106
problems with XP, 64
procedural programming languages, xxi
procedure identifier/tag (STP), 294
product conceptualization phase, 40
Product Functions section (SRS), 198
product owner in Scrum, 65
programmer/analysts, 6
programmer classifications
   amateurs, xxii
   problem with, xxiii
   programmers, xxii
      coder, xxii
      complete programmer, xxiii
      interns, xxii
      junior programmer, xxii
      Programmer I and II, xxiii
      system analyst, xxiii
      system architect, xxiii
Programmer I (programmer classification), xxiii

Programmer II (programmer classification), xxiii
programmer role in XP, 56
project head, 11
property strings (UML), 109, 112
protected class visibility (UML), 107
protocols, 119
provided interfaces
    UML components, 156
    UML composite structures, 162
pseudocode, 239
public class visibility (UML), 105
Purpose section
    in an SRS, 195
    in an STP, 290, 294

Q

qualified names in UML packages, 159
qualifiers (UML), 122
Quality Assurance department, 266
quality requirements, 185

R

RAD (Rapid Application Development) model, 49–51
    construction phase, 50
    cutover phase, 50
    design phase, 50
    requirements planning phase, 50
    risk management, 50
rake symbol (UML), 96
Rapid Application Development model. *See* RAD model
rapid prototyping, 49
readable code, xxi
{readOnly} property (UML), 112
redlines in test procedures, 307
reducing resource usage with test procedures, 290
refactoring in XP, 60
References section
    in an AR, 310
    in an SRS, 196
    in an STC, 277
ref sequence fragment (UML), 138, 139
region sequence fragment (UML), 138, 151
regression testing, 53, 276, 290
regulatory policies (SRS), 198
relationship features, UML, 117

relationship strength, UML, 114
Relationship to Other Documents section (STP), 292
release cycles in XP, 58
release planning in XP, 58
reliability (SRS), 198, 201
reproducing defects (AR), 308
request for proposal (RFP), 263
required interfaces (UML composite structures), 162
required setup for an STP, 291
requirement gaps, 46
requirement organization (SRS), 202
requirement origins, 185
requirements
    atomic, 190
    characteristics of good, 187–193
    compound, 190
    consistency, 187
    constraints, 185
    correctness, 187
    creating in SRS, 212–214
    desirable, 188
    difficult to test, 222
    feasible, 187
    gold plating, avoiding, 187
    implementation-independent, 190
    important, 188
    impractical to test, 222
    incompleteness, ambiguity as result of, 188
    modifiable, 191
    multiple in one statement, 190
    nonfunctional, 185
    nonintelligibility in, 189
    optionality, 188
    organization, 202
    overgeneralization in, 189
    passive voice in, 189
    portability, 203
    positively stated, 192
    prioritized, 187–188
    quality, 185
    reverse traceability, 192
    for SDD, 228
    subjectivity, 188
    for SyRS, 193
    tags and traceability, 192
    traceability, 192
    unbounded lists, 189
    underreference, 189
    underspecification, 188

requirements (*continued*)
    uniqueness, 191
    unnecessary, 187
    vagueness, 188
    verifiable, 190
    weak words and, 189
requirements and architecture phase in V model, 45
requirements planning phase in RAD model, 50
rerunning test procedures (STP), 290
resource usage when running tests (STP), 290
resource viewpoint (SDD), 239
respect in XP, 55
resuming tests (STP), 293
retirement phase, 42
retrospectives in XP, 64
return from subroutine in a UML sequence diagram, 145
return messages in UML sequence diagrams, 129
return type (UML), 113
return values in UML class diagrams, 110
return values in UML sequence diagram messages, 131
reusability of UML components, 155–158
reuse in computer programming, 12
reverse traceability, 171, 186, 192
    in an SRS tag, 175
Reverse Traceability Matrix. *See* RTM
review verification method (RTM), 222
RFP (request for proposal), 263
risk assessment, 263
risk-based software development models, 48
risk management in the RAD model, 50
risk management in the Spiral development model, 49
risk management in the Waterfall model, 45
robust code, xxi
roles in XP, 56
roles (UML), 119
RTM (Reverse Traceability Matrix), 170, 172, 186, 302
    adding SRL items, 274
    Allocations column, 222
    including test logs in, 308

SDD tag column, 259
Software Test/Review Cases column, 288
SRS tag column, 222
verification methods, 222
running test procedures in parallel (STP), 290
running tests (STP instructions), 293

S

satisfaction from pair programming, 61
SAT (Site Acceptance Test), 265, 289, 291
scalability in XP, 65
scaling up and down (engineering methodologies), 10, 42
scenario (use case), 86
scheduled downtime, 201
Scope section
    in an AR, 310
    in an SRS, 196
    in an STC, 277
    in an STP, 292
scrum master in Scrum, 65
Scrum methodology, 53, 65
    burn-down chart, 66
    product owner, 65
    scrum master, 65
    scrum-of-scrums, 66
    sprint restrospectives, 66
    stand-up meeting, 65
SDD (Software Design Description), 227
    completeness of, 240
    conceptual model diagrams, 44
    definition of, 170
    design concerns in a viewpoint, 229
    design constraints, 230
    design elements, 230
    design entities, 230
    design overlay, 241–242
    design patterns, 236
    design phase, 41
    design rationale, 242
    design relationship, 242
    design views, 239–240
    source element, 291
    state dynamics viewpoint, 163
    tags, 44
    target element, 230
    validation, 183
    viewpoint name, 229

viewpoints
    composition, 233–235
    context, 231–233
    database, 236
    dependency, 235–236
    design, 229–239
    information, 236
    interaction, 239
    interface, 237
    logical, 229
    patterns use, 236
    resource, 290
    structure, 237
Waterfall model, 44
SDD tag column (RTM), 259
SDLC (Software Development Life Cycle), 39–42
secondary actors in use cases, 81
security (SRS), 201
seeking better approaches to designing applications, 15
self-directed teams in XP, 64
seq sequence fragment (UML), 138, 150
sequence diagrams, UML
    activation bars, 133
    alternative flow, 135
    asynchronous messages, 129
    consider sequence fragment, 138
    «create» message in, 136–137
    creating objects, 136
    «destroy» message, 136–137
    destroying objects, 136
    differentiating between branching and long delays, 135
    dropped title box, 136
    external objects, 133
    flat messages, 129
    guard conditions, 131, 134
    ignore sequence fragment, 138, 140
    indefinite loops, 143
    interaction occurrence, 139
    interaction viewpoint, 239
    iterations, 309
    lifelines, 128
    long delays and time constraints, 132–133
    loop sequence fragment, 141–145
    message parameters, 131
    messages, 129–130
    neg sequence fragment, 148
    object lifetime, 136
    opt sequence fragment, 138, 146
    par sequence fragment, 149
    ref sequence fragment, 139
        entry point, 139
    region sequence fragment, 138, 151
    return from subroutine, 145
    return messages, 129
    seq sequence fragment, 138
    sequence numbers, 138
    showing operation order, 128
    synchronous messages, 129
    time constraints, 133
sequence fragments, UML, 137, 149
    alt, 146
    assert, 146
    break, 138
    ignore, 138
    loop, 142
    neg, 138
    opt, 138
    par, 149
    ref, 139
    region, 138, 151
    seq, 138, 150
    strict, 138, 150
sequence message labels, UML, 130
sequence numbers, UML, 130
sequential software development models, 46
setter functions, 106, 109
setup (STP), 295
showing the order of operations in UML diagrams, 128
signal handshake protocols (SRS), 198
sign-off on a test procedure (STP), 296
simple design
    guidelines for, 62
    in XP, 59, 60
simplicity in XP, 55
site acceptance (software development level), 265
Site Acceptance Test Cases, 274
Site Acceptance Test Design, 269
Site Acceptance Test Plan, 267
Site Acceptance Test Procedures, 289
Site Acceptance Test (SAT), 265, 289, 291
Site Adaptation Requirements section (SRS), 198
SIT (System Integration Test), 289, 291
small projects, 6, 10, 11

small releases (building blocks)
  in XP, 59
SMS message, 133
software allocations in an RTM, 222
software apprentices, 7, 13
software craftsman, 14
software craftsmanship, 13–15
software crisis of the 1960s, xix
Software Design Description. *See* SDD
Software Development Life Cycle
  (SDLC), 39–42
software development methodologies,
  52–68
  Agile, 52
  definition of, 52
  predictive, 52
  traditional, 52
software development models, 42–52
  Incremental, 51
  Iterative, 46–47
  lightweight, 50
  RAD, 49, 74
    risk management, 50
  risk-based, 48
  sequential models, 46
  Spiral, 48–49
    risk management, 50
  V, 45–46
  Waterfall, 44–45
software development phases
  deployment, 42
  design in RAD, 50
  maintenance, 42
  product conceptualization, 40
  retirement, 42
  testing, 41
software development testing levels
  factory acceptance, 265
  integration, 265
  site acceptance, 265
  system integration, 265
  unit, 191, 265
software engineering
  IEEE definition, 7
  invention of, 7
  original definition, 9
software engineering conventions and
  great code, xxi
software engineers, xxiv
software environmental needs
  (STC), 279
Software Interfaces section (SRS), 197

software journeyman, 7, 14–15
Software Requirements Specification
  (SRS) document. *See* SRS
Software Review List (SRL) document,
  270–274
Software System Attributes section
  (SRS)
  downtime, 201
  maintainability, 201
  portability, 203
  reliability, 201
  security, 201
Software Test Case (STC) document.
  See STC
software test document types, 262
Software Test Procedure (STP)
  document. *See* STP
Software Test/Review Cases column
  (RTM), 288
software version for a test procedure
  run (STP), 291, 295
source element (SDD), 230
Special Requirements section
  (STP), 291, 295
Specific Requirements section
  (SRS), 199
Spiral software development model,
  48–49
  risk management, 50
sprint retrospectives, 66
sprints, Agile, 53–54
SRS (Software Requirements
  Specification), 44, 170
  Apportioning of Requirements
    section, 199
  Assumptions and Dependencies
    section, 198
  attributes
    security, 201
  audit functions, 198
  Communications Interfaces
    section, 197
  Constraints section, 198
  control functions, 59
  creating requirements, 212–214
  Definitions section, 196
  Design Constraints section, 201
  External Interfaces section, 199
  Functional Requirements
    section, 200
  Hardware Interfaces section, 197
  hardware limitations, 198

high-level language
  requirements, 198
interfaces to other applications, 198
Introduction section, 195
Logical Database Requirements
  section, 200
maintainability, 201
Memory Constraints section, 197
Operations section, 197
organization by feature, 202
organization by functional
  hierarchy, 202
organization by input stimulus, 202
organization by object class, 202
organization by output
  response, 202
organization by system mode, 202
organization by user class, 202
Overview section, 288
parallel operations, 198
Performance Requirements
  section, 200
Product Functions section, 198
Purpose section, 195
References section, 196
regulatory policies, 198
requirement organization, 202
safety and security
  considerations, 198
Scope section, 292
signal handshake protocols, 198
Site Adaption Requirements
  section, 198
Software Interfaces section, 197
Specific Requirements section, 199
stakeholders, 228
Standards Compliance section, 201
supporting information, 203
tags, 175
User Characteristics section, 198
User Interfaces section, 196, 197
validating, 183
SRS tag column (RTM), 222
stakeholder in system design, 228
Standards Compliance section
  (SRS), 201
stand-up meeting, 54
start state (UML), 90
start symbol (UML), 164
statechart diagrams, UML, 163–165
  end state, 163
  start state, 163

state dynamics viewpoint (SDD), 239
statement count metric, 24
states (UML), 91
state transitions, UML, 163
{static} property (UML), 112
status of an anomaly, 309
STC (Software Test Case), 170, 261
  change history, 280
  change procedures, 280
  Context section, 278
  document identifier, 277
  environmental needs, 279
  Glossary section, 280
  hardware environmental needs, 279
  identifiers, 278
  Input section, 278
  intercase dependencies, 280
  Introduction section, 277
  Notation for Description section, 278
  Objective section, 278
  Outcome section, 279
  references, 139
  References section, 277
  Scope section, 277
  software environmental needs, 279
  special procedural requirements, 279
  validation, 184
STC tag format, 278
steering phase in XP, 58
stereotype notation (UML), 120
stop state (UML), 90
STP (Software Test Procedure), 170, 261
  Brief Description section, 294–296
  change history, 292
  Detailed Steps Required to Run
    a Test Procedure section
    (STP), 295
  document change procedures, 296
  document identifier, 292
  Instructions for Running Tests
    section, 293
  Introduction section, 292
  List of Test Cases Covered by
    Procedure section, 294
  Notation for Descriptions
    section, 290
  organizing test procedures, 290
  pass/fail criteria, 291
  procedure identifier/tag, 294
  Purpose section, 290, 294
  reducing resource usage by test
    procedures, 290

STP (*continued*)
  References section, 292
  Relationship to Other Documents section, 292
  required setup, 291
  rerunning test procedures, 290
  resuming tests, 293
  running test procedures in parallel, 56
  Scope section, 292
  setup, 46
  sign-off on test procedures, 296
  software version for a test run, 295
  Special Requirements section, 291, 295
  streamlining test procedures (STP), 288, 290
  suspended tests, 293
  Traceability section, 291
  verifying, 295
STP tag format, 292
streamlining test procedures (STP), 288, 290
strength of a relationship (UML), 114
`strict` sequence fragment (UML), 138, 150
structure viewpoint (SDD), 237
style guidelines, xxi
subjectivity (requirement), 188
subroutine entry point in a `ref` sequence fragment (UML), 139
subsystem stereotype (UML), 156
successful guarantees (use cases), 81
summary (AR), 310
supporting information (SRS), 203
suspended tests (STP), 293
sustainable pace in XP, 59, 63
Swift programming language, xxi
swim lanes (UML), 97
synchronization (UML), 96
synchronous messages (sequence diagram, UML), 129
SyRS (System Requirements Specification), 40, 44, 170, 193
  validating, 183
SyRS tag column (in RTM), 222
SyRS tags, 172
system analyst (programmer classification), xxiii

system architect (programmer classification), xxiii
system boundary diagrams (UML), 87
system documentation consistency, 171
system documentation traceability, 171
system integration (software development testing level), 265
System Integration Test, 265
System Integration Test Cases, 274
System Integration Test Design, 269
System Integration Test Plan, 267
System Integration Test Procedures, 289
System Requirements Specification (SyRS) document. *See* SyRS
system resources and great code, xxi
System Test Cases, 274
System Test Design, 269
System Test Plan, 267
system testing, 42

T

tags, 172–178, 245
  dotted sequences, 174
  requirement, 192
  SRS, 175
  STC, 177
  STP, 178
  SyRS, 172
target element (SDD), 230
team building and communication from pair programming, 61
termination (use case), 81
test case assignment to a test procedure, 294
test case dependencies, 288
test case identifier (STC), 278
test design, 269–270
test-driven development (TDD), 46, 54, 57
test logs, 306
test plans, 266
test procedures (STP), 294–296
Test Reports, 312–315
test verification method (RTM), 222
Test/verification type column in an RTM, 222
tested code, xxi

testers on XP team, 56
testing in XP, 57, 59, 60
testing phase, 41
"throwaway" programs, 43
tightly coupled classes (UML), 114
time constraints in UML sequence
    diagrams, 133
time to market, 47
traceability, 171–181, 192
Traceability section (STP), 291
tracing STP tags back to test cases and
    requirements, 303
traditional software development
    methodologies, 52
training new software apprentices, 14
transition guards, 91–92
transitions (UML), 90, 91
    state, 163
triggers
    in a requirement, 186
    state machine, 164
    UML, 94

U

UML (Unified Modeling Language)
    - (private class visibility operator), 106
    * (iteration operator in sequence diagrams), 132
    # (protected class visibility operator), 107
    + (class visibility operator), 105
    ~ (package class visibility operator), 107
    activity diagrams
        catch-all transition, 92
        expression coverage, 92
        partitions, 97
    activity diagram symbols, 89
    alternative flows, 135
    annotations, 98
    attributes
        data types, 110
        derived values, 109
        multiplicity, 111, 120
        names, 109
        syntax, 112
        visibility, 109
    ball and socket notation, 156, 163
    base values in a class, 109

changeability, 124
class attributes, 108–112
class composition relationships, 117
class diagrams, 104
class operators, 112
class relationships, 114–125
    aggregation, 116
    association, 115
    composition, 117
    dependency, 114
    inheritance, 114
collaboration diagrams, 152
comments, 98
communication links, 74
component diagrams, 155–158
«component» stereotype, 156
composite structure diagrams, 160–163, 236, 238
concurrent processing, 96
conditionals, 91
connectors, 98
constraints, 121
    {frozen}, 124
    {ordered}, 121
decision symbols, 163–165
default attribute values, 111–112
deployment diagrams, 159–160
derived classes, 253
derived values, 109
events, 94–95
fork operation, 96
guards, 91
input/output parameters, 113
interfaces, 156
join operation, 96
merge points, 93–94
message types, 129
multiple merge/decision points, 94
namespaces (packages), 76
naming a communication link, 163
navigability, 123
nodes, 159
object-oriented analysis, 103–104
object-oriented design, 103–104
objects, 125
package diagrams, 236, 238
package visibility, 107
packages, 76
partial class diagrams, 104
ports, 201
private class visibility, 106

UML (*continued*)
   property strings, 109, 112
   protected class visibility, 107
   provided interfaces, 156, 162
   public class visibility, 105
   qualified names in packages, 159
   qualifiers, 159
   rake symbol, 96
   {readOnly} property, 112
   relationship strength, 114
   required interfaces, 162
   return type, 129
   return values in sequence diagram messages, 129
   reusability of components, 155–158
   roles, 56
   sequence diagrams
      «create» message, 136–137
      creating objects, 136
      «destroy» message, 136–137
      destroying objects, 136
      differentiating between branching and long delays, 135
      dropped title box, 136
      external objects, 133
      flat messages, 129
      guard conditions, 131, 134
      indefinite loops, 143
      interaction occurrence, 139
      iterations, 309
      lifelines, 128
      long delays and time constraints, 132–133
      message parameters, 131
      messages, 129–130
      object lifetime, 136
      return from subroutine, 145
      return messages, 129
      sequence numbers, 138
      showing operation order, 128
      strict sequence fragment, 150
      synchronous messages, 129
      time constraints, 133
   sequence fragments
      alt, 146
      assert, 138
      break, 138
      consider, 138
      ignore, 138
      loop, 141–145, 142
      neg, 138, 148
      opt, 138, 146
      par, 138, 149
      ref, 139
      region, 138, 151
      seq, 138, 150
      strict, 138, 150
   sequence message labels, 130
   start state, 163
   start symbol, 164
   statechart diagrams, 163
   states, 91
   state transitions, 163
   {static} property, 112
   stereotype notation, 184
   stop state, 163
   subroutine entry point in a ref segment fragment, 139
   subroutines, 96
   subsystem stereotype, 156
   swim lanes, 97
   synchronization, 96
   system boundary diagrams, 87
   tightly coupled classes, 114
   transitions, 90, 91
   triggers, 94
   {unique} property, 112
   use cases
      description, 80
      diagrams, 231
      end conditions, 81
      «extend» keyword, 79
      extension, 79–80, 85
      Flow of Events, 81
      formality, 81
      fully dressed, 81
      generalization, 77–79
      if statements in descriptions, 84
      inclusion, 77
      minimal guarantees, 81
      narratives, 80–86
      post conditions, 81
      scenarios, 86–87, 291
      successful guarantees, 81
      termination, 81
      triggers, 80
   value parameters, 113
   visibility, 105, 108, 120

unbounded list in requirements, 188, 189
underreference in requirements, 189
underspecification in requirements, 188
Unified Modeling Language. *See* UML
{unique} property (UML), 112
uniqueness (requirement), 191
unit (software development testing level), 265
unit tasks (productivity), 18
Unit Test Cases, 274
Unit Test Design, 269
Unit Test Plan, 267
Unit Test Procedures, 289
unit testing, 41, 265
unit tests in XP, 65
unnecessary requirements, 187
unscheduled downtime, 201
updating an RTM
    with SRL information, 274
    with STC information, 288
    with STP information, 302
use cases, UML, 74, 81, 212, 214
    derived, 79
    description, 80
    diagrams, 231
    elements, 74
    end conditions, 81
    exceptions, 81
    «extend» keyword, 79
    extension, 79–80, 81, 85
    Flow of Events, 81
    generalization, 77–79
    if statements in descriptions, 84
    inclusion, 77
    minimal guarantees, 81
    narratives, 80–86
        formality of, 81–82
    post conditions, 81
    scenarios, 86–87, 291
    secondary actors, 39
    successful guarantees, 81
    termination, 81
    triggers, 94
User Characteristics section (SRS), 198
user feedback in Iterative software development models, 46
User Interfaces section (SRS), 196
user stories in XP, 56, 59

V

V software development model, 45–46
    shortcomings, 49
vagueness in requirements, 188
validation
    reducing costs via, 182
    SDD, 183
    SRS, 183
    STP, 184
    SyRS, 183
    versus verification, 46
value parameters (UML), 113
verifiable requirements, 190
verification, 46, 263
    in a test procedure, 295
    reducing costs via, 183
    versus validation, 46
verification methods in RTM, 222
version number for a test procedure, 295
visibility (UML), 105
    spectrum, 108
    of UML attribute names, 120

W

Warnier/Orr diagrams, 239
Waterfall model, 44–45
weak words, ambiguity as result of, 188, 189
white-box-generated test data, 276
whole team concept in XP, 55
workarounds to a defect (AR), 309

X

XP. *See* Extreme Programming
XP software development activities, 57
XP teams, 55

Y

You aren't gonna need it (YAGNI) design principle, 62

Write Great Code, Volume 3: Engineering Software is set in New Baskerville, Futura, and Dogma. The book was printed and bound by Sheridan Books, Inc. in Chelsea, Michigan. The paper is 60# Finch Offset, which is certified by the Forest Stewardship Council (FSC).

The book uses a layflat binding, in which the pages are bound together with a cold-set, flexible glue and the first and last pages of the resulting book block are attached to the cover. The cover is not actually glued to the book's spine, and when open, the book lies flat and the spine doesn't crack.

RESOURCES

Visit *https://nostarch.com/greatcode3/* for resources, errata, and more information.

More no-nonsense books from **NO STARCH PRESS**

WRITE GREAT CODE, VOLUME 1, 2ND EDITION
Understanding the Machine
by RANDALL HYDE
JUNE 2020, 472 PP., $49.95
ISBN: 978-1-71850-036-5

WRITE GREAT CODE, VOLUME 2, 2ND EDITION
Thinking Low-Level, Writing High-Level
by RANDALL HYDE
JULY 2020, 656 PP., $49.95
ISBN: 978-1-71850-038-9

EFFECTIVE C
An Introduction to Professional C Programming
by ROBERT C. SEACORD
JULY 2020, 272 PP., $59.95
ISBN 978-1-71850-104-1

THE RUST PROGRAMMING LANGUAGE
(Covers Rust 2018)
by STEVE KLABNIK AND CAROL NICHOLS
AUGUST 2019, 560 PP., $39.95
ISBN 978-1-71850-044-0

PYTHON CRASH COURSE, 2ND EDITION
A Hands-On, Project-Based Introduction to Programming
by ERIC MATTHES
MAY 2019, 544 PP., $39.95
ISBN 978-1-59327-928-8

THE SECRET LIFE OF PROGRAMS
Understand Computers—Craft Better Code
by JONATHAN E. STEINHART
AUGUST 2019, 504 PP., $44.95
ISBN 978-1-59327-970-7

PHONE:
1.800.420.7240 OR
1.415.863.9900

EMAIL:
SALES@NOSTARCH.COM

WEB:
WWW.NOSTARCH.COM

The Electronic Frontier Foundation (EFF) is the leading organization defending civil liberties in the digital world. We defend free speech on the Internet, fight illegal surveillance, promote the rights of innovators to develop new digital technologies, and work to ensure that the rights and freedoms we enjoy are enhanced — rather than eroded — as our use of technology grows.

EFF.ORG
ELECTRONIC FRONTIER FOUNDATION
Protecting Rights and Promoting Freedom on the Electronic Frontier